Chris Brickell has a PhD in Sociology from Victoria University of Wellington, and is Associate Professor in Gender Studies at the University of Otago. Described as 'a fascinating and pioneering exploration of a significant part of our social history', his first book, *Mates & Lovers: A History of Gay New Zealand* (2008) won the E.H. McCormick prize for best first non-fiction book in the Montana Book Awards, 2009. Several other books – *Manly Affections: The Photographs of Robert Gant, 1885-1915* (2012), *Two-by-Two: Men in Pairs* (2013), and *Southern Men: Gay Lives in Pictures* (2014) – explore men's visual histories. Chris has also published on the history and sociology of sexuality, masculinity and adolescence in numerous international journals.

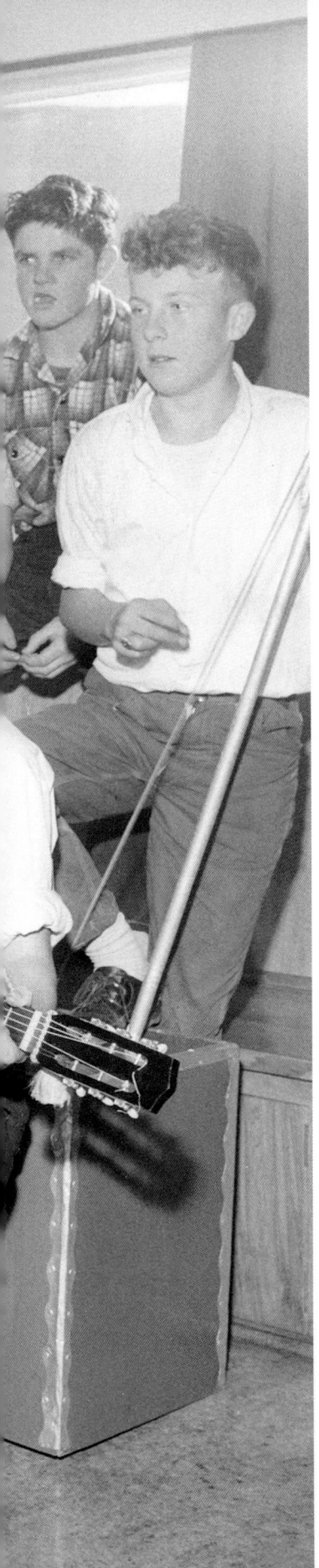

TEENAGERS
THE RISE OF YOUTH CULTURE IN NEW ZEALAND

CHRIS BRICKELL

AUCKLAND
UNIVERSITY
PRESS

First published 2017

Auckland University Press
University of Auckland
Private Bag 92019
Auckland 1142
New Zealand
www.press.auckland.ac.nz

© Chris Brickell, 2017

ISBN 978 1 86940 868 8

Publication is assisted by

A catalogue record for this book is available from the National Library of New Zealand

This book is copyright. Apart from fair dealing for the purpose of private study, research, criticism or review, as permitted under the Copyright Act, no part may be reproduced by any process without prior permission of the publisher. The moral rights of the author have been asserted.

COVER PHOTOGRAPH Teenagers celebrate New Year's Eve at Caroline Bay, 1962. South Canterbury Museum, 3690.
FRONTISPIECE At the Hutt Valley Youth Club, 1958. Alexander Turnbull Library, EP/1958/1589-F.
FRONT ENDPAPERS These North Otago boys begin their race toward the future while adults linger over the other side of the paddock, c. 1910. North Otago Museum, 1467.
BACK ENDPAPERS A group of young housemaids sits around a table in a large Christchurch house during the 1910s. Alexander Turnbull Library, 1/1-017702-G.

BOOK DESIGN Katrina Duncan
COVER DESIGN Kalee Jackson

Typeset in Tiempos, Futura Condensed and Proxima Nova
Printed on FSC® certified paper

Printed in China by Everbest Printing Co. Ltd

Contents

Introduction
Finding the Teen Age   1

Chapter One
Setting the Scene   17

Chapter Two
Adolescent Stirrings   67

Chapter Three
Jazz Age Youth   127

Chapter Four
The Teenager is Here!   189

Chapter Five
Milk-Bar Cowboys and Rock 'n' Roll   247

Conclusion
Back to the Future   313

Abbreviations   324
Notes   325
Bibliography   343
Illustration Credits   363
Acknowledgements   365
Index   368

Introduction **Finding the Teen Age**

Gertie Brookes moved from the country district of Wharehine to Auckland, a bustling city of 35,000 people, in 1889. The sixteen-year-old found somewhere to live, took up a job as a domestic servant and told those back home about her new life. Gertie's letters to her close friend Ella Marsh described her experiences. 'I like this place pretty much but there is too much work', she wrote. 'I know I won't be able to do it for very long. I keep the house scrubbed as white as it can be, of course I come in for all the heavy work.'[1] While Gertie toiled like an older woman, her youth asserted itself in ways that she found irritating, such as the rash of pimples on her face.[2] She inhabited the space between childhood and adulthood as her young body assumed grown-up burdens.

There was more to life than hard work, though: Gertie's letters tell of socialising with the young men of Auckland. 'If I go to G'ma Lichfield's there is a young man there 20-something he is, he is a lodger at G'ma's, if I go to Aunty Lizzie's, there is Stan & Percy if I go to Charlie's place over at Avondale there is a young man lives with him.' Gertie often found herself the centre of attention – and she wondered how to cope: 'I shall have to ask your advice Dear Ella what must I do,

OPPOSITE A book and a hammock on a sunny afternoon in Otago, c. 1918.

Gertie Brookes, c. 1891.

shut my eyes & never speak to them, if so mind you tell me.'[3] When Gertie received a letter from her sister Daisy, who stayed up north, she heard the gossip from home. 'I think nearly all were there except Minnie even her young man', Daisy wrote of an Arbor Day dance. 'We had a merry time of it at night we had games & dancing & kept it up till 10 then dropped.' The crowd thinned out, some among the younger set stayed behind, and 'we had a lively time of it to ourselves. I expect Minnie would be jealous if she knew we stopped till 12 then trudged home.'[4]

We are used to seeing the teenager as an invention of the 1950s, a time when rebellious young city-dwellers embraced the pleasures of an affluent post-war society: milkshakes, motorbikes, petting in the movie theatres and jiving to Elvis.[5] But the idea of the teenager did not suddenly emerge during the middle of the twentieth century. Its foundations had been laid by the time Gertie and Daisy put pen to paper.⁶ To be sure, there were no milkshakes or motorbikes during the 1880s, and definitely no rock 'n' roll, but Gertie, Daisy, Ella and their friends mooched about and chased young men anyway. 'I was surprised to hear about Mr Bridge, perhaps he is going love crazy about Minnie. I should not be the least surprised', Gertie wrote in one letter.⁷

Gertie, her sister and their friends were not teenagers in the sense we now know them, members of 'a discrete age group with its own rituals, rights and demands', but their experiences set the scene for what was to come.⁸ The late nineteenth century was a critical period here and overseas. In New Zealand, as in Australia, North America, Britain and Western Europe, young people moved from rural areas to the growing towns.⁹ While Gertie scrubbed floors and washed dishes for Auckland's well-to-do, some of her contemporaries sought employment in the big new factories. They forged an early kind of youth culture as they laboured at their machines and chatted in the lunch-rooms. School pupils also built age-specific worlds. The new secondary schools enrolled only a few young people at first – Gertie was not amongst them – but eventually they shaped the teenage experience of most New Zealanders.

The significance of the gap between childhood and adulthood has changed since the nineteenth century. The slow growth of a consumer culture, the emergence of new kinds of leisure, the advance of popular psychology and fresh rituals of romance, along with developments in work and schooling, cultivated fertile soil in which the concept of 'adolescence' took root and grew through the early decades of the twentieth century.

Teenagers do not usually occupy the centre of historians' attention. Most general histories of New Zealand focus on adults, and those in their teens appear as minor players. When historians do look at teenage lives, they usually scrutinise adults' condemnation of 'juvenile delinquency', alcohol, sex and boisterousness in general.¹⁰ But adolescence is not simply a focus for adult anxieties. It is also a phase of life that young people experience and navigate as they make their way in the world. *Teenagers: The Rise of Youth Culture in New Zealand* tries to redress the balance. This book nods towards adult concerns but it also looks beyond scandal to explore the views of teenagers themselves. The voices of people like Gertie and Daisy Brookes bring teenage history alive. Everyday activities such as talking, playing, reading and dressing are all fodder for a cultural history like this one, and so too are beliefs, bodies and emotions.[11] How did adolescents spend their leisure time? What did it feel like to be young? *Teenagers* tells of introspection, rabbit-hunting, racy French novels, hockey practice, home-made gym equipment, Bible Class camps, water pistols and idle gossip. Young people's history is at once intimate and expansive, and intricate details illustrate wider social shifts.

Text and Images

So how do we trace the life stories of school pupils, farm workers, newspaper boys, office girls, leisure seekers and young lovers, the subjects of this book? *Teenagers* draws upon a range of material gathered in communities from Kaitaia in the north to Invercargill in the south. Newspapers and government reports devote most of their time to adults' perspectives but sometimes reveal adolescents' views and voices in passing. Memoirs and oral histories take us directly into the young lives of those on whom this book focuses. For example, Wellingtonian Sophie Tindall, a teenager during the 1950s, remembers 'riding on the back of a motorbike, we were doing 90 miles from the Basin Reserve right up Adelaide Road there and I was sitting on the back, no helmet on or anything – saying "go faster go faster". We were very independent.'[12] While we need to treat such oral sources with care, for memories can fail and are often embellished over time, they also offer us direct access to a person's sense of themselves and to their memories of experiences that would otherwise be lost.[13] Interviewees like Sophie reveal events and episodes that stood out as profound or formative for them in some way.

Letters, like interviews, evoke the sensations, feelings and introspections of youth, but they also capture the immediacy of a moment. When boarding school pupils wrote home to their parents, for instance, they sought advice and relayed their hopes and fears. Bryan Helm boarded at Nelson College during the early 1940s and penned a letter to his father once a week. 'I will bear in mind what you said about conquering my feelings when in a lazy mood', he wrote earnestly, determined to better himself.[14] Brian's epistolary lapses had to be justified: 'I could not write as I did not want to post you some measle germs', he explained on another occasion.[15] The Brookes sisters' letters revealed their writers' inner-most concerns and sought reassurance. 'Ella I am a miserable girl. I do want to be good but I don't know how to. I am always doing something or saying something I shouldn't', Daisy Brookes wrote to Ella Marsh in a low moment.¹⁶

Diaries are also repositories for confessions and stories. We often assume these to be the preserve of girls and women rather than boys and men, but this is not the case in New Zealand.¹⁷ Boys' and girls' diaries tell of travel on immigrant ships, work on family farms, out-of-town holidays and walks around the fledgling cities. Many diaries are carefully structured in their form, and their writers obey conventions to varying degrees. Elsie Clogstoun lived on a farm station near Geraldine and, in 1881, at the age of sixteen, she began each diary entry with the weather. Elsie never wrote the same thing twice: 'melting day', 'unutterably hot', 'boiling', 'boilinger', 'boilinger than words can express', 'roasting, simply'.¹⁸ Having dispensed with the preliminaries, Elsie went on to amuse herself by recounting her daily experiences:

'Self'. This image from South Otago, taken at the end of the 1920s, captures an introspection often reserved for the diary, a place to confess feelings to oneself.

As a place in which to account for daily expenditure, the diary shared characteristics with the cash book. Belle Marsh's 1920s example contains a typical list of outgoings. This tells of Belle's daily routine and her social life: admission to the pictures and the Wellsford Show, a copy of *The Scarlet Pimpernel* and a pair of jazz garters.

Enjoyed the dancing. [Afterwards] Lina, Ina and I shared one medium sized double bed – we all got a fearful attack of giggles after we'd gone to bed. Giggled for about an hour without stopping. We were a good deal squashed as we're all more or less colossal. Lina and I a little over 10 stone?! and Ina 9½ – Phew! T'was warm.[19]

While Elsie's diary reveals a gentle, self-deprecating humour, diaries also record expectations about emotional and spiritual progress.[20] Agnes MacGregor, a minister's daughter, strove to be more thoughtful and less selfish as the years went on – but sometimes she disappointed herself. 'I want to turn over a new leaf this year. I was reading my silly journal from last year & find myself apparently little improved.'[21] She later added: 'I have no ambition to be an idler or dreamer.

I do wish to do God's work – to leave the world somewhat better for my having been in it.'²²

Photographs reflect other kinds of conventions. Photography was a semi-public practice in the early years when professionals, not amateurs, arranged the sitters before squeezing the bulb. On several occasions in Wellington in 1872, nineteen-year-old Mary Annie Hargreaves and her family had their 'likenesses' – as Mary put it – taken at the studio of Wrigglesworth and Binns.²³ Albums show that the extended Hargreaves family enjoyed being photographed as early as the mid-1860s. Most images were sternly posed during the 1870s and 1880s, and they give the (false) impression that nobody had any fun. But the

Fourteen-year-old Mary Annie Hargreaves in 1866. This is a rare image: there are very few surviving photographs of adolescent New Zealanders from this decade.

TEENAGERS

The photographer photographed. A rugby team at Otago Boys' High School near the end of the First World War.

conventions of image-making – especially studio photography during the Victorian era – did not always represent the way young people felt about themselves. The Clogstoun sisters' bedtime giggling never appeared in any picture, and Elsie bristled at the way she appeared in formal settings. 'I am not a bit like that', she wrote under a tiny, buttoned down photo of herself looking severe (see p. 113). A few amateur nineteenth-century photographers abandoned the studio and recorded adolescents in their daily habitats – sitting at the breakfast table, posing in backyards and lounging in doorways with their pets – but this documentary style was far from typical. Still, it helps dispel any misconception that Victorian youngsters glared humourlessly all day long.

The mass take-up of photography had to wait until the following century. The Kodak Brownie camera came on the market in 1900 and gave rise to a new informality. Young people left behind the photographic studios, grabbed a camera of their own and clicked the shutter whether their subjects were ready or not. In 1910, when thirteen-year-old Randal Burdon camped with his brother near Orari in Canterbury, he wrote: 'I found the little skunk George had got up and taken a photo of me lying under the tent asleep.'[24] Young people's photography boomed during and after the First World War. Adolescents carried cameras to school, the beach and their favourite picnic spots. Christchurch girl Alison McLeod even developed and printed her own 'snaps'. 'Quite pleased with the result. Rang Lorna up in afternoon to tell her that the negatives looked good', she noted in her diary in 1918, before confessing her guilty pleasure: 'Must try not to do quite so much photography on Sundays.'[25]

Local and Global Histories

The emergence of the modern teenager reflected international developments. Historians have recently placed New Zealand firmly in its global setting, exploring the intersections between local and global histories.[26] According to this revisionist view, New Zealand has been neither as isolated nor as exceptional as we have tended to assume. Well connected to the world economic system since the early nineteenth century, New Zealanders imported books, magazines and newspapers, and smuggled in new ideas about being young.[27] A great many immigrants made their way onto our shores too, and New Zealand-born youngsters went overseas. One local lad, Gerald Shiel, left Dunedin in 1921 to attend St Ignatius' College in Sydney. There he read Shakespeare, rowed in regattas, played cricket, took part in competitive footy ('I am as sore as a squashed cucumber') and celebrated St Patrick's Day ('hooray!').[28] Schoolboys throughout the British world participated in this kind of life, sharing activities and language across continents. Entertainment was another global phenomenon, from the acrobatic troupes and touring theatre parties of the nineteenth century to 'the pictures', popular music and dance crazes of every decade.[29]

For all this, New Zealand was no carbon copy of Britain, America or Australia. Our geography, climate, indigenous culture and successive waves of migration (both across and within our borders) shaped local lives in specific ways.[30] Relationships between Māori and Pākehā underpinned many adolescents' experiences during the early decades of British settlement and once again after the Second World War. Ideas about a pioneering spirit also moulded Pākehā expectations and experience. Adults who recalled the rough toil of their early

TEENAGERS

The milk bar is the quintessential hangout in post-war teenage history. These Auckland girls joke around during the early 1950s and remind us these were workplaces as well as leisure spaces.

years often looked dismissively upon urban lives of ease. Still, rural and urban life existed side by side during the late nineteenth century and they have done so ever since. Many townies went camping and lolled on the beaches. Thirteen-year-old Jean McLeod, who lived north of Masterton during the 1930s, mucked about under the pine trees on her family's farm before putting on her best frock, travelling into town and indulging her passion for the most glamorous of American film stars.[31]

Several key themes run through New Zealand's adolescent experience from the early nineteenth century to the 1960s: modernity, mobility, social distinctions, discipline and identity-making. The precise shape of each theme has changed significantly, but their broad parameters reveal some important continuities. By comparing these themes over a century and a half, we can see how New Zealanders' lives have changed over time and how social processes have shaped the meaning of being young.

Modernity is a slippery concept. It refers to the ways industrialisation, new technologies and various modes of mass communication come together to make a distinct type of society.[32] Young people embraced new trends from the middle of the nineteenth century, taking up emerging forms of fashion and entertainment. As historian Charlotte Macdonald writes, adolescents have long had a 'sense of living in times that were new and different'. This sense, 'at once exciting and frightening, gave contemporaries their identity as "modern". They felt and spoke of themselves as living in a world in sharp contrast to that of their parents, let alone their grandparents.'[33] Adolescents' daily lives paint a clear picture of changing technologies in New Zealand, and they provide a contrast for our own times. In the early twenty-first century there is much discussion of the 'digital generation' and the ubiquity of the internet and the smartphone, but how did older forms of technology – the typewriter, the telephone, the radio and the television – shape young people's experiences?

We have already seen how the telephone helped Alison McLeod tell her friends about her photographic successes, and the development and availability of other technologies – trains, bicycles, motorbikes and motorcars – suggest how much mobility was changing. Transport influenced the ways young people spent their time, how they moved around and the degree of independence they enjoyed.[34] The expanding railway network opened new frontiers during the late nineteenth century and allowed adolescents to travel long distances more easily than their forerunners. The bicycles and trams of the early- and mid-twentieth century made short trips easy, and the streets of the flourishing cities encouraged their own kinds of movement and territory-claiming. When young people moved around the cities and countryside, they helped shape those places in a range of ways.[35] To borrow an idea from French sociologist Michel de Certeau, they 'poached' adult terrain, re-configuring it and making it their own.[36] Officially, the city streets were spaces of adult commerce, but adolescents met up and mucked about there.

Prevailing status ideals offer another example of Certeau's concept of 'poaching'. Young people reworked ideas about status into a new array of distinctions among co-workers and groups of friends, and between adolescents and adults. Among the pages of their diaries they evaluated peers ('she is good looking, interesting, but very affected'), ranked mates ('I was not very friendly with F. but showed preference for R.C.') and judged strangers ('Mrs Mills is enormously fat with a fearfully sticking out underlip').[37] Just as adults drew their own lines around respectability, adolescents created divisions between insiders and outsiders. Sometimes they also rearranged the boundaries between the mundane and the exotic in order to drive cultural change on a wider scale. The masher of the 1880s (Chapter 2) and the flapper of the interwar years (Chapter 3) were stylish young avant-gardists who pushed the limits of fashion and shocked the conservatively minded. Still, their innovations – the masher's urbanity and the flapper's slim dress, cloche hat and jaunty dance moves – filtered into the wider society. Economic potential gave rise to style, and young people pushed New Zealand culture along.[38]

New Zealanders transformed the world around them while responding to its demands, and they tested the limits long before the 1950s dawned.[39] This was a century-long process of discipline and resistance. Adults made the rules and young people obeyed, bent or broke them. Boys smoked and showed off in Wellington's muddy byways during the 1850s; girls began loitering on street corners during the late nineteenth century; young bodies escaped their restrictive clothing as the First World War drew to a close. The expansion of secondary schooling, office jobs and factory work imposed new forms of surveillance but, as we will see along the way, they also provided opportunities for freedom.

OPPOSITE Two smartly dressed lads at the A&P Show, near Kaitaia, during the late 1950s.

Harvey Graff, an American historian, suggests that growing up represents a collective quest for maturity, autonomy and development.[40] New Zealand's boys and girls, like those everywhere else, forged a sense of themselves as they fitted in among their peers, stood out or both. Some made their way through a minefield on their way to adulthood and struggled with parents, puberty and poverty. Others had an easier time, enjoying a good education and supportive families. Many moved between identities, tried on and swapped masks, and embraced or rejected labels. In her diary Jean McLeod wrote, 'I will be a good girl (perhaps) oh yeah', and when an acquaintance said she and her sister were 'naughty girls', Jean 'ruffled his hair'.[41] Was Jean a 'good girl' or a naughty one? It depended who was talking.

A Plan of the Book

Teenagers proceeds chronologically as the book explores the lives of New Zealanders aged between thirteen and twenty. Chapter 1 tells of the contact between young Māori and British immigrants, especially in the North Island and the south of the South Island. The early migrant trickle swelled from the 1840s as sailing vessels brought increasing numbers of young people into our ports, singly and in groups, and travellers' diaries chronicle the significance of age and gender in onboard culture. On dry land, Auckland became home to adolescent convicts, Wellington's well-heeled young citizens partied and danced, and farms attracted lads seeking their fortune. The embryo of adolescence started to form in the years prior to 1870, but cohesive youth cultures had not yet come together.

Small towns grew into cities by the 1870s and adolescent lives grew more complex. Dunedin industrialised first, and Chapter 2 shows how workplaces and schools shaped a generation. A degree of cosmopolitanism accompanied the rising urban middle class, and educated boys moved into clerical jobs. As 'mashers' they developed their own sartorial styles. Others, usually working-class youths, fashioned themselves as 'larrikins', and their rough-and-ready behaviour tested adults' patience. Coherence soon gave way to complexity. Young people's worlds quickly fractured along lines of class and subculture.

Chapter 3 explores the consolidation of youth cultures in the countryside and towns during the early decades of the twentieth century. A life on the land was very different from the fast world of noisy workrooms, gossipy offices and exotic entertainments. Young New Zealanders tell us about gardening, mustering and hunting as well as domestic service and flapperdom. This was also an era of competing moral values. A new militarism disciplined young bodies, and adults began to organise adolescents' free time in this era of drill, Scouts and Guides. Sunbathing and the silent film represented the opposite end of the spectrum, while first-wave feminism occupied an awkward middle ground. New Zealand society eased back and tightened up simultaneously, and those in their teens were the most affected by these tensions.

The Great Depression and the Second World War dominated the teen years of those who appear in Chapter 4. Memoirs tell of young people living with the upheavals of the age: the slump of the 1930s and the heady atmosphere of wartime. This chapter introduces cadets, land girls, Territorials and those who revelled in the presence of military personnel. The American influence on New Zealand culture strengthened considerably during these years, especially in the realms of romance and fantasy; it was also the age of speed, 'talkies' and targeted advertising. After decades of flirting with the idea that young New Zealanders had their own enigmatic character, the newspapers pasted a new label onto them – they became 'teenagers'.

The 1950s and 1960s were dynamic decades. Chapter 5 shows how accelerating urban growth further fuelled teenage cultures. At the same time, social scientists investigated social groups, mapped teens' movements and recorded their idiom. Some young writers embraced a teenage identity and defended it in print, and energetic post-war cultures gave rise to a new political sensibility. At the same time, old ways of life rubbed along with the new: boys and girls spent days with their heads down in class, competed in sports teams, told stories at Bible Class camp and jostled in the stalls of the theatres. They carried on with their private lives as the news media subjected them to a new level of scrutiny. Chapter 5 draws to a close in 1969, by which time modern New Zealand teenagers had come into their own. Then the book's brief concluding chapter asks how recent generations of teenagers have drawn upon the past while charting a course for the future.

Chapter One **Setting the Scene**

In 1862 Charlie Brookes, his two brothers and 349 others set sail from England on the *Matilda Wattenbach*. The ship's passengers were destined for Albertland, a new settlement on the shores of the Kaipara Harbour. The trip out had been stormy and the journey on the rough roads between Auckland and Port Albert, near the present-day town of Wellsford, was a trial in itself. Charlie and his brothers wrote home to tell their parents of the ship's voyage, travels up country and their work on the land.[1] The trio owned their own block before too long, and Charlie described it in a letter. 'At last we have got our land, and a beautiful place it is. The ground is covered with beautiful grass and green food, the stuff to keep a cow on. There are no less than one hundred varieties of ferns, ferns that we cut down and burn here, which would cost a guinea each in England. It is a jolly life, an emigrant's, to go through the beautiful woods and valleys and we can say – this is my own.'[2]

Charlie, fourteen, Edwin, seventeen, and twenty-year-old Hovey left behind a comfortable English existence and set out in search of a new life. They had all the enthusiasm of youth, keen to seek their fortunes and to prove themselves in

OPPOSITE Sailing into Albertland, 1860s.

the wide open spaces of a new land. But life was not always easy. Charlie hinted at his own dislocation. He asked his parents for his sister Lizzy to be sent out from England ('she will have to come. Why? Because I say so'), and closed one letter thus: 'Goodbye. I remain your affectionate son, Loll.'[3] The insistence that Lizzy join the boys, along with the childhood nickname, hinted at Charlie's broken attachment to home.

The experiences of these young migrants resembled and differed from those of others of a similar age. The stories of many boys and girls who sailed on the immigrant ships and settled ashore tell of work, cross-cultural contact, new and old friends, love, pleasures and hardships. Age played a significant and often

The 1862 departure from London of the *Matilda Wattenbach* with 800 passengers bound for Albertland, New Zealand. Somewhere in the throng stood Charlie, Edwin and Hovey Brookes, wondering what their life would be like in the colony.

overlooked role in organising these kinds of human experience during the early- and mid-nineteenth century. 'Youth', a broad and deeply gendered category, had a wide span and a soggy middle: a seven-year-old boy was a child and a twenty-one-year-old an adult, but the space in between was tricky to define. Often, physical labour was the yardstick: size, physical strength and mental capacity signified maturity. Girls were rarely included under the rubric of 'youth', an exclusion that reflected their ongoing domestic dependence on others, whether as daughters, wives or workers. This changed later in the century when girls became increasingly autonomous and the broad male category of 'youth' gave way to a more precise and inclusive concept: 'adolescence'.

The decades prior to 1870 saw young arrivals set up rudimentary, often temporary cultures. Loose social groups began to take shape on the immigrant ships, and very small numbers forged friendships in the fledgling schools of the new country that catered for a wide – and often undifferentiated – range of ages. A handful of mutual improvement organisations set the scene for the young people's leisure organisations of later decades. In a small and transitory society, though, connections were often fleeting and not well sustained, and the prototypical youth organisation tended to be short-lived. Many of those who shared the Brookes brothers' passage on the *Matilda Wattenbach* quickly scattered across the new landscape, and atomised youths wandered the countryside in search of work. Stability of circumstances and a coalescence of culture were some way off.

Migrations and Encounters

Young people have played an important role in migration patterns since the end of the eighteenth century, and their movements gave form to the new world. Adolescent boys were well represented among the sealers, whalers and ship-borne traders who set out from Australia for New Zealand waters.[4] Many in this male-dominated world had been convicts, freed after they finished their sentences in Britain.[5] Sealing gangs from Sydney established the first stations in Murihiku (the southernmost part of the New Zealand mainland) and set up onshore huts for shelter from the elements. Many boys visited over the decades that followed, and some stayed. Jacky Marmon, the son of a convict, first visited the Bay of Islands in 1807 as a seven-year-old mascot on a whaling boat. By the time he returned in 1811 he was – in his words – 'a strapping lad of twelve, strongly built, tall beyond my years, and having seen as much "life" as many a man of thirty'. 'Though I say it myself', he wrote in his memoir, 'I was rather an acquisition to the vessel, since I was acquainted with all the parts of the ship, the ropes, the spars, the yards, and could lend a hand, with some idea how best to give my assistance.'[6]

Jacky Marmon's account highlights the importance of skill, size and physical strength in the transition from childhood to adulthood at the turn of the nineteenth century. As historian Thomas Hine suggests in the American context, physical capacity was a yardstick, an indication of the distance a youth had travelled along the road to manhood. Strength signified impending adulthood.[7] Back in the South Pacific, Jacky asserted his presence as a physically capable twelve-year-old: he was 'strapping', 'strongly built', having seen much 'life'. Jacky worked hard and drank too: 'In the foc'sle, I soon became a favourite', he boasted. 'I could sing a good song, spin a fair yarn, and do a reasonable quantity of grog with any man aboard – in a word, I was the right stuff for a sailor.'[8] Still, a degree of ambivalence remained. Jacky acknowledged his status as a kind of in-betweener as he compared himself to the men on board. We will shortly return to these definitional complexities: what was a boy, what did it mean to be in-between and what made a man?

Encounters between young Pākehā and Māori characterised these early years, especially in the northern half of the North Island where tens of thousands of Māori lived, but also around Wellington and in Murihiku. Back at Port Albert, Charlie Brookes and his brothers learned from Māori which places and practices were tapu, which local flora were edible – 'the fuschia berry makes first-rate pies' – and which items could be traded.[9] When hungry locals arrived asking 'You got any kiki?', Charlie swapped flour for pork. They 'were quite taken with my red Garibaldie', Charlie wrote, but the hat was not for sale.[10] The Brookes brothers and local Māori became close friends.

Romantic intimacies sometimes grew out of cultural contact. From the 1770s on, some Māori parents married their daughters to men on visiting boats. 'One sailor on the *Discovery* formed a mutual attachment with a young woman that was characterised by little verbal communication but much tender tactility and

SETTING THE SCENE

a desire for co-habitation', writes historian Angela Wanhalla.[11] These were customary rather than legal arrangements. They began when members of extended families debated the merits of a match and concluded when they gave their blessing. Still, Wanhalla suggests, many marriages involving Māori were love matches.[12]

Local legend and memoirs tell of inter-racial intimacies. In 1810, when chief Honekai and his warriors captured a boat crew from the sealing vessel the *Sydney Cove* on Stewart Island, the men killed five sealers but spared sixteen-year-old James Caddell. According to folklore the lad ran to the chief and touched his cloak, becoming tapu.[13] James – or 'Jimmy the Boy' – spent the next decade living among southern Māori. Around the age of twenty-one he married Tokitoki, Honekai's niece, who appeared to be around the same age.[14]

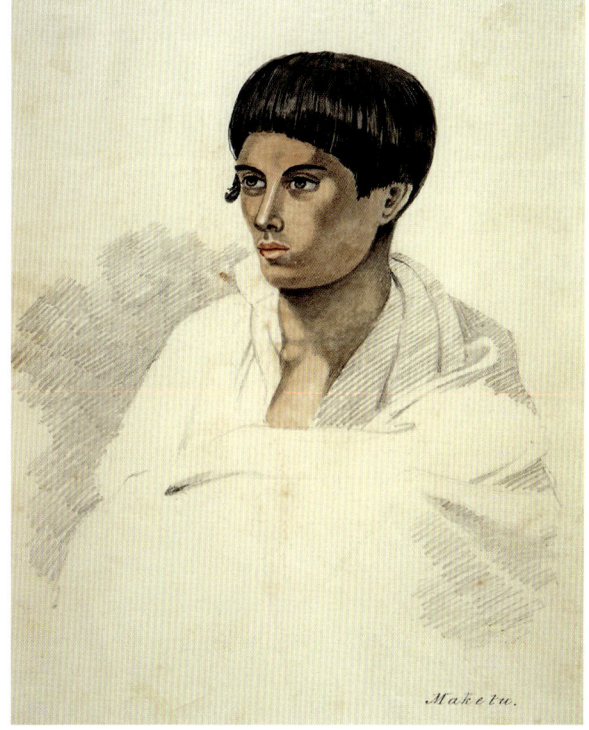

LEFT 'A youth of the Motawaka tribe studying with the Rev C. Reay for the Ministry', c. 1842. Reay had a school for young Māori students in Nelson.

RIGHT Maketu Waretotara, the son of Ruhe, a Waimate chief, 1842.

TEENAGERS

LEFT A Māori girl with a moko on her upper lip, drawn by Augustus Earle in 1832.

RIGHT A Taranaki girl, 1856, rendered in watercolour by William Strutt.

It is hard to chart the lives of young eighteenth- and nineteenth-century Māori in any real detail, and not only because written records are scarce. Few anthropologists and historians have explored the specific impact of age.[15] We do know that some young Māori, girls as well as boys, played a part in a Pacific-wide trade network centred on Sydney, 'an important imperial sub-centre' through which New Zealand produce found its way to China and Britain.[16] Tokitoki, James Caddell and 'Jacky Snapper', a Māori youth of sixteen, spent some time in Sydney exploring the possibilities for the flax trade, and others travelled there as crew on whaling vessels and boats ferrying flax, timber and other produce.[17] A few young Māori stayed with missionary Samuel Marsden at Parramatta, learning about the British world as well as Christianity.[18] These opportunities for travel and adventure proved irresistible to many Māori youth including Mowhee, a nine-year-old from the Bay of Islands. Mowhee learned of lands far away when he met a traveller recently returned from Australia. The boy talked his way onto a vessel,

SETTING THE SCENE

MOWHEE,
A young New Zealander.
Who died Dec.r 28. 1816. aged about 20 years.

Mowhee, also known as Tommy Drummond, was born about 1796 in the Bay of Islands. His adolescent years were adventuresome. In Sydney he met Reverend Samuel Marsden of the Church Missionary Society, who took the lad under his wing, and soon Mowhee became friends with Thomas Kendell. Marsden, Kendell and Mowhee – now a missionary trainee – travelled to the Bay of Islands, and then Mowhee set off on his own account for London. He died there, the victim of a virulent fever.

sailed the Pacific, and spent several years in Norfolk Island and Sydney. There Mowhee 'heard a great deal of England' and a desire to visit 'this land of wonders haunted him incessantly'.[19] In 1815, at the age of eighteen, he worked his passage to London.[20] Travel historian Jude Wilson suggests that such voyages, a chance to 'see the world', constitute the first examples of New Zealanders' 'great OE' (overseas experience).[21]

Young Māori and Pākehā had more in common than we may think. Not only did the thirst for adventure bring British travellers into New Zealand and send Māori out, but the significance of a boy's size and physical strength also crossed cultural lines. Many Māori lads trained in weaponry from fourteen or so, and much the same was true of Pākehā.[22] Gunfire rang out in every part of Taranaki in 1860 when land disputes escalated into war, and a steady stream of fifteen-year-olds found themselves in charge of guns and bayonets. At thirteen Robert Hughes was a little too young for active service, but his older brothers brought home stories of shootings, stabbings and tomahawk attacks.[23] As far as the colonial government was concerned, strong and physically capable fifteen-year-olds were ready to fight – and die – alongside older men. Fifteen-year-old Robert Brickell, my own great-great-grandfather, arrived in Auckland in 1863 with his seventeen-year-old brother John; both intended a civilian future but government agents intercepted the boys on the wharves and sent them to fight in the Waikato wars.[24]

Even though many boys in their mid-teens discharged adult responsibilities – soldiering and dangerous shipboard work were especially notable examples – they were not yet considered adults, a point Jacky Marmon tacitly conceded. Semi-independent from parents but not yet fully grown up, these lads fell under the broad category of 'youth'.[25] British historian John Gillis suggests that the designation of 'youth', shifting in its meaning and imprecisely bounded, was common in British and Western European pre-industrial society.[26] Some 'youths', including Jacky who left his parents to become a ship's mascot, and Mowhee who went to Norfolk Island and Sydney, were as young as seven or eight. Others in this category, including the scholar John Greenwood whom we will soon meet, were considerably older. Manhood and full autonomy arrived later for them, once they attained financial independence.

Young British settlers witnessed the powerful contrast between the old world and the new as they transitioned to manhood. Propagandists like Charles Hursthouse appealed to images of robust manly virtue and promoted migration as a prospect for the hardy. Hursthouse's 1857 guide for emigrants talked up the rugged encounter with nature that would quickly 'make a man' of those turning pale and pasty in an urbanising England.[27] The voyage and the new life was not for the 'feeble-minded, the emasculate, the fastidious, the timid', Hursthouse insisted, and migration offered a way out of 'grinding, social serfdom, those effeminate chains'.[28] If developing physical strength signalled the arrival of manhood, then New Zealand's rugged environment promised to accelerate the maturing process.

A youngster's relationship to serfdom and freedom, though, was not a matter of brawn alone. It also reflected his cultural capital, that is, the knowledge and training he needed for social advancement.[29] Jerningham Wakefield, the son of colonist Edward Gibbon Wakefield, was one well-off young man with a taste for adventure. Eager to leave England for antipodean shores, Jerningham first visited New Zealand in 1839 at the age of nineteen. He assumed the role of secretary to his uncle William Wakefield whose New Zealand Company scoped out the would-be colony. Jerningham's memoir *Adventure in New Zealand* records the details of his travels.[30] He set off from Wellington bound for Taranaki and met Whanganui chief Te Rangi Whakarurura at Waikanae en route. The chief offered Jerningham eight lads, including seven slaves, to accompany him and carry the baggage. Jerningham, Konatu (one of the slaves), Puke Totara (a free man, 'strong, tall and good-humoured') and their six companions set off to the north, marching over steep hills and along the shore, staying the night with local Māori or camping under trees. At Waikanae the group swapped the seaside slog for a canoe:

> We at length hoisted our sail before a fresh southerly breeze, amidst the discharge of muskets and sounds of *haere*! 'go!' about an hour before noon . . . *E Ao*, or 'the air,' a son of *E Rangi*, and half-brother of *Kuru Kanga*, was in command of the craft. Besides him, six young men, among whom was *Puke*, worked their paddles; and *Konatu* steered with a paddle . . .[31]

Jerningham Wakefield spent three more years travelling around the lower North Island reporting on political events, the relationships between Pākehā and Māori, and a range of 'struggles and perils'. Did Jerningham measure up to Charles Hursthouse's standards? Probably not. Something of a libertine, he led a life of sensuality. Governor Robert FitzRoy accused him of 'singing lewd hakas', squatting nude 'in the warm baths of Taupo' in the company of young Māori women, and 'debauching' more than fifty before returning to London to continue his dissolute ways there.[32] Jerningham's account of his early years evokes the considerable differences between an urban English life and the open, adventurous landscape of New Zealand. It also reveals the privileges available to a few: a paid passage to New Zealand, Māori youths to carry him around the country, and the money and ability to return to England. As a well-off youth Wakefield had a degree of freedom denied the military conscript or the slave, while he enacted a kind of masculinity that was at odds with the image promoted by the propagandists. Jerningham's experiences underscore the differences between colonist and colonised, centre and periphery, and different forms of youthful manhood.

TEENAGERS

The Trip Out

By 1840, a year after Jerningham Wakefield's peregrinations around the lower North Island, only 2,000 non-Māori lived in New Zealand. They truly were 'a small minority on the fringes of the Māori world', as historian Barbara Brookes writes. Soon, though, a wave of immigrants swamped New Zealand's ports.[33] The 2,000 became 20,000 by the early 1850s, and 250,000 by 1870.[34] The ships' human cargo arrived in a range of different circumstances. Many young passengers came with their families, some alone and others in pairs.

This is the 'log of the *Haddon Hall* on her voyage from London to Otago in 1874', drawn by thirteen-year-old Harold Hooper. The trip took ninety-eight days, each represented by a dot on the line. The ship made slow headway near the Equator but sped through the southern Atlantic Ocean. The *Haddon Hall* did not call ashore even once: there was nothing to relieve the social pressure-cooker effect of life on board for either adolescents or adults.

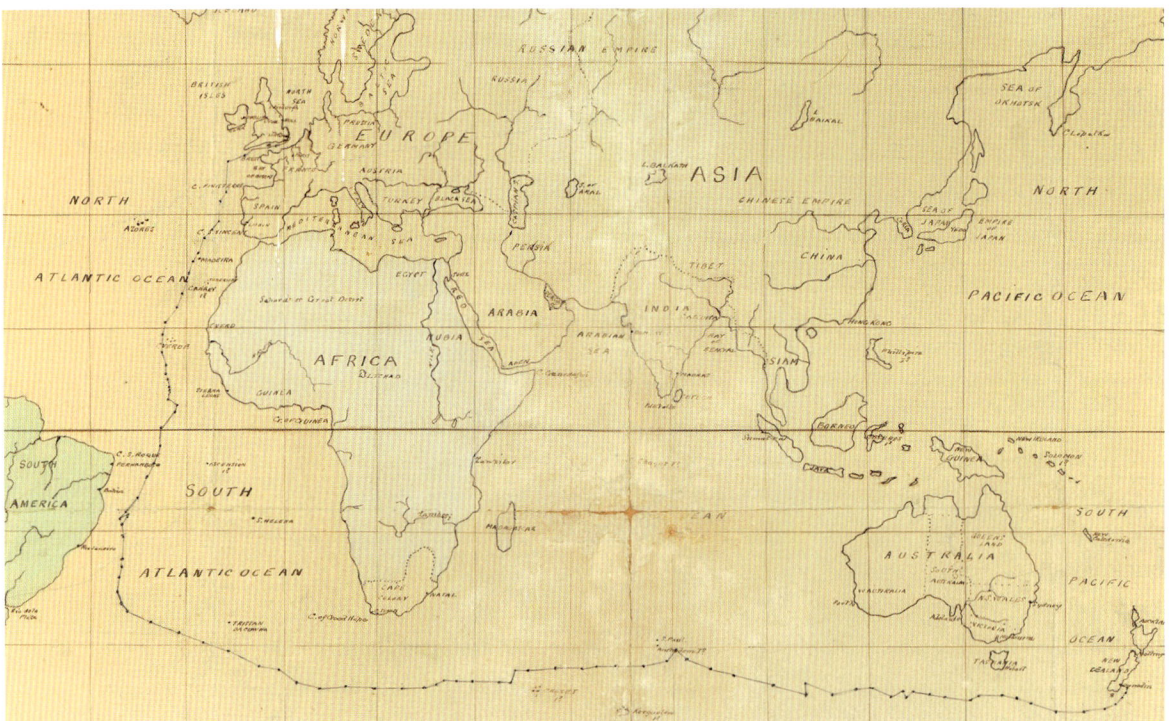

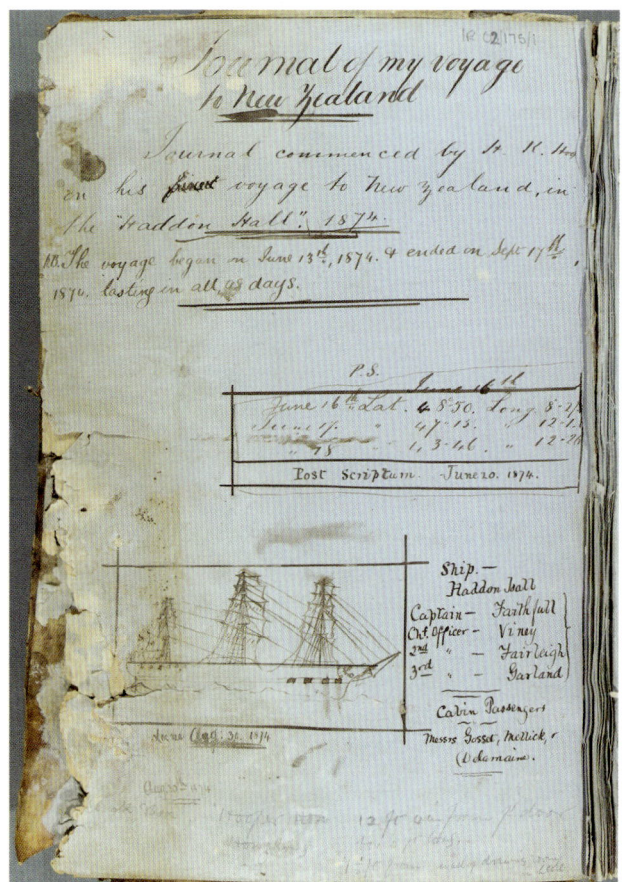

The title page of Harold Hooper's journal, one of a great many written by young people during the trip out to New Zealand.

A range of social distinctions took hold on board ship, and these had profound impacts on young immigrants. The well-off cabin class passengers, who called themselves 'colonists', had their own private compartments, while the rest (the 'emigrants') travelled below decks in the cramped confines of steerage.[35] Just as the cabins and steerage quarters separated passengers by class, the rules of steerage drew tight lines of gender and looser demarcations of age. Steerage passengers were divided into three groups, each accommodated in a separate section: married couples with children aged eleven or younger, single women, and single

Cabin passengers on board the migrant ship *Royal Dane*, 1864.

men. Families with children over the age of twelve were split up and the youngsters allocated to the single women's or single men's sections. These parts of the ships housed passengers of a low average age; most of those in the single women's and men's quarters were in their teens and early twenties.

These lines of age and gender persisted on the ships' outside decks. On the *Lady Egidia*, for instance, which sailed between London and Otago, ropes divided male from female sections of the deck with a four-foot buffer in between. 'A strict watch was kept up so that no indecent conduct might be in the ship', a young male passenger noted in his diary; 'if all things are true their [*sic*] are only five out of the seventy females on board who have not suffered from young men before.'[36] The young women were locked below decks at eight o'clock every evening. This strict segregation was enforced even when the *Lady Egidia*'s sailors struck up a band: 'the fiddles started up music and there was a dance got up by the young men but they had to confine it to themselves as the girls were not allowed to dance with them'.[37]

Not everyone appreciated such measures. Bessie Prouten set off from Gravesend aboard the *Northampton* bound for Wellington, and she chronicled the ship's regime of surveillance and her friends' attempts to thwart it. They did not like the segregation even if it was, as the shipping companies said, a measure to ensure their safety from male crew and passengers. 'There are a few rather fast', Bessie wrote in her diary in a reference to the sexually over-enthusiastic and the predatory. 'We are locked down for the night. What precious creatures we are.'[38] At first the separation between the women's and men's quarters seemed inviolable. The ship's constable maintained 'perfect order' and young women 'are not allowed to look at the young men, much more speak'.[39] On and below decks the matron kept a close eye on the *Northampton*'s single girls and young women. She was 'nice', Bessie noted, but 'too strict for some of the girls'.[40] '[W]e are like a lot of prisoners with a jailer', she added, laying out the consequences for rule-breakers:

> There was a great fuss today because one of the girls' father found that she had been corresponding with one of the young immigrants and that he had kissed her at the poop on Sunday when he went to see his sister . . . The girl spoke up and said it was not the young man's fault that she had been writing to him which the father did not believe at first. However he apologised to the young man for it. The girl told me afterwards that she liked him, she is eighteen and has another sister older than herself . . . they are very respectable girls . . .[41]

Adults' attempts at regulation met a degree of opposition. Somehow the no-speak rule failed to stop girls forming attachments to either the sailors or the lads in the single men's quarters. Most voyages took between four and five months, and they gave young people the opportunity to develop social connections and forge something of a common – if temporary – culture:

> As soon as the Constable has brought down our hot water, the door is locked – talk about being peculiar – it is almost ridiculous. When on the poop the girls are not to

look over at the young men, and when we go downstairs, the Matron stands at the bottom till every girl is down because they should not stand at the door and speak to anybody, which they will if they can. Sometimes they go up to the WC which is close to the door on purpose to get a chance of speaking to their friend but the Matron is up to them.[42]

The *Northampton* was a space of contradictory demands and possibilities. The girls found ways to unpick the knot of adult power as the ship sailed on, and the strict system of gender segregation frayed at the edges. 'We like all the sailors better than we did', Bessie wrote part way through the journey; 'although they are not allowed to speak we have a few words sometimes, some of them carry on a correspondence with the girls, but it is likely to cause a fuss.'[43] The possibilities continued to expand over time, within limits:

> Each of us three girls have got a young man at the wheel. There are four who take it in turn, including an old man. When the younger ones are there we take the opportunity when no one is in the way, to talk to them. One belongs to Edith Penn, one of the nicest girls in the mess, another to Pollie Carmen and the other to me . . . We have such few opportunities for chatting, it is too bad. We brought up a piece of pudding to give to Pollie's, but could not get a chance, too many lookers on. The other day I fetched a drink for mine, they are not allowed even to have a drink while at the wheel.[44]

The stakes were high: any seaman found chatting to a female passenger forfeited a month's pay. The *Northampton*'s constable could not be everywhere at once, though, and youthful enthusiasm won out in the end. Of the sailors and single male immigrants, Bessie wrote: 'It is fun to see them all crowd round the door when we are going below getting kisses when they can smuggle one which they do in spite of us being well guarded.'[45] 'Letter writing they have tried to prevent but cannot', she noted happily, '– the Matron says she shall not interfere, if she does it is only done more slyly.'[46] By the time the ship docked in Wellington Bessie had consolidated her friendships with the younger seamen: 'Edith and I will both be sorry to leave the ship, we have been very happy here. We have many a chat with the sailors which makes the time pass more quickly.'[47]

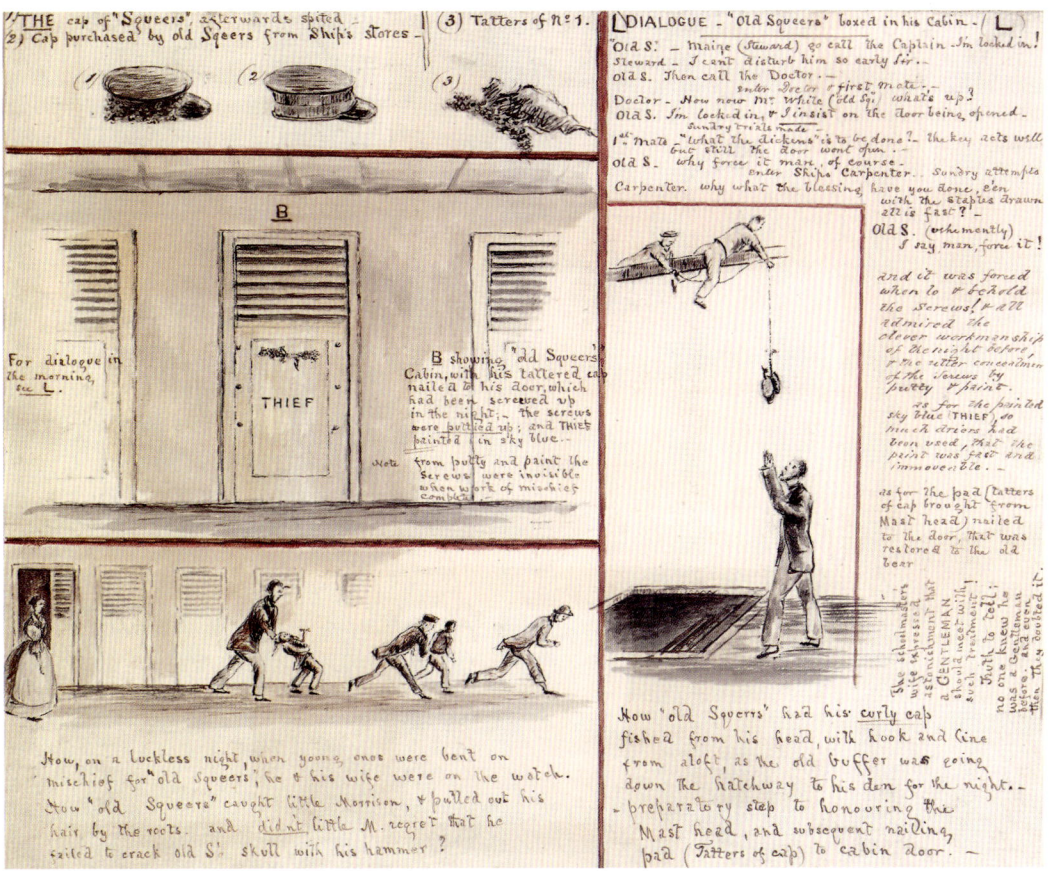

Highjinks on board the *Duke of Portland*, 1851. A group of boys played a trick on 'Old Squeers', the unpopular schoolmaster, purloining and then destroying his cap before nailing its remains to his cabin door. Then they removed the door-handle and screwed the door shut; 'the screws were puttied up and "Thief" painted in light blue'.

These girls' experiences reveal the tensions between desire, discipline, regulation and resistance, characteristics of adolescent lives then and since. Three of the *Northampton*'s passengers – Edith Penn, Pollie Carmen and Bessie herself – became the best of friends and sat together in the stern of the ship to read, write and chat. When each claimed a 'young man' for her own, she distanced herself from the older – and more controlling – constable and matron. Their shipboard lives foreshadowed later developments in the story of adolescence. The girls forged social connections on the basis of their age, and they shared a common cause: all agreed the *Northampton*'s rules were irksome and the sailors enticing. Nineteenth-century shipboard sociability, though, was fleeting in a way modern life is not. These girls' bonds broke apart when it came time to clamber ashore. 'I shall be sorry to leave some of the girls', Bessie wrote, 'but I hope I shall see them again.'[48]

Arriving and Fitting In

Although life in the hothouse of steerage helped establish several aspects of youthful cultures, friendship groups like Bessie's could be hard to sustain. Families whose young members had been separated on the ship quickly recombined upon arrival, and kin replaced friends at the centre of young immigrants' lives. Often friends dispersed in one direction, families another. A large number of girls arrived as domestics – of whom more shortly – and they also scattered to households far and wide, while many single boys began transient lives. Immigrants joined the circuits of mobility that characterised colonial life.[49]

The size of settlements made a difference to those arriving, shaping experience in particular ways. The whole of Otago had only 620 Pākehā inhabitants during the late 1840s and Auckland about 3,000.[50] The character, population and social infrastructure of these villages differed wildly from big-city Glasgow or London, the points of departure for many immigrants. Two tranches of youths – convicts who had served their sentences – bridged the gap between urban Britain and rural New Zealand, and they found the going tough. The first shipment of ninety-one lads from Parkhurst Prison on the Isle of Wight, a reformatory for petty thieves and swindlers, arrived in Auckland late in 1842 on the *St George*; the second group disembarked from the *Mandarin* the following year. Some were free agents, others apprentices bound to masters. With an average age of seventeen, these ragamuffins were small-time thieves – grinding poverty had made them steal a loaf of bread or pair of shoes – but Parkhurst was a relatively enlightened institution for its time. Its inmates obtained a basic education and some vocational training. Sometimes this met the needs of the new colony, but often it did not. Many had learned tailoring and shoemaking, but there was little demand for these skills in Auckland during the 1840s. Those who learned carpentry and bricklaying had rather more success.[51]

Assimilation was as much an ideological problem as a practical one. Local worthies judged the Parkhurst lads uncivilised and dangerous. One concerned citizen insisted that 'a convict and an emancipated one were much the same as a wild beast loose and a wild beast chained', and he worried New Zealand would become a penal colony just like New South Wales.[52] Such hostility sat side by side with concerns about the treatment meted out to the youths: 'several of them were employed on the roads without shoes or stockings. This is not by any means proper.'[53] Keen to distance their new home from the mean streets of the Old Country, colonists expected trouble from the 'juvenile delinquents of Great Britain'.[54] The Parkhurst Boys got the blame every time an Aucklander had property stolen; other settlers accused them of congregating in groups, wandering around town, stealing linen and 'committing other depredations'.[55] 'The lazy life suited some of those reprobates, and they taught Maoris evil words and actions', one colonist complained.[56] The boys felt the public disapproval most keenly. One lad wrote to a chaplain at Parkhurst and told of his reception among the colonists. His mentor replied: 'Be patient amid all the ill-usage of an ill-thinking and intemperate people, and you will soon live down the obloquy of "Parkhurst Boys". Be sure ___ that you must live it down by consistent steadiness and consistency of conduct, you cannot talk it down or force it down, still less will it do any good to show yourself vexed or angry.'[57] Young men, especially those from poor backgrounds, had to hold their tongues, seek assimilation into their new society and hope for a successful passage to full adulthood. They were not there yet.

The Parkhurst boys' experiences tell of youths finding their feet in a heady atmosphere of moral judgement, but they also reflect the continuous mobility of boys' working lives. A small settlement could not easily assimilate a substantial number of youths and once again they scattered. Many ended up breaking rocks on road-building jobs, some went to the copper mines on Great Barrier Island, a number moved onto the region's farms and others lived with rural Māori.[58]

The work lives of the Parkhurst boys' Māori counterparts were both settled and mobile. 'The everyday pattern of settlement was in small family groups, whānau, extended families, perhaps with a grandparent, two brothers, their wives and children, and some nieces and nephews', suggests archaeologist Kevin Jones, and 'community activity was organised by drawing on kin'.[59] Europeans described Māori work practices during the post-contact period. In 1861 John Gorst, a teacher, chronicled the work of boys in the Waikato. 'Three or four pairs of oxen, driven by stout, clean-limbed lads, are dragging as many ploughs through the rich loamy soil; and smaller boys are following the plough, and putting in seed potatoes.'[60] Others sowed wheat with their fathers. Gardening gave way to wandering as the crops matured. Young workers joined their elders who travelled considerable distances, 'feasting and fishing', while 'one old man or woman will take care of an entire village for weeks'.[61]

Wage labour was an itinerant business for many Pākehā youths. Some panned for gold, moving between claims and tramping around the South Island in the hope of a lucky break.[62] Many were successful: at Gabriel's Gully wandering colonial James Strachan, sixteen, amassed £100 – a small fortune – after just ten weeks' work.[63] Other youths 'moved from location to location and job to job as circumstances or seasons demanded', especially those who laboured on farms.[64] One fourteen-year-old arrived in Dunedin on the *John Wickliffe* in 1848 and went shepherding in North Otago. He 'lived near Totara in a hut, which was really half a cave, near where a big totara tree stood. There was no other living being nearer than Otepopo, which was ten miles away. Often he ran out of provisions and had to live for weeks at a time on Māori cabbage and mutton.'[65] Others drifted, picking up sporadic manual work along the way.[66] Before he set out for the goldfields James Strachan pitched his swag and wandered through the South Island, staying with kindly Māori ('I had a good feed of spuds and pork') and boarding with the ex-seamen acquaintances he had run into on his travels. James gardened, helped to build houses and rounded up stock. 'I was as strong as a young bullock', he later recalled, reasserting his claim on manhood.[67]

Sociologist Raewyn Connell uses the term 'gender order' to explain the importance of work in creating gendered relationships and ideals. The gender order is best understood as a structure of social expectations and practices that define what manhood and womanhood mean and how these shift across time and place. Work interacts with two other elements to create the gender order: cathexis, which Connell defines as 'emotionally charged social relations', and power.[68] We will shortly return to questions of power, but first it is worth seeing how itinerant forms of work provoked a range of emotional responses that shaped colonial masculinity in particular ways.

When James Strachan wrote 'I was as strong as a young bullock', he showed the pride he felt in acquitting himself as a young man. Meanwhile, his reference to boarding with Māori and ex-seamen spoke to a need for companionship and a degree of support. Others took up with work gangs as they travelled the countryside, and these provided a sense of camaraderie. On the early sheep stations boys fenced, drove stock, cleaned, rolled fleece, and spent their nights in tents, timber slab whares or mud huts with their age-mates and older men.[69] Fred Tiffen, seventeen, landed in Wellington from London in 1845. He found work with a group as a shepherd's assistant. Over nineteen days the men guided 800 sheep, six head of cattle and two pigs around the coast route to Te Ahiaruhi, a station in the Wairarapa. When the coastal trail proved impassable they ferried livestock in canoes. This was hard work but satisfying, and Fred went in search of relaxation and pleasure when he had the opportunity. At lambing time Fred thought he might get the chance to lie on the bank and watch the gambolling of the young ones, but the lambs' high spirits meant he had 'to keep going round and backwards and forwards all day to keep them within bounds'.[70]

Others longed for human company but did not quite manage it, and a sense of loneliness dominated their emotional state. Some peripatetic youths made their way into the embryonic towns, but they did not always stay long. James Strachan wound up in Wellington and stopped for a time in a boarding house. He hoped for stimulating company but 'the place was fairly full of sailors and wharf rats, nearly all hard ups', and he wandered back out into the hinterland.[71] Mark Pendry, thirteen, had no greater luck. Turned out by his veterinarian father for bad behaviour, he spent 1864 'knocking about as a stable boy amongst the hotels of Dunedin'. His father left for England and then Mark, who had 'no relative in the Colonies', led a hand-to-mouth existence.[72] The lad came to the attention of the authorities when he kicked a man out of his bed at the Steam Packet Hotel. The man attempted a sexual connection and offered money, but Mark was having none of it.[73] We do not know whether he found a form of company he preferred, or where he ended up.

The Brookes Brothers

In 1862, at the goading of his older brother Edwin, fourteen-year-old Charlie Brookes secured work with a landholder near the block farmed by his brothers. From his new situation Charlie wrote to his parents back home in England. His letters tell of a mid-century farming life, and Charlie found his rural experience more satisfying than some of his contemporaries.

> The time has at last come for me to write you a good long letter. I shall have to begin first by making excuses for not writing before, but I have none to make. Edwin would have me get work and we almost quarrelled about it, he was so proud because he was getting 3 or 4 pounds per week. So to settle it I got work and arranged my own terms so began work on the Monday morning. I am working for Mr Steventon. His tent, where I am staying, is on the other side of the hill, but I am still able to keep watch over ours. We live first rate at my place, milk, rice pudding, my favourite dish you know, meat, potatoes, plain puddings and treacle puddings, boiled rice and lots of things. I get to bed in daylight. I am making a fence now, English fashion, post and two rails. My accordion would be very nice for me, I could sit down for hours if I had the time to spare, and play myself into lands far away. I like my place very much, a kind master, good food and bed and half a crown a week is very fair for a beginner.
>
> I have been here 8 or 9 weeks, and last night, Saturday, we went to fetch groceries, the distance being about 3 miles altogether, over hills, bogs and swamp. We got three parts of the way on foot and the other part in a boat. It had been leaking so much that by the time we were half-way it was partly filled with water. At last Master said she was sinking and we pulled for the shore as fast as we could, got all the things out, fastened the rotten old boat as well as we could so that it couldn't drift away, then carried our things the rest of the journey. Was not that nice? To be rowing with water up above the knees, with the moon shining bright, casting the woods into the shade on both sides of the river. Won't you laugh? Ha, ha, ha.[74]

A little later in the year, Charlie and his brothers Edwin and Hovey were reunited on a farm overlooking the Oruawharo River where Charlie built himself a whare, but by 1868 he was dead. A storm blew up as Charlie rowed around the coast to see his lady love, his boat capsized and he drowned.

OPPOSITE Charlie's older brother Edwin sketched his own place near Port Albert. 'It will make the prettiest spot at the river', he wrote to his parents. 'Saturday I got a pig sty up and I've a little pig I bought from the natives'.

On March 31st I had my warrie nearly burnt down through the next settler setting some fern on fire. I shall never forget it. It made a humming noise like thunder. I got all my things out on the beach & expected every minute it's burning down, we got amongst it in several places & put it out, but I should think it cleared 100 acres of my land. I don't think its done any damage. I was making up my mind for the worst. I was thinking what I should do, whether I should get to Auckland or no, when towards evening we got it out, near the barrier. the fires here are just what you read of in Frank Leyton's story it's dreadful to behold a short time ago we had a fire on the Opo Block that burnt thousands of acres & lit up the country for miles round —

Rock Cottage   Red Bluff   Barrawhara

ever given you a sketch of my place but the Banks of the Arawhara it's been praised by many that it will make the prettiest spot on the river. Saturday I got a pig sty up & have a little pig I bought from the natives. I soon shall have a very pretty place if I can stop. I tried to get the boating of the evaporator stove but it seems they've given up the idea. I & the little boy we have lived on 7/- per week which is not much out here, all the time will pleasure & labour I've spent. if I leave it but I intend to stop as long as ever I can. till I have an answer to this letter if you can let me have 29£ I can have the 2 years out. not that I want it without the rest as I believe they will want as much as I do if I could see the slightest

Alder Fisher was another drifter. He arrived alone in Auckland from England in 1862 having determined 'to have a look at New Zealand and see what was to be done there'.⁷⁵ The youth travelled back and forth across the Tasman for a bit ('sailorising', as he put it) and then maintained an insecure existence around Auckland. He tried a spell as a stable hand, helped collect and sell firewood, unloaded cargo on the wharf, took on a bit of haymaking ('we slept alongside the stack') and worked on the ships ferrying livestock around New Zealand's coast.⁷⁶ Alder tried not to complain – the move to New Zealand had been his own decision, after all – but he confessed his concerns to his diary. 'Here I am in a far distant land among strangers with not a friendly face within hail', he wrote while in Auckland.⁷⁷ Social possibilities presented themselves when Alder arrived in Wellington, took up at the Ship Hotel and another fellow asked whether he would have a 'nobbler'. But the religiously minded lad resisted the temptations of a boozy kind of company. 'If inclined that way at all off you go nobblerising from morning till night . . . I do not wonder at so many young fellows going astray when they come out here. Believe me 'tis a hard struggle to keep on the right path.'⁷⁸

These youths' experiences reflected their relative inexperience and their status as recent immigrants. They tried hard to establish themselves in a land where a great many men wandered the landscape in search of work and company.⁷⁹ Their emotions – pride, pleasure, a sense of accomplishment or loneliness – arose out of their daily life and work and also reflected the broader patterns of colonial masculinity. Drink lubricated male bonds, albeit temporarily, but youths with an aversion to alcohol, those who moved around a lot, and inhabitants of isolated localities all found it difficult to obtain social support and emotional stability. Even those with weak ties to other young men discovered that itinerancy hampered the emergence of sustained youth-centred cultures.

Inevitably, immigrants had different feelings about their freedom and mobility. While James Strachan saw his peripatetic life as an adventure, Alder Fisher yearned to swap incessant mobility for domestic contentment. 'I do not like this way of living at all, I mean boarding at a public house', Alder told his diary. 'It will be a happy time indeed when I have a house to go to.'⁸⁰ Achieving domestic happiness was often slow, though, and few boys married. Precarious colonial circumstances gave rise to unsettled private lives.

Girls' Work

Few historians have acknowledged that the nineteenth-century category of 'youth' is profoundly gendered. Gillis, for instance, writes of 'youth' as a time of semi-independence and he relays the experiences of boys – farmers, apprentices and scholars – but does not consider whether girls occupied the category in the same way, or whether in fact they occupied it at all.[81] In New Zealand, at least, they did not. Paid labour did not define adulthood for young women in the same way it did for young men, and shifting forms of dependence, not semi-independence, shaped antipodean girls' lives before the 1870s. When most girls left home they went in one of two directions: marriage or domestic service. Girls had the right to marry at twelve, as long as their parents agreed, and they tied the knot at an earlier age than boys. During the 1850s the median age of a first-time bride was a little over twenty-one. Twenty-five was the median age for grooms.[82] Girls, then, were much more likely than boys to trade the support of their parents for a married life. Others took up paid domestic work and remained closely tied to hearth and family, someone else's rather than their own. Few young women enjoyed anything resembling true independence.

By the end of the 1860s, three-fifths of all female workers were domestic servants.[83] The New Zealand government kept an eye on the need for domestics and offered free passage into the country for single girls and women between the ages of twelve and thirty-five.[84] Many singletons on the immigrant ships, some of whom walked straight from London's workhouses to the wharves, set out to New Zealand to take up opportunities here.[85] They had a clear incentive: employers' demand for servants outstripped the available supply, and rates of pay were more than twice as high as those in England.[86] Some prospective servants showed themselves proficient at their work but others did not. Elizabeth Sangster was matron on the *Oamaru*, a ship that conveyed its human cargo from Glasgow to Dunedin. She felt that many of her charges 'have no idea of either sewing or knitting anything into shape', and some 'are so stupid but surely they will improve'.[87] Either way, desperate householders snapped them up as soon as they landed.

Girls between assignments and those not provided with live-in accommodation found shelter and rations at the immigration barracks, private boarding establishments and servants' homes set up in a few towns.[88] In Christchurch in

1863, Maria Rye, herself young and unmarried, launched a fundraising drive for a 'safe and respectable home for young women of good character'. She received sufficient support from public subscriptions to open the Christchurch Female Home in January 1864. There were rules to be followed:

1. That girls of good character only shall be admitted;
2. That each girl shall pay 12s per week, in advance, towards her board and lodging;
3. That a girl may be admitted twice in one year, provided her character remains good, and that no debts in her name remain on the book;
4. That each girl shall be at liberty to attend that place of worship in the town of Christchurch which she prefers;
5. That the girls shall rise at 7 a.m. Every girl to be at home by 8 p.m., and all lights out by 10 o'clock each day in the year.[89]

Girls' domestic situations reinforced their dependence. Like the servants who boarded with their employers, those who took up a place at Maria Rye's were subject to continued surveillance. They returned home after a day toiling for their masters and mistresses only to defer to their pseudo-parents at the Female Home. Maria Rye's refuge for respectability had over 200 boarders – no doubt many signed up out of necessity, not a desire for being closely guarded – although it closed four years later when its funding ran out.

Power played an important role in the organisation of female domestic labour, as it did in the nineteenth-century gender order more generally. Some employers treated girls as lackeys, subjecting them to long hours, a never-ending array of tasks and frequent reminders of their station in life. Those engaged as general household help had the roughest time. One lass woke on December 25th to be told: 'You are to go on with your work as usual today; Christmas is not meant for servants.'[90] Later in the century, Gertie Brookes, whom we met at the start of this book, reported she 'worked so hard that I feel as though there is no life in me' and she described a servant acquaintance by alluding to American slavery: 'she works like a nigger'.[91] Gertie wrote a sympathetic letter to another friend in service: 'Oh dear alas, you don't know how sorry I feel for you having to work so hard. I'm quite sure it isn't your duty to work there until you are ill.'[92] Some mistresses misused their power to the point of tyranny. The newspapers relayed the

OPPOSITE In Wellington, c. 1860, Mrs Jessie Crawford takes a seat while her melancholic-looking young servants stand behind her.

sad case of Dunedin servant Katherine Telfer. She slept on the floor and left the property only twice in five months; her employer beat her and deprived her of food. Katherine turned witness at a coroner's inquest after another servant in the same household starved to death.[93]

Positions involving childcare also involved long hours and high levels of accountability, but they proved less monotonous, offering greater human contact and affording a degree of emotional satisfaction. A woman near Whakatane hired Pare, 'a big strong Māori girl', to help with the children who soon became very attached to her.[94] In 1851 Motueka mistress Sarah Greenwood wrote fondly of her servant: 'My damsel is very good tempered, good natured, fond of children and willing to take advice though, with the usual giddiness of 15, she does not always act upon it. Altogether I feel her such an immense comfort that I cannot be very severe upon her shortcomings.'[95] Sarah Greenwood's reference to 'comfort' suggests she valued her damsel's emotional as well as practical assistance – intimate bonds sometimes ran both ways – although the word 'giddiness' signals the impact of youthful inexperience as well as the hierarchy of the working relationship.

Not all domestic servants achieved the same status. While the general household help stood on the lowest rung of the ladder, the governess, a combination of servant, childcarer and teacher, occupied the highest. Openings were scarce and only the lucky few secured a position. Mary Haselden arrived in Auckland in 1861 and made enquiries. 'One Wednesday, Maria, Mamma, Fanny and I went to call on Mrs Stratford, the doctor's lady at Parnell, which is considered quite an aristocratic part of Auckland, to see if she could use her influence to get us governesses' positions, but she did not give us much hope, says there are as many governesses as pupils.'[96] Mary waited some weeks before finding a suitable situation in Auckland, but her appointment lasted only briefly: she lost her job after her mistress' money ran out. Some months later Mary moved north to Doubtless Bay to become a governess for a magistrate. The job was not especially burdensome: 'There are five little girls, the eldest nearly nine, but the eldest two are now in Auckland. So I have only to teach about an hour and a half a day. The youngest are Katie, Fanny and Baby. Katie is five years old. Today we have been for a row across the bay and called on Mrs D . . . who has a family of five daughters and two sons. It has been a lovely day and I enjoyed the row very much indeed.'[97]

The propagandists for immigration, including Charles Hursthouse, marketed New Zealand as a land of opportunity, and not all immigrants undertook an arduous sea journey only to become second-class citizens. Just as many young female passengers wriggled free of onboard surveillance, once on land some girls resisted the subordinate position mapped out for them. The typical antipodean servant arrived with expectations of a new, less class-bound life, and she had little interest in putting her mistress on a pedestal. The well-off did not always appreciate this fact.[98] A Wellington couple complained about the fifteen-year-old girl to whom they paid five shillings each week to do the dirtiest tasks. Their 'little maid' insisted someone else light the fires 'and thinks she does wonders by getting up, when we call her at seven, and doing the sitting room (twelve feet square) before breakfast'.[99] Not only that, their lass responded to instructions with 'saucy answers'. Other settlers complained that their domestics wore clothes too similar to their own and insisted on having their friends over.[100] Still, hierarchies bent a little in a land where servants remained in short supply.[101] One mistress had no choice but to turn a blind eye to her maid's truculence as 'there is *literally* no one else to be had'.[102]

Was it possible for girls to side-step domestic controls even further and gain a degree of autonomy? Some of them tried, although few managed to escape the prescriptions of the gender order. Some set themselves up on the goldfields, selling sly grog or working as 'hebes' (barmaids) or dancing girls.[103] Older men tended to glamorise young women decked out in ringlets, crinolines and jewellery, and to see them as being above 'service'. 'Why it would be almost an insult to ask so much smiling beauty to bring you beer', suggested a traveller in Hokitika. 'They were, of course, of all types from blondes to brunettes, mostly with Junoesque figures and engaging smiles.'[104] But the reality of bar work was far from romantic, and freedom remained elusive. At Kaniere on the West Coast, a sixteen-year-old dancer performed each evening until eleven o'clock and was then expected to entertain miners at cards, sometimes until six in the morning. Her employer sued her for breach of contract after her health broke down and her sister took her away from the saloon.[105]

More than a few goldfields girls sold sexual services to the miners. Some swapped favours for money upstairs in the saloons and others worked in separate brothels run by older women.[106] In 1872, fourteen-year-old former domestic

OVERLEAF Girls and young women lived on the margins of the goldfields' male society. Here, in the settlement of Napoleon Hill near Ahaura in 1866, three dancing girls peer from the doorway of the Casino de Venise.

servant Margaret Glen reportedly associated with 'common prostitutes' in the goldfields town of Thames and she 'led a very depraved life'. The local detective warned her to 'quit the company of bad characters or she would be locked up'.[107] She did not, and a judge jailed her for a year. Margaret's case reveals how girls' work intersected with gendered notions of reputation. The language used to describe Margaret's case – 'depraved', 'bad characters' and 'ill-fame' – signalled the division between reputable and disreputable girlhood. Indeed, historian Sarah Carr suggests that the link between work and respectability underpinned women's identity during the 1860s.[108] The stakes were particularly high among the young, and unwitting girls could be corrupted and driven from respectability more or less permanently. The *Observer*, an Auckland newspaper, told its readers of fifteen-year-old girls living in brothels, 'merry-eyed children circling like moths round the flame of vice'. The tale was shocking, and the term 'children' intensified the sense of moral outrage.

While a Thames judge imprisoned Margaret Glen, boys and men benefited from the sexual double standard. Their role in paid sexual exchange was overlooked and the shame and punishment was heaped upon girls' and women's shoulders instead. Police arrested fourteen-year-old Eliza Lambert for prostitution and rowdy behaviour. An 1859 arrival through the port at Lyttelton, she hung around the theatre in Christchurch's Gloucester Street using foul language and throwing stones through hotel windows. The authorities released her from custody in the hope she would leave the province. She did not, and they flung her back in gaol.[109] If Eliza refused to discipline herself then the state would do it for her. Her case, along with Margaret Glen's, underlines a broader point: while economic independence precipitated boys' transition from childhood to adulthood, a girl matured when she learned to obey the rules of respectability. The right sort of work set a boy on the road to manhood, but the wrong sort led a girl into ruin. Although the language of respectability has since lost its currency, the sexual double standard lives on today.

These examples gesture towards the profound differences in girls' and boys' lives during the middle of the nineteenth century. The young domestic servant remained dependent on her employer in a close-bound and controlled way, while the itinerant youth ranged across a wide geographical territory and his social ties remained loose. Girls' ongoing domestic dependence meant that their life transitions were less strongly marked than boys', and usually they slipped from girlhood to womanhood with little fanfare. Only a challenge to prevailing codes of respectability, like those issued by Margaret Glen and Eliza Lambert, attracted attention. These gendered transitions would take a new shape later in the century when new kinds of paid employment separated home life from work life, brought together large numbers of girls to build their own culture and created new geographies of adolescence. Secondary education greatly altered young New Zealanders' lives too, although its beginnings were small in scale and imperfectly formed.

Schooling the Few

New Zealand had a haphazard school system in the years before 1870, and few in-betweeners enjoyed any secondary training.[110]

Some young immigrants arrived in New Zealand with an education already under their belts. Charlie Brookes went to a church school near Oxford before he set out for the Albertland settlement, and the well-off Jerningham Wakefield studied at King's College, London. Teachers on the immigrant ships informally conveyed their knowledge to anyone interested.[111]

During the early decades of European settlement, social status, parental incomes and religion determined access to education. Missionaries and church groups set up schools for their own purposes in the north of the North Island. They trained personnel for the church and 'civilised' Māori in order to ease their conversion to Christianity.[112] In Paihia in 1826, Jane and Marianne Williams educated Māori girls at their private school. The Williams sisters emphasised the niceties of English gentility, although it is not clear whether academic subjects entered the picture alongside the 'catechism and embroidery, hymn-singing and laundering'.[113] However, other missionary schools taught reading, writing and arithmetic right across the age range, and a visitor to one mission noted: 'I observed all ranks and ages, Chiefs and subjects, old and young, bound and free, receiving and communicating instruction with a degree of decorum and regularity that would have reflected credit on a school of the same kind in England.'[114] This focus on literacy bore fruit: by the late 1850s roughly half of Māori adults could read the Māori language and one-third could write it.[115]

TEENAGERS

ABOVE Benjamin Ashwell's Māori school at Taupiri in the Waikato. Girls and women learned domestic tasks, boys and men did farming and carpentry, and all received an academic education: reading, writing, arithmetic and scriptural history. This sketch is based on a faded photograph from 1859.

The state was slower to establish a school system. Provincial governments set up some primary schools during the 1850s and 1860s for children under the age of fourteen.[116] From 1867 the first government-run 'native schools' taught English language, mathematics and manual skills to Māori under the age of thirteen or so, and fifty-seven such schools were established in the ten years that followed.[117] All schooling was optional, though: not until 1877 did legislation provide free and compulsory education for seven- to thirteen-year-olds.

Those over the age of thirteen attended school only if their parents could afford the tuition fees, and private educational institutions sprang up in the main centres. John Gorrie's Auckland Academy offered a classical education that was taught in three sessions each day: ten until two, two until four, and an evening class from six until nine.[118] Gorrie laid out his curriculum in the local newspaper: 'English reading and Grammar, Writing, Arithmetic, Geography, Mathematics, Latin, Greek, &c.'[119] Charles Grace set up the Wellington Academy, and the short-lived Dunedin Academy, established in 1855 by James Grant, also offered a classical bill of fare.[120] These schools educated 'young ladies' as well as 'young gentlemen' while maintaining a respectful separation of teaching times. The Wellington Academy, for instance, catered for the former at lunch-times and the latter in the mornings.[121] Girls had other options too: older women, often unmarried, ran small private schools for female colonials. These reinforced the connections between femininity and familial domesticity when their proprietors,

BELOW Part of a panorama of St John the Evangelist school, Tamaki. From left to right: the printing office, wash house, Bishop's house, English school, hall, kitchen, Māori adult school, weaving room, surgery, Rangitoto, St Thomas' church, college chapel, Māori boys' school and the primary school.

like their counterparts in similar English schools, adopted a maternal role towards those in their care.[122]

Other English educational traditions took new forms in a New Zealand context. Churches set up schools with secondary departments, including St John the Evangelist in Tamaki, established by Bishop George Selwyn in 1843 to teach both Māori and Pākehā, and in 1854 the Anglicans opened Te Aute College for Māori boys in the Hawke's Bay.[123] St John's, an antipodean version of the English public school Eton, trained boys and young men for ordination.[124] Selwyn attempted to bring together Māori and Pākehā youths on equal terms. He taught young Māori the ways of English civilisation and checked those English lads who thought themselves better than their Māori counterparts.[125] Eighteen-year-old John Greenwood studied at St John's, and his 1850 diary entries tell of days reading Shakespeare and practising his Greek and Latin. School was simultaneously a place of regulation and relative freedom. John rose early in the morning and turned in late at night, studying in between, but he often took time out from the formal curriculum, whiling away hours playing cricket, tootling on his flute, reading Molière aloud and gardening with the Māori pupils. He enjoyed regular breaks for 'talk, kai, rest' and went out to visit children at the nearby kāinga (Māori village).[126]

St John's offered the sort of outdoor education Etonians could only dream of. In 1851 John Greenwood set off on a voyage from Auckland to Stewart Island with Selwyn and several fellow pupils in the sailboat *Undine*. He spent mornings studying Greek and the art of navigation, and the afternoons doing Selwyn's accounts and looking after the stores on board: a box of bees that travelled with the party, and Selwyn's ever-expanding collection of seaweed. John seized the opportunity to 'take the sun' whenever he could. The Bishop was not always the best expedition organiser. John complained that Selwyn's 'ruling passion seems to be the love of power, to gratify which he will interfere and meddle in the most frivolous as well as the most important things. Now as an example take the matter of provisions. In the Navy, men get flour, rations, pease [*sic*], preserved meats, lime juice (and fresh meat in harbour), none of which things have we had since we left Auckland.'[127] In a few places, John crossed out his references to Selwyn, presumably for fear of the consequences if 'His Lordship', as John called the Bishop, happened across the diary. Next to a mess of ink obscuring several words,

John Greenwood, aged about sixteen, painted in 1848 by his mother Sarah.

John later explained: 'This means that the Bishop exploded about something or other.'[128]

John Greenwood's experiences stand in marked contrast to those of itinerant youths and domestic servants. John tells of a privileged family background and a semi-established social world. No wonder he wrote of his school, 'In spite of any grievances, real & imaginary, I am very happy here.'[129] Some of his classmates – and perhaps John as well – enjoyed themselves a little too much. In 1852 homo-erotic dalliances came to the attention of the church authorities and the ensuing scandal rocked St John's. 'Evil practices', as one senior staff member called them, had gone on 'almost from the commencement of the college',[130] beginning among the Pākehā lads who then 'corrupted' the Māori pupils. Selwyn tried to limit the damage. His teachers kept a closer eye on the boys and tutors began checking

TEENAGERS

Designed in England in 1850, Big School opened at Christ's College in 1863. The total enrolment was small: forty-four pupils in 1857, eighty-two in 1862, fifty-nine by the end of 1863 and sixty-seven in 1864. These numbers represented a thin top slice of Canterbury society and a wide range of ages: Christ's College catered for youths between the ages of seven and seventeen. Fifth and sixth formers sat at the desks in the far left corner, third and fourth formers in the right corner, and first and the second formers next to them. The headmaster sat behind the lecturn-like desk at the lower left of this photograph that corresponds to the centre of the room. Only later were schoolboys allocated to separate rooms according to their form, and increasing age segregation helped transform youth cultures.

the bedrooms every night, but it all proved too much and the school went into abeyance in 1853.[131]

During the late 1840s Reverend and Mrs Kissling opened St Stephen's Native Girls' School at Kohimarama as a counterpart to St John's. At the building's inauguration 'several of the lads from St John's College presented offerings as tokens of regard for the girls of St Stephen's'.[132] Bishop Selwyn fervently hoped students of St John's and St Stephen's would meet and mingle. He wanted his 'trained Māori youths' to marry the Kisslings' educated young women.[133] Selwyn was no rigidly minded patriarch, and he felt girls as well as boys deserved a secondary training. So too did Reverend Walter Lawry, who set up the Wesleyan College and Seminary in upper Queen Street in 1850. This early example of a co-educational school, established primarily for Pākehā, catered for the offspring of missionaries and others 'who looked for a superior education'.[134] Girls and boys learned arithmetic, physiology and the classics, a gender-neutral curriculum that carried on in New Zealand schools for the rest of the century.

Schools contributed to the development of young people's cultures slowly and irregularly. The numbers of pupils were tiny at first: St John's taught only seven in the college and fifteen in the Māori boys' section in 1850 when John Greenwood attended.[135] By 1863 Christ's College in Christchurch, a fee-charging Anglican school, had sixty pupils. Like St John's and the first state secondary schools – Nelson College (1853), Otago Boys' High School (1863) and Wellington College (1867) – Christ's College taught boys aged between seven and the late teens.[136] A proven ability to learn – and parents' willingness to pay fees – determined whether a boy would be enrolled, not his age.

If small numbers and a broad age range constrained the development of age-specific cultures, so too did educational architecture. Most schools taught everyone more or less together. Upon the completion of Christ's College's Big School in 1863, for instance, all sixty pupils received lessons in one large room. They were separated only by the spaces between clusters of seats. Boys had little opportunity to spend time with those their own age when eight-year-olds and eighteen-year-olds learned in the same classroom. That would have to wait until schools grew in size and spatial complexity. These fledgling educational institutions hinted at what was to come, but they did not yet sharpen the lines between youths of different ages.

TEENAGERS

Colonial Entertainments

Leisure, like education, would play an important role in shaping adolescence as a social force. At first, though, opportunities were relatively circumscribed and the social infrastructure sparse. One early arrival remembered Auckland during the 1840s when 'everything was in a very primeval state – no free libraries for young men, no regular amusement except the billiard rooms or the hotel'.[137] As he hinted, the first hostelries sprang up very early indeed. Before 1881, when an age of sixteen was imposed, no national licensing law stipulated a minimum age to drink in a bar.[138] (In 1904 eighteen became the national drinking age and this rose to twenty-one in 1910.) Young New Zealanders had as much right as their adult counterparts to imbibe a pint at Auckland's Royal – which opened its doors in 1841 – or the Exchange which took first orders soon after. Some publicans, including the proprietor of the Swan Inn at Motueka near Nelson, added to the entertainment by building a skittle alley: a long, low wooden structure set up for ten-pin bowling.[139]

The village of Auckland in 1843 with its boggy ground, rough paths and a scattering of wooden buildings. Entertainment was restricted to two hotels, a billiard room and make-your-own fun. High-spirited youths rang doorbells, removed door mats and shifted a board marked '→ To the Cemetery', placing it 'in Dr Fischer's grounds, pointing to his residence'.

A lad peruses the entertainment on offer in Christchurch in January 1866. The Christy's Minstrels – variety players offering skits and 'blackface' – have come to town; there is also a 'Boxing Night' and the Lyttelton Regatta. Young New Zealanders enjoyed other diversions too. 'Sensation novels' dealt with insanity, sexual irregularities and cases of mistaken identity. They were widely available and popular; New Zealand booksellers sold *The Woman in White* (1859), *East Lynne* (1860) and *Armadale* (1864) through mail order. Critics attacked them as corrosive of morals, addictive for their shocks and thrills. A conservative periodical worried that such novels would rouse youthful passions, being 'greedily devoured' at the expense of more wholesome titles. By the mid-1860s the colony's theatres – not the most reputable of hangouts – showed stage adaptations of *East Lynne* and the other novels to eager audiences.

Two kinds of entertainment emerged in the early colonial setting: mixed-age leisure, by far the most common kind, and the rudimentary youth-focussed leisure I explore in the next section. Youths and adults socialised together in mixed-age settings, including the hostelries and skittle alleys as well as the chess and book clubs that sprang up during the 1850s.[140] Horse racing amused young and old alike, and some went to considerable lengths to enjoy the spectacle. In the summer of 1846, when seventeen-year-old Fred Tiffen had time off from his job on a Wairarapa sheep run, he decided to visit the races at Te Aro Flat in Wellington – 'being on pleasure bent'. Fred walked all the way around the coastline and arrived at the racecourse four days later.[141]

Well-off Wellingtonians also danced at Barrett's Hotel where young people enjoyed 'having society', as one lass put it, in the company of adults.[142] A bullock wagon with an awning conveyed the girls and women to one Barrett's dance in 1843, for it was hard to maintain a lady-like get-up on the muddy streets of the frontier town.[143] Further north, Auckland governess Mary Haselden also loved going to the ball and she spent many pleasant evenings whirling about the floor with a range of partners.[144] The dance card, a pre-arranged list that recorded partners for each dance, regulated social interactions. Sometimes dances ran until dawn when the light of the rising sun allowed revellers to make their way home through the streets, and girls were carefully chaperoned by men whom their parents carefully vetted. The ball was a highly formal affair patronised mostly by the well-to-do, but other kinds of dances had a different tone. In Christchurch the itinerant James Strachan wandered down to Cook's Boarding House where he and others participated in 'a sort of Free and Easy'. Some participants chatted, others took to the dance floor, and boys and girls provided the entertainment. At Cook's, Strachan wrote, 'the music was supplied by a young lady with a tambourine, and her brother, a young lad who had a box organ and a triangle'.[145]

Mixed-age leisure took place in the schools, too, where social occasions brought together pupils and staff. At St John's College in 1851, John Greenwood had a whale of a time at an informal concert with 'games, songs, Maori war dance &c, agreeably interspersed with Kai'. It all 'made a very merry and very noisy evening. Certainly Mr and Mrs Lloyd and Co. did laugh with right goodwill. I must say some of the charades were very funny, though I say it, who should not say it, being one of the actors. Mrs Lloyd was quite frightened when a number of the Maories [sic] came in with mats & spears and danced the war dance with appropriate yells &c. Altogether the whole affair went off capitally and I went to bed very tired, stiff & hoarse.'[146]

While the St John's concert offered a distinctly New Zealand take on a British cultural tradition, other mixed-age entertainments arrived from the Old Country more or less intact. The 'penny gaffs' offered a mixture of farce, melodrama and singing, all performed 'through a haze of rank tobacco smoke to a raucous,

A Certain Freedom

Wellington had only recently become home to Pākehā when, in 1843, seventeen-year-old Mary Ann Petre arrived with her husband Henry. Mary grew up in a convent and the pair were married in 1841. They travelled from Portsmouth on the *Thomas Sparks*, stopped for a time in Cape Town and later arrived among the bush-covered hills of Port Nicholson. Mary eagerly explored the new landscape. She wandered the rough tracks to Karori with a friend, spent hours in bush around the city, waded through streams and rode horses along the gravelled road to Petone. There were mosses, ferns and insects to collect, and pies to make from the berries growing along the way. Mary's diary, a small volume bound in alligator skin, reveals an extensive round of visiting and reciprocity among the well-heeled settlers. Francis Molesworth turned up armed with melons and cucumbers from his fertile garden in the Hutt, the Fitzgeralds put on dinner (although it was 'such a squash' in their tiny house) and Mrs Fitzgerald taught Mary to play the guitar.[147] The Featherstones threw 'a very stupid party', as Mary called it, but she enjoyed spending time with the Daniells, another family.[148] After dinner there one evening, she wrote: 'how I like this free, happy life'.[149]

Of all Mary's leisure activities, dancing made her happiest of all. There was a 'most delightful ball' at Mrs Joyes that began at nine o'clock and continued till three in the morning; 'Henry danced a great deal.'[150] On hearing the news of another ball to come, Mary jotted: 'I danced about the room for joy.'[151] Not always were such amusements conducted on dry land. On board a visiting ship, she wrote, 'we were received with all possible French politeness. The vessel was very prettily fitted up. We had a dejeuner and we walked up and down the deck for an hour while the band played. The captain said we should if we liked have a dance onboard. I should think we did like!'[152]

Mary Petre as a young woman.

Vauxhall Gardens as depicted in *Otago Punch*. There are plenty of opportunities for youthful dissipation. Pleasure-loving Dunedinites danced, rode horses, canoodled in the bushes and lazed about while listening to a band. Such pleasures were not confined to Dunedin: Cantabrians made the most of Kohler's pleasure gardens in Lincoln Road, but any untoward goings-on in Kohler's maze and leafy walkways stayed out of the newspapers.

all-male audience'.[153] Auckland's first penny gaff opened in 1841 at the back of Watson's Exchange Coffee Rooms. The audience listened to a band and sang along with 'Larry Rooney and the Monkey' and other lively tunes.[154]

Commercial pleasure gardens were another English import. Dunedin's Vauxhall Gardens took its name from a south London establishment of a similar type and opened for business in 1862. Vauxhall offered its pleasure-seekers a range of amusements: teas, dance bands, a shooting gallery, swimming pools, football and fireworks displays. There was an altogether more sensuous side as well. Girls and boys enjoyed games with suggestive names like Whipping the Goose, Groping for Silver and Catching the Cock, and on a grassy hill they played 'kiss-in-the-ring', a game with its roots in the fertility rituals of pre-Roman England.[155] Often they abandoned the kissing to throw hay at one another.[156] In New Zealand, just as in England, the pleasure gardens quickly became contradictory social spaces associated with vice as well as peaceful recreation.[157] Young women worked behind Vauxhall's bar and, it was often claimed, ladies of the night solicited their trade outside.[158] The public flocked to the gardens to 'look and to be looked at, to dance and to pose, to touch and to flirt' and, unsurprisingly, respectable New Zealanders worried about moral corruption.[159] 'It is wrong to lure boys and girls, young men and women, over the waters to Vauxhall' thundered the puritanical James Grant, sometime principal of the Dunedin Academy. He railed against shady corners with such names as 'Venus' Arbour' and 'Cupid's Retreat'.[160] Henry Farley, Vauxhall's developer, airily dismissed such claims. There was no 'Venus' Arbour', he retorted, tongue in cheek; detractors must have been thinking of 'Lovers' Walk'.[161]

This debate ran deeper than the doings in Vauxhall Gardens. Suggestive signposts, kissing games and hay-throwing all incited worrisome feelings. An increasing number of American commentators wrote that young people longed for happiness and pleasure to such a degree that vast and volatile outpourings of emotion governed their actions. Such impulses, they concluded, required careful control.[162] In New Zealand, a Nelson lecturer spoke of 'the cultivation of the senses and the discipline of the mind', insisting that colt-like youths 'must be broken to the bit'. While 'the exercise of the senses is naturally pleasurable to children and young people', he added, self-control and discipline made an adult.[163] Small wonder the theatres – 'spiritual pest-houses', Grant called them – caused concern.[164] What happened on their stages told of mystery, adventure, criminality and lust, and prostitutes often fought in the lobbies.[165] Morally upright citizens worried that dancing also rendered young people powerless in the face of their baser instincts. A writer in *The Evangelist*, a Presbyterian magazine published in the Otago goldfields town of Lawrence, warned that the 'young maiden gives way to the love of dress and fondness of company – yields herself up to the fascinations and excitement of the ball-room, the theatre, and such-like ensnaring vanities' and is soon reduced to a 'mere butterfly existence'.[166]

Such religiously motivated commentators engaged the trope of sensation to draw social distinctions. *The Evangelist*'s writer thundered: 'The syren voice of pleasure, with its merry laugh and witching song, lures on and on, and faster, ever faster glides the current with its gay, thoughtless victim.'[167] Boys were not immune to temptation. Too many of them turned 'vain' and 'light-minded' – and careened towards perilous futures as 'libertines', 'rakes', or, even worse, 'gross, degraded debauchees'.[168] This was an argument about gender and generation: youth were attached to a form of sensation so excessive it compromised their mental faculties. Sensation marked an important boundary: hedonistic young people occupied one side of the line, and self-aware, disciplined adults lived on the other.[169]

Self-improvement and the New Significance of Youth

Churchgoers responded to the risk of youthful exuberance by setting up organisations to foster appropriate kinds of fellowship and train young minds. In the process, they provided an alternative to mixed-age leisure and helped young people's cultures to coalesce. The Young Men's Christian Association (YMCA) is the most well-known early example. Established in London in 1844, the association offered spiritual uplift and companionship by providing bible study and prayer groups.[170] In 1853 a twenty-nine-year-old English immigrant by the name of Richard Barcham Shalders, an erstwhile member of the London YMCA, wandered Auckland's muddy streets and invited young men to a 'Scriptural Conversation Class' at his Queen Street home. Six youths aged in their teens and early twenties went along, then a dozen, then thirty.[171] Two years later the Auckland YMCA came into being, and soon a cosy reference library and reading room – complete with lace curtains and a warm fire – opened in Durham Street. This proved especially popular when the English mails arrived, and wandering colonial youths found a social environment where they could read letters from 'home'.[172] The library also hosted a regular lecture series on such topics as the 'formation of character' and 'the demand of the age for self-improvement'.[173] The benefits of such events soon spread to other centres: the YMCA was set up in Dunedin in 1861 and in Christchurch a year after that.

While the YMCA had British origins, the young men's mutual improvement societies of the 1850s and 1860s used an American template. Designed for a frontier society, the American mutual improvement model was well suited to New Zealand's socially fractured, itinerant male population. Youths who meandered across the countryside could look up the closest chapter and find companionship. Loosely affiliated to the Protestant churches, like the YMCA these societies gave their members an opportunity to discuss scientific and 'improving' subjects.[174] Led by a churchman and a lawyer, the Christchurch Young Men's Literary Association was fairly typical. Its members established themselves as arbiters of taste by debating whether 'Tennyson is overrated' and 'Burns is a truer poet than Longfellow', and they readied themselves for future civic leadership by discussing the economy, the death penalty and the idea that the South Island should seek independence from the North.[175]

Age-wise, these associations reflected the imprecise, shifting and gendered spectrum of 'youth'. A boy had to be at least sixteen to join the Nelson Young Men's Mutual Improvement Society, whose members met in a hay loft to study the literary classics, and most members were aged in their late teens and early twenties.[176] For the first time the particular significance of the teen years hoved into view. In 1862, medical doctor Edward Blackmore lectured young Nelsonians on their importance. 'The seven years named the teens are the most precious of all years', Blackmore told the lads. 'They are the springtime of human life, the formative period of the permanent personal qualities of the mind.' To youths who unwisely spurned the opportunity to read widely, develop the mind, and build up social and intellectual capital, Blackmore had a stern warning: 'the summer and autumn and winter of your mental life will be a scene of barrenness and dismal desolation'.[177]

As they listened to these kinds of improving speeches, members of the Nelson Young Men's Mutual Improvement Society and its brother organisations imbibed an important message: youth in general, and the teens in particular, constituted a significant stage of life in social, moral and developmental terms. Calm heads and wise counsel would guide impetuous youth through this challenging period. In 1862, when Blackmore addressed Nelson's youths, he reminded them that the teen years were the right time for young men to shape their personality, turn their backs on impulsive passions and embrace sound judgement. Blackmore's talk

made ripples across the wider community too: the *Colonist* newspaper printed every word for local readers to ponder.

The literary associations were small in scale but they played a significant role in the history of young New Zealanders. By providing opportunities for youths across a fairly wide age range and disseminating ideas about the teen years' importance, they led the way as embryonic examples of a youth-focussed leisure. Conservative reactions against untrammelled sensation, it turned out, had a transformative outcome.

Conclusion: Blurry Boundaries

It was not always easy to see where mid-nineteenth-century childhood ended and adulthood began. Only a few commentators spoke of the 'teens', and the male category of 'youth' denoted the uneasy space between the most dependent of children and fully autonomous adult citizens. Countless boys – James Strachan, Fred Tiffen, Alder Fisher and a vast number of others whose experiences went unrecorded – were sufficiently big, strong and independent to play a key economic role in the colony. They roamed the colonial landscape, went droving or shepherding, and panned for gold. Sometimes they took up with mates, often for just a while; they also made their way on their own. Fifteen-year-old soldiers met a different fate: their commanders fed them into the killing machine. Youthful experiences varied geographically. North Islanders were more likely than their southern counterparts to find themselves as soldiers, embroiled in wars over land.[178]

Youths occupied an ambiguous world. Sometimes they were child-like and at other times they assumed adult responsibilities, but none had full legal citizenship. Male New Zealanders had to be twenty-one to vote, and only those who owned property or paid high rents had that privilege. Girls earned even less recognition. No female colonist could cast a vote before 1893, and her passage from girlhood to womanhood attracted little public attention. She was excluded from the category of 'youth', and no organisations catered to her leisure needs. The YMCA's first members joined in 1855, and the young men's mutual improvement societies held their first meetings during the same decade, but young

OPPOSITE A sulky lad on a blank set in William Harding's Whanganui studio, photographed some time during the late 1860s or early 1870s.

women's organisations, including the Young Women's Christian Association (YWCA), did not come together until the 1870s. Instead, girls' dependence defined their place in society. The captains and matrons on the immigrant ships tried to make sure they stayed sequestered and under adult control. On land, those who rejected ideals of respectability – the likes of Margaret Glen on the Thames goldfields and Eliza Lambert in the streets of Christchurch – risked shame, ostracism and punishment. Most girls, though, slipped seamlessly from one kind of domestic duty into another: home life, paid service, and a future as a wife and mother.

Everyday terminologies reflected these gendered differences. Young female colonials had only one word to describe them: 'girl'. Until they became 'women', a status often marked by matrimony, they had the same designation as a young child. Publicly, at least, boys were the first in-betweeners. The diary of New Plymouth thirteen-year-old Robert Hughes provides an example of this age gradation. 'February 24, 1861', Robert wrote, 'a youth named R. Chilman who was bathing in the Henui River with two boys was drowned today.'[179] At some point – Robert did not say when – a 'boy' turned into a 'youth', then a 'youth' into a 'man'.

New Zealanders saw the occasional glimmer of what was to come. In 1857 the Reverend J. Buller gave a speech to members of the Wellington YMCA in which he hinted at young men's self-assertion and boundary-pushing:

> It is truly a pitiable sight to behold a youth just entered his teens, strutting along our streets, with an air of self importance rivalling that of a Mogul, the cigar in one corner of the mouth, and from the other, at studied intervals he puffs the smoke with an affected grace . . . our youth of the present day conceive as the insignia of manliness [that] they must wear a moustache and smoke a cigar.[180]

Buller echoed other colonists' ambivalence about pleasure in a Pākehā society undergoing its own kind of adolescence. Adult complaints about adolescent dissipation have a long history indeed, but look again: Buller's objections were as much a revelation as an outright condemnation. The Reverend anticipated the youth culture of the decades that followed, with its strutting, smoking and self-confidence. Buller also revealed the peculiarities of the colonial experience when he compared New Zealand to Britain:

> 'Our young men' are the future fathers, citizens and rulers of our country . . . In the old country the privileges of manhood are scarcely thought of until the age of twenty, or twenty-one; here the lad of sixteen will deem himself insulted if called a boy. In England (at least among the middle classes) a long period intervenes between boyhood and manhood, during which the youth is serving a term of apprenticeship under the discipline of a master's authority; or he is engaged in a curriculum to fit him for his destined profession: here the lad has hardly escaped from the ferule of the school master when he assumes all the importance of mature age.[181]

As Buller pointed out, the rise of apprenticeships and secondary education had begun to transform the status of British youth by the middle of the nineteenth century but the same was not yet true of New Zealand. Few boys became apprentices before the 1870s, when industrial production ramped up, and the secondary education system remained fragmentary at best.[182] Even most well-off parents felt their sons would be better off working than studying.[183] New Zealand drew heavily on the Old Country for immigrants, social mores and imported goods, but this was no Little Britain. The small size of antipodean settlements, the colony's need for physical labour, the frequency of cross-cultural contact and the challenges posed by New Zealand's geography all shaped youthful experience in particular ways.

Change was in the wind, though. Soon boys became less independent and girls more so. As the pre-industrial category of 'youth' loosened its hold, the newer concept of adolescence was forming. Boys and girls alike required greater education and a degree of care, and they forged their own social milieux as New Zealand society grew in complexity. The image of the mostly independent male 'youth' would soon lose ground to the new, semi-dependent 'adolescent', a category that included girls as well as boys.

Chapter Two **Adolescent Stirrings**

On Tuesday 16 November 1880, fifteen-year-old Elsie Clogstoun wrote in her diary:

> Roasting, simply. I never felt such fearful weather before. Gertrude and I have been to learn Spanish by ourselves. We have done 5 jolly exercises and 4 pieces of translation and some grammar. It is such an easy language and so nice to learn. Found a hedge sparrow's nest with one nearly fledged bird and 3 eggs in it. Blew the eggs. Two were inoffensive, but oh l'odeur of the other!! It was almost unblowable. For the last 3 or 4 nights G. and I have pottered about the garden and swing and parallel bars at about 10pm. It is so balmy and enjoyable. We ate large quantities of seed cake, jam and cream in the dairy in the dead of night.[1]

Elsie grew up on a farm station, Five Forks, inland from Geraldine, and her parents were friends with other runholders in Canterbury. Although Elsie's diary captures the idiom of a well-to-do young Cantabrian, its jolly Englishness reflects the way many middle- and upper-class adolescents talked and wrote. Elsie also

OPPOSITE 'Breakfast', eaten with great seriousness near Masterton, c. 1888.

TEENAGERS

tells of bridging country and town: the family spent days in Christchurch while their father was on business there. Elsie's world revolved around her family and friends, some of them her own age. Her diary also reveals a certain irreverence, challenging our assumptions about Victorian girls' modesty and decorum. Like many boys and girls in their teens, Elsie was rude about those she did not like. En route between Christchurch and Orari by rail in 1880 she noted: 'There was a most wonderfully and indescribably ugly woman in the train. Such a nasty sort of ugliness. Very fat face and gooseberry eyes and sticking out lips.'[2]

Elsie's life was both similar to and different from the lives of other adolescents in the later decades of the nineteenth century. She spent much of her time on the family farm, but unlike a majority of fifteen-year-olds she received a secondary education, a privilege reserved for a small but growing number of New Zealanders in their teens. As a runholder's daughter Elsie had a great deal of leisure time. While domestic servants toiled and other youngsters filed into the factories that sprang up after 1870, Elsie played tennis and croquet, climbed hills and looked forward to the holidays.[3]

The later decades of the nineteenth century were years of contrast: the leisured lives of the well-to-do seemed a world away from the daily drudgery of the less fortunate, and the towns accommodated young people's cultures that were different from those seen in rural New Zealand. The concept of 'adolescence' came into focus and doctors and newspaper editors disseminated it to a wider audience. Unlike the older category of 'youth', 'adolescence' gathered together girls and boys, while the first sub-groups – masher, girl masher, larrikin, larrikiness – suggested new modes of self-creation in an increasingly fractious and class-conscious society. Paradoxically, the late nineteenth century was a time of coming together and pulling apart: just as population growth gave rise to greater social complexity, the new adolescent cultures began to splinter along lines of status and style.

Work and the Emergence of Adolescence

Work retained its significance in young people's lives. Girls on farms took responsibility for domestic tasks and childcare, boys did the heavier outdoor labour,

OPPOSITE A collection of late-nineteenth-century adolescent portraits. Those identified are Alice von Sturmer (*top left*), Markham Sherwill (*top row, centre*), H.B. Dyer (*middle row, centre*), Cecilia Sherwill (*middle right*), a daughter of the Kemsley family (*bottom left*) and John Grace (*bottom right*).

TEENAGERS

and everyone milked cows and harvested crops. Henry Wood lived in Taranaki during the 1880s. At the age of eighteen he moved off the family farm to work for bush-felling contractors near Maxwelltown, and he toiled for twelve hours each day, Monday to Saturday, in exchange for twenty-five shillings per week. Henry lived in a tent and subsisted on potatoes and meat; when he broke his ankle he carried on regardless. He soon tried his hand at several other jobs. As a road-builder he loaded drays with stone, then he went logging with his sixteen-year-old brother ('a good axe-man').

Near the Southland town of Riverton, two sons of sawmiller James More attend to their bullock team during the 1890s.

Henry's experiences hint at changing attitudes towards adolescent male labour. On the road-building job his supervisor told him 'that as I was only a boy he would give me £1 a week and explained that boys were not expected to do heavy work but were expected to be smart in their movements'.[4] During the middle of the century an eighteen-year-old labourer was expected to be able to do the same work as an older man, but by the 1880s, when Henry's boss described him as a 'boy', social boundaries had begun to shift. There were other differences too. Henry had received intermittent schooling during his mid-teens, a luxury denied most working boys in earlier decades. Henry's memoir also tells of his search for emotional support. While milking on a dairy farm he found something of a surrogate family to care for him. 'On the whole I was much happier here as the work was much lighter than the bush felling, and I enjoyed the company of Mr and Mrs Marchant, and also the employees, including the young housemaid.'[5] Henry, and other adolescents like him, were less independent than their mid-nineteenth-century forebears. They required special consideration in the workplace and at school and continued familial care.[6]

The pace of change quickened in the urban centres and significantly transformed young lives. Mere villages during the 1840s, by 1880 Auckland and Wellington were home to 22,400 and 28,000 people respectively. Dunedin grew quickly on the back of gold and pastoralism, and 45,400 souls lived there in 1880.[7] The frequent contact between Pākehā and Māori that characterised the 1840s and 1850s began to weaken as the towns grew in size and an urban/rural divide became more pronounced. Industrial employment expanded: young people in the cities flocked to work for confectioners, bakers and joiners, and took jobs in factories that made shoes, bricks and ropes.[8] The manufacturing sector grew quickly: New Zealand had 1,857 factories by 1892 and 6,438 just eight years later.[9]

Social trends influenced the composition of factory workforces. By the 1890s most girls took a job once they left school at thirteen or fourteen, and, conversely, women usually retired from paid labour when they married. As a result, girls between fourteen and twenty-one comprised 60 percent of the female labour force by 1900, and they clustered in particular sectors. Almost 80 percent of workers in the clothing industry were girls or women.[10] They spent their days in the sewing, labelling and packing departments of large factories, while the boys and men tackled the heavier jobs like cutting and pressing.[11] Of those girls and

There are very few surviving photographs of young nineteenth-century women engaged in domestic tasks. Here Jean Nicholson and Eva Williams do the washing in Central Otago, 1896, but this is a highly posed shot. The apron was standard washday wear but a fancy hat definitely was not.

young women not in the garment trade, many worked for bootmakers or in the woollen mills.[12]

Several pieces of legislation governed factory work, each drawing a slightly different line between childhood and adolescence. The 1873 Employment of Females Act stipulated that girls and women would work no longer than eight hours each day (there was no such limit for boys), and an 1875 amendment set ten as the lowest age for work in a factory. The 1881 Employment of Females and Others Act raised this age to twelve, and ten years later the 1891 Factories Act defined the upper limit of 'childhood': thirteen for boys and fourteen for girls.[13] These laws were not always observed, but they did mark the point at which a child became an adolescent. Among boys, a growing number of apprenticeships marked the boundary at the opposite end of the adolescent age range.[14] Apprentices became journeymen as they entered their early twenties: a shift in job titles and wage rates coincided perfectly with a lad's shift into adulthood. As a category and constellation of experience, adolescence took shape in a context of increasing industrialisation.

Not always were factories the easiest places for in-betweeners to spend their days. In 1890 the government's 'Sweating Commission' unearthed some grim conditions and discovered that many adolescent boys worked tirelessly.[15] Lads in one Canterbury tailors' shop toiled sixteen hours a day.[16] There were other depredations too. Not all factory owners provided lunch-rooms, and some bosses turned workers out into the wind, rain and snow at lunch-time.[17] One boy told the Commission of long days working at Hopkins' bakery in Dunedin, with its stifling air and poor facilities:

> The ventilation was very bad. The room was underground, and there was only one grating to it. When you went down the first flight of steps there was another small flight, about seven steps, down to another bake house [...] Then there was another place where the butter would not get soft, but when the gas was turned out it was so dark you could not see your finger before you. When I went there my employer said I was to work from 7 in the morning till 7 at night, but the rest worked on and I worked on too. There were about six there younger than I was – about fifteen. There was no fixed time for meals, and we got our meals on the benches in the bake house. There were no sanitary conveniences; you had to go outside to the station or to the saleyards.[18]

Hopkins' bakery was an unpleasant workplace, but factories had their benefits too: they helped shape new kinds of youth culture. Proximity and age-separation counted for a lot. For many girls, busy workrooms full of young people offered an attractive alternative to the limited social contact of domestic labour with its isolated and degrading grind of blacking gratings, scrubbing chamber pots, and attending to their masters and mistresses from dawn until dusk.[19] There was fun to be had, and the Sweating Commission unearthed a fair amount of skylarking. Some boys amused themselves by running about, throwing things and 'scribbling indecent lines'.[20] An 1895 report suggested girls working in boot factories were prone to 'rowdiness', 'coarseness' and 'rough behaviour'.[21] Boys and girls egged each other on as well. Reverend Vicesimus Lush, an Auckland churchman who saw the factories as breeding grounds for moral decadence, claimed that 'foul stories and jokes' circulated among boys and girls in crowded workrooms.[22] Lush's comments, published in the *New Zealand Herald*, hint at social interactions, chat and banter unchecked by adult overseers. In the railway workshops across the country – Newmarket, East Town, Petone, Addington and Hillside – male trainees became fitters, turners, boilermakers, blacksmiths, pattern makers, painters and carpenters. Young apprentices forged strong and enduring friendships. They began at the age of fourteen or fifteen and many continued in the same workplace, with their well-established group of mates, for most of their lives.[23]

Factories changed the relationships between young workers and adult authority. Not only did they provide social opportunities, but the new division between home space and workplace also afforded girls a new independence. No longer were they directly surveilled by their parents, masters and mistresses, for factory discipline was remoter and much less focussed than its domestic equivalent. Unlike the domestic servant, the factory worker was only one of many under the supervisor's eye and, as the Sweating Commission's report reveals, girls as well as boys mucked about with impunity. In addition, factory workers had more obvious leisure. While domestic servants assisted with dinner and washed dishes afterwards, factory hands left their work behind and enjoyed a social life well away from their supervisor's watchful gaze. Girls nattered with one another as they made their way home, and the evenings and weekends opened up for leisure.[24]

No sooner had adolescent work cultures begun to coalesce than they fractured like cooling toffee; by the 1890s new divisions of status separated groups of young people from one another. Sometimes adults drew the line. One shirt and mantle manufacturer insisted she only employed 'respectable' girls, suggesting that her workers were socially superior to others.[25] Often, though, adolescents made the distinctions themselves. The owner of one Dunedin shirt factory mentioned his workers' desire to distance themselves from those employed by other companies: 'Our girls do not like our place to be called a factory . . . They think it is a "Young Ladies' Shirt-making Establishment".'[26] Up the line in Christchurch, the manager

A young apprentice (*centre*) works in the bindery of Dunedin's *Evening Star*. The newspaper industry was one of many employers of adolescent workers.

of Ballantyne's, a department store with its own manufacturing arm, told the Sweating Commission that 'the milliners will not mix with the dressmakers, or the dressmakers with the tailoresses'. This was partly a matter of pride, he thought, but also stemmed from the clustering together of those with similar roles in a large staff of 200.[27] As soon as the factories brought together large numbers of adolescent New Zealanders, the members of the new generation divided themselves into cliques.

Educating the In-Betweener

The expanding school system joined the industrial sector as a creator of modern adolescence. Gillis suggests 'the lines newly-drawn between primary and secondary education' helped divide childhood – those of primary age – from the

TEENAGERS

These sketches of classmates from Wellington College – with their school caps and a range of other clothing – are from Austin Strong's 1895–98 sketchbook.

adolescents enrolled in secondary education.[28] There are two important elements here: the first is a significant growth in secondary rolls.[29] In 1878, the first year for which statistics are available, 6,465 boys and girls over thirteen, the school leaving age, attended the public schools. This figure climbed to nearly 10,000 three years later.[30] Some fourteen-year-olds stayed on in the top classes of the primary schools, but the growth flowed through into dedicated secondary schools as well. Christ's College, which taught sixty boys in 1863, now had 187 pupils, and the other colleges recorded similar growth.[31] By 1888 nearly 20,000 New Zealanders over thirteen received a state education, a figure that sagged during the economic slump of the late 1880s and recovered by the turn of the century.[32]

Space is the second part of the equation. We have already seen how early New Zealand schools herded together small numbers of pupils across a wide age range and taught them all in the same room. By the 1870s, though, primary and secondary-age youngsters began to occupy different physical spaces within New Zealand's education system, just as they did in Britain.[33] This was sometimes because both primary and secondary schools became available in some areas, and single-sex colleges stopped enrolling younger children. In the new 'district high schools', many of them in the smaller towns, older pupils took their lessons in detached buildings because there was space to do so. Like the factories, the newer buildings allowed age-specific cultures to develop.

The dream of an egalitarian society had been a selling point for new settlers but it further unravelled during the 1880s. 'Social divisions did exist', writes historian Jeanine Graham, 'and they were based upon wealth.'[34] Schooling perpetuated these distinctions. The Junior Civil Service exam (popularly called 'the Junior Civil') served as a gateway into the expanding government service and the proliferating commercial sector that chose office clerks from the same pool. Parental wealth usually determined who had the chance to sit the exam, for the high schools charged fees. Among the less affluent, a small number of high achievers obtained scholarships. A secondary school education, economically restricted to a relative few, provided a ticket to the rapidly expanding middle class.

Fred Gibbs attended Nelson College as a day pupil and his diary documents the minutiae of a middle-class schoolboy's life. Fred took his schoolwork seriously and threw himself into literature and ideas. In the midst of a trigonometry class the sixteen-year-old became 'absolutely entangled in a discussion political, theological etc, re Protestant v. Roman Catholic', and often at home he had his head in the clouds and ignored his siblings.[35] He would rather sit quietly over breakfast, contemplating the philosophy of Thomas Carlyle, than chat to his brothers and sisters.[36] Literature and philosophy were the cornerstones of a liberal middle-class education; pupils decided what they liked and nailed their colours to the mast. Dreamy Fred stood his ground when one acquaintance tried to make him 'prefer Byron to Tennyson, an impossibility'.[37]

Scholarly expectations were high in late-nineteenth-century New Zealand, and an endless stream of exams dominated pupils' waking hours. Fred told his diary about the 'very long, stiff' entrance Latin paper for 'Matriculation', a university entrance examination. He also sat the 'Junior Civil', and a further set of papers qualified him for a university Junior Scholarship: 'An infinite amount of work now & working at Trig and Shakespeare pretty hard', Fred wrote; 'swotting tremendously all round.'[38] These kinds of pressures came to the attention of concerned adults. The newspapers told tales of overworked adolescents going mad or dying of study-induced 'brain fever', and Truby King, superintendent of Seacliff Lunatic

School Life

Thirteen-year-old Herries Beattie attended Gore School. Like the other state primary schools, Gore taught pupils up to the age of fifteen.[39] In 1898 Herries penned lively portraits of his thirteen- and fourteen-year-old class-mates. Vincent Pyke ('Big Vin') was 'thin and rather gawkish', 'a nervous shy kind of boy [who] shied clear of girls. I was his chum and many a time we went for a bathe together and hunted for birds-nests together as we were both collectors'. William McKenzie ('Billy Mac') 'filched lollies which we chewed surreptitiously.' A 'hard case', Billy 'was always ready to do anything and was foremost in all larks'. Henry Lakeman, Herries' 'great chum', knew his mind and was not afraid to speak it. A bold advocate of temperance, his pronouncements attracted much 'hooting and taunting' but Henry stood his ground, became 'fired up', upset a few of his antagonists 'and kicked their behinds'. Henry was 'a bright intelligent boy', a 'good scholar' and a 'tough citizen'.[40] These boys had different interests and moods, and several kinds of colonial masculinity found a place in Herries' affections.

Herries also described the girls in his class. Jeanie Wilson was a great joke-teller with a strong temper and arms of iron. 'I remember once that when I displeased her, she got me such a cuff that it nearly knocked me over and then when I tried to hold her hands I could not do it – she was too lithe and strong. She was about or was the best runner in all the girls at that period.'[41] Jeanie Pollock 'could and did barrack the boys worst of all'. On the latter, Herries added: 'One good thing about her was that she would not stand rough or coarse jests like lots of girls do. In character she was resolute and impervious like all haughty girls.' Herries, Lulu Coutts, Jessie Baldwin and Billy Mac 'had real lively times' at Gore School, but their shy friend Leslie Pyke, Big Vin's brother, was not quite so lucky. Some of the girls 'teased him a lot stuck hatpins in him kicked him etc and nearly drove him mad'.[42] The mêlée did not last. At fourteen Herries Beattie left behind the tumult of Gore School and went to board at Southland Boys' High.

ADOLESCENT STIRRINGS

At first glance this group of sixth formers at Wellington Girls' High School, photographed in 1887, mostly look innocent, even a little pious. In fact, nineteenth-century schoolgirls could give as good as they got. In 1883 several pupils at the newly opened Nelson College for Girls pelted a teacher with stones in the street, and a number were caught cheating. 'Most (if not all) [at the] school had done so at some time or other, every girl having to write a confession or apology', wrote Fred Gibbs who attended Nelson College several blocks away.

Asylum near Dunedin, thought 'cram' paved the way to 'general instability of the nervous system'.[43] Like his European and American counterparts, King regarded adolescence, a term he often used in his lectures and public writings, as a perilous stage of life that required careful mental and moral guidance, not overwork.[44]

Fred Gibbs never developed 'brain fever' even though he worked hard, and the young Nelsonian survived the rigours of study. His diary tells of physical as well as mental exertions: gym, swimming and rugby. Nelson College had an especially close link with the last item on this list: the school hosted New Zealand's first rugby union match in 1870. Fred and his mates played rough, 'having skin off arms and thigh and neck, a bad ankle etc but nothing serious'.[45] As members of the school team, Fred and his brother Sid sailed Cook Strait to take on Wellington College. His diary describes the match in some detail, recounting an altercation with Wellington's weather as well as the opposing team:

> Soon after dinner went to play our match on a slippery ground & with a Wellington gale blowing dead across the ground. Our team was in very bad training but we were about matched in weight & our backs were superior, so we still hoped to win. They were trained to a nicety by Firth, & I have never seen a team play so skillfully. Firth of course was directing them all the time & inciting them to do their utmost. The game resulted in a victory for W. College by 2 tries to nil. I really believe we should have more than matched them but for the wind. For our forwards could have held their own, had not our backs helplessly broken down. For the latter were not used to kicking a gale of wind & actually failed to get their kicks off at all, dropping the ball several feet alongside of them instead of in front of them.[46]

Fred's diary records the antagonisms that continued in the dormitory afterwards:

> Next morning I was awakened by a pillow & then several others were thrown at Sid & self as occupying the end beds of 2 rows. We took it half in good part merely taking possession of the pillows, in order not to make a row although I mentally determined to do something afterwards, as they came from Oldham, Cresswell and other young cads. They even dared to try & retake a pillow from Sid, whose firmness however soon made them desist. They then began to pitch them at Jones whose want of tact & extreme unpopularity soon involved him in a fracas.[47]

OPPOSITE A group of Nelson College rowers around the turn of the century.

Jim and Ernie, two Wairarapa lads, during the late 1880s.

Fred painted a vivid picture of middle-class male adolescence, one that readily illustrates the tension between swotting and games. If intensive study granted access to the new white-collar jobs, then rigorous sports instilled the necessary character. The idea that sport inculcated manliness took hold long before Fred scraped his arms and strained his ankle.[48] During the late eighteenth century, Western Europeans believed risk, danger and pain defined a truly masculine life; a hundred years later many educationalists embraced rough physical training.[49] New Plymouth-born Truby King, who had grown up a sickly and bookish boy, saw rigorous physical exercise – 'properly clad in flannels for the purpose' – as an antidote to the brain-melting dissipations of 'cram'.[50] A healthy body, he figured, was the perfect container for a well-developed mind.

Some adolescent girls also enjoyed a secondary education. Roughly similar numbers of thirteen- and fourteen- year-old boys and girls attended the public schools, but girls predominated among fifteen- and sixteen-year-olds. In 1878 there were 50 percent more girls over fifteen than boys of the same age, a ratio that slowly reduced as the 1880s and 1890s wore on. By 1900, though, girls still had the edge in this age group.[51] This suggests a surprising degree of equality: contrary to our usual assumptions, girls over the age of thirteen were considered no less worthy of an education than boys. Few parents expected female scholars to study different subjects or to make less of an effort.[52] The early girls' secondary schools offered the same kinds of topics as the boys': French and German literature, Chaucer, Shakespeare, algebra, geometry, trigonometry, botany and chemistry.[53] The first such institution, Otago Girls' High School, opened in 1871. It owed its existence to successful lobbying by the educationalist Learmonth Dalrymple, a persuasive figure who wanted girls to have the intellectual opportunities she had been denied in her native Scotland.[54]

Hukarere College for Māori girls, another early secondary school, opened in Napier in 1875 to train a Māori elite. This group of 'brown-skinned, English middle-class women' would adhere to and proselytise 'Pākehā norms', writes educationalist Kay Morris Matthews, and Māori would be 'classified and stratified according to a Pākehā hierarchy'.[55] An education at Hukarere was more than simply an expression of colonising ideology, though; it expanded girls' horizons too.[56]

Schools are complex institutions. Their rules, curricula and classroom regimes tend to maintain and reproduce social hierarchies, but they also bestow cultural capital, assist social mobility and (sometimes) provide a degree of emotional support. As the numbers of sixteen- and seventeen-year-olds in secondary education increased from a relatively small base, a growing number of pupils found a generally amenable system that upheld high standards for girls and boys alike. Jessie Hetherington, a pupil at the co-educational Prince Albert College in Auckland, remembered her favourite teacher, a Miss Rainforth, 'much beloved by all of us for her gentleness and her understanding sympathy with our troubles and griefs, although she could be caustic when the occasion demanded it'.[57] Teachers like Miss Rainforth offered emotional sustenance to their young charges, smoothing their passage through adolescence.

Like everyone, the pupils at Otago Boys' High endured a lot of exams – Harold Hooper sat seven over two days in the winter of 1874 – but there were concessions. The headmaster called impromptu half holidays from time to time, the boys wandered into town to take lunch at the popular Watson's Dining Rooms, and they headed home when, as Harold wrote, there was 'nothing doing at school'.[58] These

'Diagrammatic view of one side of whare at Waihohama on Jan.22.90.' Three of the five heads are labelled: 'red hat, white nightcap, brown hat'. These five lads, Wanganui Collegiate pupils, set out on foot in order to 'penetrate the heart of the North Island and to ascend the heights of its great volcanic centre'. A written journal records the walking, views and blisters as the group headed up the river, and how they enjoyed the hospitality of local Māori and slogged up Ruapehu. Then 'we were sitting, half frozen it is true, but triumphant [at] the actual summit'. Within sight of Ngauruhoe, the day's walking over, 'we were lying snugly in a comfortable Maori whare, with the immediate prospect of enjoying a hearty tea'.

examples reflect the prevailing pattern in mid-nineteenth-century America, where light-handed regulation and a degree of informality carried the day.[59] In New Zealand this approach was also made possible by the small size of schools. In 1881, for instance, Nelson College had 134 boys, Otago Girls' High had 144 girls, and Auckland Girls', the largest secondary school in the colony, provided an education for 245.[60] Small institutions also offered ready social opportunities. Pupils at Nelson College for Girls enjoyed music recitals, debates and picnics, while Dunedin boys and girls laughed, whistled and stomped their way through concerts at All Saints' Schoolroom.⁶¹ Only during the twentieth century would discipline tighten and headmasters reshape school life along quasi-military lines.

Continued expansion at the secondary level gave rise to new kinds of institutions. The first technical schools offered evening classes to adults and adolescents during the 1890s and expanded to accommodate day pupils after 1900.⁶² Then they split in two: the classes for adolescent day pupils evolved into technical high schools and the trades training sections formed the nucleus of New Zealand's polytechnic system.⁶³ Tertiary education developed on the back of an expanding secondary school population. The universities catered for the well-off and the academically inclined. Otago University opened its doors to male students in 1869, and young women joined them in 1871.⁶⁴ Otago became part of the University

The first Canterbury College play, *Much Ado About Nothing*, was performed during the 1870s. Helen Connon, on the far left, was the second female arts graduate in the British Empire and the first woman to gain a degree with honours. At the age of eighteen, while still a university student, she began teaching at the newly established Christchurch Girls' High School.

The Rise of Adolescent Slang

Words provide ways to think about identity, reinforce social expectations and differences, and help people forge a sense of solidarity. New Zealand's in-betweeners have drawn from the shifting idiom while developing a code of their own. A very few terms made an early appearance – by the 1840s a 'stupid' party was boring or pathetic, and a 'capital' one was the best possible fun – but slang became widespread during the 1870s as local youth cultures grew in earnest.

A 'fast' person was precocious or slightly dangerous; a 'flash' one was highly fashionable. Some girls described their male friends as 'cures': good time boys. 'Mr A. is certainly a "Cure"', Mary Hargreaves wrote in 1871. (Mary often placed informal words in quote marks.) 'He pretends he doesn't care one bit for "the women" (as he calls them) which is all nonsense. I think he is a flirt.'[65] Life was not always romantic, though. 'School was the most horrible rot', thirteen-year-old Edward Roberts wrote in his diary in 1896, although he did not say why. 'Stinking school.'[66]

Before the 1930s, when the 'talkies' (movies with dialogue) began to shape New Zealanders' linguistic worlds, most locally used slang terms had British origins. These reflected popular school stories and the *Boy's Own* and *Girl's Own* magazines. A situation or suggestion might be 'beastly' or 'bosh' (bad), 'bonza', 'bosker', 'grand', 'ripping' or 'spiffing' (good), while an incorrigible friend who liked 'japes' and 'larks' was 'a hard case' or 'a proper brick'. John Morpeth enjoyed the Duke of York's visit to Waitaki Boys' High School in 1927: 'Jack Hamilton gave me six chews – decent – quite fine by midday – Duke of York came – great crowd in hall – gave him a haka and decorations looked jake.'[67] Not everyone's actions were laudable, though. A 'blab tongue' was a boy or girl who gossiped without restraint.

Some words and phrases familiar to us now – 'knocked up', 'savage', 'rude' – had different meanings during the nineteenth and early twentieth centuries. 'Knocked up' originally meant tired rather than pregnant, 'savage' was angry, and 'went rude' meant 'got mad'. Other terms retained their popularity. 'Rowdy' youngsters had 'heaps' of fun during the 1870s, just as they do now.

of New Zealand in 1874, an umbrella institution that incorporated Canterbury University (established in 1873), Auckland (1883), Victoria (1897) and Canterbury Agricultural College (later Lincoln, 1896).

Like many of the early secondary schools, the early universities were small and generally supportive of their students. Jessie Hetherington went to Auckland University College in 1899 when the Bachelor of Arts required six subjects including the compulsory trio of Latin, Mathematics and English. She enjoyed the Latin lectures most, 'for Professor Tubbs' style was vigorous and his comments salty'. 'Korero Club' (also known as 'Talktalky') catered to the female students too shy to speak in full debates.[68] Social opportunities came along too: 'a few Saturday night dances in the old St. Andrews Hall in Symonds Street or the Masonic Hall in Princes Street, picnics to the island of Motutapu or Kohimarama Bay, College Reviews full of skits upon the Professors'.[69] Jessie left Auckland University College in 1903 and went to England the following year to study law before returning to New Zealand.[70] She was a rare breed: nearly three-quarters of the young women who graduated from university between 1878 and 1920 went straight into teaching, most of them in high schools.[71] Only a handful studied law like Jessie, or medicine.[72] Decades passed before a university education would widen the range of opportunities for large numbers of young women.

The Colonial Girl

If work and education represent two legs on the tripod of adolescent history, leisure is the third. Adolescent cultures grew in casual and formal settings that reflected changing geographies and new gendered patterns. The 'colonial girl' made her appearance during the later decades of the nineteenth century. Her local origins lay in the early years of Pākehā settlement when necessity dictated an outdoor existence. Thirteen-year-old Jane Bannerman, an immigrant from Glasgow, arrived in Dunedin in 1847. She clambered ashore with her family and made the most of an open-air life. 'We were in excellent health', Jane later wrote in her memoir; 'there was something so gladsome in the climate, and novelty in all our surroundings. Everyone alike was roughing, and all were cheery and hopeful.'[73] Jane's pragmatic approach to 'roughing [it]' carried on

OVERLEAF The Bicknell girls on a sunny afternoon near Oamaru, 1896.

A colonial girl, Ruby Wilkinson of Ophir, poses with her catch from the rabbit-infested Central Otago countryside one day in 1895.

through the century and girls as well as boys fished, hunted and adventured. 'The children were the first colonists to make themselves fully at home, the first to take full advantage of physical freedom', writes historian Erik Olssen.[74]

Colonial girls made the most of New Zealand's wide open spaces. They played impromptu games of rugby, if not with a ball then an inflated bladder from a recently killed pig.[75] Jessie Hetherington pestered her brother until he 'found me simply a nuisance, wanting to join in football games', and she was far from the only one.[76] Elsie Clogstoun's brother was more amenable to his sister's leisure interests, and he took her 'rinking' (roller skating) in a mid-Canterbury grain store with a seventeen-year-old male acquaintance.[77] From the top of the country to the bottom, girls saddled up their horses and headed off for day trips, or fished off the sides of boats.[78] A group of friends speared flounder as they toured the coast of Stewart Island, cultivating a healthy appetite and eating 'an enormous supper' made from their bounty.[79]

Girls of the late 1860s embraced a new mentality that reflected their surroundings. One woman complained that her granddaughters were 'rather too colonial – not exactly fast but rather too sharp and satirical'.[80] This new attitude combined a love of fresh air, energy, fearlessness and an independent spirit. It shaped the lives of those in rural areas who adapted English ideas of feminine respectability in an arcadian setting, and also in the cities where new job opportunities loosened the association between femininity and domesticity. Clothing, though, took a long time to catch up with the colonial girl's ambitions and activities. Her heavy blouse and narrow skirts did little to help her mobility, although she persisted nevertheless. The occasional sartorial pragmatist offered a helping hand: a few girls' schools adopted bloomer uniforms, and these allowed easier movement.[81] Outside of school, those who sewed their own clothes tweaked them within the dictates of fashion. The contradiction between confining attire and an active life would resolve itself during the first decade of the new century when female fashions finally caught up with colonial realities.

Sometimes Victorian girls jettisoned their clothes entirely and revelled in the sun and bare flesh. Elsie Clogstoun wrote about a naked swim: 'Father, Ina and I walked to the Hai Hai Timoana in the afternoon, taking tea things as before.' A degree of segregation assured the preservation of modesty. 'F. bathed in the toppest hole, and I[na] and I in the bottomest one. Perfect, jumping off the rock into the deepest part.'[82]

Leisure and Pleasure

Boys also told of the pleasures of nude bathing. One time, Fred Gibbs wrote: 'It was a glorious summer's day & we were in the highest spirits . . . We went to Sunday [swimming] hole and went round the upper end, where we took off shoes & socks, waded across, & undressed on margin on other side . . . We had a delightful bathe though not a long one.'[83] Fred's diaries are full of feeling: his 'rapturous' response

to a nature ramble, the 'delight' of a bathe and the attachments of friends. After a swim, he suggested climbing the hills:

> Taking the beautiful walk I had discovered some weeks before, [the others] heartily assented & off we went chatting all the way . . . we examined carefully all the landscape beneath us & revelled in its beauty. Kelly seemed to feel it immensely. We constantly stopped to talk[;] now and again [we] raced [and] Kelly and I kept nearly abreast with Jones far behind. As we got close down by Hunter-Brown's hill, a beautiful sunset took place . . . Then suddenly remembering that the other two were in a greater hurry than myself to get home I turned to descend, when Kelly in his simple way, expressed admiration at my description [of the sunset] and both declared I was a poet etc, Kelly remarking to Jones 'He speaks like a book, doesn't he?' which happens to be one of the phrases I hate most, though of course I never hinted that. We got down at dusk having spent a most delightful afternoon, in fact it was the most rapturous time I ever had.[84]

Wide-open spaces invited mucking about. These young Wairarapa folk – including Minnie May D'Arcy (*left centre*) and her fiancé Charlie Blackburn (*right centre*), both in their late teens – amuse themselves among the haystacks, c. 1889.

Nineteenth-century adolescents read voraciously, including books and serials imported from England and America. Jessie Hetherington's family read *Strand Magazine*, which included the Sherlock Holmes mysteries in instalments; *Pearson's*, a mixture of literature and socialism; and *Boy's Own* and *Girl's Own*. The authors represented on the Hetheringtons' shelves included Dickens, Thackeray, Tennyson and George Eliot. Elsie Clogstoun enjoyed serials *Punch* and *Sporting and Dramatic*, Mark Twain's *The Adventures of Tom Sawyer*, Mary Elizabeth Braddon's occasionally feminist love story *Vixen* ('rather liked it') and the irresistibly titled *That Aggravating Schoolgirl*. Christchurch law student Charles Knight read quickly and widely: Tolstoy, Hardy, Browning, Cicero, Plato, Burke, Shakespeare and the South African feminist Olive Schreiner. This sketch of a girl reading is by eighteen-year-old Frances Hodgkins who went on to attend the Dunedin School of Art and become one of New Zealand's most well-known painters.

Intensity infuses every sentence of this paragraph: an enjoyment of natural beauty and the sensuous pleasures of a bathe helped deepen the relationships between Fred and his friends. We do not usually associate such sensuousness with Victorian culture, but pleasure profoundly shaped adolescent life.

Leisure patterns became increasingly complex during the late nineteenth century. Elsie Clogstoun's and Fred Gibbs's experiences remind us that youngsters spent their leisure time in a mixture of adult and adolescent company. Elsie and Fred mucked about with their parents and siblings, as well as friends their own age. While secondary schools and factories fostered friendships between age-mates, some New Zealanders built youth-specific cultures in overwhelmingly adult settings. Mary Hargreaves and her friends enjoyed the atmosphere in Wellington's ballrooms in 1872 when they claimed slivers of space for themselves. Mary wrote of 'flirtation corners', those nooks and stairways where adolescents stole a quiet moment away from their chaperones.⁸⁵ Mary went to a great many dances, and there were plenty of opportunities to mingle. 'I have been very gay', she wrote. 'I had some delicious dances.' Mr Alberson 'is a great flirt I hear', she added. 'He is great to dance with.' Another time, Mary, Aggie and Diana 'gossiped away' while 'Ada was having a quiet flirtation with Mr Gilpin'.⁸⁶ Some years later, in 1889, Gertie Brookes wrote to a friend about slipping the noose of adult surveillance. 'My goodness Ella you can't think how I am dying to hear all about this school party & above all things who you danced with', she exclaimed excitedly. 'If I had only been there to have had a peep at you shouldn't I have been shocked to see you with some young man's arms around you. I am sure I hope you had a fine spree & I hope to goodness Miss Minnie wasn't watching every little thing you did.'⁸⁷ As New Zealand's population increased and these kinds of occasions became more common, adolescents claimed a little more space for themselves.

Dances were highly public occasions, but private spaces had their uses too. As the small dwellings of the early colonial period gave way to larger residences,

Elsie Clogstoun described her love of dancing and sketched the clothes she and her sisters wore: 'Started at 7.15 p.m. in the wagon for Waitui, for a ball. I enjoyed it awfully. What sickening wretches I have made us in our portraits. My dress was cream coloured summer serge trimmed with a creamy lace and a puckered creamy Latin plastron. It is a very pretty dress. Ina's is the pale blue English stuff, the plastron and sleeve slashings are of the dark red satin.'

The Railway Revolution

New modes of transport greatly enhanced adolescents' mobility. Several cities – Auckland, Wellington, Christchurch, Dunedin and Invercargill – had small steam or horse tram networks by the early 1880s, and these afforded access around town. The most dramatic change came with the arrival of the railways. Railways provided labouring jobs for many young men and gave rise to a vast new world of experiences for travellers. Elsie Clogstoun was bored as well as captivated by a train trip from Orari to Dunedin in 1881, parents in tow. In her characteristic manner she told her diary: 'From Orari to Timaru was flat and stupid, but a little way this side of Timaru', where the line hugged the coast, 'it was delicious.'[88] In Dunedin, Elsie and her parents peered through shop windows and amused themselves at lunch:

[We] went to a fiendish little shop with 'Pies and Coffee' written over the door. We were each given a pie, hot with pallid gravy swimming about on the top of the crust, and a teaspoon to eat it with! It nearly made us sick. We all 3 (Father Mother and I) sat and giggled so hopelessly that by the time we'd stopped we couldn't possibly have eaten them so we paid and went.[89]

Dunedin Railway Station near the end of the century.

Elsie was no stiff-upper-lip Victorian. Of her Dunedin holiday, she wrote: 'I enjoyed these 2 days frantically.'[90]

Fred Gibbs and his mates were the beneficiaries of the railway line between Nelson and its hinterland, terminating at the tiny village of Belgrove. They hopped on and off the trains on their way to a tramp or a spell at a swimming hole, moving freely around the district. 'Train to Bishopdale & then to bush', read a typical entry in Fred's diary.[91] These lads, and many like them, found a ready mobility on rail.

the houses of the well-to-do provided room for domestic parties and spaces in which young people's cultures took shape. Adults and adolescents usually retreated to separate rooms during mixed-age soirées, and parents sometimes went out for the evening and left the younger set to its own devices. Mary Hargreaves spent some 'jolly' evenings playing cards with other youngsters and occasionally attended 'juvenile parties'. One winter's evening, when she and her siblings had their house to themselves, 'Ned Dransfield came over, we were most awfully rowdy, for I got a hold of a book of Fred's and read something that he didn't wish me to see, and he rushed after me & tried to get it from me, we did "kick up a row". I get as wild as those boys when I am with them, they are "Cures".'[92] Mary's acquaintance Robert, in contrast, was no 'cure'. Mary disparagingly described him as 'not a very lively youth'.[93]

The Colonial City

Urban growth, and the slowly expanding consumer culture that accompanied it, profoundly shaped adolescents' leisure worlds. Many young New Zealanders had to request goods from overseas during the early years of Pākehā settlement – in 1841 one Wellington girl wrote to her family in England to ask for clothes, shoes and sewing supplies – but mass importing and local manufacturing expanded in the years that followed.[94] By the early 1860s the 'fancy goods bazaar' had emerged, a rudimentary variety store selling toys, sports equipment, grooming accessories and general bric-a-brac, and the first department stores evolved out of the bazaars and drapery shops. Before long a growing array of stores offered treasures to enthusiastic young shoppers.

Young people wandered, found food and knocked about in groups their own age. Mary Hargreaves ran into friends in Wellington's streets and they perused the stores together before popping into Daisy's tea shop to 'do' a bun each.[95] Gertrude Dyer described her peregrinations around Dunedin at Christmas time in 1898: 'In the evening I went up town with Flora. It was the largest gathering of people promenading around town that I have seen for a long time. All the shops looked very bright and the people in them appeared to be very busy.' The pair visited drapers Brown Ewing to see the 'enchanted Grotto' in the cellar and they loved browsing in

Princes Street, Dunedin, early 1880s. The streets are muddy but the buildings are grand; a tram connects the north and south of the city and adults and youths mingle on the footpaths.

Braithwaites, a veritable Aladdin's cave of books, ornaments, toys and jewellery.[96] Mary, Gertrude and Flora became flâneuses, to borrow a metaphor from continental Europe. They wandered the pavements, window-shopped and soaked up the atmosphere.[97] The flâneuse, the shop window and the department store were all powerful symbols of late-nineteenth-century modernity, and crowds of milling shoppers were soon an everyday phenomenon.[98]

Some in-betweeners enjoyed consumer pleasures more than others, and not every girl was quite as lucky as the flâneuse. The working day for shop girls was long: many stores stayed open until 8 pm most nights, 11 pm on Fridays and midnight on Saturdays.[99] Young shop assistants told the Sweating Commission their legs ached from hours of standing, and an *Otago Daily Times* correspondent roundly criticised adult shoppers' 'inhuman desire to see the young lives of suffering shop girls offered up on the sacrificial altar of aesthetic tastes'.[100] One youngster's pleasure was another's pain. At the same time, the shop girl, like the factory worker, had a greater degree of freedom than her domestic servant counterpart, and the cities encouraged a new independence for shopper and worker alike.

The Larrikin Menace

Boys' public lives could be boisterous. While Dunedin's young women browsed Braithwaites, southern lads made their presence felt in ever more assertive ways. In 1872 a youth wrote about his mates skylarking in the city's thoroughfares. The lads wandered aimlessly down Princes Street, a rough byway lined with low timber and stone buildings, and they met two more friends. All four wove their way down the middle of the thoroughfare, amusing themselves 'by trying to trip one another', grabbing their friends' hats and exacting revenge by making one another 'kiss the ground'. The boys mooched about for a further hour before going their separate ways.[101]

Well aware of boys' rambunctious behaviour, some adults worried that the growing towns and cities had become increasingly menacing and that the hours after dark threatened moral danger.[102] The news media complained about 'knots of young men and boys' who loitered at night, engaged in 'horseplay' and used 'ribald language'.[103] Some of these characters earned themselves a sobriquet: 'larrikins'. An antipodean translation of the European 'hooligan', the term emerged in both New Zealand and Australia by 1870.[104] Wellington's *Evening Post* described the larrikin as a 'colonial street boy' with a love of the night:

> A larrikin is rarely or never seen in daylight. Indeed in most cases it is only after dusk that he becomes a larrikin. During the day he is a school-boy, errand-boy, office-boy, factory-boy, or butcher-boy, and maintains this disguise with tolerable success until the shades of night have fallen . . . [then he enjoys] smoking in clumps at street corners, spitting on the pavement, and insulting females.[105]

Larrikins caroused in the streets, sometimes in 'gangs' of twenty or so, 'yelling like fiends, and generally making themselves merry'.[106] They embodied the uncontained sensation of recklessness that so perturbed nineteenth-century adults. 'It is by his pleasures that the larrikin is diagnosed', declared the *Grey River Argus*; 'he lives for enjoyment.' These pleasures were often antisocial: 'heckling Chinamen at all hours', 'hustling Europeans at night', interrupting public meetings, pushing over drunks and setting fire to women's skirts as they passed by.[107] One particular subset was known as 'theatre larrikins'. They sat in the cheap seats and hurled insults at those enjoying the entertainment.[108]

In a similar vein, Dunedin's 'adolescent thugs' took over Farley's Arcade on Saturday nights. Visitors to Farley's – a covered thoroughfare modelled on the arcades of Paris – saw youths shouting, jostling and fighting. The *Evening Star* commented that these 'local hoodlums flitted like immature imps up and down, straining their inventive faculties to attain some higher flight of diabolism than usual'.[109] The frontier masculinity of Australian bushranger Ned Kelly and his gang made an appearance in the parks of New Zealand's cities – and newspapers all around the country reported these boys' antics.[110] In Auckland a group of nineteen larrikins, mostly aged between fourteen and seventeen, lurked in Albert Park; one fellow 'had a toy pistol and, burlesquing the Kelly gang at intervals, was firing off caps'.[111]

The hard work and pious abstemiousness of the rising middle class, whose members denounced the general 'waywardness of colonial children', set the standard for acceptable urban behaviour.[112] Keen to uphold such divisions, a well-to-do Auckland father reminded his scruffy son that 'one of the grand distinctions in society is between the washed and the unwashed', and urged him to tidy himself up. A well-born boy should not be mistaken for a ruffian.[113] These middle-class values shaped the state's response to larrikinism, and politicians toyed with the idea of regulating working-class street culture.[114] Deeply worried about the dissipating influence of the night, some parliamentarians tried to pass a series of Bills that would empower police to arrest under-sixteens wandering the streets after 10 pm. Such extreme measures generated widespread opposition, and their proponents eventually gave up.[115]

New Zealand's parliamentary crusaders did not act alone. Instead, they took their lead from the international 'child-saving' movement.[116] Increasingly anxious that individual behaviour reflected collective ideals of national morality, middle-class child-savers tried to protect young people – especially those of the working class – from the perils of the night.[117] But how to stop lads unleashing their energies on the nocturnal streets? Boys' Brigade began in Glasgow in 1883 as an attempt to hone boys' physical and moral qualities. The brigade arrived in New Zealand soon after, and local lads learned self-discipline by playing rugby and cricket, and marching in straight lines.[118] Larrikins who ignored such values and committed crimes against property and people began to fill the dormitories of the early 'industrial schools'. The one at Burnham, established near Christchurch in 1874, was the best known.[119]

There is no denying the angst among respectable New Zealanders, but we can see the larrikin as more than simply a cipher of adults' anxieties. By engaging in 'a politics of gesture, symbol and metaphor', as British cultural theorist Dick Hebdige puts it, they built cultures of their own.[120] Some larrikins fashioned a particular look: striped shirt, patterned scarf, grey jacket, bell-bottomed pants and high-heeled boots.[121] The larrikin's staunch pose included pranks, practical jokes and coarse language. 'You bloody rotten whore, you stinking bugger', a Taranaki larrikin yelled at local residents one evening in 1883.[122] Just as clothes, language and violence identified larrikins to the general public, these elements helped distinguish these lads from other boys their own age.[123] In 1894 members of Auckland's would-be Ned Kelly gang accentuated the contrast by 'thrashing' boys who walked across their turf,[124] intensifying the social distinction between rough and respectable youths. Even those tamed by the child-savers asserted themselves in the face of officialdom: when Christchurch's mayor addressed a group of Boys' Brigaders as 'gentlemen', they distanced themselves from his term of address by 'stamping, clapping and whistling'.[125]

Not every late-nineteenth-century girl confined herself to sedate wandering and window shopping. The 'female larrikin', or 'larrikiness', was typically aged between twelve and sixteen, and like her male analogue she took pleasure in her new-found independence and street-smart style.[126] The gossipy columnists at the *Observer* had this to say about a Sunday night dance in the Waikato township of Te Aroha:

> The female larrikin element was well represented, under their well-known leader. No doubt they thought their conduct excited admiration in the breasts of the gentlemen present but had they only known the disgust which was felt at their immodest whispers and bold glances, they would perhaps have conducted themselves better.[127]

THE LAUNDRY

Girls toil in the laundry of Burnham Industrial School. The industrial schools were designed to accommodate and educate young people from impoverished backgrounds who might otherwise descend into crime. In its early years Burnham housed eighty 'inmates', boys as well as girls. Here, on the laundry walls, Bible verses urged young transgressors to embrace the word of Jesus and repent their sins.

While the prudish *Observer* wagged its finger at such outrageous behaviour, the horse had already bolted. As the nineteenth century drew to a close, an increasing number of girls joined their male counterparts on the street corners at night. 'Karangahape Road is becoming a regular beauty parade in the evenings', Auckland's *Star* claimed in 1892. 'Shortly after seven o'clock girls of all ages, sizes and descriptions begin to wander up and down the footpath for the benefit of the boys, who line the kerbstone.' Not content to sit quietly, the larrikiness made her presence felt. 'Some apparently respectable girls make as much noise as the larrikins of the sterner sex', the *Star* told its readers.[128] The *Otago Witness* filled out the picture, referring to Australian larrikinesses who turned out in their 'gaudy finery' to 'parade about with their "boys"'. They scoffed, giggled, jeered and sneered, and 'sped along the road to Destruction in short frocks and frizzled hair'.[129]

The larrikiness and the reaction against her assertive behaviour tell of a transformation in ideals of gender and propriety. Unlike the emboldened girls of ships' steerage whom we met in the previous chapter, and the dancers who sneaked into the corners of New Zealand's halls to gossip and flirt, the female larrikin issued a fully public challenge. She cocked a snook at adult surveillance and paraded up and down the streets – often at night – laughing at those who would restrain her. They could cling to their bourgeois ethic and complain all they liked, but they struggled to prevent her from colonising the footpaths – or worse. In November 1889 a judge tried fourteen-year-old Emily Brooks in the Dunedin City Police Court and sent her to jail for four months on charges of larceny and false pretences. Her purloinings included a cape, boots, skirt, hats, jam, cocoa, biscuits, bacon and potatoes. She disappeared from the care of her grandmother and obtained lodgings in hotels by claiming the police had sent her. Two years later, at sixteen, Emily was tried again for theft – this time for stealing 'male attire'

Were these two members of the larrikin tribe? In 1889 Emily Brooks, fourteen, consorted with other 'girls of very bad morals' and landed in prison for four months. The same year, Wellington police charged William Wright, also fourteen, with breaching the peace. A judge jailed him for a month. Dick Hebdige suggests that nineteenth-century English girls and boys of the streets usually appeared in photographs only when they came into contact with the repressive state or zealous social reformers. The same is true for New Zealand. These are coerced poses; prisoners raised their hands in order to reveal any identifying marks in the years before fingerprinting developed as a forensic technology.

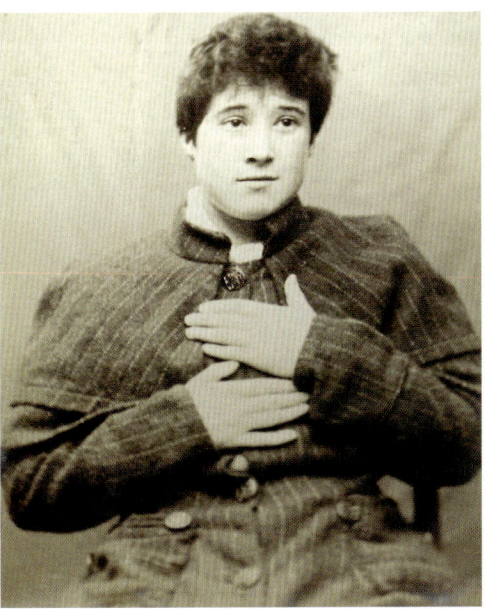 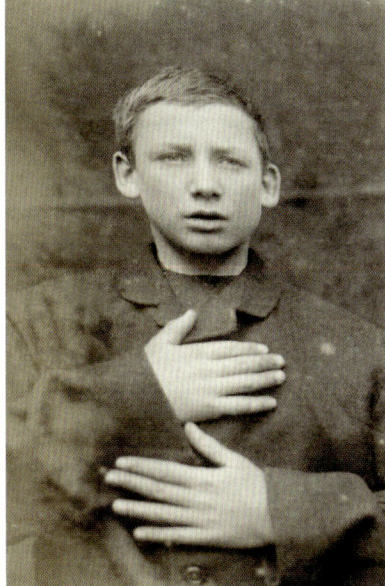

– and sentenced to twelve months' hard labour. As well as her pilfering, she kept company with girls of dubious 'morals'. A police sergeant summed up the situation when he said Emily 'had been living a very bad life'.[130]

Youth cultures continued to split along the fault lines of status, taste and respectability. In 1872 Mary Hargreaves complained about larrikins disrupting a Wellington concert. They made 'such a row', she said. A year later a group of 'larakins' gatecrashed a private party in Dunedin and the young partygoers called the police on their peers.[131] Gore schoolboy Herries Beattie wrote of his friend Charles ('Cooky') Cook's patchy school attendance: 'Wagged it. Larrikin now. Working at Thorn's Boot Store making boots.'[132] Herries, it seems, did not find such a pose wholly agreeable. Others in Gore held even firmer views. Members of the town's Young Men's Literary Society frowned upon local fellows 'who have as much backbone as a jelly-fish, and their chief aim is to see who can drink the most whisky without getting drunk'.[133] When it came to reading matter, Gore's respectable youngsters agreed with newspaper editors' complaints about 'factory hands, pit boys and telegraph boys' devouring 'penny dreadfuls' and 'fill[ing] their foolish brains with rubbish about highwaymen, pirates, and other objectionable people'.[134] Such titles as *Sweeny Todd*, *Varney the Vampire* and *Deadwood Dick* irritated Gore's literary boys, and they decried anyone craving 'literature of a frivolous and trashy nature'.[135] Young New Zealanders, including those in Gore, held a range of opinions about the cultures emerging in their midst.

Mashers, Dudes and the Changing Gender Order

The larrikin was not the only type of male adolescent who occupied the streets of New Zealand's towns and cities. The 'masher' and the 'dude' emerged as the middle class expanded. Wellington's civil service provided a most congenial habitat for these characters during the 1880s, and so too did the privately owned offices that offered clerical jobs.[136] These lads were young – 'the silken down of adolescence peeps faintly above his tender mouth', Auckland's *Observer* said of the dude – and their monikers hinted at sensuality: 'masher' came from the verb 'mash', Victorian slang for flirt, while the 'dude' took his name from 'duds', common lingo for clothes.[137] Both identities were imported: the dude hailed from

America while the masher was English, an habitué of London's West End theatres and the raffish streets of Soho.[138]

New Zealand's newspapers subjected mashers to endless, often voyeuristic analysis. The *Otago Witness* defined them as latter-day dandies: 'The modern masher of the most pronounced type is nothing if not an aesthete whose whole force goes to the worship of beauty, grace, and delicacy. His small moustache is fine and trim; his skin is smooth and fair; sometimes his complexion is artificial, and it is always scientifically preserved.'[139] Mashers and dudes turned their backs on the rough pioneer work ethic that had shaped their parents' lives. They rarely toiled at physical labour, preferring 'caramels, cigarettes and late hours'.[140] The *Observer* sensed the ambivalent masculinity at play, and ridiculed the young bucks:

> Pick it up tenderly!
>   Touch it with care!
> Fashioned so slenderly!
>   Give it some air!
> Let not the wind brush it
>   With touch that is rude.
> There, soft! You may crush it,
>   For it is a dude![141]
>
> His bang-tail coat, cigaw,
>   His cane of pattern snobbery
> His style of saying 'Aw',
>   And all that sort of bobbery
> He minces on the herb,
>   Like frying bacon-rasher,
> Oh! he is most superb,
>   This dude, this lady masher.[142]

This doggerel described the masher's effeteness. He was a long way from real manhood, the *Observer* implied, unlike his robust labouring counterpart from the early colonial period. In contrast, the masher worshipped 'beauty, grace and delicacy' and his clothes had 'a certain effeminacy of prettiness'. When it came to literature, the *Otago Witness* revealed, he preferred 'erratic poetry' and 'luscious fiction'.[143]

Journalists could scoff as much as they liked, but many girls found mashers highly desirable. In 1891 one wrote to a friend: 'I have not found a masher yet to suit me, I think I will have to wait a very long time for one.'[144] Some masher-hunters did get their man, even if they had to share him with others. In 1890 Whangarei's 'Mairtown Masher' was seen 'doing the heavy with two young ladies', while law student Charles Knight told of a holiday in Sydney in 1893: 'Alias seems to have blossomed out as the masher of Neutral Bay & fallen a victim to Carmel and Norma.'[145] The suave, sophisticated masher made other fellows jealous, as a Wairarapa paper reminded its readers:

> A report has reached us of a misadventure which befell a certain Adonis living in Masterton, through the jealousy of others of the 'masher' tribe, who find themselves totally eclipsed in the feminine circle whenever this handsome youth appears to view. Burning with revenge and wounded self-esteem a party of them awaited his approach just as the shades of eve came slowly down, and the morepork awakened from her dell. They waited and stood on a bridge and as the innocent favourite of the fair sex essayed to cross the structure he was ruthlessly seized by his less fortunate rivals and remorselessly plumped into the cress grown creek beneath.[146]

The masher's existence provides further evidence of a diversifying late-nineteenth-century youth culture, even in a small society. New Zealand's urban settlements were a great deal less developed than the cities of the northern hemisphere. Masterton's mashers shared their town with 2,000 other inhabitants in 1890, while 5.5 million people lived in Greater London, the masher's spiritual home. The sensual streets of Soho and bustling theatres of the West End were very different from the muddy byways, cress-grown creeks and low timber-fronted buildings of the Wairarapa settlements.[147] Still, New Zealand's mashers embraced local conditions and enjoyed the pleasures offered by small-town life. Masterton's Theatre Royal hosted a constant stream of minstrel shows, touring singers, Shakespearean plays, and the latest musicals by Gilbert and Sullivan.[148] There was plenty for a masher to like, even in a smallish borough.

A Dandy Thief

A flash style and bad behaviour sometimes went together, and a few youths carried out their misdemeanours with real panache. The flamboyant Thomas Gleeson, a stock rider-turned-burglar from Auckland, attracted considerable attention. Eighteen-year-old Thomas was arrested in Invercargill in November 1888 for a series of Christchurch thefts. Hundreds of curious onlookers thronged to see him disembark from the train at Dunedin station under police escort. Word of his thefts had preceded him: watches and chains, rings, lockets, a selection of revolvers, silk handkerchiefs, scarves with green spots. Some he on-sold, others he wore: a coat and a slouch hat from one shop, 'an elaborate silk dress and fittings', cosmetics. Thomas went in for disguises of all sorts, dressed one moment as a stylish gentlewoman and then as an older man with a clip-on beard and large moustache. Each disguise enhanced the potential for subterfuge. Locked up in Dunedin Gaol, he escaped by sawing through his cell's bars with a file and went a-thieving twice more. He took money, ham and boots from a butchery, and a wedding cake, plain fruit cake and a dozen pastries from a bakery.[149]

Thomas was a youth of few words. In the train from Invercargill to Dunedin he told police: 'I did not think you were so close on my track'; when captured after his daring escape he spat: 'If I only had a revolver I would shoot the pair of you.'[150] The press presumed him an unlikely criminal. 'Wholly guiltless of moustache or beard, his expression being somewhat feminine', the newspapers reported, 'he stands 5ft 7¼ in., is slight made but wiry, with fresh complexion, dark hair and blue eyes. There is nothing in his face or demeanour to indicate he would be the author of such exploits as burglary or prison breaking.'[151] The stolen slouch hat was an item of larrikin uniform and Thomas' police photo reveals that he held himself with style: clean shaven, he wore a neat haircut and a tie held with a ring. New Zealanders were entranced by the exploits of this larrikin-masher, a daring dandy with an incorrigible streak.

Thomas Gleeson.

In Masterton during the late 1880s, Jack von Sturmer, son of the local magistrate, poses for the camera in his masher outfit.

Not every middle-class lad wished to try on this particular mask of modernity.[152] Some resisted the very idea of the masher, and not always out of jealousy. In 1885, Nelsonian Fred Gibbs viewed the type with disdain: 'Melville making short stay with Hudsons 2 doors off', he wrote in his diary. 'Has come out awful masher with stick etc! Of course I take no notice but am rather disgusted. Elder brother's influence I suppose.'[153] While Fred's acquaintance Melville experimented with the masher mask – coached, perhaps, by his older sibling – such light-hearted silliness did not appeal to Fred's serious self-image. Fred shared the *Observer*'s belief that mashers rejected the manly self-presentation required in

ADOLESCENT STIRRINGS

Early youth subcultures were not always clearly demarcated. Here, during the 1880s, masher and larrikin styles overlapped: young Whanganui resident Mr Hooper, on the left, sports the masher cane, but the waistcoat and loosely knotted tie are worn in a slouchy larrikin pose. Both he and his companion Mr Silcock wear working boots rather than the toothpick shoes favoured by Jack von Sturmer on the opposite page, although Silcock's daring shirt is as much masher as larrikin.

Frances Hodgkins' rendering of the dudine's masculine suit with its wide lapels, 1880s.

the colony. He went on to deride such fellows as 'fops'. 'I was utterly disgusted at his manner', he wrote of one.[154]

Just as boy mashers nudged prevailing codes of masculinity, the girl masher, a middle-class version of the larrikiness, challenged feminine ideals. The *Otago Witness* described her as an 'angular, bony, hard-mouthed girl' given to 'masculine pursuits and masculine imitation'.[155] She embodied the new female independence by talking rather too loudly, laughing uproariously and shoving adults out of the way in the streets. 'There is no slang or popular vulgarity with which she is not acquainted', the *Observer* complained.[156] The 'dudine', the corollary of the dude, also assumed a masculine look. She dabbled in male attire and wore a hat, waistcoats and 'trim little jacket' made at men's outfitters, a high collar and tie.[157] 'The girl dude is absurd', sulked *The Press*, 'for she never succeeds in looking either ladylike or gentlemanly.'[158] The timing of such complaints was far from coincidental. Suffragists had begun to agitate for women's right to vote during the 1880s, and a parliamentary Bill introduced universal franchise in 1893. The widespread representations of suffragists as 'manly women' seeped across into newspapers' coverage of adolescent girls as well. Young women did not necessarily object to this portrayal. Some adopted the tie and waistcoat as their own and became the 'New Women' of the 1890s.[159] They helped transform the gender order as the new century approached.

Innocence and Temptation

Reactions to the new types of adolescents, especially the larrikiness, hinted at a semi-public discussion of youthful sexuality. French philosopher Michel Foucault famously rejected the idea of Victorian sexual 'repression', arguing instead that an explosion of sexual discourse characterised the period.[160] This is certainly true of New Zealand, where newspaper editors complained about 'precocious' girls wandering the streets and boys eagerly searching for information about sex. Dunedin youths browsed Braithwaites for suggestive pamphlets and told each other about their finds. An eighteen-year-old clerk in the head office of drapers Bing Harris and Co. showed his mates 'a pamphlet written in a dramatic sentimental kind of way in high flown old fashioned language that describes vividly various sexual crimes and how they were done'.[161]

Such examples suggest a sexual double movement. 'Liberalising forces' gave rise to risqué books and pictures, which then prompted a conservative reaction.[162] Seacliff superintendent Truby King, an enthusiastic pontificator on questions of public morals, loudly complained about the 'corrupt publications' that 'circulate freely among the youth of the colony'.[163] He claimed they threatened proper psychological development and did not provide the careful guidance the adolescent required. King's moral-sounding objections were not unusual for doctors at the time: a great many physicians took Christian ideas about sin and guilt and refashioned them into arguments about healthy minds and bodies.[164]

This terrain of sexual thought and debate was heavily gendered. Boys were assumed to be sexually curious, prone to excitation, rapacious even. Much to King's disgust, many pored over the Australian newspaper *The Dead Bird* and a

The Dead Bird, 10 November 1889: breasts, bloomers and challenges to Victorian modesty. Some of the images are numbered and captioned: number 2 is 'She's got "a little ankle, a pretty little foot"', and number 4 reads 'They're afloat'. Detractors decried *The Dead Bird* as 'vile and impure'; they complained about the text – young readers could indulge themselves in tales of divorce, debauchery and sodomy – and the saucy cartoons. The newspaper bore a resemblance to the comic genres of later decades.

popular book titled *Elements of Social Science; Or Physical, Sexual and Natural Religion*. This volume advocated frequent intercourse among the young, King said. He added, as if he could possibly know, that half of all New Zealand boys had read it.[165] Youths also congregated in the public galleries of courtrooms when sexual cases came to trial and they revelled in proceedings.[166] King and other doctors found such excitations deeply worrying. If a boy's nascent sexual desires were not carefully handled then he might become sexually incorrigible. King's colleague Herbert Barraclough wrote that adolescence 'is the period when the omnipresent problem of sex obtrudes itself with irresistible force . . . the moral sense at the time of puberty is in a state of flux'.[167] By 1890 doctors had begun to re-cast ideas about runaway sensation in psychological terms.[168]

Girls ran up against a different – and often impossible – set of social expectations. They were meant to retain their innocence while, paradoxically, knowing how to fend off unwanted advances from men and boys. Those who successfully trod this tightrope were 'good' girls, but those who failed to control male sexuality – or worse, gave in of their own accord – were widely dismissed as 'bad' girls on the road to ruin. Child-saving organisations like the Girls' Friendly Society, an Anglican organisation set up in 1883 as a local iteration of an English group, tried to 'rescue' the wayward.[169] The society built boarding houses for immigrant girls over the age of thirteen and, like the proprietors of the domestic servants' homes of the 1860s, its good officers tried to shelter their charges from the perils of urban life.[170] But some girls needed more intensive intervention. A Catholic order opened the Magdalen Asylum near Christchurch for those requiring sanctuary from 'the glittering temptation to loathsome vices'.[171] Not everyone could be saved, however, and unrepentant lasses sidestepped such rescue attempts. Some were 'constantly attracted for immoral purposes on board of vessels' tied up at Wellington's wharves and others wandered Auckland's alleyways 'in company with hoodlums of the other sex'.[172]

The tightrope was not an easy one to walk. How could a girl possibly remain sexually innocent and know how to dampen men's ardour? Gertie Brookes revealed the double-bind when she wrote to Ella Marsh in 1889:

> On Saturday night when I was going into Newton some man came bumping up against me (I fancy he was a little bit drunk) & when he just got past he stopped & said good

night, I did not say anything but hurried on as fast as ever I could but like my luck I herd [*sic*] him following me, well he soon overtook me then he started to ask me ever such a lot of questions & all I said was just 'yes' or 'no' (he went on) aren't you frightened to go out by yourself at night, I said no, you are not one of the timid sort then & he was just going to put his arm around me I gave myself a shake & said <u>get away you miserable thing do</u> & didn't I cut, he stopped & stared at me & then I think he must have turned back for he did not follow me again, don't you think that was an insult Ella, I know I was scared at the time I thought the old beast was going to kiss me.[173]

Gertie's drunk interlocutor had tried to ascertain what kind of a girl she was, assuming that a 'timid' (that is, innocent) lass would be safely locked away at home at night, or at the very least would feel nervous about being out. Anyone who stood her ground in public must be a bold, disreputable girl who would welcome such an embrace.[174] When the drunk man failed to make sense of Gertie's assertive response, he could only stare in surprise.

Gertie negotiated a web of social norms as she wandered Auckland's streets. She was far from a willing participant in her assailant's plans, but nor was she a timid wallflower happy to retreat indoors. Gertie enjoyed the attention of younger men, and she conveyed her feelings to Ella with an ironic pen: 'My word Ella if you want a sweetheart just come down here, of course I have not got one yet but I never pass a young man without he nearly stares his eyes out at me but that is not my fault.'[175]

Others in Gertie's circle discussed the persistent sexual double standard. In a letter to Ella Marsh, Hettie Stott told of Mary Smith who had fallen pregnant and was 'taken to the Costly Home. Now you know what girls are taken there for & why.' By way of further explanation, Hettie added: 'I am awfully sorry for the girl she was not fit to be in town, Auckland is getting so vile worse every year.' She finished with a sermon: 'What poor weak creatures we are, & how easy we are led astray, a girl wants to have her wits about her in town or else it is all up with them.'[176] Hettie suggested that Auckland had become a sexually dangerous place for girls, and not only because men took liberties. Some girls struggled to hold the line when confronted with the city's temptations.[177]

As Gertie Brookes and Hettie Stott intimated, adolescent girls were not themselves without desire. Some were circumspect in public but confessed their

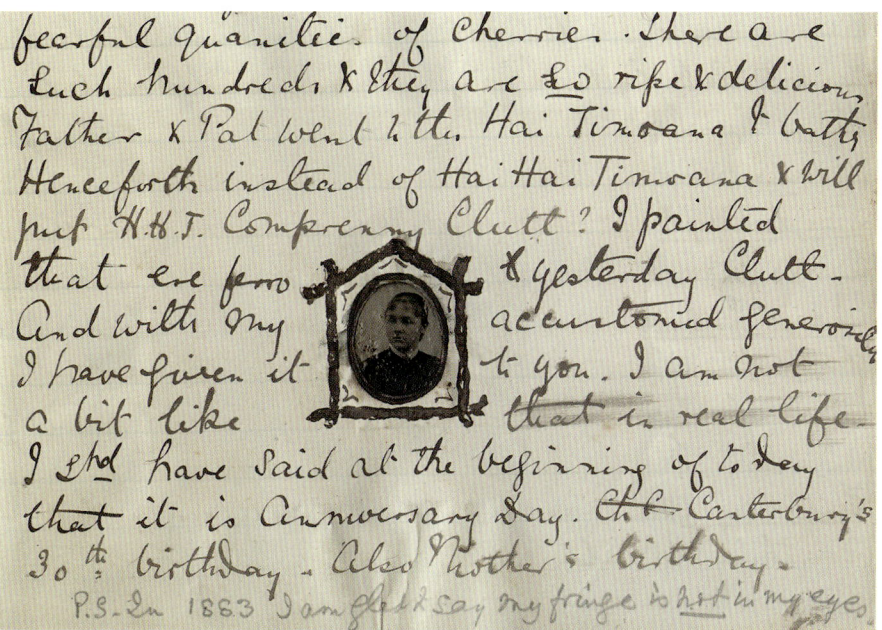

'I am not a bit like that in real life': A lively lass, Elsie Clogstoun took issue with the stern demeanour in the photograph she glued into her diary and surrounded with a frame in ink. 'Clutt' is the name Elsie gave her diary; 'Comprenny' is an anglicising of the French 'Comprenez': 'do you understand?' Elsie's diary was a friend in whom she confided.

longings in their diaries and shared details with their confidantes.[178] In 1881, Cantabrian Elsie Clogstoun wrote of a visit to the estate of a local gentry family where she and her sisters encountered Barton and Dudley Mills, two 'grizly youths'. Barton was 'fearfully conceited' and Dudley 'awfully ugly', Elsie reported, but her sister Ina told of a dream in which she 'violently wanted the eldest of the youths to get onto the bed. Dreams are odd.'[179] Helen Anderson was even more forthright about what she wanted. On a boat trip around Stewart Island in 1899 she harboured longings for the ship's mate, a 'short quarter cast boy of 18. He is extremely jolly and entertaining, fascinating, adorable, beautiful, lovable – charming – everyone is in love with him including me.'[180] She went to a concert ashore, and 'best of all I made love to a Stewart Island native in the corner!'[181] Such expressions of feeling were largely acceptable as long as the girls adhered to the rules: during the nineteenth century the term 'making love' referred to flirting and cuddling, not sexual intimacy, and a public dance had its overseers after all. Light snogging in a corner, where respectable adults maintained ultimate control, was not the same as a fumble down a grimy alleyway. Even so, Helen's frisson of pleasure is palpable.

Debates over the age of consent offer up another example of Victorian sexual ideologies and reveal the tensions between male and female desires. Following pressure from first-wave feminists, including those in the Women's Christian Temperance Union (WCTU), the age of consent rose from twelve to fourteen in 1889, fifteen in 1894 and sixteen in 1896. Campaigners argued that an increased age of consent would hold men responsible for their sexual advances, restrict their access to female bodies and protect girls' respectability.[182] The rapid (although incremental) increase reflected the art of political compromise: many feminists supported an age of sixteen from the outset, but parliamentarians needed several years of coaxing.

Some WCTU feminists wanted to place control on female as well as male sexuality. Girls' brains, they proposed, could not restrain the 'purely sexual instincts' until their early twenties, and they argued that the age of consent should be as high as twenty-one in order to protect young women from their own sexual urges.[183] They were not intent on redefining female sexuality, and rejected the ideas about female independence that circulated in the factories and among larrikinesses and girl mashers. Instead, they focussed on sexual danger, which, as Barbara Brookes writes, 'made them uncomprehending of women who experimented with sexuality outside of marriage'.[184] Their complicated reactions are borne out in their attitudes towards marriage. The reformers did not seem to mind that boys and girls were able to marry at very early ages: after all, wedlock protected reputations and upheld moral virtue. The age of consent regulated precocious girls and rapacious single men, not wives and husbands.[185]

Devoted Friends

Some adolescents preferred the intimate company of their own sex. There is very little historical evidence of sex between young women, although we do know more about intense emotional friendships. In Nelson, Fred Gibbs' sister Resa developed an attachment to a Miss Furlong who declared, as Resa's ardour began to cool, 'Oh Resa I used to love you more than any one in the world & to think you near perfection as possible, & I used to sleep with your likeness under my pillow, kiss it last thing at night & show it to my friends saying "there's the girl", etc!'[186] Such florid expressions of devotion, which Fred noted in his diary, mirror the pattern of romantic friendship that prevailed in Western Europe and North America.[187] Like the overseas versions, some New Zealanders' romantic friendships incorporated erotic elements and others did not, but it is not easy to know which was which. Resa and Miss Furlong sometimes slept in the same bed, but bed-sharing was common in large families at the time and the practice reveals little about those who engaged in it. Fred worried that Miss Furlong had strung Resa along – 'does she laugh at Resa & think what a fool she is making of her' – but he had no problem with the sentiment itself.[188]

Then again, Fred's own intimate interests lay with men alone. Fred, who never married, was deeply ambivalent about young women and went out of his way to avoid them. 'Only danced with a girl', he wrote one evening in 1884, 'and didn't like it much.'[189] No girl could compete with Fred Kelly, the son of a foundry-man who secured a scholarship to attend Nelson College and became Fred Gibbs' 'greatest friend'. 'Without realising it I was far more confidential with him than with anyone else. We could always enter into and sympathise with one another's moods, which I now perceive to be the greatest proof of true friendship', Gibbs wrote.[190] He was heartbroken when another pupil accidentally shot Kelly dead during school rifle practice.[191] As a sixteen-year-old, Fred admired only men: one public figure was 'a fine looking fellow', he wrote, and another 'gave me tremendous impulse'.[192] Four years later, then a twenty-year-old schoolteacher, he described an evening with a male colleague: 'H. & self necessarily interfere with one another, while the most unfortunate result is that I get nervous & unnatural.'[193] Fred did not elaborate on the precise nature of this 'interference' and 'unnaturalness', but his description is highly suggestive: the euphemism 'unnatural' usually referred to a sexual connection between men.

New Zealand law proscribed some types of sexual encounter between males. Until 1893 only anal sex ('sodomy') was illegal, at which point Parliament criminalised all other sexual activities under the term 'indecent assault'.[194]

This pair steals a quiet moment on a yacht in the Auckland area at the turn of the century.

Still, convictions were relatively rare. Almost every case involved an older man, and he was usually the only one punished. Younger partners, including those who swapped sexual favours for cash and access to alcohol, concerts and the music hall, were generally thought to be led astray or strong-armed by the older party. There is no doubt some encounters were coercive: in the Waitaki Valley in 1896, for instance, fifteen-year-old cow boy Syd Jamieson complained to a clerk on his sheep station after a seventy-year-old labourer sexually assaulted him in a tent.[195] Other times, though, lads were fully complicit in the liaison and prosecutions took place only if parents found out.[196] The prevailing assumption about young innocents and older corrupters came into focus by the end of the century, an example of the deepening social divide between adolescents and adults.[197] Significantly, though, police had little interest in regulating sex between adolescent boys. Lying beyond the concern of New Zealand's parliamentarians and middle-class moralists, it went unnoticed and unpunished until the following century.

From this Day Forward

Of those adolescents who sought out a sweetheart of the opposite sex, fewer married as the nineteenth century progressed. In 1876, 1 percent of men and 21 percent of women married in their teens, but the 21 percent figure dropped to 12 percent by 1896 as the median age of first marriage increased.[198] This upwards trajectory helped to further distinguish adolescence from adulthood, for greater numbers of girls took up paid employment in the years between home and matrimony. Demographers suggest that young women's changing patterns of decision-making also played a part. Increasing numbers of brides took their time to check out the field and assess 'the prospects of any groom'.[199] But the question of prospects did not always favour would-be grooms of a young age. In a public lecture in Blenheim in 1882, a Reverend Lee told his audience that love in marriage was 'crucial' but that young women had to consider their beau's likely financial success. 'A beardless youth still in his teens would most likely, and certainly by a sensible young woman, be rejected without thanks.'[200] While girls assessed the possibilities and applied their own criteria, parents often controlled the process and scrutinised young men's earning potential as well. Some middle-class parents determined whether they would allow a suitor to 'pay his addresses' to their daughters, and they broke up courtships if they did not approve of their offspring's partners' prospects.[201] One Whanganui lass was apparently 'rather nice looking' but, as she had 'rather a common manner and way of behaving', her beau's parents terminated the courtship.[202]

Reverend Lee and the status-conscious folk of Whanganui clearly expected romance to play second fiddle to a suitor's prospects, but romantic and sentimental ideals flowered in broader Victorian culture.[203] Charles Knight bared his soul to Di, a would-be girlfriend, as the pair ambled through Hagley Park in 1893:

I then told her how I had gradually fallen in love with her. If to always think of one person, to model one's life as one thinks another would wish, waking always thinking of her, to let one person dominate one's existence is to love then I loved. She listened and said no-one had ever yet entered into her life that she could say dominated her life. 'Silliness'. I bridled at this and said that I did not think of the noblest emotions and thought silliness.[204]

Crushed, Charles extricated himself from the situation. 'Goodbye. Her face lit up by the crescent moon. I turned and fled hurriedly down Armagh Street.' He had a little more luck with Christiana Walter, but she soon departed the district and left Charles broken-hearted: 'Oh day of parting. Goodbye my love we now must sever.' He took flowers and grapes to Christiana's hotel, talked to her on board ship, then, heavy-hearted, watched her sail away.[205]

Among romantics – or, at least, those not completely beholden to prospects – personal compatibility counted for a lot. Daisy Brookes described her priorities in a letter to her friend Ella Marsh:

> Have you come in with a nice young man yet. I think it is high time you had one now ... I think I have done with W.G. he's too much of the stuck up for me, perhaps I will go back to O.P. after all he seems a nice chap and is one of my sort no stuck up in him so we will see by and by we don't know none of us what will happen between now and then.[206]

As Daisy's attitude to snobbery demonstrates – 'too much of the stuck up', to use her phrase – the ideals and practices of courting were fragile threads in a delicate cloth of social expectations. While Daisy and her domestic servant friends moved freely through social spaces, upper-middle-class offspring had to negotiate the minefield of respectability. Many such girls headed out of an evening with a chaperone to guard them, just like their forbears, and those who arrived at a social event in a group were escorted home afterwards. The newspapers publicly shamed boys who refused to act as escorts and looked down upon girls who 'stepped out' without adequate oversight. The wrong kind of public associations had dire consequences, especially during the 1870s.[207] A lass named Katie Marshall featured in the gossip column of the local paper after she was seen

OPPOSITE **Ruth Harding** married land agent Jim Crawford at the age of nineteen; Jim was a fair bit older. Ruth's mother allowed Jim to 'pay his addresses' to her daughter, and Ruth wrote of their subsequent courtship: 'I felt I could not kiss a strange man so old and big – but he implored and begged so much that I just put my lips to his face and then felt dreadful thinking he would think me bold'. There is no such carry-on in this photograph taken by Ruth's father, William Harding.

promenading in Whanganui's streets with a male admirer, a music teacher. 'A perambulatory young music teacher was soundly thrashed by an indignant father for walking about at unseemly hours with his daughter', the paper reported salaciously. The parents of Katie's pal Ruth Harding, who recounted the tale in her own memoir, forbade her from seeing Katie ever again.[208]

Some adolescents found ways to bend the rules in the midst of such strictness. Chaperonage sometimes gave rise to its own pleasures, as a Dunedin lad revealed after his return from a party:

> I hardly need mention I needed no pressing to the invitation to see two young ladies (sisters) home. They lived about a quarter of a mile away, the walk under ordinary circumstances would not have taken above three minutes, but somehow or other it took us a little over an hour; we must have mistaken the road or something. I know we passed the gate several times and either wouldn't or couldn't find the latch; perhaps we never tried. I leave you to conjecture which.[209]

Charlie Blackburn and his bride-to-be Minnie May D'Arcy, c. 1889.

Although chaperonage helped maintain middle-class ideals of gender and respectability, this form of social regulation began to weaken by the 1890s.[210] Boys' and girls' relationships to the night shifted, led first by young working-class people and then those from the middle class. Girls became more independent, and, even though the child-savers tried to rein in working-class adolescents, the most restrictive examples of adult control slowly loosened their grip. Adults' regulation of adolescents took different forms over time, and Chapter 3 outlines new foci for control: a militaristic attitude and the deliberate, carefully structured organisation of leisure time.

Conclusion: Organised Uncertainty

At the end of 1880, two days before Christmas, Elsie Clogstoun expressed her frustration at the attitude of a friend who went by the nickname 'The Hanmer'. He 'isn't a man', she wrote testily. 'He is only 17, but has to be called "Mr" – Yah.'[211] If Elsie's friend's claim was laughable – 'Yah' was a popular term of dismissal, after all – then what did it mean to be seventeen in 1880? Was such a person a child, an adult or something in between? There was no clear consensus and Elsie wavered on the subject. After all, she thought that attaining the age of sixteen would make her 'hopelessly and irretrievably old'. 'Oh woe is me', she sighed.[212]

Elsie's prevarications reflected an increasingly organised uncertainty: the category of adolescence now occupied the liminal space between childhood and adulthood. The Factories Act of 1891 defined a 'child' as a boy under thirteen and a girl under fourteen, as we have seen, and historian Jeanine Graham suggests that such Acts of Parliament helped define young people as being on 'the threshold to adulthood'.[213] But we should not jump to this conclusion too quickly. Thirteen- and fourteen-year-olds were no longer children, to be sure, but neither were they adults: they were adolescents. Sometimes the concept was implicit – employers told older boys they were not expected to work as hard as men and paid them less, for instance, and they hinted at youngsters' reduced physical capacity – but the new terminology made an appearance too. Newspapers began to chatter about 'adolescent vigour' and 'adolescent foolishness' during the 1870s and 1880s, in relation to girls as well as boys.[214] The ranks of high-spirited factory labourers

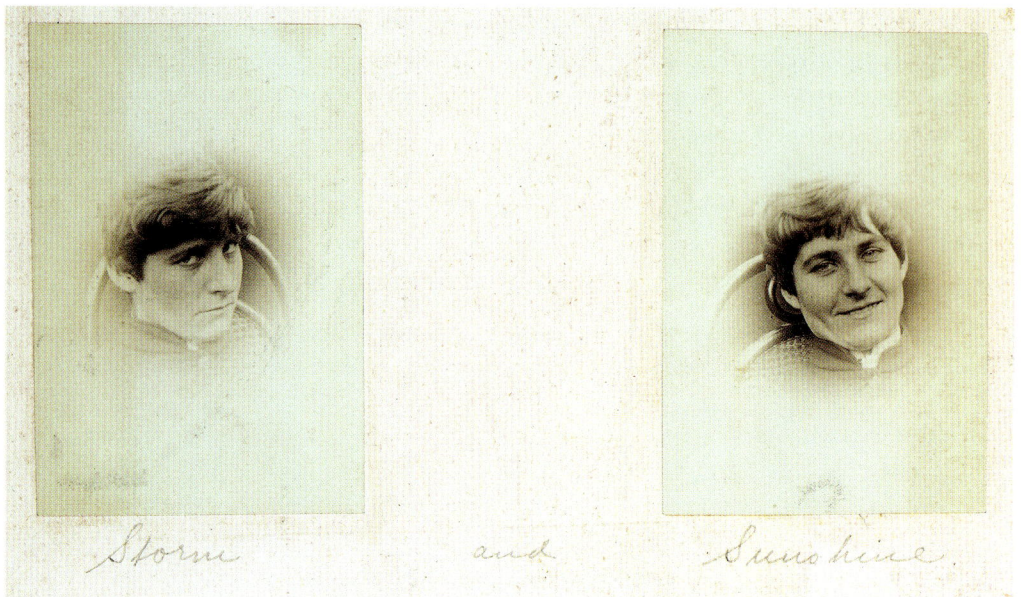

'Storm and Sunshine', a pair of photos by Masterton photographer Robert Gant, c. 1889. The idea that adolescence is a time of 'storm and stress' dates from the early 1880s, and Truby King published on the perils of youth in the *New Zealand Medical Journal* in 1890. Drawing from the work of international psychiatrists Bevan Lewis and Thomas Clouston, King saw adolescence as a particularly important – if unstable – stage of psychosocial development. Some of King's views, including the need for self-control and sexual restraint among the young, are still popular today. Other ideas – that adolescents never fully appreciate the work of Shakespeare, for instance – are voiced less often.

and street-loiterers included both, after all; 'adolescence' was gendered quite differently from the older idea of 'youth'. The concept of adolescence had become firmly embedded in the national consciousness by the early 1890s when Truby King told New Zealanders all about the intricacies of young people's development.

Boarding school life demonstrated adolescents' semi-dependence. Jessie Mackersey's sons Lindsay and Norman boarded in Hastings and constantly wrote home for provisions and money: 'another tucker box, please', '10/- for gunpowder and shot', 'a pair of running shoes'. 'Do not forget about the tin of cakes you promised me', Lindsay reminded his mother.[215] These boys made choices about their leisure time, but they needed parents to fund their exploits. As inhabitants of the space between childhood dependence and adult responsibility, adolescents like Lindsay and Norman lived in an ambiguous world.

Young folk pondered the meaning of this curious in-between state. This anonymous writer put pen to paper in 1873 and told of his fellows:

> Most youths desire to arrive at old age, some exhibit this wish in different ways to others; one for instance you will see pay a visit to his father's office, perch himself on a stool in the office, put a pen behind his ear, and look round with an expression that says 'don't I look a man', another commences at an early age to shave himself so that his whiskers may grow the sooner and thus look manly. There is another class of youths whose attempt to look manly is not very praiseworthy. I refer to that class of youths who stalk up and down the street with a pipe in their mouths and a stick in their hands.[216]

The pipe-and-stick crowd – those who attempted to 'look manly' but were not yet fully grown men – became the dudes and mashers of the 1880s, the lads with a penchant for 'the newest slang and the latest flash song', as the *Otago Witness* put it.[217] The suggestion that a 'class' of youths paraded the streets with canes and pipes tells of the increasing visibility of young people's cultures, something journalists perpetuated when they furnished their readers with the details. Those who paid attention learned where these new types hung out, what they wore and how they shaped a style.

Urban life allowed a more sustained sense of youthful collectivity than the momentary alliances and itinerancies of the earlier decades. The towns and cities provided spaces for larrikins, larrikinesses, mashers and dudes to rework international styles and challenge ideas about appropriate gendered behaviour.[218] The 'flight from rural to urban life' invited encounters 'with the urban crowd, and the freedom and perils these provided', as Amy Srebnick writes in her history of sex and culture in nineteenth-century New York.[219] Auckland and Dunedin were a far cry from the large North American and European cities but, like their overseas cousins, young antipodeans enjoyed the shops, theatres and street life, and made friends in the schools and factories.

In-betweeners wanted to spend time with their own kind, and the growing gap between mixed-age and youth-focussed leisure served to reinforce the distinction

TEENAGERS

between young people and adults. But youth cultures divided along lines of class and style as soon as they took shape. Diverse young New Zealanders embodied class and gender in particular ways, and they did not always see eye to eye. In 1880 a Christchurch newspaper correspondent complained about the clerks in banks and the government service, status climbers who excluded 'shop girls' from their social events.[220] In a world of penny dreadfuls, beer and cigarettes, the abstemious lads of the Gore Young Men's Literary Society judged their fellows harshly. The reverse was true as well: those who preferred highwaymen to high-brow no doubt dismissed Gore's cultural gatekeepers as a pack of nobs.

Life with pets. In Masterton Jack von Sturmer poses with Dandy the dog; near Oamaru a girl spends time with her best friend.

The most personal aspects of daily life retained their significance as New Zealand society changed. 'Had a bathe at Pelichet Bay in the afternoon with Forsyth, Brown, McFarlane, and Bligh. Our puppy is missing', wrote thirteen-year-old Harold Hooper as he pondered the perilousness of existence: 'Edward Penny one of my schoolfellows died yesterday at 13 yrs. A warning to all.'[221] Agnes MacGregor, fifteen-year-old minister's daughter, pondered her developing personality: 'I am afraid I am very, very selfish. I do not feel like the same girl who wrote the beginning of this book – perhaps it is because I am older. I hope I am growing a little better, but Oh, I'm awfully bad yet.' A year later, Agnes resolved to 'turn over a new leaf' and 'become more thoughtful than I have been'. She knew adolescence signified a transition to an adulthood which, she hoped, would be socially worthy.[222]

While Agnes chronicled her changing self-perception, Elsie Clogstoun lived in the moment. 'I'm writing on the lawn', she jotted in her diary during the summer of 1881, 'and it would be quite perfect if sandflies weren't trying by hundreds to devour me. A weka yelling in the bush and the boot-boy trying to play the concertina are the only 2 discording [*sic*] elements. Who wouldn't live in New Zealand?'[223] Urbanity shaped antipodean adolescence for increasing numbers of young people during the 1880s, but rural arcadia still defined a New Zealand life for many. This tension between the cities and the countryside continued to shape in-betweeners' experience in the decades that followed.

Chapter Three Jazz Age Youth

The typewriter changed girls' lives dramatically. As the nineteenth century gave way to the twentieth, the number of office jobs exploded under the influence of this new machine with its clacking keys and smudgy black ribbon. Women began to displace men in clerical roles. In 1881 only 1 percent of office workers in the private and government sectors were women; by 1911 that figure had swollen to 24 percent.[1] A great many were young, typically aged between seventeen and twenty-one, and the newspapers used the term 'flapper' to define them.[2] The *Star* first told of the flapper in 1905, describing her as 'the latest product of the New Age: the lady typewriter'.[3] The *Evening Post* picked up the theme in 1914, suggesting that the flapper wore 'fashionable clothes' and 'ran about offices at the most critical time of her life'.[4] When she ventured outdoors she talked loudly in the streets, giggling and swearing.[5] On weekends she headed for the seaside to sunbathe, show off and go out surfing: she held her own 'with men in this new sport'.[6]

Readers of the *Grey River Argus* learned more about the flapper's social aspirations:

OPPOSITE At Days Bay, Wellington, during the 1920s.

There is one vast upheaval which as yet we are hardly aware of. It is the sudden emergence of the Flapper as a force in society. Yesterday there was no such person. To-day she is all over the place [. . .] Long before they are marriageable our girls are sure of themselves and sure of us. The Georgian maiden of 15 has more devil in her than the Victorian matron of 50. Indeed, the younger she is the more intractable and untameable she is apt to be. The rising generation are drunk with the new wine of liberty. They are born free, and they laugh when any Rip van Winkle offers them a pretty little set of chains to wear in a dainty little doll's house [. . .] The Flapper knows all there is to be known about life long before she is supposed to have commenced to live.[7]

If the larrikiness and the girl masher were the flappers' nineteenth-century predecessors, parading along the pavements, wearing confronting clothing and openly courting male attention, the confident and intractable flapper challenged adult perceptions even more.[8] Some grown-ups worried about her freedom and a loosening of sexual morals, but she intrigued others.[9] The *Mirror*, a fashionable magazine, published many articles referring to the 'modern girl' and her love of stylish clothing, independence and late hours.[10]

As a cultural phenomenon the flapper spoke to a pair of competing trends that emerged during the late nineteenth century and shaped the decades that followed.[11] James Belich suggests that New Zealand society tightened up 'like a giant spanner', the result of a successful 'moral crusade' by those who promoted self-restraint, temperance and probity. 'Its after effects', he adds, 'kept things tight until the 1960s.'[12] But this is a considerable oversimplification.[13] The moral crusaders were noisy and they notched up some successes, but New Zealand society also eased back during the period. This was in fact a double movement. New types of organised leisure – Bible Class, Scouts, Guides and the rest – regulated young lives while making room for a new sociability. A resurgent militarism worked to rigidify boys' experiences but continuing urbanisation enabled a bohemianism of sorts. The commercialisation of everyday life was no less complex. Advertisers reasserted ideals of domesticity at the same time as girls' work choices expanded. The cinema, a revolutionary force, showcased flapperdom, incited sexual pleasures and fanned the flames of moral anxiety. With adolescence now firmly established as a concept and a way of life, formal and informal youth cultures expanded during these radical and conservative years.

The Body Transformed

Adolescent bodies symbolised social change during the first decades of the new century. Girls' hair went up, then down, then radically reduced in volume. Pinned-up hair signified maturity during the early 1900s. Late in 1906, Dunedin fifteen-year-old Dora de Beer wrote about her sister's transition: 'Kate put up her hair, and school has broken up.'[14] Four years later, an eager lad named Erle wrote from boarding school to his sister Tommy: 'I look forward to seeing you with your hair up. I will look forward to having some fun with you then.'[15] The first flappers bucked this trend and wore their hair down. The word 'flapper' described the way shorter, newly liberated locks dangled and swayed against their owner's neck. The baggy dresses of the early flappers also heralded change by displacing the tight-laced look of the 1890s.

Grace (*left*) and Nola, 'The Heavenly Twins at Waimarama Picnic: Flappers'. Office assistant Nola Pratt and her friend Grace lived in Hawke's Bay. Their photograph, from the early 1910s, shows the transitional style: Nola's hair is long and flowing and the girls wear loose baggy dresses. The pillarbox dress and the cloche hat came later.

Newspaper editors complained about the 'New Woman', that 'creature determined to kill grace, beauty, charm, all those gifts by which women rule the world; a creature of short hair and long ideas', but feminism's promise of freer movement appealed to many girls.[16] Rational dress and bodily mobility were signs of modernity, and British historians suggest that girls embraced feminism as a revolt against the world of their parents.[17] In New Zealand, Hilda Lovell-Smith and her Christchurch friends counted themselves among this number: in 1907 they wanted clothes that better enabled an active life, and they considered the corseted waist an 'absurd and indeed wicked fashion'.[18] Likewise, Dora de Beer was a highly mobile teenager who hung about with 'a very naughty American girl about town', played tennis with her Dunedin friends and went in for competitive hockey.[19] She also embraced the broader concept of women's rights:

> Mrs Cotton has a little sewing class on Monday afternoons down at the Metaphysical Rooms, to which Kate, Lossie, Dorothy Trimble and myself go. We talk of most things on Heaven and Earth, and to-day we discussed 'Women's Rights'. I wonder when their rights will be acknowledged for the time must come when men see that they are above being classed as 'children and idiots'![20]

A young writer in the *Star* also gestured towards new horizons. 'We are evolving into a race of tumultuous, tornado-like girls, whose hearts rebel against housewifery', she proclaimed. 'Modern girls think "it isn't good enough" to marry on small means. They crave for sport, amusements, "week-ending," and playing – instead of working – at life.'[21] The bicycle, an important accessory to New Womanhood, invited such mobility and playfulness. 'I was out learning to ride the bike the other night with my mate, and we got in some fine old spills', a fifteen-year-old girl told the *Otago Witness* in 1901.[22]

The ins and outs of early-twentieth-century feminism appear contradictory to a twenty-first century mind. On the one hand, first-wave feminists encouraged girls to move about and build up their bodies, and the physical culture craze appealed to many. In 1903 the German strongman Eugene Sandow toured New Zealand and women as well as men thrilled at his flexing muscles.[23] Hilda Lovell-Smith's Christchurch friends took up bodybuilding with great enthusiasm. In 1907, in their hand-written magazine *The Clansman*, they noted that

'Marie is renewing her acquaintance with dumb-bells and spirometer and attends a class of Sandow enthusiasts on Tuesday evenings', while Muriel 'superintends a girls' physical culture class at St Albans' that promised a rigorous workout with much 'muscular exercise'.[24] Other girls asserted their physical strength too. In Wellington in 1909, a thirteen-year-old initiated a sexual dalliance with a twenty-four-year-old sailor (see p. 159), and she later told police: 'I go in a lot for physical culture and am well developed, and I can box.'[25] New ideas about bodily mobility suited colonial girls' lives better than the corseted containment of the late nineteenth century.

Girls and young women take part in a gymnastics class at the Leys Institute, Ponsonby, Auckland, in 1906. The sign on the wall reads 'Mens Sana in Corpore Sano' ('a sound mind in a sound body').

At the same time, new modes of social regulation impeded girls' demands for self-determination. Belich suggests that most early-twentieth-century feminists supported moral evangelists' attempts to achieve the 'tight society'. There is no doubt many first-wave feminists held traditional views about family life, and they wanted to reinforce and revalue 'the traditional roles of wife and mother'.[26] Prominent feminist writers and activists, including well-known sex educator Ettie Rout, also endorsed eugenics. This increasingly popular, pseudo-scientific philosophy held women responsible for bearing 'good stock', and its proponents saw physically fit girls as the breeding machines of the future.[27] Strong, healthy mothers would bear robust babies and strengthen the colonies of the British Empire. This concern became pressing at a time when Pākehā fertility rates fell dramatically, from 5.3 births per woman in 1883 to 3.4 in 1906.[28]

Moving about in spite of voluminous picnic clothes: a turn-of-the-century running race, probably at Port Albert.

Girls' embodiment changed again leading up to and during the First World War. Flappers' fashions, for instance, underwent a transformation as the 1910s drew to a close. Heavy fabrics and baggy dresses gave way to light cotton in 'pillar box' styles with higher hems, costume jewellery and the faintest smudge of lipstick ('just enough to make a difference').[29] Self-styled flappers re-did their hair in a 'Buster cut' with sweeping fringe and bangs, or the more radically cropped 'shingle cut', and jammed a cloche hat on top. Silk stockings made their debut too. The new look ushered in a more overt form of heterosexual display. Dunedin resident Eileen Soper, a flapper of the 1920s, later remembered: 'We played on our charm and would flirt terribly, we showed off and made eyes and really flaunted good form. A friend of mine, a doctor's daughter, would do something very terrible that the rest of us wouldn't dare. It was a time of wearing very pretty underclothes and at parties this lass would turn a series of cartwheels showing her pretty legs and frilly underthings.'[30] Eileen Soper's friend was not entirely out of step with wider social changes. Her boldness indicated that previously private desires had become increasingly public.

By the mid-1920s the cloche had become ubiquitous and girls revealed their legs more often than not. These young women pose in a beauty competition in Timaru in 1927. The first Miss New Zealand competition was held a year earlier when nineteen-year-old Miss Otago Thelma MacMillan won. Mavis Pycroft, Miss Canterbury, was only fifteen.

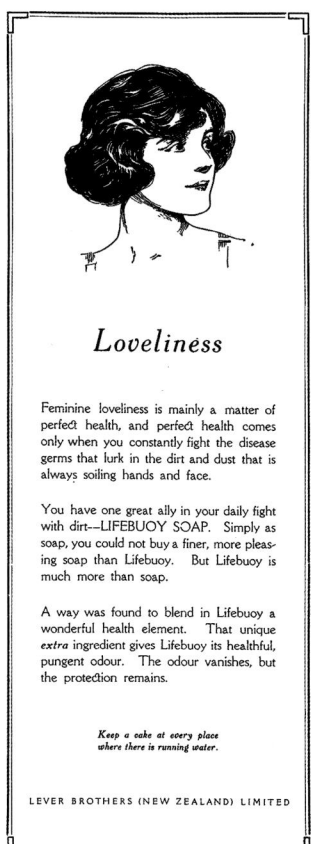

Advertisers of the 1920s began to target young women by appealing to femininity. These advertisements appeared in the magazine *Dominion Girl Guide*.

Consumer society played an increasingly important role in the lives of girls. Advertisers tapped into this movement and peddled an attractive, alluring femininity. While it is commonly assumed that this occurred in the 1950s, in fact advertisers directed their attentions to adolescent girls during the 1920s.[31] Nineteenth-century boys had been the first 'youths', but twentieth-century girls were the first teen consumers. Advertisements in the *Mirror* and the *New Zealand Girl*, the latter published by the YWCA, targeted a young female market.[32] Lithe models in flapper styles extolled the virtues of shoes, stockings and soap. 'Be a Rexona Girl!' exhorted one ad in the *Mirror* in 1926; 'Be pretty, be dainty, be attractive!'³³ Readers of another magazine, the *Dominion Girl Guide*, learned that 'feminine loveliness' could be found in a packet of Lifebuoy soap.³⁴

Consumption laid bare the tensions between freedom and regulation. Some girls honed their image and 'put on style', treating themselves to store-bought ball gowns and splashing out on fancy hats.³⁵ Ruby Abdallah studied in the commercial course at Auckland's Seddon Memorial Technical College in 1914, and her teacher wrote on her school report: 'Too much concerned about her personal appearance.'³⁶ Others, though, were reluctant to embrace the flapper look in its entirety, and they resisted its tendency to enforce a new form of conformity. Some found the cloche hat uncomfortable – its low brim blocked a girl's view – while the short, shapeless dress required a 'straight up and down' body type.³⁷ Mabel McIndoe, a student at Dunedin's Archerfield School, asked: 'what could we bosomy girls do but hook ourselves into tight up and down "corselettes" and chest flattening bras?'³⁸ This stand-off between revolution and restriction, and bodily restraint and pleasure underlined the tensions of the flapper era. The modern girl was expected to keep up a reasonable degree of fitness, follow fashion, train for an office job and look forward to starting a family. A product of complex shifts in the gender order, the flapper pushed some of femininity's boundaries while maintaining others.

Cissy Boys and the Perils of Modernity

Tensions between freedom and control were not solely a girl's domain. Even though advertisers did not target adolescent boys – and they would not begin to do so until the 1960s – some youths sought out fancy clothes anyway. A few followed in the footsteps of the masher of the 1880s and struck a bohemian pose. In 1913 the *Dominion* told its readers about the 'nut', a 'callow young man' with long fringe, low-cut waistcoat, cane, cigarette, black silk tie and 'passionate socks'.³⁹ Related types included the 'boy flapper' and the 'jazz boy', a 'modern, gay young rooster' who sported a skirted coat with a split up the back, a shirt with a four-inch collar, a wide necktie, and a green or pink handkerchief.⁴⁰

Some adults disapproved of the new developments, and they treated the jazz boy more harshly than they had his masher predecessor. *New Zealand Truth* was

Christchurch photographer Adam Henry Pearson McLay captured the different faces of youthful masculinity during the 1920s, from the sporty get-up of the cyclist (*left*) to the effete pose and (probably) colourful tie (*right*).

a widely read tabloid, a self-proclaimed champion of the working man with an often-salacious focus on popular culture, and in 1925 the paper described the 'dress sins of the cissy boy':

> Perhaps these peculiar young persons consider that since the 'female of the species' is casting so much off in the way of clothing nowadays it is up to them to put a little more on. The chief article appears to be a huge, wide tie of flaming stripes, checks, or spots. Next in furiosity come the socks, ringed, striped, or 'clocked,' of every conceivable hue. The trousers are turned well up to show the full effect – which is truly 'striking.' Frequently there is a white or coloured waistcoat, with imitation pearl

buttons, while a blazing muffler is thrown carefully around the neck [...] the whole ensemble is topped by a hat of marked shading, worn with a rakish tilt. Add to this a cigarette smoked in a long holder, and you have a picture of the perfect modern Adonis.[41]

This flamboyant lad greatly bothered *Truth*'s writers. They appointed themselves the enforcers of gender norms and publicly derided the new modes of masculinity. 'If this sort of thing continues', the paper said of cissy boys, 'some of them will run a grave risk of being shot in mistake for pheasants. The real pheasant is of more value than his imitation in that he has the gastronomical virtue of being edible.'[42] In another example, *Truth* described the behaviours of a

John Ewing (*left*) and Ernie Webber in 1924, 'a year after leaving college'. The lads were on holiday in Invercargill with a third friend, the photographer Doug Wraight. The Al Capone hats are worn with aplomb; John sports a natty bow tie and Ernie a striped shirt.

group of four 'decently dressed' lads – 'boy flappers' – on the last train from Upper Hutt to Wellington one Sunday evening in 1922. Out came the cards and the camp talk: 'What'll it be Queenie, five hundred or bridge?', and 'Make it euchre, Birdie old dear – I can't get the hang of the others.' *Truth* went on: 'And how delightfully smartly they burbled! They had been having a "sporting" day, and told all about it – to everyone.' Impatient with such enthusiasms, *Truth* insisted 'this sort of thing is a positive infliction'.[43] Like the masher and the dude, the semi-bohemian cissy boy, with his flamboyant gestures and style, compared unfavourably with the earthy, farm-based manliness of the pioneer ideal. *Truth*, 'the down-market face of moral evangelism', as Belich aptly describes the newspaper, reacted with evident hostility.[44]

How many boys fashioned themselves in this way on New Zealand's streets, and in the trains and theatres? It is difficult to tell, but James Courage was certainly one of them. James grew up on a farm station near Amberley and received an education in Christchurch. At the age of seventeen he confided in his diary: 'I have now got a confession to make to myself. I am passionately fond of clothes. To have nice clothes and to look smart is one of my ambitions. It is in fact part of me, like my love for music and for beautiful things.'[45] A year later, in 1921, he reiterated: 'I love clothes and pretty things, and have great opinions on art. I am sensual, I am self-centred, I am a snob.'[46]

James was acutely aware of his departure from prevailing norms of masculinity: his sensuality, artistic nature and fondness for beauty set him apart, but so too did his class. The son of a runholder, he saw himself as a trend-setter, and it is clear that class shaped adolescent cultures, just as it had done during the late nineteenth century. Few youths could aspire to James's level of consumption, and only a few could afford his taste. 'I have at last managed to attain an allowance for £80 per year for clothes and pocket money', he wrote. This was a small fortune, and James was not wrong when he added: 'I will be able to have heaps of nice clothes.'[47] Although James was a well-born exception, some among the less-well-off augmented their existing wardrobes with the occasional new fashion item. Photographs hint that individual items of clothing – the broad tie, the wide-legged trousers known as 'Oxford Bags' and the outrageously coloured socks – percolated through the youthful population, in the towns and cities at least.

OPPOSITE Young Māori were overwhelmingly rural during the 1910s when Opunake photographer Sam Feaver welcomed these boys into his studio. Over ninety percent lived in villages or worked as labourers on Pākehā farms and in the timber industry. Unfortunately we do not know the names of this smartly-dressed pair – or their particular circumstances.

Militarism and War

Truth was not the only defender of a robust sort of masculinity. A resurgent militarism cut right across the cosmopolitanism that spurred James Courage's love of clothes and the jazz boy's bright socks. In the wake of the Boer War, imperialists fretted about the strength and vitality of the youth called upon to fight on overseas battlefields.[48] What would happen when they had to do so again? A public lecture titled 'Physical Needs of the Empire', given by a Francis Fisher under the auspices of the Christchurch Physical Culture Society in 1905, ran the usual line. Fisher told his audience that many of New Zealand's boys and young men were too physically 'anemic' to make reliable soldiers in times of military need, and they needed bulking up.[49]

Some parents agreed that strength maketh the man and sent their sons to the gymnasiums to harden them. Wellingtonian Charles Taylor went along to Dovey's gym, made friends there and later wrote: 'I know it did me a lot of good.'[50] Other boys objected: 'Physical Culture rotten as ever', one noted in his diary without further elaboration.[51] Secondary schools' cadet units provided another plank in the militaristic platform. The Defence Act of 1909 ordered those aged between twelve (soon revised upwards to fourteen) and eighteen to take part in cadet training.[52] Cadets arranged themselves in rows and gripped their guns while solemn men in military uniforms ordered them about. Charles Taylor described his school's cadet unit in Wellington:

> [W]e wore jerseys, black with blue cuffs and collars and glengarry caps and had wooden guns that fired caps, but it was regular drill and marching, with an officer from the permanent force who came over at times to inspect us and put us through our drill, our schoolmasters were our own officers, but the big boys were picked out for sergeants and corporals.[53]

Charles Taylor did not mind his time in the cadets. He and his friends lined Wellington's streets as a guard of honour when the Duke and Duchess of Cornwall and York came to the city in 1927. 'We were splashed and covered in wet mud but we didn't care much as we had a good view of everything.'[54] Charles even had a trip away with his unit:

A uniformed Oamaru lad poses with his sister and mother during the First World War. If he was over eighteen and younger than twenty, as seems likely, the uniform signified his involvement in the Territorial force. Oamaru had a signal unit, a mounted rifles squadron and an infantry company. The lad's mother looks proud and the sister sombre.

> There was a big Exhibition at Christchurch and we cadets had a trip down to see it, we were encamped in Hagley Park and had a wonderful time, the routine was just the same as for regular soldiers, we were awakened in the morning by bugle, with our soap and towels we marched down to the River Avon and washed ourselves then marched back and dressed ready for breakfast . . . to keep order, from each troup certain of us were picked and given a badge with MP on it, which of course stood for 'Military Police'. This let us out of drills and parades, all we had to do was round up the stragglers and keep order, most afternoons were free, when we could go to the Exhibition or anywhere else we chose.[55]

Many boys, including Charles, made the most of such occasions and enjoyed the free time between adult-organised activities. They also enjoyed experiences, including a trip to the exhibition, they would not otherwise have had. This process of nationalistic manhood-making, with its rituals, special events and sense of adventure, and the imposition of ideology – in this case the glorious pursuit of Empire – did not stop these lads from having fun.

Fun was one thing, but there was a deadlier agenda at play. Recruits' time became more carefully controlled once the First World War broke out in 1914, and the stakes increased considerably. Until 1917 men had to be twenty in order to sign up for overseas service, then the age of enlistment fell to nineteen.[56] Eighteen-year-olds like Arthur Ross joined the Territorials.[57] He settled into camp life at the Wyndham racecourse as a mostly diligent trainee, but freedom beckoned from time to time. Arthur sometimes 'told a few fibs' and absconded to a dance at a local school.[58] A year later, at the age of twenty, he followed in the footsteps of many before him and enlisted in the army. Young men like Arthur travelled to Trentham army camp and transferred to Tauherenikau where the rigours of training awaited: marching, physical jerks, leaky tents, 'Reveille', the 'Last Post', a weekend's leave in Wellington and a voyage to Europe on an overcrowded troop ship.[59]

Young men experienced harrowing introductions to combat. Along with the rest of his battalion, twenty-year-old Alexander Aitken, a Dunedin youth, occupied a set of terraces just behind the front line near Chunuk Bair. On this Turkish hilltop, where the troops of the British Empire fought the Ottoman defenders, Alexander witnessed death for the first time. The intensity of his experience is palpable:

> The gradient at the steepest part of this ascent could not have been much less than one-in-one; I never did harder work than climbing that short distance in fighting kit. At last, panting, we stood clear on these artificial terraces, 600 feet above sea-level; between two worlds, Chunuk felt but not seen (had we seen it, it would have seen us) beyond the crest above, and behind us to the west, thirty miles of the Aegean. My spirits rose as I turned to the magnificent view, but were quickly damped by an ordinary incident of trench warfare. From the trench mouth, just at hand, a stretcher-party was emerging, carrying a man of the Wellington Battalion, shot through the head and dying, a friend of my own good friend Frank Tucker. A glance was enough to show that he would be dead in a few minutes. My feeling of reverent awe never recurred so strongly when such sights had become familiar. The bearers passed down the slope; the next morning would show another wooden cross in the small cemetery at the head of the Dere. I date this initiation of mine as 12th November 1915.[60]

The grim reality of war was a world away from the rhetoric that held sway over many New Zealanders back home, especially in school classrooms.[61] Adolescent boys who keenly followed news of the war believed the sacrifices were heroic and they talked about themselves as future combatants. In 1915 one lad wrote to the *Otago Witness* and expressed his longing to train as a soldier. 'Things are getting very serious, and I am afraid it will be months before the war is over. The Germans are pretty strong, and will take some crushing.'[62]

Lured by patriotism and a sense of adventure, many boys lied about their age and enlisted for service abroad. We do not know what proportion of the 100,000 personnel who served with the New Zealand Expeditionary Force were under age. Historians have concluded that high numbers of British and American under-nineteens went to the front, and the same was probably true of New Zealand.[63] Gisborne lad Eruera Kawhia was only fifteen or sixteen when he enlisted and went to France. He died of war wounds in Armentières two years later, in 1916.[64] Victor Manson Spencer also claimed to be older than he was. The engineer's apprentice from Otautau, Southland, joined the First Otago Batallion at the age of eighteen and served in Gallipoli.[65] In July 1916 Victor was blown up, buried alive for four days and suffered from shell shock; he subsequently absconded and was imprisoned for nine months. Once released he escaped again, only to be arrested four months later.[66] He had been living in a house in the countryside with a French woman and two children. Victor told the military court: 'my health has not been good and my nerve has been completely destroyed. I attribute my present position to this fact and to drink.'[67] Victor, like many others, paid a high price for his involvement in the war. He was charged with desertion and, in February 1918, at a lonely crossroads in a remote spot near Ypres in Belgium, he was shot and killed by a firing squad of his peers. The realities of life at the front – mud, madness, desertion and death – were a far cry from the adventure stories eagerly consumed by the young.

Borstals and Special Schools

Prevailing ideas about national fitness were not confined to the theatre of war: they also influenced the state's philosophies about education and law

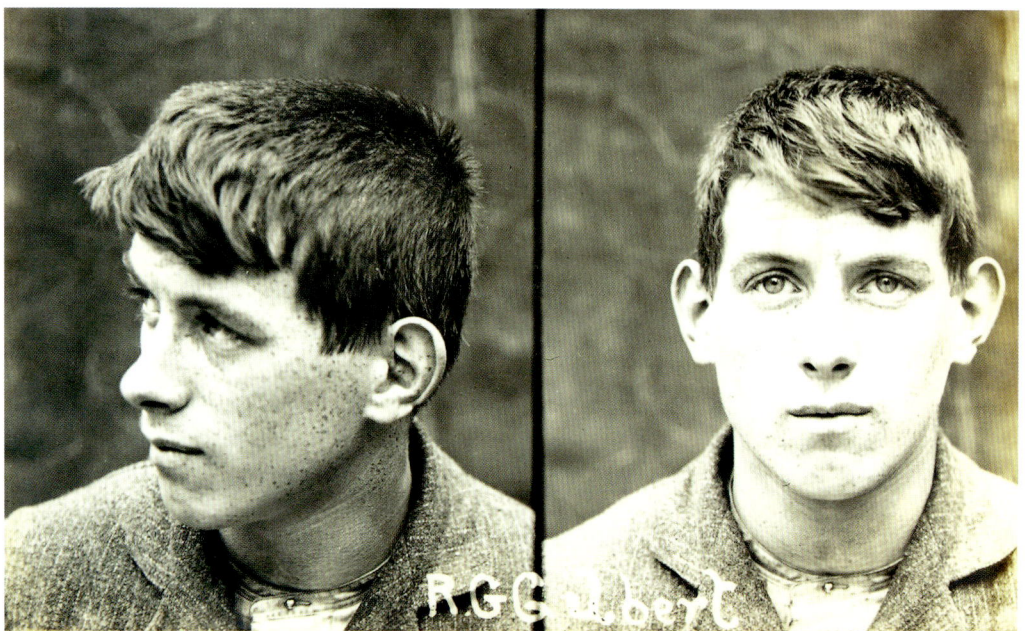

Seventeen-year-old Robert Grant Gilbert, alias George Moore, was charged with burglary in Christchurch in 1908. He ended up in a reformatory, probably Burnham. Robert escaped, was caught thieving in Auckland and landed in jail. His entry in the police register reveals he had been a porter in his native Tasmania, had a small scar on his left wrist and a burn mark on his right arm. The official record does not mention the chunk out of his left ear.

enforcement. Increasing numbers of adolescents found themselves in residential institutions during the early decades of the century.[68] Several new reformatories and 'special schools' opened, spurred on by a number of factors: population growth, a continuing push from the child-savers, and eugenic arguments about segregating the morally and mentally 'unfit' from everyone else. The reform-minded George Hogben, a former school principal who became Inspector General of Schools in 1899, set about classifying inmates by age, gender and behaviour.[69]

Young male and female offenders were incarcerated for different reasons and housed separately. Girls were most likely to be institutionalised for crossing the lines of middle-class respectability. Eugenicists advocated the separation of 'sexually promiscuous girls' from the rest of society, and by 1901 a specific institution catered for them: the Te Oranga reformatory in the Christchurch suburb of Burwood.[70] Confined within the moral safety of Te Oranga's forbidding walls, those accused of 'carrying on with boys' and 'laughing and roaring in the street' would be reconstituted as docile domestic servants.[71] They washed laundry and carried out other domestic work, prayed and endured hours of drill. Inmates resisted Te Oranga's harsh discipline by picking fights with staff members and one another, but the matrons restored order by strapping offenders, boxing their ears and locking them up in solitary confinement.[72] Although staff at Te Oranga had the upper hand in the war of moral enforcement, they could not control their charges forever. When released from the reformatory many wandered the streets, stole, smoked and took up with the 'wrong' kinds of boys.[73] If Te Oranga represented an attempt to tighten society, some of its erstwhile inmates preferred a life of sexual and social freedom.

Most boys and young men faced arrest for thefts or public disturbances rather than for sexual misdemeanours.[74] Michael McKay was one of them. Desperately drunk, the Dunedin twenty-year-old wandered past a group of men and women on their way to church one day in 1908 and yelled: 'Look at that pack of Roman Catholic bastards standing there. They are a lot of fucking cunts. They are all cons [convicts] and prick suckers.'[75] A disgusted judge locked him up for three months. Larrikins also stormed back onto the streets. The newspapers had been quiet about them as the century ticked over, but they paid new attention during the 1920s. Larrikins formed themselves into loosely organised 'gangs' that poached public spaces and turned them to their own uses. One New Year's Eve, Christchurch larrikins assembled in the Square wearing 'false noses and bizarre hats' and began 'scrumming', fighting and jostling with police.[76] In 1927 members of two rival gangs battled it out in the West End Picture Theatre in Auckland's Ponsonby Road where 'there was a good deal of punching going on'. 'Try and put me out!' yelled one youth, and a second loudly threatened to 'clean up' his foes.[77] Even though New Zealand boys used their fists, not the guns popular among their Australian counterparts, many made their way into the government system of youth detention.[78]

In pursuit of his segregation philosophy, George Hogben turned the nineteenth-century institution at Burnham from a co-educational industrial school into a boys-only reformatory. A dumping ground for the most hardened of delinquents, Burnham soon became infamous for its spartan conditions, the roughness of its charges and the floggings meted out by warders.[79] The reformatory's most famous inmate, future Labour MP John A. Lee, ended up there in 1906 after two convictions for theft. He found Burnham 'a sterilising hell' where boys had no access to books, newspapers or worthwhile skills training.[80] The many escapees, John included, were routinely captured, returned to the reformatory and flogged.

While Burnham and Te Oranga took 'delinquent' adolescents, in 1908 Hogben established Otekaieke Special School near Kurow, a remote spot in North Otago. Otekaieke catered for 'feeble minded' boys whom the authorities, in child-saving mode, hoped to rescue through education.[81] A large leather-bound register records details of boys in the care of headmaster George Benstead. Benstead took his cue from Hogben's new classification of institutionalised youth, weeding out those who belonged elsewhere. He took one look at nineteen-year-old Oscar Fry, whom he described as a 'lazy, indolent boy much given to loafing, cigarette smoking, hanging round street corners, an admirer of the music halls', and dispatched him to Burnham to join the other 'larrikins'.[82] Benstead transferred a few other lads – 'custodial cases' who showed no signs of improvement – to the asylum at Seacliff. He also separated boys within Otekaieke itself. Older and younger boys lived in separate buildings for the sake of the younger lads' 'morals'. The older ones, one inspector wrote, were 'too degenerate and peculiar even for the approval of the least prudish of critics'.[83] Quite a few of Benstead's charges were inclined to 'dirty actions with boys similarly inclined': a euphemistic reference to mutual masturbation.[84] These 'hopelessly bad boys', Benstead wrote, were 'a constant source of contamination to the others'.[85]

In spite of Otekaieke's particularities – its geographical isolation, constant surveillance and enforced segregations – Benstead's views reflected wider social concerns. When the headmaster worried that masturbation sapped boys' will to work – 'on [the] slightest pretence [a particular seventeen-year-old] would absent himself to try to indulge in the solitary vice which is sapping his strength and manhood', Benstead wrote – he reiterated the nineteenth-century notion that the capacity for labour unlocked the door to manhood.[86] This idea had profound material consequences: those who restrained their lusts and worked hard might find their way out of state care. Some Otekaieke boys made progress as time went on, marching slowly towards their goal. One 'developed into a fairly good worker & took an interest in outdoor farm and garden work', while another gave an indication that institutionalisation may have reformed him: 'I still think eventually he may be given a chance to go out into the world.'[87] A number of Benstead's charges learned to constitute themselves as the moral subjects of their own actions. 'Habit of loafing, but now a better worker', Benstead noted of one lad. 'Habit of self-abuse almost cured.'[88] The moulding of disadvantaged youths into socially useful and respectable citizens was the child-saver's ultimate goal. Sometimes Benstead succeeded, but often he did not: many boys spent the rest of their lives in custodial care and some died at Otekaieke.

Jobs in Town and Country

The early-twentieth-century work world was one of transition, not only between childhood and adulthood, as many colonists believed and George Benstead demonstrated at Otekaieke, but also between agrarian and industrial production. This shift had begun during the late nineteenth century but now it picked up pace. Offices swallowed increasing numbers of adolescent workers, and so too did the factories that transformed life in the larger cities. Their number tripled between 1900 and 1930 to reach a total of 17,000.[89] Girls continued to play a crucial role in the workshops of the nation. Some twenty young men were employed to lug heavy trays at the Hudson chocolate factory in Dunedin but Hudson's female workforce was much larger. One hundred and ninety women, most of them aged between sixteen and twenty-four, filled trays with chocolate and slammed them down to free any air bubbles, fed individual confections into wrapping machines and packed the tin-foiled delicacies into cartons.[90] At the Wax Vesta factory in another part of town, girls spent their days standing in one place and putting matches into boxes.[91]

Factory girls helped transform urban femininity.[92] The Wax Vesta girls were clean and well-behaved at work, but in their lunch-hours and at night they became 'matchy tarts', yahooing in the streets and hurling slang at passers-by.[93] Belich's 'tight society' failed to control them. Instead, their experience hints that

Among the hum of the belts and fragrance of soap, adolescent workers pack boxes at the Lever Bros plant in Petone, c. 1925. A great many girls found employment in the packing rooms of the country's factories. The text on the wall spurs them along: 'Our work must be right. Good enough won't do.'

public expressions of enthusiasm supplemented the indoor boisterousness of the nineteenth-century factory girl. These workers were not entirely independent in an economic sense – most girls handed their wage packets to their parents and received an allowance in return – but still female factory workers had more money – and much more autonomy – than ever before.[94]

Male employment also changed as the towns and cities grew. Delivery jobs boomed during the early years of the century. Practically every seed merchant, drapery store and pharmacist employed a boy on a bicycle; some were junior members of the permanent staff, others part-time workers with an after-school round.[95] A great many boys found employment in the post office delivering telegrams. Oamaru had a total population of only 5,000 in 1918 and yet a photograph of the telegraph gallery shows a workforce of fifty-four boys and young men that same year. Prevailing notions of mobility and respectability explain why employers hired adolescent boys for such jobs. American historian Gregory Downey suggests that telegraph messengers 'had to be able to access places and activities in the city that most urban women could not', without threatening the wages and status of adult men.[96] Like their American counterparts, New Zealand's telegraph boys sallied forth wherever a message needed to be delivered: through darkened lanes and empty streets, into rough huts and the houses of the well-to-do.

Telegraph boys developed a culture of their own. They often worked evenings and knocked about between assignments. Members of Wellington's youthful workforce loitered in the doorways of the Chief Post Office and the premises of the *Times* newspaper, both in Lambton Quay, and chatted idly.[97] Boys from Hamilton's post office set off to the city's picture theatres, confectionery shops and tearooms after finishing their shifts. Some listened to bands in the parks, others went to the shooting gallery.[98] The bicycle was a tool of the trade, but it also let messengers escape adult surveillance and explore the city together. These boys enjoyed varying degrees of freedom alongside their work obligations.

Some of Oamaru's fleet of telegraph boys, photographed at the end of the war.

Growing factory work and the new squadrons of messengers were in marked contrast to older patterns of employment, especially in the countryside. Periods of itinerancy still shaped the working lives of many, including those like John A. Lee who wandered around Otago after his escape from Burnham and sought out employment on farms. 'The work exhausted and then made me whipcord fit', he wrote in his account of the time.[99] Some girls set out from home to become teachers and travelled considerable distances to remote locations. In 1923 seventeen-year-old Ivy Bell journeyed from her southern Otago home by mail car, two trains and then an open-sided bus – it was 'no comfort at all' – to reach her assignment in the tiny far-away hamlet of Timaru River near Lake Hawea.[100] Ivy put up with the isolation for a year before moving to a job closer to home.

Some rural working patterns had even earlier beginnings. Many parents sent their offspring into service with neighbours, sometimes for pay but often in exchange for board and food. Daughters cooked and cleaned while sons worked as labourers or cow boys.[101] Perhaps unwittingly, they continued a practice common in parts of pre-industrial Europe. Boarding out was common when a plot of land could not sustain a family's children; their offspring may not be paid, parents figured, but at least they would not starve.[102] In New Zealand this mismatch between farm size and family size, combined with continued industrialisation, fuelled migration into the towns and cities.

Among those who did stay on the land, boys' farm diaries record a long list of the jobs they were expected to attend to on their family farms: watering, weeding and manuring crops; chopping wood; cutting hay; fencing; making butter; shearing; and tending horses and looking after lambs.[103] Thirteen-year-old Hugh McMaster worked on his parents' farm at Outram, near Dunedin, and his diary details his usual tasks: '28th Fine but cloudy. Went to creamery. Thinned turnips till dinnertime. Cut hay and ricked some today. Father and I set a dozen traps tonight and looked [at] them about 9 o'clock. Caught two rabbits.'[104] Other diaries reiterate the repetitive nature of boys' farm work: one lad, on a farm near Owaka in southern Otago, thinned turnips and set traps day after day, week after week.[105]

Researchers and oral history informants agree about the nature of boys' work – mostly it took place outdoors – but the labour of rural girls is rather more contested. Historian Caroline Daley suggests girls only worked outside if their parents had no sons to help out around the farm, while most oral interviews

OPPOSITE Workers at the meat works near Balclutha early in the century. Adolescent boys, like the two on the left of this image, usually began with the menial jobs: pushing waste around the floor with a broom and hosing away blood.

from the 1980s and 1990s, including those conducted by Daley and sociologist Claire Toynbee, corroborate the belief that early-twentieth-century farm girls worked almost exclusively indoors.[106] 'There were no carpets in those days, mostly linoleum, and yes, you had to scrub the floors and the big kitchen table', one woman remembered of her younger days. 'We had a long kitchen table as you can imagine, and this had to be scrubbed and scrubbed, and the steps. You had to scrub them every day.'[107] Other interviewees agreed, referring to childcare, sewing, baking and cleaning.

Farm diaries, though, reveal a different labour pattern among rural girls, perhaps because they recorded daily events and were not retrospectively altered by climates of opinion and gendered divisions of labour. Many girls did indeed work outdoors.[108] At Outram, Hugh McMaster's sixteen-year-old sister Lizzie

A great deal of adolescent labour was unpaid, in both town and country: vegetable growing, wood chopping, coal carrying, and tending pets and livestock. Here a young fellow contemplates the garden he has just dug, c. 1918.

The Irrepressible Charlie Cook

Did rural work in New Zealand offer an antidote to the grime and moral decay of England's industrial cities? Farmer and philanthropist Percy Sargood certainly thought so. In 1914 Sargood brought twelve disadvantaged English boys to Wanaka as farming cadets. He thought fresh air and the chance to work hard would offer new opportunities and discipline for the sixteen- and seventeen-year-olds. As Sargood wrote in his notebook, this was something of a 'social experiment'.

Most of Sargood's boys were diligent and well-behaved under the guidance of a chaperone named Vorley, but Charlie Cook tested his handler's patience. 'A big, curly-hair [sic] boy, rather playful, very strong', sixteen-year-old Charlie had worked as an office boy and a packer for a boilermaker at the Union Docks in London. He was 'the only mis-behaved and unruly member of the party' aboard the *Tainui* on the way out to New Zealand. Charlie tried to interest the other lads in his japes and 'was always the cause of the other boys being unruly'. More than once he had to be turned away from the dinner table 'because of his piggish behaviour'. The notebook's summary of behaviour tells us that he was 'also reported to have thrown a bed-chamber into the sea, and to have thought it great fun when told [off] about it'. When discovered with £1 6s 6d that had been stolen from Vorley's coat pocket, Charlie mysteriously insisted it had been given to him by one of the stewards 'for services rendered'.[109]

Charlie Cook.

Once he settled in Wanaka Charlie did as he pleased much of the time. His supervisor found him 'lax in general behaviour, idle and slow', and if not closely watched he would 'shirk work'. Although the local shopkeeper had been asked not to sell cigarettes to the boys, 'Cook however managed to get them by some means or other' and he smoked them in defiance of the rules.

Percy Sargood hoped his charge would outgrow the incorrigible behaviour of youth, but he may have waited a long time. We do not know whether Charlie settled into his rural life or not: did the city lure him back?

regularly milked cows with her brother: 'Hugh and I had all the cows done except one when mother came home', she wrote one January day.[110] Lizzie had other outdoor jobs too: watering crops, harvesting potatoes and berries, smoking beehives, carrying messages, feeding cattle and emptying rabbit traps. She also mustered sheep from the back of her 'frisky' horse Salem. Pragmatism ruled on the McMaster farm, not gendered ideals. Everyone had to help out in an era when few tasks were mechanised. On a busy afternoon, Lizzie noted, 'all hands but the cook' were needed outside.[111]

Lizzie McMaster was not the only colonial girl who genuinely liked outdoor work. A great many others milked cows and killed chickens ('had good fun', one girl wrote of her neck-wringing spree), while rabbit-shooting was something of a national pastime for girls and boys alike.[112] 'Killed 3, & hit three more which got away. Enjoyed it fine', a Canterbury lass wrote in 1918.[113] While rural New Zealanders acknowledged a gendered division of labour, they allowed the boundary to blur when pragmatism – and girls' sense of adventure – intervened. These descendants of the first colonial girls felt the lure of freedom decades later. While rural and urban girls' lives differed markedly, a feisty attitude sometimes unified them. Perhaps the rabbit-shooters and the 'matchy tarts' had more in common than they ever imagined.

In and Out of the Classroom

New Zealand's secondary school system changed the lives of more and more young people as the twentieth century rolled along. The leaving age rose to fourteen in 1901 and the secondary education system received another boost two years later when the government introduced its free place scheme. This provided two free years of secondary education to those who passed the Standard 6 Proficiency Exam. Pupils who wanted to extend their schooling could sit the Junior Civil Service Examination in the fourth form, and a successful performance bestowed a 'senior free place'. The enrolment of state-educated secondary pupils over the age of thirteen grew slowly but steadily on the back of these changes. Numbers increased from 19,139 in 1900 to 22,505 in 1910, by which time free-place holders accounted for 70 percent of pupils in the state secondary

Not all young Māori attended the denominational schools; some trained within the state system. Tenga-o-te-Rangi Te Hore Takarangi, a fourteen-year-old pupil at Wanganui Collegiate, poses with his rowing and rugby trophies in 1914. Conversely, a few Pākehā attended the likes of Te Aute College. Erle Crawford was one of them; letters to his family reveal a ratio of seven Pākehā to sixty Māori in 1910. Erle had a 'jolly time'. He shared a room with another Pākehā, and like the Māori pupils he learned 'carpentering' as well as academic subjects, enjoyed the constant games of rugby and had 'a grand time playing tennis'. Te Aute produced leaders, including Āpirana Ngata and Peter Buck. Between 1919 and 1948, scholarship students from the Cook Islands, Niue and Samoa also attended Te Aute and its sister school for girls, Hukarere.

schools.[114] Enrolments climbed further to 28,831 in 1920.[115] A growing number of private establishments sprang up alongside the state schools, including new church-run Māori colleges like Queen Victoria School for girls in Auckland and Hikurangi for boys in the Wairarapa.

Secondary schools allowed increasing numbers of teens to build youth-centered social worlds.[116] At Archerfield in Dunedin, Mabel McIndoe and her friends giggled at the back of the class, marched in formation to the Municipal Baths, hid in the summer house to avoid netball and did their 'prep' (homework) together in the sun.[117] Schools were the seed-beds for friendships, cliques and

MAORI COLLEGE CLAREVILLE 1904.

Hikurangi College, an Anglican Māori boys' school, opened at Clareville in the Wairarapa in 1903. Pupils received free board and the curriculum included English, religious studies and technical training. The school catered for relatively small numbers: twenty-four boarders. Hikurangi closed in 1932 after the main building burned down.

new antagonisms, and extra-curricular activities allowed pupils to express their talents. Sport proved hugely popular, and school magazines chronicled players' shortcomings and successes, especially on the rugby field: 'Talbot and McLean are both sound, though not brilliant', read a typical report in the *Christ's College Register*. Cox played 'a dashing but not always safe game', while Johnston 'is weak in tackling, and a little slow in handling'.[118] New sports joined traditional games in the list of options. Basketball, an invention of the American YMCA, arrived here in 1908 and quickly spread around the country. Soccer was introduced during the First World War and became popular during the 1920s.

Other types of extra-curricular activities nurtured new expressions of identity. A growing number of camera clubs reflected the widespread take-up of snapshot photography after 1900, and glee clubs and dramatic societies sprang into life at the same time.[119] Christ's College pupil James Courage played a range of dramatic roles. These included Dick Bultitude in *Vice Versa*, a mystical play in which father and son use a magic stone to swap bodies – 'I got so many compliments it nearly turned my head', James told his diary, blushing as he wrote – then he was Mrs Fairplay in the farce *Simpkins' Little Breakfast Party*, and Miss Clara Manners in *A Pair of Lunatics*.[120] When preparing to perform as Ruth Pemberton, the female lead in *Holed Out in One*, James wrote: 'I don't know how I shall get on, but my usual slight streak of effeminacy will no doubt help me.'[121] These roles set the scene for a future career as a novelist and playwright, and James also came to see his artistic temperament as a marker of his own homosexuality. The association between same-sex desire and effeminacy slowly took hold during the 1920s – it is implicit in *Truth*'s account of the burbling 'boy flappers' on the Upper Hutt train – and James' artistic experiences provided the foundations for his sexual

Photos captured a look, a pose and an attitude. This image tells of an afternoon at Waitaki Boys' High School in Oamaru, c. 1918. Hardy, Hall, Dundas, Fulton and another boy kill time on the field. The school uniform looks strikingly modern.

Learning About Sex

'Through the window opposite I saw the landlady dressing, the spectacle was quite diverting, the first part of it chiefly.' These were the words of thirteen-year-old Randal Burdon who wrote in his diary while staying in a hotel in 1910.[122] Early-twentieth-century moral crusaders felt sure many boys – not just Randal – let sexual impulses rule their lives.[123] Physician Herbert Barraclough insisted that the 'great physiological crisis' of adolescence gave rise to 'strange new feelings' that were 'readily perverted to evil', while Henry Field, a university researcher, said that boys made matters worse by circulating pornographic stories among their classmates.[124]

Some commentators thought sex education would stem the tide of immorality. Richard Bligh from the Australasian White Cross League, an organisation modelled on a British counterpart, visited schools to urge sexual restraint upon the pupils.[125] He distributed Australian pamphlets with titles like *Purity and Impurity* and *Confidential Talks with Young Men*, and handed out cards pledging their holders to a moral life. *Truth* newspaper complained that Bligh spread 'purity piffle', awakened curiosities that were better left dormant and showed physiological diagrams that made schoolboys faint – but many youths simply jeered at Bligh's exhortations and tore up their pledge cards.[126] A 1922 parliamentary inquiry into venereal disease demanded a 'sane' literature that might counter the 'evil' of ignorance, but much of the available material was generated by those, like Bligh, with religious axes to grind.[127]

Many adults worried that the 'solitary vice' (also known as 'the secret sin') threatened young men's 'strength and manhood', but some of the information on masturbation caused as much concern as the practice itself.[128] Quacks advertised in the newspapers, invited boys to write to them about their 'problems' and threatened to contact correspondents' fathers if money was not forthcoming for the quacks' dubious 'cures'.[129] Truby King went undercover as a seventeen-year-old in order to catch out the unscrupulous operators. He felt sure impartial information would 'aid in guiding youths past shoals which frequently wreck or mar them'.[130]

Not until the 1950s would sex educators publicly acknowledge that girls masturbated too, but the courts heard of other sexual exploits. In 1909, thirteen-year-old Mary Stephen, who often spent time on the wharves, met a twenty-four-year-old sailor off the HMS *Challenger* in Wellington Harbour and wrote to him again the following day:

> Wellington 3/5/1909
> Dear Mr Johnson,
> Expect me down by the 'Challenger' at ten to four on Thursday afternoon. I will be there even if it rains all day. This afternoon I walked up Lambton Quay four times to see if I could see you in town, but I suppose you were not ashore on Monday. I've been thinking of you ever since yesterday, and I'm longing to see you again. I must close now and remain with much love.
> Your own sweetheart
> X Rays May
> xxxxxxxxxx
> xxxxxxxxxx   xxxxxxx
> xxxxxxxxxxxx
> xxxxxxxxxxxx[131]

Holding hands in Otago during the late 1910s.

Police arrested the sailor after he fondled Mary under a tree near the railway line in Thorndon. Mary later recalled that the seafarer put his hand inside her bloomers, unbuttoned her drawers, and touched her legs and then her breasts. He then 'exposed himself to me, saying "Look here"' and 'said if I was eighteen he would marry me tomorrow'. Unrepentant, Mary took this in her stride. 'I visit any warship I can get on', she proudly told police.[132] When newspaper editors heard about cases like this they insisted that boys were often led astray by female counterparts to whom 'the mystery and secret of sex are no mystery or secret at all'.[133] Like their Victorian predecessors, girls and women were meant to be sexually innocent and passive, not eager participants.[134]

Doing the high jump at Waitaki Boys' High.

self-making.[135] As a young adult he referred to himself as an 'invert', a term we revisit in the following chapter.

School dramatics encouraged pupils to play with gender – a great many boys and girls enjoyed mucking about with personae on stage – but some adults worried that the education system did not adequately prepare young people for later life. Eugenicists and some physicians insisted that a rigorous academic education for girls overshadowed the importance of motherhood and domesticity.[136] Truby King, an eager proponent of the 'tight society', was the most outspoken on the topic. He denounced a gender-neutral education as 'one of the most preposterous farces ever perpetuated'.[137] Women who had grown up in the nineteenth-century school system vehemently disagreed with King. An anonymous correspondent wrote to the *Dominion* to say schools should provide a solid education for 'the girl who looks over the hedge and longs for the open road that leads to the mountain peaks of knowledge'.[138] Politicians, though, came down on the side of King and his cronies, and in 1917 they changed the law. No longer would boys' and girls' curricula run along similar lines – Greek, Latin, mathematics, chemistry and the rest – but all girls holding free places would also learn household economics, hygiene, cooking and needlecraft.[139]

Such belated attempts to impose gendered restrictions had only limited success, for the move to differentiate girls' from boys' education failed to stem the social changes of its time. Many girls resisted the idea that they should train for a life of domestic servitude, and those with a disinclination for academic study gravitated towards the new commercial courses that sprang up around the country. Typing, the main subject, prepared eager girls for office work.[140] Much to Truby King's dismay, jobs often took priority over domesticity and motherhood among the younger set. Seventy percent of women in their early twenties

At the Christchurch School of Domestic Instruction, c. 1915. The school had been set up in 1893 to train domestic servants. There were 225 pupils by 1900, many of them sent directly from primary school. They learned 'practical and theoretical cookery', the arts of table service and cleaning skills. In 1907 the school became a department of Christchurch Technical College.

remained single in 1916, and a sizeable proportion of them – along with those in their teens – moved into office jobs.[141] The schools were happy to meet the demands of a modern world. They responded to the needs of their own communities, not the exhortations of conservative politicians, and the secondary education system fostered a new social and occupational mobility.[142]

Co-educational schools slowly became more common, and these allowed an easy mixing of boys and girls. Charles Taylor remembered a lively time at Wellington Technical School when, in 1905, he started out as a fourteen-year-old student of electrical engineering. Boys and girls rushed around the buildings together and slid down the bannisters, went to the teachers' houses for 'jolly parties' and developed crushes on their elders. Charles and his friends adored the 'lovely' English mistress Kate Lawson and drawing mistress Sybil Johnstone.[143] The informality suggested by Charles's memory of his teachers' first names – still fresh in his mind when he wrote his memoir many decades later – dissipated during the decades to come.

University students mingled either comfortably or unhappily, depending on their temperament. Some young men enjoyed the company of their female counterparts. At Auckland University College they met over the ping-pong table outside the men's common room and forged strong friendships in a small, intense world where everyone came to know everybody else.[144] Women made up a quarter of Auckland's student body during the 1920s, and they were well represented at Canterbury and Otago too.[145] Some Otago students cheerfully drank together at balls and congregated afterwards in Dunedin's 'primitive roadhouses'.[146] Other male students sulkily demanded women resume their place as 'divine creatures content to win and keep a good man and raise a family', but their female counterparts brushed aside the sentiment.[147] Opportunities, values and relationships ebbed and flowed in this contradictory era.

Regimented Free Time

Adults played an increasing role in establishing and regulating adolescent leisure. Although the child-savers' first attempts took shape during the 1880s, a much broader movement to instruct young people in moral worthiness

PREVIOUS PAGE Procession day at Canterbury College during the 1920s. Costumes spanned a wide range, from ghosts to professors, policemen, clergy and aviators. Cross-dressing and fake noses were popular. Capping shows with titles like *The King of Kawau* and *Just as You Say Dear* entertained audiences during the 1910s. Their printed programmes celebrated graduates' successes and provided summaries of the entertainment on offer. When it came time for 'Procesh', students wandered through the main streets in their fantastic attire. These years saw the public emergence of a university student culture, affording young people greater visibility in the streets of the bigger cities.

dawned along with the twentieth century. Chaperonage declined and growing numbers of girls and boys occupied the streets with increasing confidence, but malleable young people were regarded as easily directed to evil deeds. The child-savers saw the 'model adolescent' as an 'organised youth, dependent but secure from temptation'.[148] With this view firmly in mind, they tried to reshape the way young New Zealanders understood their bodies, their friendships and their place in society.

Religious organisations helped organise in-betweeners' leisure time.[149] Some small-town Protestant churches set up youth groups and branches of the Young People's Society of Christian Endeavour, while the Wesley Young Men's Institute convened in Auckland in 1901.[150] The Bible Class movement catered for young New Zealanders over the age of twelve and took the baton of self-enhancement from the embryonic mutual improvement and literary societies of the nineteenth century.[151] Under careful guidance, members pored over the 'good book', stretched their muscles in physical culture classes, and debated moral and ethical issues. In 1916, members of the Woodville Methodist Young People's Society learned about philosophies of justice and the roots of criminal behaviour. Their study reflected an increasing focus on moral reconstitution and the new institutionalisation demonstrated in the growth of reformatories like Burnham, Te Oranga and Otekaieke.[152]

The new Christian organisations sorted adolescents into groups by dividing the religious from the agnostic, the youngest from the oldest, and boys from girls. Faced with a very occasional meeting between the male and female wings, Bible Class members reacted with shyness or barely suppressed enthusiasm.[153] The ideology of separate spheres for boys and girls was, in part, a response to the 'white blouse revolution', as Olssen labels the effect of office careers on feminine ideals, and anxieties about turbid masculinity.[154] 'Muscular Christianity' offered an antidote to such dissipations, and boys gathered together to celebrate and practise the values of 'adventure, heroism, virtue and valour'.[155] *The Young Man's Magazine*, published by St John's Bible Class, proselytised Muscular Christianity under the motto 'be strong and shew thyself a man'. It advertised Sandow competitions, opportunities for adolescents to show off their muscles, and promoted the camps where the valiant Christian lad would 'win a half-mile, play a good game at three-quarter, eat a square meal, give a good lusty Māori war-cry,

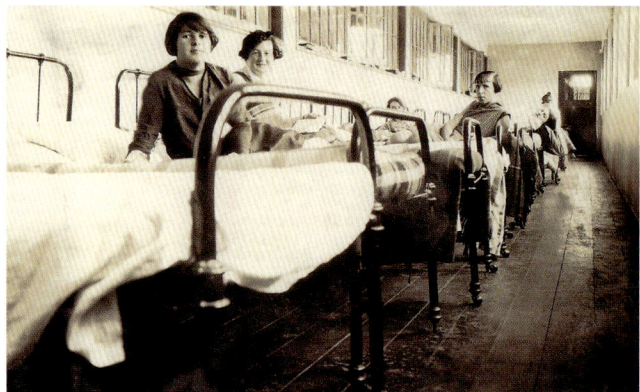

Although the Bible Class movement catered to adults as well as adolescents, it was a crucible of youth culture. *Clockwise from left:* 'The Babes', at the Otago Young Women's Bible Class camp at Milton, 1929; 'When We Were Very Young', 1920s; 'Rest Hour', at Paerata Dominion Camp south of Auckland.

and then go afterwards to his tent and read a chapter'.[156] The similarities with early-twentieth-century eugenics and state-sponsored militarism could not have been clearer: muscular male Christians would take their place in the ranks of the morally and physically fit.

But church-based organisations did more than just keep an eye on the moral tone of the nation. They also played a productive role by giving rise to a critical mass of young people. Huge Bible Class camps sprouted on school grounds,

Clockwise from left: 'Washing Up', Wellington Executive Young Women's Bible Class weekend retreat, c. 1929; 'The Maids'; 'Apiti Boys Ready for the Fray', moments before an informal rugby match at the Apiti Bible Class Rally in the Manawatu.

racecourses and anywhere else with room for an overabundance of tents, while cross-denominational sports tournaments brought together adolescents from all around the country.[157] Bible Class groups fostered a youthful mobility and a degree of socialising that few had enjoyed during the nineteenth century.

Bible Class was not the only mass movement. Scouting roared into life in 1908 when Lieutenant-General Robert Baden-Powell, an officer in the British army, published the famous manual *Scouting for Boys*. Scouting had spiritual elements, but unlike Bible Class it was not overtly religious. Instead, the Scouting movement promulgated values like abstemiousness, honour and physical fitness while promoting a vigorous outdoor life.[158] Scottish-born Colonel David Cossgrove led the local movement. He migrated here at an early age, met Baden-Powell when both men served in the Boer War and carried his new friend's vision to southern shores. Growth was rapid. By the end of 1909 some 500 New Zealand Scout troops catered for 6,000 lads.[159] Belich and other historians suggest Scouting attempted to 'tame' the young and prepare them for the teamwork and self-sacrifice of war, and some boys keenly felt the Scouts' contribution to the zeitgeist.[160] Ernie Ashby joined in Dunedin in 1916 and imbibed the 'militaristic flavour'. He later remembered 'corporals and sergeants and things like that', lots of 'marching and so on, of course, everyone had to have their bugle band in those days'.[161]

Still, the regimented aspects of the Scouts, like the cadet corps and Bible Class, did not stop youths from having fun. While the boys diligently learned teamwork, drill and signalling, they led themselves into happily chaotic scrapes. In 1912 a group of Wellington Scouts recorded their visit to the hills of South Karori:

> Some of the Scouts had some signalling practice, while some others more energetic proceeded to dam up the stream. Then we had a bathe and some tried to swim in about eighteen inches of water, but hopelessly failed. After which we boiled the billy and left for home about 5 o'clock. After winding along the tortuous stream and a long climb up the hill, we came out above the Upper Karori reservoir. Proceeding along its banks, some of us came near finding a watery grave owing to the banks being loose shingle. Happily this terrible catastrophe was averted and having come out on the road we separated and wended our very weary homeward ways.[162]

Back in Britain, girls heard about Scouts' adventures. They presented themselves to Baden-Powell and demanded to join their brothers. Like many of his adult contemporaries, though, the lieutenant-general did not want girls and boys mingling. Instead, Baden-Powell's sister Agnes took charge of the first Girl Scouts, an organisation that promised to produce 'a new generation of healthy, clean-minded, patriotic mothers'.[163] For Agnes, a believer in the womanly arts, eugenic concerns about health and fitness went hand in hand with traditional modes of femininity. Colonial girls also clamoured to take part in their own kind

'Personalities, by Phil.': this sketch introduces an assessment of the girls attending the Buttercup Farm YWCA camp in Otago in the summer of 1919–20. The 'twins' were responsible for 'any little deeds of mischief', Phil had 'a charming but "gummy" smile', Tiny was 'brainy at Bible study', and Bessie was 'the life of the camp . . . wholly taken up with fun'.

of Scouting, and the New Zealand model mirrored the London set-up very closely indeed. David Cossgrove's daughter Muriel followed in Agnes Baden-Powell's footsteps when she organised the Girl Peace Scouts, a group that later merged into the Girl Guides.

Muriel Cossgrove placed a 'a strong emphasis on being ladylike', but Guiding had a more complex impact on the gender order than it appears at first glance.[164] On the one hand, the official Guide literature encouraged decorous behaviour and a feminine appearance. Diligently conducted 'exercises for beauty' would produce slim waists, shapely legs and nice ankles, while those wanting to 'improve the bust' could extend the arms and propel them in circles six times over.[165] But a broader form of female citizenship took hold too. Guides learned about judo, maps, signalling and camping out; they studied wildlife photography, hut-building and astronomy.[166] The adventurous aspects of Guiding proved highly compatible with the outdoor ethos at the heart of colonial girlhood.[167]

Like their male equivalents, girls' organisations provided social opportunities. In 1919, at a YWCA camp near Dunedin, girls played hockey and basketball and spent time at the beach. 'In the evening we played strenuous games on the sands in the moonlight, which was ripping', wrote one girl. Back inside, 'the "kissing" game in the evening was great fun and Miss Black proved adept at the game'. Then,

'Oh her Appetite!' Two hungry girls at the YWCA's Kia Ora camp, 1920, in the wilds of Otago.

'in a picturesque costume Mrs Wolfe and Miss Powell sang a touching love-sick duet'.[168] These happy days combined exercise, mucking about and female bonding. At an Easter Bible Class camp at Paerata in 1927, friendly girls with 'eager faces' played at ghosts in purloined bed sheets, squirted one another with water pistols, performed cartwheels, played cricket, swam in swamps and 'penetrated impassable forests'. There were concerts, camp fires and food raids in the dead of night followed by surreptitious scoffing.

Some girls bent the rules. At Paerata, Rita sneaked off for 'a meet at the gate'.[169] That Rita had to go all the way to the front fence shows the level of gender segregation: boys were barred, literally. Other girls barged straight through the barricades of respectability: not content to loiter at the gate they headed for the wharves. A particularly naughty group of Girl Scouts boarded a man-of-war in Wellington Harbour and behaved 'in such a way that the Officer Commanding the Military

District had to call on Colonel Cossgrove to restrain them'.[170] Records do not reveal the kinds of behaviour that required restraint, but it surely had to do with male personnel on the ship.

As popular modes of organised leisure, the Bible Class movement, Scouts and Guides provided carefully controlled social opportunities that reflected adults' demands for fitness, order and obedience while answering young people's calls for companionship. The category of adolescence consolidated when New Zealanders in their teens took part in activities designed for them and embodied what it meant to be young, strong and (mostly) disciplined. Girl Guides developed their bodies by learning judo skills and Boy Scouts learned the discipline of marching in a straight line. Still, these new organisations were not simply the tools of the 'tight society'. They also rounded up large numbers of young people, gave rise to a sense of solidarity and, like the factories and the schools, helped bring adolescents together en masse.

Informal Pleasures

Young people's leisure hours took very different forms. Not everybody wanted to be marched here and monitored over there, at least not all the time. Just knocking about could be good too. Groups of fellows spent time together in the small Southland hamlets during the 1910s:

> About twenty young chaps aged from sixteen to twenty used to ride hacks down to Mataura on a Saturday night and what a time we used to have, we did not have much money but could always manage a pack of cigarettes and a pie for supper. Every Saturday night a band would play, the pipe band one week and the next week the brass band. Seeing the south express in was a must. On the way home we would have horse races, and in summer on a hot night I with two others used to have a swim in a flooded coal pit. We swam in the nude and we let our clothes dry us as we put them on.[171]

Like Mole and Rat in the well-known children's novel *The Wind in the Willows*, other boys messed about in boats. 'I went for a ride to Days Bay on my bike with Ray and Mclean and Bridson', a Wellington schoolboy wrote in his diary. 'We had

This beach shot, from Kathleen Macklin's album, dates from the 1920s. It reveals a marked generational contrast during the 'Roaring Twenties'. In-betweeners show their bare arms while adults wear suits and coats in the middle distance.

a good time went out in Bridson's boat and met rain at Petone coming back it was just a shower and we did not get wet.'[172] Those without their own craft could hire boats for a row.[173]

Others ate together. Wellington's young apprentices met at Garland's Restaurant for a feed each night while they waited for technical college classes to begin.[174] Christchurch girls found their way into tearooms, punctuating their shopping trips with visits to the Rendezvous or Cooke's for strawberries and ice-cream.[175] House-to-house visiting was a common ritual in rural areas, small towns and cities, a way to consolidate and slowly expand social networks.[176] In Dunedin, Dora de Beer spent time in her friends' rooms. 'Mary and I went up to Margery's', she wrote in her diary in 1906. 'We sat round a dear wee gas fire in her bedroom, ate chocolates, and talked scandal.'[177] Dora's account of eating and gossiping with friends in bedrooms tells of a kind of low-key adolescent culture-building familiar to modern readers.

So far, most of these examples – schoolboys' boating, the Mataura lads' horse-riding and Dora's fireside chitchat – tell of gender-segregated leisure. Many young New Zealanders sorted themselves into groups of girls or boys even when no adult dictated who was acceptable company. These arrangements mirrored the single-gender leisure pattern enforced in Bible Class meetings and Scouts' rambles. At other times, though, boys and girls intermingled like never before. Photograph albums reveal a great many mixed groups, especially after the First World War when the camera became a common accessory. As the cloche hat, the bathing costume and the t-shirt revolutionised young people's dress, groups of boys and girls headed for the beaches where they lay on the sand and draped themselves over one another. Pictures show tangles of bare arms and legs, a stark contrast to the fully dressed adults hovering in the background. The beach was a 'new frontier for self expression', a space where in-betweeners enjoyed themselves unchaperoned.[178] Sombre adults had to be content to bear witness. The contrast between controlled and independent leisure reveals the schism between the 'tight society' and something very much looser.

Commercial Freedoms

Organised leisure activities faced their biggest ideological competitor not in the nation's streets or bedrooms, but in the new citadels of commercialism. The movies (also known as 'the flicks' or 'the pictures') seized hold of New Zealanders' imaginations during the first decade of the twentieth century.[179] In 1906, *The Story of the Kelly Gang*, the world's first feature-length film, resonated with an antipodean audience. Crowds up and down the country crammed into community halls to watch the antics of the infamous bushranger and his law-breaking associates.[180] A new generation of larrikins revelled in the escapades of their Australian heroes.[181] In 1911, five years after Ned and his mates enthralled young New Zealanders, the first purpose-built movie theatre opened in Wellington. Cinemas soon sprouted like mushrooms, and by 1915 Aucklanders had a choice of thirteen picture palaces in the inner city alone.[182] Young viewers loved the comfort of the air-cushioned seats, the strains of the live orchestral music and larger-than-life action on the giant screen.[183]

Harrold and His Friends

'Got up at five this morning & went up to the Church to help to cut up the sandwiches etc for the picnic. After breakfast I took father's bicycle & rode to the old Town & Suburban Racecourse. Here I had a grand time playing cricket and other games. At the former I made 29 runs against Ted Smyth's & others' bowling. Went for a swim in the afternoon & then riding back home, packed up & rode around to the wharf. Viv, Dave Nelson & myself in the same cabin, & after leaving at 8.30, got to bed and were soon fast asleep.'[184] Harrold Ennor made this entry in his diary on New Year's Day in 1907. At first glance there is nothing special about this record of an eighteen-year-old's summer in provincial New Zealand, but look again. Harrold's writing evokes sociability, leisure and mobility: he chatted, swam and played cricket. His ride to Napier's wharf was the first leg in a sea-bound journey back to Gisborne, his usual place of residence.

Harrold's diary reveals the rhythm of an adolescent life: his work as a law clerk, study for Matriculation exams and his leisure hours. Some of his spare time was highly organised. He went to church twice on Sundays, belonged to Christian Endeavour and Bible Class ('had a real good time in prayer'), volunteered as secretary at the local YMCA and dutifully traipsed off to drill practice.[185] Less formal pursuits filled in the gaps. Harrold collected stamps, developed his own photographs, played cards and Ludo with his siblings, and one afternoon he and his

Gisborne about 1908, when Harrold and the others wandered around town and hopped into boats.

friends 'biked out to the Rev. Walker's at Ormond. There Alf, Cliff & I had a ramble over the hills & some somersaulting into manuka bushes, then we got onto our machines & rode home.'[186] The boys also strolled aimlessly about Gisborne's streets, stopping at the local tearooms for a feed and a yarn. The houses, hills and roads provided the setting for these adolescent lives.

Just as church-organised activities alternated with relaxation, not all free time was segregated by gender. Boys and girls ran into one another in the streets, visited each other's houses, rowed boats, played bowls and generally 'went around' together. One afternoon Alf, George, Grant, Harrold, Viv, Vera and Grace took a boat out on the river. 'Got back at 6.30. Had tea at "The Elms", then played a few games & set out for home.'[187] After work Harrold 'met Miss Hill, Miss Primrose & Ted Church & we had a real good time eating, drinking & making merry'.[188] These youngsters indulged in intrigue, barracked one another and swapped allegiances. Some weeks after the outing in the row boat, Vera began to give Harrold 'sarcastic' looks and spread rumours about him. Luckily Freda was there. One day after church Harrold 'went home with Freda & had a grand talk with her for ¾ of an hour. My, she's just alright. Think she leans my way a little.'[189] The two became confidants. They looked out for one another and tried to work out what Vera was up to. Harrold's diary does not tell us whether they figured out Vera's motives.

Harrold Ennor's diary is a little history of an early-twentieth-century adolescent life with its social connections, pleasures and frustrations. It shows us that adults' concerns about young people – preoccupations with self-control and national fitness, for instance – paled into insignificance when compared to everyday social demands.

Boys' bucolic pleasures: camping at Pounawea in the Catlins, a few years after Harrold wrote his diary.

Wellington's fantasy theatre, the Regent, photographed in 1926, the year it opened. The silent movie era still had a few years to run. One young fan of Christchurch's Regent described his experience: 'It had stars in the ceiling which twinkled . . . the atmosphere was somewhere between a cathedral and a palace. On cold days, we would duck out of the cinema at interval, funds permitting, to a nearby pie shop. It took a while, and you nearly always arrived back in your seat juggling a boiling hot pie in the darkness.'

The cinema catapulted American popular culture into New Zealanders' consciousness. By 1916 American films accounted for 95 percent of those shown here and a third of all New Zealanders, many of them young, went to the pictures each week.[190] One Wellington schoolboy attended twice a day, slipping down to the movie theatre in between various domestic tasks:

July Tuesday 12th. Very wet and windy, wind a northerly and cold. Stayed at home from school all day, mended the puncture in the football. Went out in the afternoon to the pictures with Jack. Went out again to the pictures in the evening with Jack.

July Friday 22nd. Fine no rain windy, wind a northerly. Did not go to school but stayed at home and made a hat stand in the afternoon. I went to the pictures with Jack. Geoff came down in the evening and I went again to the pictures with Jack and I saw Mother and Geoff in the same pictures.[191]

The silent movies bred an exotic crop of stars: glamorous Greta Garbo, boyish flapper Clara Bow, deadpan stuntman Buster Keaton, Western hero Gary Cooper and the ever-alluring Rudolph Valentino. In 1918 Christchurch lass Alison McLeod swooned at the sight of Elmo Lincoln in *Tarzan of the Apes* – and envied Enid Markey her role as Jane:

> [Lincoln] has such a refined gentle yet strong face & such a massive frame & limbs. He was the man for the part. He looked so handsome, too. He must be a handsome man even when he is dressed modernly. Of course, as Tarzan, he had only a skin round his waist. The way he swung through the trees was marvellous. From bough to bough, leaping & swinging through the tree tops. And climb! He must be very strong, too, because in one part he swung up & down by the branches & supple-jacks, with the girl clinging to him. Some fun, being that girl![192]

Others also celebrated the appeal of movieland, including a group of young Dunedin fans. A 1927 Otago University study collated their views. They especially enjoyed cowboy pictures, comedies, whodunits and war films. One fourteen-year-old girl loved seeing mystery films at the Empire on a darkened evening. 'It makes it seem more real to me', she said.[193] A boy of fourteen wrote: 'The pictures I like best are the wild western romance, the chief stars of which are Ken Maynard, Fred Thompson, Tom Mix, Buck Jones, and Hoot Gibson. It is exciting to see one of them in a fight, or galloping over the Praier [*sic*] on their fine horses.'[194] Gender made a difference at the movies. Boys and girls often attended the pictures together but they preferred different genres. Male viewers, especially the youngest, did not always enjoy the sentimentalism of the romantic genre. 'I absolutely hate the love films. The senseless way the lovers gulp at each other for hours and sob and kiss and fall into each other's arms', one lad complained. 'Lunatics, bachelors and old maids may like them, but the majority do not, for only subnormals would act in the way these lovers do.'[195]

Youngsters were not the only ones to voice their occasional disapproval. Movies, even the silent type, threatened to transform culture in unpredictable ways, and serious-minded adults worried about the potential for hyperstimulus and titillation in general. 'Crook films', as they described the crime thrillers, perpetuated 'a craze for fun, frolic, adventure' and celebrated 'extravagant self-display'.[196] A government report suggested that 'the darkened hall', the 'atmosphere of crowd excitement' and the 'intensely sensational character of the emotional scenes' led youngsters astray.[197] This criticism took nineteenth-century concerns about sensation in a new direction. The smoking and the swearing were troublesome – words like 'Damn!' appeared in large letters on the screen – and, to top it all off, girls and boys watched such depravities together. Cinematic pleasure threatened to leap off the screen and into the darkened back rows. Still, this was not quite a free-for-all. The New Zealand government did not censor films before 1915 but, as a film historian explains it, the 'consciences of the respectable' held sway when it came to selecting screenings.[198] Perhaps the guardians of public morality had a measure of success. One early American genre is notably absent from the movie listings of New Zealand newspapers: sexually salacious comedies with titles like *The Boardinghouse Bathroom* and *The Broadway Massage Parlour*.[199]

Censorship, though, was not the only form of social control. Like the advertisements that began targeting young female consumers, films also moulded adolescent selfhood and desire in commercially acceptable ways. The movie moguls became highly skilled at the latter, and shareholders held all the cards in Hollywood.[200] Films shaped gender identities not by barking orders and organising camps as others had done. Instead, they spun fantasies, disseminated new fashion trends and built upon the rudimentary fan cultures of the early 1900s. The international 'postcard craze' took hold in the first decade of the century and adolescents, especially girls, swapped pictures of stage stars: Phyllis Dare, Grace Palotta, Tittell Brune, and a great many other 'goddesses of charm and luxury', as one theatre historian puts it.[201] Collectors absorbed the glamour of their 'beautiful imaginary friends' and pondered the meaning of style, even though few ever laid eyes on the stars whose likenesses they collected. Brune, who toured New Zealand to great acclaim, was an exception.[202] Ten years later the movie industry gave these early fan cultures a significant boost. Large numbers of girls modelled themselves on their heroines. Although very few could emulate the lifestyles offered in movieland, they did adopt markers of modernity like bobbed hair and shorter skirts.[203]

What of these viewers' male counterparts? The newspapers tried to persuade their readers that Valentino's films were 'full of action' as well as 'splendid romance', but the actor promoted a masculine image that made many New Zealand men uneasy.[204] He was the silver screen's greatest lover: suave, passionate

 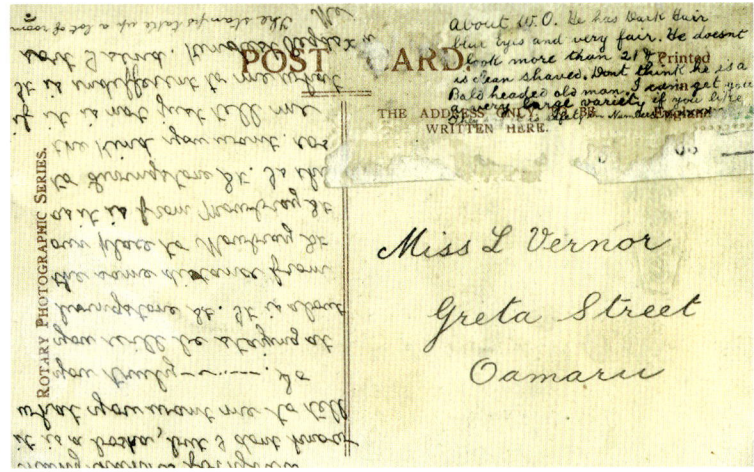

This postcard of stage star Phyllis Dare, sent to young Miss Vernor in Oamaru by a friend, tells of adolescent fan culture during the early twentieth century. The coded 'mirror writing' refers to postcard collecting: 'Many thanks for yours, it is a boska', the sender writes approvingly. 'Is this the kind you want cos if it is not just tell me.'

and hugely popular with female viewers, but was he overly slick and too eager to please? The cissy boy and the boy flapper took a leaf out of Valentino's book, but other lads – including those who expressed their scorn for 'love films' – remained unmoved. Male New Zealanders dragged the chain when it came to romantic gestures, and boys in some theatres burst an inflated paper bag each time the actors kissed.[205]

Bunny Hug and Black Bottom

Cinema-going and fan cultures were the beacons of modernity. They reached a new level during the 1930s and 1940s, as we will see in the next chapter. Dancing, in partial contrast, had old and new characteristics. A recent arrival to the Otago town of Alexandra told of the ongoing importance of dances in small communities:

> I was amazed when I came here, the girls of my age and even a bit younger, they had beaus paid them attention, men. There were men everywhere. We had dances in the school at Earnscleugh … The boys, they were so numerous that they had to rush for a dance. My word, the girls had a good time then. It was a really lovely life. The boys flocked, the girls flocked, and a lot of courting was done at those places.[206]

In a similar vein, eighteen-year-old Arthur Ross met his future wife – 'a brown eyed girl, her age just sweet sixteen' – at a dance at Boghead in a remote part of Southland. 'This was the first dance she had been to and naturally she was shy. After having a couple of dances with her I plucked up enough courage to ask her if I could see her home. When she said yes I could have hugged myself so pleased I was.' The pair kissed goodnight and 'she was so thrilled with that kiss that she did not wash it off her face'.[207]

The scene soon changed in the larger centres where the tentacles of American culture reached out and tickled those on the dance floor. Few lads wanted to be Rudolph Valentino but their dancing took a slick new turn during the 1910s. Jazz fans tore up the old-fashioned dance cards that recorded who would dance with whom and in which order. 'Cutting in' had become an accepted practice.[208] Jazz transformed the dance floor, and new moves, many of them inspired by black American culture, wowed enthusiasts. 'Full of frenzied energy and tempestuous vitality', the foxtrot first made news in 1915, and it soon became mainstream.[209] Other 'freak dances', as aficionados called them, were less conventional. These included the Peabody, the Black Bottom, the Tango and an enduring symbol of the jazz age: the Charleston. Dunedin school pupil Mabel McIndoe and her friends took to jazz like ducks to water, eagerly embracing the new style:

> In our early and middle teens we girls organised dances in our own homes. Carpets would be lifted, floors french chalked, trifles, jellies and sandwiches made and gramophones wound up. In the arms of schoolboys and callow young men, mostly our friends' brothers, we foxtrotted and pumphandled our way through these records. To us such music meant only one thing – you got up and danced. We learned the Charleston and, in our short, slinky dresses we crossed our hands alternately and rhythmically to our knees while our legs flew out in the corners.[210]

Dancers all around the country revelled in the Charleston, but the Bunny Hug, a dance in which partners strode about the floor cheek-to-cheek with their arms wrapped around one another's shoulders, stirred more controversy. Some claimed this dance first appeared in the brothels of San Francisco.[211] Never a newspaper to let a scandal slip past, *Truth* leapt on the new innovations. 'Pimply-faced boys and giggling flappers' congregated 'beyond parental vision', its editors claimed piously; the youngsters revelled in the 'immodest steps' of the new dances. *Truth* journalists insisted, with little supporting evidence, that Dunedin adolescents took part in 'jazz orgies' in the Town Belt at midnight.[212] Having made the outlandish claim, the usually loquacious paper refused to provide any more details.

Why all the fuss? While closely organised adolescent leisure often threw a cordon around lively youngsters, jazz headed in the opposite direction. The new dances freed young bodies to move in close quarters and explore a new sensuality.[213] Girls' dancing clothes looked and felt much slinkier than those of their predecessors, and those who danced the Bunny Hug celebrated a sexual freedom

Modernity reaches a small community: a dance at the Port Albert Hall north of Auckland during the 1920s.

that the 'tight society' types – Truby King, the Cossgroves and the rest – disowned most forcefully. Jazz loosened the very stays the moralists tried to tighten.[214] One British cultural theorist suggests that jazz promised some of the 'forbidden danger' that rock 'n' roll later acquired, and this was true of New Zealand too.[215]

Like the movies, jazz tapped into the new commercial leisure scene. Privately owned dance halls and cabarets imported the hedonistic dances into our cities and towns, and their owners paid professional dancers to demonstrate the new moves.[216] Opportunities for unchaperoned fun abounded. Mabel McIndoe sallied forth to The Hydro, a dance hall on the seafront at St Clair. She took to the floor with Pat McCassie, a big, confident boy with a 'very disturbed complexion' and bitten fingernails who 'took me home in exchange for some petting in draughty seafront shelters along the way'.[217]

Gladys Hadley, a sixteen-year-old Aucklander, truly embodied the new sensibility. *Truth* told of her life under the salacious headline 'Flapper's Startling Story of Gay Doings in Flat'. Gladys, a land agent's assistant, flatted with another young woman and one day she met 'a dapper young man' at the flash Dixieland Dance Hall. She went for 'joy-rides', had sex with the youth in his car and again at a flat in Waterloo Quadrant, and popped in to the city's hotels for a 'spot' (a boozy drink).[218] Commercial dance halls gave licence to the modern, highly mobile lives of adolescent girls, a fact not lost on *Truth*. Gladys started frequenting the Dixieland at thirteen, and her easy associations across gender lines strayed from the segregation assiduously enforced by Bible Class, Scouts, Guides and the like. Her adventurous and public refusal to regard sexual intimacy as possible only within marriage exemplified the sensual side of modern life. Gladys, a young working woman, showed no interest in the 'tight society'. Instead, her tale of joy-rides, sex and drinking, and *Truth*'s response to such pleasures, lay bare the interplay of rigid rules and new freedoms that prevailed during the 1920s. Gladys Hadley embraced modernity and lived life to the full.

Conclusion: Contradictory Times

Gender norms swirled, shifted and settled during the early decades of the century. The 'foot soldiers of modernity', as Erik Olssen calls the young, unmarried women

Cadets in rows, North Otago.

of the time, were 'the driving force behind social change'.[219] The flapper led the way at a time when physical culture and new fashions transformed young female bodies. A mix of factors both liberated and constrained her. Advertisers appealed to femininity, bodily freedoms and female desire all at once, reinforcing and reworking expectations of glamour and beauty. Growing financial independence, first-wave feminism, eugenic notions of national fitness and the steady expansion of secondary schooling profoundly reshaped girls' lives.

Ideas about boyhood and the transition to manhood were complex too. Youths lined up in rows as war beckoned; many gripped their guns and dreamed of the ultimate sacrifice. Even so, more than one form of masculinity held sway during the period. Militarism's grip was not total, and regimented stoicism did not entirely displace the nineteenth-century mode of 'warm male friendship'.[220] Youths still enjoyed idyllic and chaotic leisure hours with their mates, and even the cadet scheme provided opportunities for socialising. By the 1920s, headlines like 'Dress sins of the cissy boy' and 'Jazz boy versus flapper' focussed attention on flamboyant lads obsessed with clothes and luxury. Old ironies abounded: those who complained about youth culture also acted as publicists, just as they had done for the masher of the 1880s. Stylish boys learned about the latest look, and they tried it on for themselves.

Bob and Alaster, South Otago.

Social life proved just as contradictory. Mixed-age leisure continued its appeal, and young people went along to the family picnics, group outings, balls and concerts that so amused their Victorian forebears. 'Not a bad concert. Hall crowded. Had a pretty good time', Belle Marsh wrote of one such event, although she was less enamoured by another: 'Went to a mouldy old picnic at Blackburn's beach.'[221] Church socials and dances brought together many young people, and some of them went on to marry.[222] When it came to the organised, gender-segregated forms of youth-centred leisure – the Girl Guides and Boy Scouts, YMCA and YWCA – these achieved more than one thing. Bible Class camps taught piety but they also hosted water fights, ghost pranks and midnight feasts. They separated boys and girls while intensifying the allure: a sneaky

A group of Otago lads, 1916.

Constrained exuberance: a sack race at Hataitai, Wellington, in 1915.

meeting at the gate was all the more delicious for being illicit. Ultimately, these upholders of morality promoted youth culture, sometimes on a large scale.

Competing social trends weakened the extent of gender segregation. Church stalwarts were suspicious of the cinema, but many of their young parishioners spent their evenings at 'the flicks' in mixed company. A range of other spaces also afforded opportunities for boys and girls to spend time together. Harrold Ennor was a devout churchgoer, and a member of the YMCA and Bible Class, but his diary also chronicles his comings and goings in Gisborne's streets, in private houses and on the river. He and his friends, girls as well as boys, wandered about together with little parental oversight. The sunny sensuality of those who lazed on the beaches and had their photos taken for posterity offer a stark contrast to khaki uniforms, tents in rows and books of rules. But this was not an era of hard and fast distinctions: sometimes young people, including Harrold and his friends, picked up both strands simultaneously.

How did New Zealanders describe those between thirteen and twenty during these complex decades? The term 'teen' slowly extended its reach but 'teenagers' had not yet made their debut.[223] One Sunday School organiser led the way when he spoke of 'the needs of the teen age', suggesting that an 'overflowing energy' and an 'openness to spiritual truth' characterised this time of life.[224] Very occasionally, 'teen age' appeared as an adjective: in 1926 the YWCA told of its work among 'teen age girls'.[225] Given the role of the churches in promoting young people's culture, it comes as little surprise to discover the new term appearing in religious contexts. Similarly, the advertising company, another key player, began to appeal to 'teen age maidens'.[226] Still, descriptive language remained loose, and the ubiquitous categories of 'boy' and 'girl' held sway too. George Benstead, headmaster at Otekaieke Special School, assumed that any male unable to earn a living was a 'boy'. Nothing less than financial independence would turn him into a man.[227] Nineteenth-century ideas about work and masculinity continued to define life transitions for many, and they stayed strong for many years to come. Old and new ideas jostled for attention.

Everything, it seemed, happened at once. Many young people wanted to ease back even as many adults tried to tighten New Zealand's social order. Flapper and dance hall habitué Gladys Hadley took this trend to an extreme, while others – adventurous Guides, suave cissy boys and high school glee clubbers – tried on a less threatening version for size. This impulse did not always last a lifetime, though. Some New Zealanders, although probably not Gladys, later forgot the wilder aspects of their youth and their role in the development of adolescent culture: their participation in new forms of leisure, their invention of fan culture and their embrace of jazz. They became the uptight forty- and fifty-somethings of the 1950s who advocated a set of 1910s and 1920s remedies for youthful excess: tightly organised leisure and a good dose of drill. But another group would take shape in the interregnum between these two generations: the first teenagers.

Chapter Four The Teenager is Here!

'This evening Maurice and I biked down to Sumner leaving around 6.10. We went for a swim . . . perfect sea, big breakers, warm and no undertow. We ran to Cave Rock, walked to Shag Rock, then back to the dressing shed. Then we climbed the steep road at Scarborough and turned back at the top when Taylors Mistake came in sight.'[1] David Wildey, nineteen, wrote these lines in his diary in the summer of 1940. His prose captures the outdoor lives of generations of young New Zealanders, the easy accessibility of beaches and hills. Such leisure spaces were never far away, even in cities like Christchurch. David lived near the centre of town, and trams, trains and bicycles afforded him and his friends easy access to places to enjoy. But the beach was not David's only playground. Most Friday evenings he and his brother Evie turned up at the Milky Way milk bar in High Street to enjoy the fare – ice-cream cost nine pence, three waffles were sixpence, ice-cream and fruit salad one shilling and threepence – before wandering out into the night.[2] Several streets away, the YMCA had a gym: 'All apparatus exercise', David noted in his diary, 'no one in charge. Spent about twenty minutes under a hot shower, then a plunge and a few lengths in the icy pool.'[3] During the summer

OPPOSITE A pair of trampers during the 1940s.

Nineteen-year-old
David Wildey in 1940.

David went along to the YMCA's camps and enjoyed sunbathing, soccer, cricket, skittles and 'educational' films.[4]

The 1940s saw the rise of the 'teenager', a term that first appeared in America around 1930.[5] Like their adolescent predecessors, teenagers were semi-autonomous subjects who navigated the demands of parents, school and work as they fumbled their way towards adulthood. The teenager label also suggested a heightened relationship between youth and popular culture, especially the increasing influence of American consumerism. The Depression slowed rather than stalled the development of adolescent consumer cultures, and then the

Second World War brought American troops and their sophisticated ways to southern shores.[6] A new generation of movies, the 'talkies', spread cultural imagery, style and slang as they captivated young audiences, while the jitterbug, the speedway, and for the lucky few the motorbike and the motorcar, symbolised a new era of speed. The 'scrapbook self', a pastiche of cultural influences and diverging social norms, arose from the continued interaction of youth and consumer culture. In the booths of the Milky Way, the tents and gyms of the YMCA, David Wildey and his friends embodied the new teenagehood whether they realised it or not.

The Sugarbag Years

The 1930s dawned to the hardships of the Great Depression. The American stock market had crashed in October 1929, and jobs dried up amid falling profits. New Zealand's exports to Britain fell.[7] A great many antipodeans went without work, although we do not know exact numbers: official unemployment figures are imprecise at best.[8] Life was tough for many, and innumerable town-dwellers left for the country as the downturn hit.[9] Adult men toiled on relief projects while impoverished adolescents made a little money as best they could. For some at least, culture-building took a back seat to day-to-day survival. One Hokianga lass scraped together a meagre income by picking and selling the fungus growing on rotten trees.[10] A Taranaki girl worked in a bookshop for a while, lost her job and then helped out on a farm. She laboured seven days a week so she could afford to replace her leaky shoes. 'I was always looking for bits of cardboard to shape and fit in them so that my feet would not hurt', she said: eventually the makeshift solution wore out.[11]

Many who remained in the cities did it tough. Homeless and jobless youths slept rough in Auckland Domain and survived on scraps.[12] Factory, retail and office jobs shrank in number, and young workers had their incomes cut. The fact that adolescents earned lower wages than adults spared them even greater levels of unemployment, but young New Zealanders were far from expendable. Sixteen-year-old Mary Findlay had a succession of jobs as a domestic servant in Wellington's large houses. Her mistresses doled out humiliation, her masters

Boys' Hardships

Some boys lived footloose lives during the Depression and the Second World War. Pushed from one job to the next, they moved around in search of work. South Islander Sam Morrison left school in 1934 when 'jobs were hard to get' and he shuttled through a number of short-term assignments. Sam worked in a biscuit factory for a while, then a paint shop for a few months and he became a fleecer for his uncle's shearing gang in the Mackenzie Country. 'I had to pick the fleece up off the floor and throw it on a table where there would be uncles and cousins of mine sorting it out and cleaning it, ready for putting it on the press.' Then he left to labour at a lime works, a job he hated. 'Lifting stuff in the winter months,

Boys stack and cut kindling in 1932 at the height of the Great Depression. A range of local schemes helped out-of-work boys. A Whanganui scheme registered them and offered a weekly allowance of four shillings a week for those attending classes in gardening, woodwork and boot repair. Another made boys available for odd jobs and farm work, while a base at the YMCA provided free gym facilities, educational lectures and movies.

your fingers would start to bleed, burnt lime would get in them and they burned from the tips, it was horrible.'[13]

Sam never worked by himself but other boys suffered from isolation and loneliness.[14] The war had scarcely begun when thirteen-year-old Robert Stapleton left his Timaru orphanage bound for the Hawke's Bay. He wound up at a backblocks farm in the Waipawa district and his new digs – a small house with no electricity, a quarter of a mile from the homestead – was a dispiriting departure from the constant company of the twelve boys in the orphanage's dormitory. Robert milked cows, plucked poultry, and scrubbed pots and floors. He objected to being treated as a 'slushy' so his employers trained him as a shepherd. Constantly 'under the thumb' of the station owner, Robert gradually saved up enough money to buy a second-hand bicycle as a way to escape his seclusion. 'Then I used to bike into Waipawa every Saturday morning. I'd spend the day there, with the sole object of going to the pictures on the Saturday afternoon. Now those roads were 17 miles and they were shingle roads, and I did this because I could get away from the environment and go to the pictures.' A permanent escape came at the age of sixteen when he returned to the South Island to go lambing on a large station in the Mackenzie Country. There were plenty of other young fellows there and Robert's loneliness abated.[15]

Like their nineteenth-century counterparts, boys like Robert and Sam lingered in a peripatetic no-man's-land between precariousness and independence. Their position in the labour market was tenuous to say the least, and they had nobody to look out for them.

A Wellington lad in his work apron.

and their sons sexually assaulted her, and she was constantly packing her bags in search of the next assignment.[16] Each time Mary walked off the job she met desperate young women queueing at the front door for an interview.

Mary changed tack in the face of such hopelessness. She pleaded with the manager of a department store to give her a job, and soon began as a junior in the millinery section where she earned eleven shillings and twopence a week. She dusted three times a day, packed hats in tissue paper and ran messages. Her supervisor was tyrannical but she enjoyed the gossip among the junior staff, the scents wafting around the cosmetics counter and the opportunity to touch up her lipstick behind the scenes. The respite did not last long. The store's finances worsened, Mary lost her job and once again she trudged the streets in search of work.[17]

The worst of the Depression had passed by 1935. Seventeen-year-old Margaret Stevenson moved from Piriaka, near Taumarunui, to work at the Sanitarium café in Wellington. This was a radically new experience for her:

> What with the hard work and poor pay I still loved the city. It was so very different from what I had been used to. The crowds of people, the shops full of such beautiful things even if all I could do was feast my eyes on them. Riding on the tram-cars, having the conductors make eyes at you, wolf whistles from young carpenters on building sites, things I have never in my life before experienced. How could I not be expected to enjoy it, hard work, poverty and all. I was really living, I was growing up.[18]

Paid work offered more than an income: it also gave girls a sense of freedom and an entry to the adult world.[19] Although Margaret's work was hard, the pay poor and she often wondered whether she had swapped 'one kind of slavery for another', the move to Wellington was a revelation. She lived with girlfriends in a series of inner-city rooming houses and had 'a continual stream of drunks winding their way home past our door, every night'.[20] The young women firmly bolted the door and never left the house after dark. Margaret's experience combined peril and pleasure in equal measure, but she would not have swapped it for anything.

Margaret's story tells of the novelty of city life for those who grew up in the small towns and farming districts. Whereas the slump had sent young people

These young nurses muck about at Kaitangata during the 1930s. Seventeen was the age of entry into nursing. Many hospitals and nurses' homes were run quite strictly – 'the ward sisters really were dragons' – but there was some fun to be had. A former Hamilton nurse told of 'the occasional flare up when we would all pile into a taxi for 2/6- and go down to the local diner and buy a feed of fish and chips' or swap cash for crates of beer at a pub a little way out of town.

out of the cities, the subsequent economic recovery sucked them back in,[21] and as jobs became more plentiful, especially in the manufacturing sector, patterns of internal migration swiftly reversed. Youth employment quickly recovered. By 1937, as Michael Joseph Savage's crusading Labour government settled into office, the vocational master at Wellington Technical School fielded endless requests from employers. They wanted boys as clerks, junior salesmen, electrical engineers and messengers. The civil service soaked up almost all of the 'senior engineering boys' and 'clerical lads' the college could train.[22] Business owners called out for increasing numbers of young female workers too: typists, clerical staff, shop assistants and factory hands. A 1939 report by the Vocational Guidance Association encouraged schoolgirls to prepare themselves 'for the professions of women'.[23] The promise of economic independence reappeared after the hiatus of the Depression, and teenagers became an economic force in their own right.

The talk of 'professions' also signalled an ongoing shift in the gender order. Historian Melanie Nolan suggests that the government spoke with two voices on women's paid labour. 'The New Zealand state was neither liberator nor gaoler', she writes; 'its role was ambiguous.'[24] Politicians prioritised women's domesticity while unemployment remained high but changed their tune as soon as the economy rallied. The demand for workers in businesses and government departments trumped the notion that women belonged in the home. Primary school rolls shrank during the Depression and married female teachers were pushed out of the profession, but teenage teachers joined married women in school staffrooms when rolls bounced back during the late 1930s.[25] The white blouse revolution continued apace. As the proportion of girls and women in the labour force rose, so too did their pay. The female statutory minimum wage climbed from 47 percent of men's hourly rate in 1936 to 60 percent in 1946.[26]

Shirley Albiston's experiences reflect some of these shifts. Shirley and her friends went to Wellington East Girls' College and divided themselves into two groups. The academically minded among them took subjects like French, history and mathematics and anticipated careers as teachers. Those in the other group looked to factory work and office jobs. The thought of factory labour filled Shirley with 'repulsion', and at first she pitied the young women arrayed in rows in commercial offices.[27] As time went on, though, she faced stacks of history homework with waning enthusiasm and eventually changed her mind. Shirley's teachers recoiled at her betrayal: anybody who left school to become 'an ordinary office girl', they told her, gave up 'a noble profession for an ignoble one'.[28] Only a career like teaching, they insisted, would allow a young woman to fulfill her intellectual potential.

But Shirley's mind was made up. In 1938 she graduated from Gilby's Commercial College and looked for an office job. She had no difficulty finding work in post-Depression Wellington. 'There is a great demand for typists and practically no supply', she wrote, 'so I can pick and choose.'[29] Shirley liked her first employer, a Mr Ross. He was 'a lot of blow', as one of her friends described

Studiousness and nice clothes at the Dunedin art school, King Edward Technical College, during the 1930s.

him, 'but he is so very considerate and never keeps me longer than 5 o'clock and I have a holiday every second Saturday'.[30] Shirley got on well with her other colleagues too: Miss McIntosh, the head typist, was 'very dexterous at her work, and is very good to me', while Eric impressed Shirley as well: 'I think he must be very intellectual and has an admirable command of the very unusual words in the language.'[31] The work suited Shirley, but she got itchy feet and soon took up a job in a government department. Her diaries lay bare a now-familiar contradiction: paid employment gave young women income and a degree of independence, but it could also be monotonous. When Shirley's government job made her feel like an 'automaton', she looked once again at her options and returned to the private sector.[32]

Wandering the Country

The previous chapter outlined the three kinds of leisure that consolidated during the interwar period. Teenagers divided their time between organised recreation, informal knocking about and rapidly expanding commercial opportunities. These categories persisted, and sometimes intersected, through the middle decades of the century.

One form of lightly organised leisure owed more to Europe than America. Turn-of-the-century German adolescents formed themselves into the Wandervogel, a youth network whose name translates into English as 'wandering bird'. The Wandervogel's keen adventurers hiked around the countryside for weeks at a time and slept rough.[33] Wandervogel ideas made their way into New Zealand thirty years later when the youth hostel movement, another German invention, reached our shores. The timing was hardly coincidental. The new Labour government took an interest in outdoor education alongside its focus on public health. Savage's ministers wanted greater emphasis on sports in order to 'keep the young people fit during the rest of their lives'.[34] The rate of urban growth also played a part. As New Zealand's cities grew in size, some townies sought to escape, in one commentator's words, the 'rush, trams, noise, smoke and city in an over mechanised world'.[35] The same imperative had driven the Wandervogel, a by-product of Germany's rapid industrialisation.

The near-ubiquity of the bicycle – and the steadily improving state of the country's roads – added another dimension to the New Zealand version of Wandervogel. Many boys' diaries of the 1930s tell of Scout troops and groups of friends who left town during the summer holidays. Boys put their bikes in trains' luggage vans, disembarked hundreds of miles down the line, and meandered home over a period of days or weeks. Burton Collins and his Christchurch mates biked all over Banks Peninsula. They pedalled hard and compensated for their toil by swimming in streams and lazing in paddocks. 'It was powerful hot. We are all

These sketches adorn the pages of the Takatuma Scout Crew's log book. This Wellington-based rovers' group recorded its activities during the early 1930s: tent-pitching, cooking, singing, basketball, parading and pillow-fights.

sore from sunburn except Mac who is brown', Burton jotted in his diary.[36] 'Pushed up in blazing sun . . . Road good so far. We saw the bays & got a drink at a house.' By evening Burton and his friends were exhausted: 'Tent & bed 9pm.'[37] Jim Parnell, a Whanganui Boy Scout, recounted thumbing lifts from passing trucks, dossing down in strangers' sheds and cooking over open fires. '10 miles from Greymouth, Mike's bike head broke and he went for a nice dive. We patched him up and stopped a passing van. Camped in pouring rain in the driver's wash-house at his home. Slept well.'[38]

Boys' leisure culture reflected an ongoing gender separation. Girls were not as mobile as boys, and they tended to travel much shorter distances. Up until the

1940s most girls' forays into the countryside, whether by bike or horse, were day trips. In Taranaki, a teenaged Dorothy Mackay climbed Mt Egmont and walked for miles round the rocks and bays of the coastline, while teachers at Christchurch's St Margaret's College dragged their girls around the hills.[39] One afternoon they began in Lyttelton and carried on through Governors Bay to Cashmere, a distance of twelve miles. 'We could hardly hobble in from the tram stop', a pupil wrote to her parents afterwards. 'We must have looked mad.'[40] The YWCA and the Girl Guides organised camps to take girls into the great outdoors, but these were short day walks rather than multi-day trips covering large swathes of countryside. One group of Rangers camped at Trentham race course and did not venture far at all, although they went for one hike. 'Peggy, Joyce, Eva and Violet thought their last hour had come when a mad horse chased them but as only the good die young they escaped with their lives and a tear in Violet's dress.'[41] The walk – if not

Four Scouts and a rope bridge.

the mishap with the horse – was fairly typical of an afternoon's activities at a girls' camp during the 1930s.

While boys' log books chronicled exertion and deprivation, girls detailed the homely aspects of camp life: sheltering from the rain, filling paillasses with straw and playing the gramophone before bed. So what happened to the colonial girl during these post-colonial decades? The sassy adventurer had not disappeared, but like her nineteenth-century counterpart her geographical range remained limited. Some young women took part in the early tramping clubs, a few of which – including the Hutt Valley Tramping Club and the Victoria College Tramping Club – encouraged them to join.[42] The male members of other clubs, though, felt that long-range mobility was a male prerogative. More profound shifts in gendered mobility had to wait for the widespread availability of the motorcar during the 1950s and 1960s.

Nelson College rugby during the 1930s. Bryan Helm's letters to his father and brother in Motueka mention reasonably high rates of injury: players were often taken to hospital in ambulances. Younger boys had to perform a haka for the First XV. They practised every morning, Bryan wrote, 'which makes us very hoarse'.

Milkshakes and Modern Leisure

The teenage bodies that toiled, pedalled and wandered also needed feeding. Jim Parnell told of his haphazard approach to the subject while biking around Nelson: 'dinner to be bought at Kawatiri but we passed it. Pub at Owen Springs would not sell us any food apart from 2 cakes of chocolate. We then had half a cake each.'[43] Food and drink loomed large in the minds of teenagers in the cities too. The number of eating places slowly increased after the First World War. Cooke's Tudor Tearoom in Christchurch was a popular hangout during the 1930s, while the Plaza and the Ritz appealed to young Wellingtonians.[44] A Ritz regular described the establishment as a 'rather posh little tearooms in Cuba Street'.[45] These were places to meet, to be seen and to make new friends. Another girl worked at the tearooms in small-town Taranaki: 'There was a crowd of young men camping in Opunake, repairing the railway lines and bridges. They would come into the tearooms for meals so we got to know them quite well. So of course there were lots of parties and pictures to go to, to say nothing of the rides on jiggers out into the country.'[46] Other eating establishments provided new options. Railways apprentices and trainee nurses enjoyed the 'bohemian atmosphere' in Auckland's two Chinese cafés, where they were given a welcome respite from hostel tucker.[47]

Geographies of food and drink changed as the image of the teenager consolidated. The first in-betweeners, including the Dunedin schoolboys who frequented Watson's Dining Rooms during the 1870s and Harrold Ennor's friends who sat around Gisborne's tearooms in 1907, occupied the predominantly adult spaces of the cafés with little claim on the territory. The milk bars changed all that. These first appeared during the 1920s and offered patrons ice-creams, tea, coffee, pies and doughnuts.[48] Over the following thirty years, as they refined their appeal, teenagers made them more their own. The milk bar's neon street sign announced its modernity, its booths were ideal for intimate socialising and jukeboxes added to the atmosphere during the war. Popular American literature portrayed the pleasures of the 'soda shop', the milk bar's US equivalent. The comic book series *Archie* debuted in 1942, and young New Zealanders read about the everyday dramas of a group of friends – Jughead, Archie, Betty and Veronica – who whiled away their spare time at a soda joint called the Chocklit Shop in the fictional town

Photographs of New Zealand's milk bars are almost always devoid of patrons, and this, the Sunshine Milk Bar in Wellington, is no exception. The 1940s booth-type seating and the soda fountain were fundamental to milk-bar architecture; there appears to be no jukebox but the 'alcove' at the back was no doubt popular with teenagers. The menu at the end of the counter features strawberries and ice-cream, fruit salad and sundaes – along with baked beans, spaghetti and Bovril on toast.

of Riverdale.[49] Like their northern hemisphere counterparts, New Zealanders began to associate the milk bar with teenage culture.

As the 1940s drew to a close, respectable adults regarded the milk bar as a place for 'delinquent' youths rather than the 'kinder, gentler, *nicer*' type of milkshake-loving teenager.[50] In both America and New Zealand, the milk bar's image became sullied by the taint of juvenile delinquency. One study of Auckland delinquents blamed the pleasures of urban life for loose behaviour and told of 'petty thieving, malingering, and frequent loitering around milk bars'.[51] These concerns reflected teenagers' adoption of these establishments as their own. A growing critical mass of milk-bar aficionados – some of them at least – were no longer content to blend in and focus on their ice-creams.

Milk bars were not the only symbols of progress and pleasure in the post-Depression years, and teenage modernity took a particularly fast and mechanical turn. Speedways sprang up in the larger centres. Thirteen-year-old Len Gale and his thrill-seeker brothers spent countless happy hours at Auckland's Western Springs: 'Another world, fumes, noise and thrills! We were drawn to the pits between the races to see our heroes and to soak up the whole man machine atmosphere. The smell of hot oil and fuel was exciting. Mechanics would be adjusting the engines of the midget cars and motorbikes. The drivers in their leathers, looking very important and drinking beer straight from the bottle.'[52] Len described the feeling when the Hell Drivers visited from America: 'we were drawn to the Speedway like iron filings to a magnet'.[53] Down at the speedway, a circuit of commercialised thrills, the drivers became celebrities.

Automobiles also represented speed. Few New Zealand teens had access to cars during the thirties and forties, either their own or their parents', but still they could dream. Girls and boys slipped coins into milk bars' jukeboxes and listened, enthralled, as Nat King Cole extolled the pleasures of the road trip: 'If you ever plan to motor west / Travel my way, take the highway that is best. Get your kicks on Route 66.'[54] An impatient few took matters into their own hands: a new kind of 'youth gang' specialised in stealing cars from city streets. The cleverest thieves disguised their pilfering with stolen number plates and evaded arrest for months.[55] Still, neither the car nor the motorbike was the ultimate symbol in this new age of speed; the flying machine took that honour. Shirley Albiston wrote with awe about the slick, stainless steel Lockheed Electra, 'a huge aeroplane which nearly deafens you every time it lands', that carried ten passengers on the route between Auckland and Wellington. 'And so the march of science goes on.'[56] In 1938 Shirley and her workmates watched an air show from the windows of another modern emblem, Wellington's nine-storey Hope Gibbons Building, practically a skyscraper in its day. 'Gordon, the boy in the office, was so thrilled about it all the week', Shirley jotted in her diary. 'In the end he was counting the hours to when it was to begin.'[57]

Many youthful diversions drew heavily upon technology and gadgets, 'the marvellous inventions of science', as one historian describes them.[58] David Wildey popped in to the Christchurch Industries Fair one drizzly winter's evening in 1940 and his shilling bought a round on the Ferris wheel.[59] The same year, the rides at

OPPOSITE Speedway was the sensation of the 1930s, hugely popular with teenage audiences. Its stars included Fay Taylour, a visitor from Ireland and one of the few women to race competitively, and New Zealander Charlie Spinks. Professional photographers posed the riders as though they were movie stars, and no doubt many fans saw them that way.

A quiet afternoon at the fun fair, the roller coaster ready for action once this pair have paid their admission.

the Centennial Exhibition in Wellington – the Cyclone roller coaster, the dodgems and the Octopus – attracted some 2.9 million passengers. New Zealand's total population was only 1.6 million at the time.⁶⁰ Amusement arcades, the forerunners of the 1980s 'spacies parlours', grew in popularity too. Chock-full of fortune-telling machines and photoscopes (a kind of coin-operated peep show), they provided table football, roulette, and games with exotic-sounding monikers such as Bally Roll, Bally Racer, Magic Ball and Master Brain.⁶¹ Shooting galleries catered for trigger-happy teenagers.

Back at home, the quieter hobbies of Meccano and radio-listening became popular. Thirteen-year-old Cantabrian Burton Collins and his brother Noel, both members of the local Meccano club, made 'a horizontal oscillating type steam engine', a steam lorry and a range of other mechanical gadgets; *Meccano Magazine* provided the inspiration.⁶² The government set up the National Broadcasting Service in 1936 and radio stations proliferated. They aired serials with titles like *Soldier of Fortune*, *The Mystery Club* and *Ghosts of the Tower* that eager listeners enjoyed each week. The electronically minded also made their own radio receivers from sockets, valves and terminals they had bought or scrounged. A few boys earned Scout badges in recognition of their skills.[63]

Meccano Magazine, Burton Collins' favourite, was an example of the increasingly specialised world of print media. While young New Zealanders continued to read the *Auckland Weekly News*, the *Truth* and other mass-circulation newspapers aimed at an adult readership, a new range of overseas magazines – especially those from the US – catered more specifically to their particular interests. The American title *Seventeen*, aimed directly at adolescent girls, first went on sale in 1944 and quickly became popular here. It covered such topics as work and shopping, and columnists provided advice to the lovelorn. *Seventeen*, like *Archie*, is still in production today: these two print culture threads connect twenty-first century teenagers to their wartime predecessors.

While *Seventeen*'s style tips and *Archie*'s soda shop pals proved innocuous, the characters in many comics and 'pulp' paperbacks were much less virtuous. These latter-day 'penny dreadfuls' poured into New Zealand by the boatload during the Second World War. They portrayed 'a world of sin and sex and drugs

The bicycle race was a feature of a speed-filled life: these lads competed for trophies in the Nelson area some time during the 1940s.

and booze', as American cultural theorist Susan Stryker puts it, catering to barely acknowledged fantasies of fulfillment, betrayal, passion and violence.[64] New Zealand newspapers attacked these new competitors and fuelled a pious anti-pulp crusade. In 1937 *Truth* declared that '30,000 copies of magazine filth pollute New Zealand', many of them advertising contraceptives to their young readers.[65] *Korero*, a magazine printed for the armed forces during the war, described comics as 'hypodermic injections of sex and murder' that pushed their way into adolescents' consciousness as easily as a needle slid into an arm.[66] Such proclamations told of an intensifying transcontinental panic. In Australia, Britain, Canada and the US, morally minded adults blamed comics for corrupting innocents and threatening family life.[67]

Hollywood and the Scrapbook Self

The magazines and comics that addressed teenagers as a distinctive social group were far from the only American influence during this period. Clothing retailers adopted American sales techniques during the 1940s, a time of generous minimum wages, a growing demand for workers and high disposable incomes.[68] Advertisers of the 1920s had begun to target adolescent girls as a market for particular products, but the connections between young people and shopping intensified in the decades that followed. Department stores and boutiques began to address the 'teen-ager and modern miss' as consumers.[69] In 1941 Shirley Albiston and a friend visited Zummees, a Wellington clothes shop. They were mesmerised by 'a vociferous sales girl with red hair and tangerine lipstick' who insisted that each dress the friends looked at 'was more perfect than the last. It seemed absolutely impossible to stop trying them on.' The shop girl 'was unconsciously a perfect proponent of the American system of "third degree"', Shirley concluded. 'When we escaped it was twelve o'clock.'[70] Even though clothes were rationed during the war, Zummees had plenty for sale – and teens were keen to shop. Young New Zealanders' enthusiasm for consuming quickly picked up pace during the late 1940s as rationing receded.

Just as it had been during the 1920s, the cinema was the most influential vehicle of American popular culture. Chapter 3 chronicled the rise of 'the flicks' but the industry reached a new level of sophistication after 1930. The loquacious 'talkies' replaced the occasional on-screen 'Damn! and 'Kapow!' with actors' real voices. From 1935 a few films – including the famous *Gone With the Wind* – appeared in vivid Technicolor.[71] A whole new genre arrived too: the early teen film in which young stars rehearsed the ins and outs of adolescent life. Mickey Rooney played Andy Hardy, the all-American boy from a 'typical American family', and Judy Garland was girl-next-door Betsy Booth.[72] This duo starred in over a dozen films that told of romantic entanglements, unforeseen circumstances and teenage embarrassments. Teenagers all around New Zealand saw aspects of their own lives reflected on the silver screen. The Andy Hardy films were not confined to the cities: one road show took them to the small settlements of Banks Peninsula and the tiny towns of Central Otago.

The currents of American youth culture did more than scoop up our teenagers in their slip-stream: antipodeans actively sought out the pleasures of the cinema. By the 1940s New Zealand had twice the number of seats to patrons as the movie-mad United States.[73] Shirley Albiston wandered through Wellington and described the sparkle of the city's movie wonderland. 'When I went down into the town the coloured lights outside the picture shows were sparkling and glancing on and off. And there were young girls without hats, laughing and leaning on the arms of tall boys.'[74] Inside the theatre, darkened rows of seats provided an ideal setting for these giggling teenagers' courtships.[75] Whether or not they engaged in their own romantic liaisons, movie-goers immersed themselves in the glamour and escapism of Hollywood. Thirteen-year-old Jean McLeod grew up on a farm station north of Masterton alongside her brother, sister, parents and several farm workers, and she took to the pictures with a passion. The lucky family had a car to whisk Jean and the others from Mt Bruce to Masterton, a distance of about eight miles, and they saw every film on offer at the Regent. Jean adored Olivia de Havilland and Merle Oberon, and fell in love with the suave Robert Taylor.[76]

The movie industry went into hyperdrive during the 1930s. Fan cultures grew like topsy and teenage adoration reached new heights.[77] June Hill and her Hamilton friends swooned over male stars at the local cinema ('isn't he gorgeous?') before writing away to the film studios for pin ups. 'We'd get a big poster back with something written along the bottom, and we used to swap them.'[78] New Zealand teenagers – especially girls – avidly collected the new

movie magazines that flooded an eager market. Jean McLeod bought copies of *Screenland*, *Movie Mirror*, *Modern Screen*, *Screen Romances*, *Hollywood*, *Photoplay* and *Motion Picture Magazine* from the bookshops in Masterton and compiled scrapbooks with the images. Her brother Nev and sister Norn donated pictures of Jean's cherished stars, and Jean and Norn cut out 'Grace Moore, Norn's latest "pash"'.[79] Jean's scissors knew no conscience. 'I cut out pictures of Lady Alice & any other I fancied. I cut them from Jack's *Daily Mirrors*.' She showed Jack, the rabbiter on the family farm, what she had excised from his newspapers and all he said was 'Um'.[80]

Jean's barely under-control hobby told of teenage lives increasingly influenced by the popular media and a growing belief that leisure and consumption provided a pathway to self-fulfillment. Advertisers and the movie industry actively promulgated this therapeutic ethos: the pleasures of popular media, they insisted, compensated for the monotony of daily life.[81] Commercialised leisure also provided the context for the 'scrapbook self', to coin a phrase. Growing numbers of teenagers selected, sorted and displayed media representations in order to assemble a media-savvy identity. Sometimes they decorated the space around them. A wall covered in movie star cut-outs became a staple of the teenage bedroom, and there were variations on the theme. Nev McLeod, Jean's brother, turned the walls of his bedroom into an art gallery. He took most of his pictures – scenery, mainly – from the *Auckland Weekly News*, and his sisters Jean and Norn kept an eye out for other photos he might like. Jean overheard him murmuring 'impressive' as he pinned up the pictures that passed muster.[82] Nev, like Jean and her friends, fashioned himself as an arbiter of style and taste.

Teenagers also decorated their own bodies. Many tried on clothes and make-up in order to imitate their heroines. Jean McLeod and her friends smeared blackberry juice on their cheeks to impersonate movie stars, but they abandoned the experiment when the teacher 'said he didn't approve of rouge in school'.[83] Their scrapbooking took place in a distinctive early-teenage way. These thirteen-year-old girls experimented with adult styles, well aware that they were only imitating womanhood: blackberry juice was not real make-up. Three days later they made another attempt: 'Phyllis brought powder & a puff and we played at make-up saloons. I was Madame Marina and Phyllis was Dame Loretta.'[84] Jean wanted more. At home, with the help of the family's maid, she first tried on

OPPOSITE On the bleachers at a swimming pool somewhere in the South Island, with the necessary props: cigarettes, a camera case and clothes set aside for later.

American Slang

Most nineteenth- and early-twentieth-century slang was British in origin. Many such informal terms retained their currency through the 1930s and 1940s, and some evolved over time. 'Swot', for instance, meant 'to study' in 1880, and by the 1930s the adjective 'swotty' meant 'nerdy', as we would say now. Teenagers often applied it, with mild derision, to one another. Secondary schools generated their own language, and terms like 'new bug' (a third former) and 'day bug' (a day pupil) became widespread. American popular culture also had a huge impact on young New Zealanders' slang after 1930. Teenagers headed to 'the pictures' (pronounced 'pitchers') where they 'went nuts' for the 'movie stars' and the 'heart throbs' of Hollywood.

They took up movie slang with alacrity. 'Gee', 'yeah', 'super' and 'lousy' are examples from the 1930s. No doubt teenagers also learned the words banned by the censors during the following decade: 'broad' (when applied to a woman), 'tomcat' (when applied to a man), 'goose' (when used 'in a vulgar sense'), 'punk', 'stick 'em up' and 'shag'.[85] 'Big knuckle' and 'rumble', two synonyms for fighting, also had cinematic origins. When a gang member left his gang for a respectable life, he 'turned square' or became 'a proper square'. Less contentiously, 'cool', 'groovy', 'hip' and 'man' (as in 'yeah man'), and jazz-culture combinations like 'hip cat', took hold during the 1950s.[86]

The syntax of slang evokes young people's experience. 'Had tea at Slyfields. Dick showed us his motor-bike while the others were at church. Corker', Burton Collins jotted in his diary in 1930.[87] 'Nothing exciting has happened this week', schoolgirl Lizzy Page wrote to her parents during the 1940s. 'We didn't go to the flicks after all, and the dance was off, but we flossied ourselves up and jazzed off to the College sports yesterday afternoon.'[88]

Some words have all but disappeared: few disagreeable people are now referred to as 'stink bombs', and nobody uses the verb 'smooge' to describe kissing and cuddling any more. Still, some terms have their newer equivalents. In 1936, Jean McLeod's mother ordered her to strip her bed and Jean refused. 'Bake me!', she exclaimed, as if to say 'So what, I don't care!' Her twenty-first-century counterpart would probably say 'Bite me!' Language, as much as clothing styles, school routines and leisure time, encodes the meanings of youth.

OPPOSITE The motorbike was an increasingly popular mode of transport among older male teens, but riders met their share of misfortune. Eighteen-year-old Aucklander John Marsh wrote to his parents about a mishap, and he revealed some of the slang of the 1930s. 'On Wednesday night I was going round to Laurie's for my togs, when I had a real good smash. I was about 300 yards from Laurie's when a Maori named Dave Wade & his brother ran into me with an old Essex car. I was well on my right side of the road, and was almost stopped to let them pass, but they never saw me until they were right on me & hit me with their right hand mudguard striking me sort of a glancing blow & me & the bike just fell in the road just about where we were hit. Just now I've a stiff knee & a small cut on my leg, a few beautiful bruises on my legs & on my head but otherwise wasn't hurt. But the bike!! Gee it's well smashed.'

Music at home continued its popularity well into the twentieth century. On 7 July 1933, Dot Marsh (fourteen) and her brothers John (seventeen) and Doug (nineteen) are the 'Down and Outs', playing with family friends.

lipstick: 'Liked it!'[89] Few of those inspired by movieland's feminine style had a maid to assist with their cosmetics, but Dunedin's factory girls imitated Joan Crawford, with her 'sort of square mouth', and flattened their hair as a tribute. 'I've never had straight hair', one of them later recalled; 'I remember once I was trying to flatten it down, trying to not look in the mirror. Oh dear oh dear. It was a ghastly sight.'[90]

As Nev McLeod's interior decorating reveals, popular culture provided scrapbook fodder for boys as well as girls. Not always was the look a success. 'Oh, he's been going to too many moving pictures', Beatrice McCahon dismissively wrote of Edgar, a lad with whom she had an on-again, off-again friendship in Dunedin.

'He sounded so conventional & hackneyed all the time, dotting his remarks with "Hells" & "Gods" that I wanted to laugh at him.'[91] While Edgar's attempts to refashion himself fell flat, speedway fans, even those without a motorbike, modelled themselves on the stars of the race track. Len Gale and his brothers 'became interested in speed, human speed. My brother Jim was the best runner so we decided to train him for the school sports.'[92]

The scrapbook self revealed social distinctions at the same time that it reflected teenage creativity. Beatrice McCahon laughed at Edgar's attempt to present himself as worldly and sophisticated, while young Jim Gale wanted to beat other runners and prove his superior ability as a hybrid boy-machine. Other technologies spawned different social divisions. When boys wrote to the radio stations to request rollicking swing hits like Tommy Dorsey's 'Well, Git It' and other 'hot' tracks, they crafted an image of themselves as modern lads who knew a good thing when they heard it. These boys distanced themselves from the staid world of their parents and their own conservatively minded contemporaries.[93] The new teen self emerged at the intersection of technology, pleasure and the influence of the commercial world.

Romantic Longings

The fantasies promulgated by movie-makers seeped into everyday life. Not content just to watch on-screen romances, many teenagers sought out a rollicking passion of their own. Like an antipodean Andy Hardy, Burton Collins longed for a female companion his own age. The earnestly religious fifteen-year-old searched for a quiet Christian girl with a good singing voice, an interest in reading and a proficiency at domestic duties. 'Somehow I feel dis-satisfied & long for a girl-friend who understands', Burton told his diary.[94] He made little progress in the search for a devout domestic companion, and three years later he still wallowed in self-pity: 'this isolation & solo love is no good. I'm tired of being alone.'[95] By the end of 1936, now aged nineteen, Burton began to write more explicitly. His religiosity had waned and he no longer felt guilty about listing what he wanted: a girlfriend 'with a good figure which she would let me see & feel'.[96] He had no luck there either.

TEENAGERS

A teenager is presented at a debutante ball, Oamaru, 1940s. For decades girls took part in civic events where they 'came out' into adult society at the age of eighteen or nineteen, 'presented' by a male companion. Down the road in Dunedin, Doris Carne's brother presented her to the Bishop. 'There was much rivalry about gowns, hairdos, bouquets. You had to have a special white dress and a bouquet of flowers. And have your hair done at the hairdresser which didn't in those days happen often, unless you were getting married or something really special.'

The American practice of dating emerged during the 1920s and became widespread during the 1930s. This differed from, but did not entirely displace, the older practice whereby boys gave their attention to one girl at a time. Dates took place unchaperoned, in a public place like a cinema or milk bar and sometimes as a part of a group. This move away from adult surveillance afforded a greater degree of privacy than ever before, even, ironically enough, in public. Those who dated a lot accrued social status.[97] Burton Collins wasted no time embracing the zeitgeist. Through the winter of 1936 he managed a dizzying array of outings with Daphne, Jean, Ngaire, Betty, Marjorie, Pat and Helen, and he tabulated the details

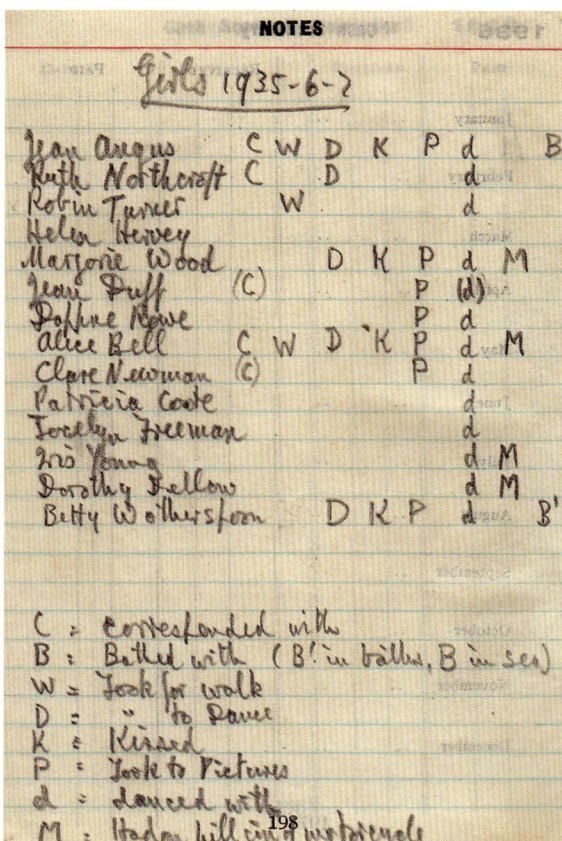

Burton Collins' table, 'Girls 1935-6-7'. In the best list-keeping tradition of the diary, the lad meticulously documented his social activities with the teenaged girls of Christchurch, and he provided a translation of the table's fine-grained coding at the bottom of the page. 'Took to a dance' was not the same as 'danced with'; bathing could be done at the pool (B') or in the sea (B). A lucky few had a ride on the pillion of Burton's motorcycle (M).

at the back of his diary: 'took for walk', 'took to dance', 'took to pictures', 'kissed'. Not every girl embraced Burton's charms. Margaret refused an invitation to Popeye's Party – an event named after the cartoon sailor, no doubt – and Burton noted how he felt: 'Boo Hoo.'[98] He rapidly 'lost his passion' (as he put it) for Helen and Jean, and decided Betty wasn't for him. Then there was Alice: 'she is in love with me & I don't like her!'[99] Dating was a two-way street, and girls were just as likely to express their reservations before ditching boys who proved unsatisfactory. Burton took Marjorie to a dance and then to a debate at Canterbury University's Dialectic Society, there was a chat 'at her gate & 1st kiss!', but Marjorie

A group photographed at a dance in the Auckland region. Shyness, contentment and diffidence all appear on the faces of these teens. The dance could be a place of judgement and dissatisfaction as well as entertainment. In a letter to her parents, Christchurch schoolgirl Lizzy Page described one occasion when St Margaret's College held a dance with a nearby boys' school: 'I had a horrid little partner with smelly red hair till about half past eight. I asked him if he knew any other girls there, but he didn't seem to take the hint. I wouldn't talk to him and threw him off in the end. About two or three dances before supper I got a partner who didn't have smelly hair, and who could dance, and didn't come up to my shoulder.' After supper, she continued, 'we had a moonlight dance. The horrible little twerp with red hair wanted to, but I told him it was reserved.'

would not go out with Burton again. She told him he was too self-absorbed and didn't 'consider other people'.[100]

Dating also reflected the increasing importance of high school cultures. In 1936 the government made fifth-, sixth- and seventh-form education free, and in 1944 the leaving age rose to fifteen. Enrolments continued to increase: 40 percent of fifteen-year-olds attended secondary schools in 1939, and ten years later 60 percent did.[101] Teenage experiences differed from school to school. Daytime social mixing between girls and boys proved difficult for those enrolled in a single-sex boarding school, although sports days and dances allowed some mingling. One evening, at a dance with the lads from a Christchurch boys' school, St Margaret's pupil Lizzy Page 'had most of the dances with the same

Single-sex and Co-ed Schools

'Swot, swot, swot, that's what I should be doing but I don't', wrote thirteen-year-old Burton Collins at exam time in 1930.[102] Either his guilt got the better of him or he exaggerated his lack of enthusiasm, for several years later he became Dux of Christchurch Boys' High School. Burton belonged to the school astronomy club, the camera club and the lifesaving team; he was a monitor, librarian, platoon commander and a frequent visitor to the nearby pie cart. Most of Burton's activities would be familiar to recent generations of intellectually minded schoolboys.

Diaries, letters and school magazines tell of a range of school cultures. Lizzy Page, a boarder, enjoyed school even though she missed her parents. 'Please don't ring me up for my birthday because I know I'd cry or do something silly', she wrote in one of her many letters home.[103] She and her friends shared their 'woes and secrets', did their hair, and spent bored afternoons 'snapping and biting at each other'.[104] Teachers at St Margaret's fostered cordial relationships with their pupils. The house mistresses loaned a sympathetic ear and played dance records with the girls at night.

Boys' boarding schools could be less hospitable.[105] Rolls grew, an increasingly militaristic attitude took hold and teaching staff lost the easygoing attitude of earlier years.[106] A third former at Nelson College, Bryan Helm told his father about his many thrashings for laughing in 'prep', submitting late homework and forgetting his French verbs.[107] Senior boys joined the teachers in dishing out punishments. Bryan 'got a hiding with a pingpong bat which broke, from a prefect, for not learning the

Pupils from Tokomaru Bay School at Wellington Zoo during a trip to the capital. Having won a waiata contest on the East Coast, the pupils came to Wellington to sing for the Broadcasting Service.

A science lab at Nelson College for Girls.

College Song', and the Head Boy lashed him for 'fooling at the dinner table'.[108] He scored his belt for each beating and wrote home to ask about protocol. 'On Thursday night I got three with a sand-shoe from Hazelwood, who is head of the boarders, and am not sure whether to nitch my belt, can you advise?'[109]

Stand-alone high schools became more common during the thirties and forties. Some were recent incarnations of the technical schools. Others, including the one in Whakatane, evolved out of the district high schools. Yearbooks tell of Whakatane pupils' sporting prowess, school trips and messing about: 'it is a little distracting when a prominent member of the Sixth who, upon entering the room and slamming the door, proceeds by fox-trotting half-way across the room. After completing the distance to her desk with a rhumbah, she exclaims in a loud voice, to her co-magpies: "The French [test] was just corking. They were dinky little questions, weren't they girls?"'[110]

The Brylcreem era arrived along with the war, and boys fussed over their appearance. One, 'a beautiful boy who has won world-wide renown as the laziest boy at school, spends half an hour before the mirror each morning arranging his locks in sweeps and swirls with the aid of curling pins, tongs, brush and comb, water, hair oil, and his two young sisters'.[111] Boys acquired gaudy ties and 'evil-smelling hair oil' for weeks before the annual school dance.[112] Hair turned up in a fourth former's poem too:

There's Pauline, our shorty, who blushes very red,
And Leith whose face is always being fed,
There's Maureen whose hair is long down her back,

And Jackie and Kitty whose tongues never slack.
Here too is Valerie – angelic thing –
Just tap her head and it may ring.
Last there's Barbara, a studious soul,
And Lorna P – whose head is never whole.

Johnny T – is very smart.
Trying to break the ladies' hearts.
Then there's Townie – always witty –
Although he's not the least bit pretty.
David's hair is always slick,
Because the oil he uses is very thick.
And last of all is bashful Roy,
Who's always looking very coy.[113]

David, mentioned in the poem above, was a trend-setter, a fact unappreciated by his school mates. Still, he tapped into a longer history of boys caring for their appearance: the masher and the cissy boy were his stylistic ancestors.

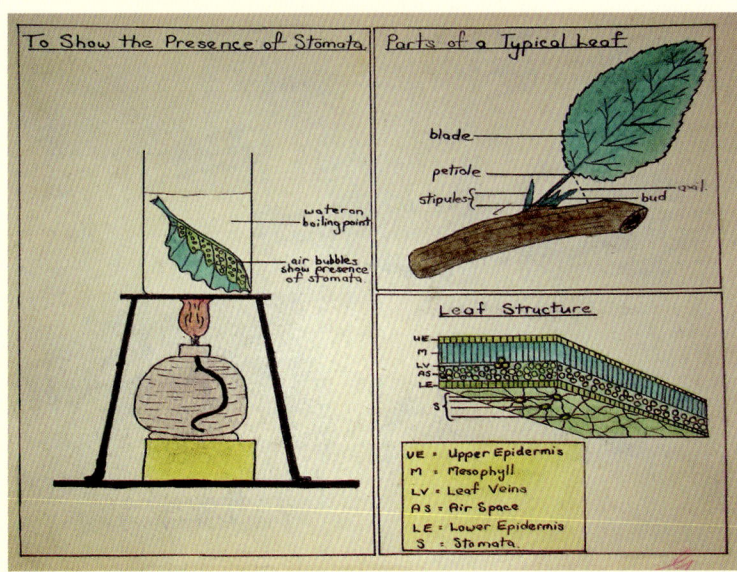

This page of a science exercise book, with its images of a type familiar to generations of pupils, is the creation of Arthur Stoddart from Owaka District High School.

A Yugoslav Society Kolo group, Auckland, 1948. Most dancers were in their late teens. One remembers: 'We practised twice a week and it was very physically demanding. The climax of all the practices was our performance at the annual Yugoslav ball.'

boy' and spent the next day 'being nearly teased to death'.[114] On another occasion, out watching a play, she wrote breathlessly: 'I saw our friend Diana Maunsell, complete with hair, lipstick, boyfriend.'[115]

Girls in day schools had more free time than those who boarded. Shirley Albiston's diaries show her Wellington East Girls' College friends making the most of their evenings and weekends. Shirley wrote about the amorous adventures of Rena and her 'special boyfriend' Ross, 'whom we call for no special reason Bottlebrush'; Valerie's boyfriend John Irvine who had eye lashes like 'willows overshadowing rippling brooks'; and a boy from Stratford who sat chatting with June in the gutter outside Valerie's house. Shirley greeted the news of the latter with morbid fascination: she thought it less than proper to talk to a beau in the gutter, even though 'June was having the time of her life.'[116] Some lads arrived from even further afield. 'Last week a sailor-boy quite captivated the heart of Bella, a French one too', Shirley wrote in her diary. 'Now alas he has gone away and Bella is alone until the next ship comes in. Meanwhile she consoles herself by composing letters in French to him.'[117] Cultures of mixed-gender leisure, which slowly developed after the First World War, rapidly expanded and now took hold in a range of urban spaces. Bella might have made the acquaintance of her French amour almost anywhere: in the street, at the movies or on the wharves.

The movie theatre, milk bar and footpath were not the only places with romantic potential. Transport played an important role too. The tramway and railway systems reached their zenith during the 1930s and 1940s, and they provided platforms for public flirting. Sometimes the authorities tried to pre-empt such fraternising. School trains on the Nelson line had separate carriages for boys and girls, and young travellers had to be content to wave at one another out the window when the train went around a bend.[118] Trams, though, became portable display stands on which teenagers appraised one another. When Valerie persuaded Shirley Albiston to catch the same tram she caught with her beau John, Shirley approached the situation with a degree of annoyance. 'Really of course she wanted to show him off. When we at last boarded the tram, Valerie sat in the corner, and made me get out of the way so that she could see him – so that he could see her of course – and then began to blush, so that she looked like a conceited little ass.'[119] Three months after Valerie put John on display, she lied to her parents, met John 'at the tram stop at a quarter to eight' and rode off to the movies on an evening date. Shirley could see the appeal of a mobile love affair, even though she thought John 'a most uncouth looking creature'.[120] 'Valerie tells us that she knows she should not do it but she could not bear to refuse him', Shirley wrote in her diary, 'it's so clandestine, and oh so romantic.'[121] The tram provided a stage in a teenage play and Valerie performed a heady mix of display, secrecy and defiance.

Boats were also platforms for a drama, especially in Auckland. Several teens set out one day in 1941, and one later told the story: 'Stan had promised us a trip to Waiheke on his 24-foot Mullet boat. This we were eager to do. Camping gear was transferred to the yacht, and more food bought to go with a dozen beers. The trip coincided with leave our girl friends had from the hospital. It was a crowded yacht that set out from Matiatia. We had heard about the dances and sizzling hula demonstrations at Oneroa.'[122] The emboldened party engineered a scene:

> And so it was that a dare was proposed. Yes! Jean would do it! There was some debate about where she would stand and for how long – but it was agreed. Under fore sail the gaff rigged yacht ghosted into Matiatia. The ferry had not long docked; yachts were at their moorings. People were boarding buses and a few cars. There, shock horror, one of the girls was bare from the waist up! Fellow yachties cheered, old men gaped; children were enclosed in summer dresses lest their innocent eyes witness such depravity. The bay was in turmoil.[123]

Valerie's defiance on Wellington's trams had nothing on Jean's public breast-baring. These teenage Aucklanders fizzed at adults' instant reactions and revelled in the commotion. Jean's unruly display did not come from nowhere, though; it was the latest in a long line of slow disrobings. The corset loosened its grip after 1900, hemlines rose during the 1910s, and young beachgoers bared their arms and legs after the First World War. In-betweeners' clothes were more than adornments: they signified self-expression and social change. Jean's assertion of a young woman's freedom extended the long and complicated history of the adolescent body by pushing the boundaries even further.

Valerie's and Jean's adventures raise broader questions about teenage autonomy. Those who showed off on trains, trams and boats asserted their independence for all to see, but not everything had changed. Parents still regulated aspects of teenage lives; Valerie confirmed as much when she sneaked out of an evening and met John at the tram stop. Even though unsupervised dating had grown in popularity, chaperonage was not quite dead. Adults and older siblings maintained varying degrees of oversight. Brothers watched over younger sisters at dances and parents continued to impose constraints when romances got too serious. Mothers and fathers who disapproved of a relationship sometimes piled on the pressure until it broke down, while others intervened directly.[124] Parents also called the shots when it came to marriage prospects, much as their nineteenth-century predecessors had done. Rotorua lass Witarina Mitchell was instructed to 'cut' several boyfriends after her mother exclaimed 'Over my dead body!'[125] Others succumbed to arguments about religious compatibility and abandoned a relationship when parents ruled out a future mixed marriage.[126] Modes of dating, commercial entertainments and young people's clothes had all changed since the late nineteenth century, but still parents kept a close eye on the liaisons of their offspring.

Pashes, Physicians and Policemen

One of Doris Carne's brothers usually watched over her when she attended church dances. In his role of MC he glanced in Doris's direction now and then. 'I wasn't able to get up to any nonsense there!', she said. 'They had me fenced in, I tell you.' But soon something happened to lessen her family's concern: Doris made friends with a young gay chap by the name of Harold. 'Whenever he needed a female on his arm, I was the one! We even danced on the stage at the Town Hall together, a demonstration of ballroom dancing. And when I was young I always felt very safe with him.'[127] Doris and Harold roamed the streets and dance halls of Dunedin, and Doris's brothers stayed out of the way. Doris's parents knew Harold and trusted him. This friendship opened new doors at a time when few New Zealanders openly discussed the topic of homosexuality – but Doris's parents sensed Harold's secret: 'I think my mother was quite happy because she might've known more than I did!'[128] Doris' and Harold's story hints that changing ideas about same-sex relationships accompanied the new patterns of dating and mixed-gender socialising. Some parents, including Doris's, regarded a gay friend as a reliable consort and a safe pair of hands.

Attachments between girls and among boys also took a range of forms during these decades. The 'smash' or 'pash' had emerged in the dormitories and classrooms of girls' schools in Western Europe and North America during the nineteenth century, survived the weakening of gender-segregated cultures and became noticeably apparent in New Zealand during the 1930s.[129] At Wellington East Girls' College, Shirley Albiston's friend Nancy 'was very thrilled' when she realised that Olga, a student from Russia, 'had such a "pash" on her'. Opposites attract, Shirley figured, with 'Olga so passionate and Nancy so reticent'.[130] Pashes could be fleeting, but sometimes they turned into a friendship of a more enduring kind. Shirley had her own intense attachment to Nancy: 'I have leant on her,

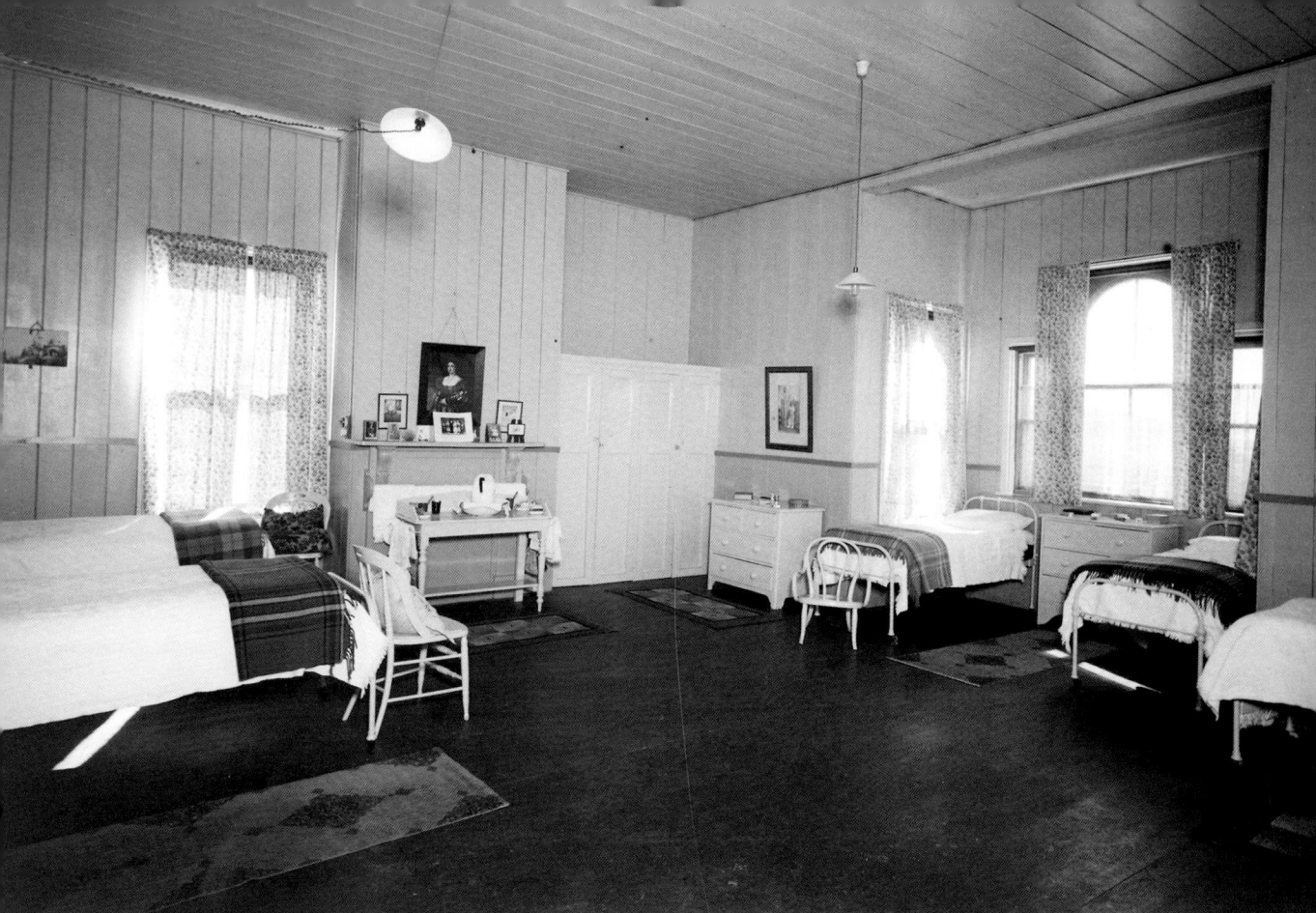

A dormitory for boarders at Nelson College for Girls.

all the time she has been a kind of protection for me from the outside world', Shirley confided in her diary. 'It was like creeping inside a good strong hollow tree during a storm – you know you are safe, the tree can never bend.'[131]

Girls also harboured 'pashes' for school staff. Shirley loved and worshipped Miss Gardiner, a thirty-something teacher with a 'sweet' demeanour, 'eyes such a lovely blue' and 'cheeks so pink'.[132] Only belatedly – nearly a year later – did she realise her teacher was 'an ordinary human being instead of a species of deity'.[133] This was not an exclusive pash, though: Shirley betrayed not the slightest trace of jealousy when Nancy and a girl named Paula also fell under the teacher's spell. Nor did the pash necessitate any long-standing gender commitment on the enthusiasts' part. Some girls, including Nancy who expressed an interest in a tall, handsome fellow named Ted, pashed on teachers while also desiring boys. Shirley, though, did not fit this particular mould. She professed no interest in boys and had nothing good to say about those she met along the way: not only did she think Valerie's John 'uncouth' but she declared that Colin, Valerie's previous beau, looked 'like a cabbage'.[134] In later adolescence Shirley airily reported: 'I have so much to occupy my time, there is no room to think about boys.'[135]

A popular psychology of youthful sexuality appeared in the local newspapers during the 1920s and maintained its influence through the thirties and forties.[136] The English physician Havelock Ellis suggested that girls pass through a 'homosexual phase' on their way to heterosexuality. 'In its varying aspects of differing intensity all the gradations of sexual sentiment may be expressed', Ellis wrote about attachments like the pash.[137] New Zealand's journalists, doctors and youth workers disseminated Ellis's views. In 1929 Dr Jessie Scott told a Christchurch audience that intense female friendships reflected the existence of a 'homo-sexual period'.[138] Thirteen years later, in 1942, a YWCA guidebook instructed camp leaders to make sure their adolescent charges 'become heterosexual', although they did not say how.[139] Shirley echoed some of these ideas in her diary. She felt sure her 'childish adoration' for Miss Gardiner would die away as she got older, and instead she would become aware of 'the opposite sex': 'another growing menace', she called it.[140] There were other tantalising connections too. Ellis suggested 'female inverts', as he called lesbian women, possessed male souls, and once again Shirley hinted at such an idea. 'Valerie White says that [a teacher] is neither feminine nor masculine', she wrote warily, 'which is rather horrid because it might insinuate anything.'[141] Did she also recognise herself in this description? We cannot know for sure. Shirley stopped writing diaries at the age of twenty-one, still unmoved by young men's charms.

The 'pash' was not limited to the lives of schoolgirls. David Wildey confessed a 'non-sexual' crush on a handsome, muscular gym instructor at the YMCA in Christchurch, and he developed an erotic attachment to a close male friend.[142] His reveries drove him to 'a frenzy of sexual desire . . . and frustration!'[143] David's crush and his erotically charged friendship, which involved a single messy episode of oral sex ('he shot all over my face and pillow') were closely related: unlike some other teenagers with same-sex crushes, David later came out as gay.[144]

David never had any trouble with the police, but the law's long arm grabbed other Christchurch boys by the scruff of the neck. Having previously focussed on cases involving adult men, by the 1940s police began paying attention to sex

David Wildey (*left*) and his friend Maurice on the beach at Sumner in 1939. David was eighteen at the time, Maurice twenty.

between boys. Four Christchurch lads, aged sixteen, seventeen and twenty-one, met at St Paul's Church in 1944. They paired off in private Papanui houses, took photos of one another, went to the pictures and kissed each other goodbye as they headed home on the trams.[145] Somehow a local detective became aware of the boys' fun and had them arrested, but their probation officer recommended leniency. Each lad hailed from a respectable family, he said, and he wanted to give them the opportunity to re-establish themselves 'in the eyes of the community'.[146] For some, the idea of the 'homosexual period' applied to boys as well as girls, and need not last a lifetime.[147] The existential benefits of this idea were two-fold. It exempted teenagers from the increasingly pathologised category of homosexuality while reinforcing the deepening division between adolescents' and adults' sexuality in an era when the concept of the teenager took shape. At the same time, the idea of a homosexual period required a new level of policing when it came to boys' behaviour. There was a risk the period might become permanent if precocious lads were not carefully monitored.

While these stories of regulation and control gesture towards the law's repressive potential, they also reveal the comings and goings of adolescents' intimate lives. Court files show us that homoerotically inclined boys found one another while sitting on the steps outside Auckland's Ferry Building, browsing Wellington's shops and loitering in Dunedin's Queens Gardens, and they went on to create their own circles of friends.[148] Two Oamaru boys – one eighteen, the other a little younger – started chatting in front of a shop on Wansbeck Street. They met again in the doorway of the Empire Hotel, went together to the Opera House,

Trevor Nunweek (*right*), aged about eighteen, and a friend. One of the defendants in the Papanui court case, Trevor worked in a glove factory and had enlisted in the Air Force before his arrest. Afterwards he fled to Australia but returned to move once again in queer Christchurch circles.

The Perils of Puberty

The physiological aspects of puberty caused annoyance and anxiety for a great many boys and girls in their teens. In 1883 Fred Gibbs threw tea dregs at his brother Dick who teased him about growing whiskers. Six years later domestic servant Gertie Brookes tried to find out about acne. 'I think I get uglier every day of my life', she wrote to her friend Ella Marsh; 'you know all those pimples I had on my face at home, well they have not all gone away yet. Mrs Baker asked a lady doctor the other week what caused them & if I could take something to make them go away & she said that nearly all young girls at my age had them.'[149]

Elizabeth Mason's friends were kept entirely in the dark about puberty during the 1920s. One said that 'when her pubic hair began to appear, her elder sisters  told her that they suffered from the same affliction and that it was a shameful peculiarity limited to the McGrath family and had to be kept secret. As for menstruation, that was another frightful disease which only the McGraths suffered from.'[150]

Menstruation was the most taboo issue of all. It is barely mentioned in nineteenth-century sources, even in the most private of diaries.[151] The veil of silence continued through the thirties and forties although a few magazines began to advertise menstrual pads and tampons. They did so with euphemistic references to freedom, comfort and fluffy cotton fillings.[152] Some girls knew nothing about periods and thought they were dying when they first saw blood. The mother of Wyndham lass Ailsa Dawson kept her daughter in the dark, and Ailsa had her first period while staying with family friends in another town. One of her hosts 'was so kind and cleaned me up and made me feel better and helped me understand that it was quite normal'. Back home she did not let on until she could conceal matters no longer. Her mother 'produced a pile of sewn flannelette cloths along with a belt and safety pins' and 'matter of factly told me to pull myself together as all girls had to put up with this'. Menstruation was strictly women's business. Ailsa 'had a great fear my brothers would find out, Mum made it quite clear they were not to know'.[153]

Sex education was offered haphazardly during the war years. Some commentators wanted sex instruction for school pupils and young factory workers, but few such classes took place. Instead, there were pamphlets with titles like *Young Manhood*, *Sex, Love and Marriage* and *Digest of Hygiene for Father and Son*.[154] These described the bodily changes of puberty and warned of the consequent perils.[155] In 1941 evangelical writer Mary Manse published under the pen-name 'Purity'. She suggested that masturbators had a pale, sickly appearance and a 'shamefaced look'.[156] Local magazines took a different tack by publicising newer psychological ideas: one suggested masturbation was often used as an 'emotional anaesthetic' or indicated a 'repressed' homosexuality or an unconscious 'resentment against being a girl'.[157] One way or another, the physiological effects of puberty still worried a great many adults.

A parasol (*opposite*) and the back seat of a bus (*above*) during the 1930s.

bought ice-creams, had supper at the pie cart and retired to the younger lad's house. 'On the way to his home I hugged him', the older one said and they later had sex in an out-building. 'The two of us then went into the house and I hugged and kissed him in the kitchen.' The relationship became semi-regular: 'I went to table-tennis with him on Monday night the 27/9/48, and later when I was leaving him at his home I kissed him at the door.'[158] Their string of dates was tragically cut short. One night, as the pair readied themselves to go to the theatre, a detective appeared as if from nowhere; the court records do not say how police learned about the relationship. Still, these boys' story conjures up the general spaces of teenage life in a medium-sized provincial town – streets, ice-cream stalls, pie carts and the table-tennis club – and show that outlawed attachments took shape on the same urban terrain as socially respectable ones.

War's Impacts

The Great Depression paved the way for the Second World War, an international crisis that further shaped the development of teenage culture. David Wildey was twenty-one in 1941 when the army called him up for service. He trained at Burnham camp near Christchurch and took part in 'route marches, afternoon and whole day manoeuvres, fatigues, lectures and leave' before joining the medical corps and sailing to New Caledonia to serve in a hospital there.[159] David's friend Maurice was drafted too, but his poor eyesight relegated him to domestic duties. Parliamentarians murmured about the fitness of New Zealand's youth, briefly reprising the eugenicist moment of the early 1900s, but they soon concluded that the vast body of young men, 'by their gallant conduct, have confounded their critics'.[160] Three decades of drill had paid off after all.

War put young people in unusual situations and tested them in ways not seen for a generation. In 1940 the military conscripted those over the age of nineteen and sent them overseas at twenty-one (or twenty, if their parents agreed). Like their progenitors during the First World War, some teens lied about their age in order to serve abroad. Others turned their hands to a range of tasks in New Zealand.[161] The state drafted eighteen-year-olds for home service. Jack Hutchison, 'a skinny barely 6½ stone pale faced child/man', had spent his early adolescent years reading military action stories and replaying famous battles in the backyard 'with sticks and saucepan lid hats and peaches or plums serving as grenades'.[162] He was eager to serve in battle and reported to Auckland's Rutland Street Drill Hall to join the Territorials. The prospect of war seemed 'euphoric and glorious' to many lads, like Jack, who had grown up in peacetime. Spurred along by a slew of books that romanticised battlefield horror for a new generation, they looked enviously upon the sacrifices of the First World War.[163]

By 1942 boys of sixteen or seventeen began to volunteer for the Home Guard.[164] Along with older men they patrolled the coastline to keep a lookout for Japanese attacks, but they were ill-prepared and sometimes afraid. 'Us young boys and old

Cadets, possibly members of the Air Training Corps. Established in 1941, this Corps trained boys between the ages of sixteen to eighteen who expressed an interest in the Air Force. Many then trod the path that led from ATC to Air Force.

Schools replicated military regimentation. Here is such a display at Nelson College, some time during the 1940s.

men were supposed to patrol the beach areas and live under canvas at the base of Paritutu', one later wrote of his time in Taranaki. 'It was real scary patrolling at night on Moturoa Beach and I was glad to have the company of three of four dogs.'[165]

Those still at school rehearsed their war-readiness. The youths in Wanganui Technical College's Air Training Corps practised small-bore rifle shooting and camped at Ohakea Air Force Station where they spent hours in physical training, lectures, marching ('square bashing') and target practice.[166] Some schools set up signalling corps too. A reluctant Waimate boy inherited 'a squad of third formers to lick into shape' and he made an unlikely Lance Corporal. 'On one famous occasion at manoeuvres I confused left and right and they marched right through another squad.'[167] This young chap developed a life-long hatred of militarism. While some young men embraced what they saw as an exciting, glorious departure from the routine of everyday life, others chafed against the discipline and jingoism.

Girls fared somewhat differently: the Second World War significantly expanded the horizons of many. Those aged over eighteen could volunteer for the Women's Royal New Zealand Naval Service (Wrens), the Women's Auxiliary Army Corps (WAAC) or the Women's Auxiliary Air Force (WAAF) to work as typists, cooks, clerks, signallers or telegraphists, but none in their teens saw overseas service: auxiliary members had to be older than twenty-three for that.[168] Younger girls had other options. Fifteen-year-old Valda Tyson joined the ANA (Army, Navy and Air Force) club in New Plymouth. The ANA hosted servicemen on leave, providing them with a tightly controlled environment in which they could socialise with carefully vetted female partners:

> Us girls were rostered to help in the kitchen. The purpose was to give the boys on leave somewhere to go for an evening meal and then there was dancing until 10pm when a bus would take the boys back to base. Well us teenage girls thought this was wonderful, as we never had to wash or dry the dishes, the boys were falling over themselves to get into the kitchen and put their hands into those huge sinks, and then of course they had partners for at least the first dance or two . . . We mostly had Airmen in New Plymouth as the base at Bell Block was a training station where the boys came for six months. Us girls had a wonderful time as we had a fresh batch of keen young men every few months.[169]

For Valda and many other teenagers, this particular form of applied housework also provided opportunities for fun: lots of boys met lots of girls. Valda was too young to realise her dream of joining the auxiliary forces, and the ANA was the closest she ever got to a life in uniform. Not every social opportunity drew upon traditional gendered ideals of domesticity, though, and the range of options for girls continued to grow. Valda surfed with other teens at Fitzroy Beach

Young WAACs, 1944.

Many girls continued to work in factories during the 1940s. These photographs document those in the Ross & Glendining clothing factory in Dunedin. *Clockwise from top left:* Working in the hatmaking department under the supervisor's eagle eye; the cutting-out table; machining handkerchiefs; the dining room, a facility provided in the better-provisioned factories. Two researchers suggested that Ross & Glendining's bootmakers 'wage a constant warfare with the forewoman', but the young hatmakers lacked their counterparts' 'bold brave spirits'. Still, they chatted and sang during their work, and on weekends went to the pictures together. These girls came to work on a Monday morning singing the latest from Bing Crosby, Gene Kelly and the rest.

and a local man convinced them to start a surf lifesaving club. 'I believe we were one of the first women's teams in New Zealand. The only facilities we had were two reels which we poked under a few sheets of iron nailed together, our blue woollen swim suits for competition and a standard for the march pasts. But we all trained and managed to get our surf medals and saved a few lives.'[170] Tradition alternated with new prospects, and the boundaries of female teenagehood continued expanding.

Exceptional circumstances forced two changes upon young women in the world of work: compulsion and new kinds of tasks. Industrial conscription ('manpowering') came into force in 1942, and eighteen- and nineteen-year-olds joined older women in production lines making ammunition, engineering components, battledress and footwear.[171] 'We'd work on a bench where we filled the tops of the bullets with lead', a Hamilton woman later told an interviewer. 'Then we'd lift heavy boxes with the parts of bullets and they went into big machines and through the hoppers and we made sure they didn't jam and that sort of thing. I enjoyed that, it was great.'[172] Other girls received letters drafting them into abattoirs and canneries, hotels and hospitals.[173] Manpowering radically reshaped career plans. One eighteen-year-old had her heart set on teaching, found herself working in a telephone exchange and the post office trained her in shorthand once the war was over. She never did stand in front of a class.[174] Young female conscripts approached the situation in different ways. Some girls resented the manpowering programme, especially when it sent them in directions not of their choosing. Others, though, relished their escape from jobs they hated. Happily for some, the war delivered the final blow to the drudgery of the servant: domestic service died, unlamented by generations of slaveys.[175]

Internal migrations continued their ebb and flow during the 1940s. Just as post-Depression cities drew young people in, the war sent some back out. Girls aged over seventeen could volunteer for the Women's Land Service – some 4,290 did – and they swapped their office clothes for overalls and gumboots. Their experiences varied widely. Some 'land girls' lived in rough whares and were treated like servants. Others escaped from the 'monotony' of 'the same old daily grind in office or shop' and enjoyed genial company.[176] Being a land girl could be an adventure. Townies gained confidence and new skills when they attempted tasks unlike anything they had known before. Ruth Atchison remembered her work on an isolated Taranaki farm at the age of eighteen:

> We land-girls skinned cattle and sheep, plucked dead sheep and often brought home wild pigs to eat. We had to tie them onto the saddles to bring them home, and the horses didn't appreciate it a bit! We often had to cut the throats of wild pigs when they attacked our dogs, and getting into the middle of those fights was full of danger ... We made one large paddock of hay and we hand-scythed that and

forked it on to the horse and sledge, and took it home to the homestead, tied on securely with ropes.[177]

Many women looked back fondly upon these adventuresome years. 'It was a great life and I learned so much. Looking back, I'm surprised at what I did do. I could never kill or pluck a dead sheep now.'[178]

The war laid bare incipient tensions in the gender order. Some women eagerly seized upon changing social norms. The *New Zealand Woman's Weekly* and the *Mirror* celebrated women's contribution to the war effort, reminded their readers that 'our girls proved themselves to be the equal of their brothers' and began agitating for equal pay on this basis.[179] On the other hand, some land girls struggled with the chauvinism of men who considered farm work unsuitable for a woman and muttered about 'Amazons' who 'reject their sex'.[180] Government officials recognised the value of young female labour while worrying about girls' moral safety, and they kept manpowered teenagers close to home.[181] Would girls be penned in or set free? These debates echoed the strains and contradictions of earlier decades. Teenagers worked out what they wanted, tested prevailing cultural assumptions and forged their own paths as best they could.

The clash of values came to a head in 1942 when the uniformed troops of the 'American Invasion' landed on New Zealand's shores. This influx of US servicemen represented a transnational swap: our government agreed to leave troops in the Middle East as long as American forces would repel any Japanese advance into the South Pacific.[182] Up to 50,000 Americans were in New Zealand at any one time. Many of the 'doughboys' (soldiers) and 'leathernecks' (marines) were only eighteen or nineteen, two or three years younger than the young New Zealand men who saw overseas service, and they lived in camps near Auckland and Wellington. Glamour was their stock in trade. 'The Hollywood cinema screen had suddenly erupted into life in our own city', and local women 'succumbed to gifts and attention'.[183] Many girls found it hard to resist the well-paid, well-mannered, confident Americans who 'rose to their feet as if on springs when a woman approached', doffed their hats in the streets and surrendered their seats in trams.[184] The invaders showered female locals with smokes and stockings from their camp stores, and girls often found them 'wittier and less serious' than New Zealand men.[185]

The 'American Invasion' was not entirely novel. It tapped into and intensified the Americanisation of New Zealand culture that had taken root during the interwar years. Hotdogs and hamburgers, for instance, had already arrived in a rudimentary form.[186] Likewise the jitterbug, a swing-style dance of an especially fast and bouncy kind, landed on our shores in 1938.[187] Still, the American visitors generated a lot of excitement and there is no doubt they further embedded American innovations in New Zealand society. Parties and dances amused the bright young things, and teenagers danced on the naval ships and in the cabarets ashore. Some locals held parties for the invaders:[188] one Auckland watersider met marines on the wharves and invited them home. 'Crates of beer clinked as they

On the banks of the Waikanae River during the late 1940s or early 1950s.

were hoisted onto the front verandah and cartons of cigarettes appeared as if from nowhere. There were three teenage girls in the family and they brought their girl friends along, naturally the Americans thought this was a great idea. There was singing and dancing till the small hours.'[189] The jitterbug's popularity spiked in 1943 and teenage girls eagerly sought out the lads in uniforms., The Americans taught Wellingtonian Mihipeka Edwards and her friends how to jive:

> The Yanks are beautiful dancers, and a lot of new hits are played by the bands: such songs as 'In the Mood', that was really 'hep', as the Yanks used to say; the very catchy 'Chattanooga Choo-Choo'; and the 'Boogie-Woogie Bugle Boy from Company B'. We jive to 'Johnny Doughboy Found a Rose in Ireland' and many others coming on the scene. Oh, I have never had as much fun in all my life.[190]

However, not everyone welcomed the foreigners. Church groups and newspaper editors complained about girls who formed disorderly queues outside the army bases and drunkenly danced in clubs with American servicemen.[191] Some local men did not hide the resentment they felt towards the Marines, and many New Zealanders of both sexes expressed their discomfort when women dated Americans. 'Neighbours twitched curtains and gossiped when women were seen stepping out with Yanks.'[192] American Marines offered a welcome tonic to the drabness of the home front but they were also unsettling foreigners who threatened to destabilise the social order.

The gendered effects of war are clear to see. The fighting had a profound personal impact on boys and young men, especially those who served in the forces. Some came home physically maimed and psychologically damaged, walking embodiments of the old associations between masculinity, sacrifice and pain. Many younger lads imagined war to be a noble sacrifice, just like their First World War predecessors, and some no doubt saw the 'Yanks', barely older than themselves, as heroic embodiments of military glory. For girls, war work opened up a new range of possibilities. The *Mirror* and *Woman's Weekly* started talking about equal pay; and *Freedom*, the National Party's newspaper, told its readers about new 'careers for girls': law, architecture and accountancy. The war increased teenage girls' independence and provided more fuel for the ongoing white blouse revolution.

Conclusion: Facing the Modern World

'Teenagers': finally New Zealanders between thirteen and nineteen had a serviceable name for themselves, a modern alternative to the vagueness of 'youth' and the scientific-sounding 'adolescent'. A number of ingredients had come together in the making of teenage identity, many of them from popular culture. In particular, American influences came to the fore as young mid-century antipodeans created lives for themselves. The streamlined milk bar reflected an American aesthetic, comics showcased teenage hangouts and the Marines popularised the jive. The US practice of dating aligned perfectly with New Zealanders' movie mania, and movie-goers enacted Andy Hardy's on-screen escapades in their personal lives. A trip to the cinema, where well-dressed girls

A Wairarapa netball team during the 1930s. Netball evolved out of basketball, a game invented by the YMCA in America in 1891 and taken up in New Zealand around 1908.

TEENAGERS

leaned on the arms of tall boys, was an expression of the wish for freedom and independence as well as the basis of a night out.

Not always did New Zealanders' teenage experience rest on the American values of commercialised leisure and consumer desire, however. The camping trip and bicycle tour owed more to the youth-centred Wandervogel movement of early-twentieth-century Germany. Increasing numbers of teenagers, especially boys, headed into the countryside with those of their own age. The near-ubiquity of the bicycle generated new pleasures and youth-focussed opportunities far away from adult surveillance. Lads pedalled for miles, relied upon the helpfulness of strangers, batted away sandflies, and greeted daylight in sodden tents.

The legacy of colonial girlhood lived on too. Jean McLeod, Masterton's most ardent movie fan, was a typical antipodean as well as an eager internationalist. She played cricket, cannibals, detectives and escaped convicts with brother Nev, sister Norn, Nancy and other friends: 'We acted it up in the pines', Jean wrote.

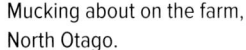

Mucking about on the farm, North Otago.

'Nancy was goofy.'[193] In an ironic concession to femininity, she added: 'Threw the footy for our figures' sake.' In fact the boys never managed to get hold of the ball and the girls beat them soundly.[194] Later Jean laughed with glee when she put bits of Norfolk Pine tree down Nev's neck and 'made him irate'.[195] The sass, stamina and strength of girls and young women resonated down the decades too, in schools, offices and factories as well as on the farm.

Many adults greeted teenagehood with scepticism. In a reprise of nineteenth-century discourse, grown-ups complained about feckless boys and girls who spurned good, honest toil. Newer concerns appeared as well. Doctors, journalists and social workers alluded to adolescents' 'special problems': materialism, individualism and a worrisome tendency to self-gratification spurred on by increasing national wealth.[196] A Catholic youth group leader was not alone when he suggested that post-war life had 'brought into being a race of emancipated young people for whom practically no provision has been made in the older forms of society'.[197] Resurgent worries about juvenile delinquency drew upon similar anxieties: alienated from social controls and with too much time on their hands, wayward teens hung around milk bars, stole cars and made a general nuisance of themselves.[198] As a catch-all concept, juvenile delinquency signalled a vague sense of unease about adolescent independence, gendered social shifts and weakening familial control. Teenage life, English author Jon Savage observes, became 'a blank canvas onto which adults could project their fears'.[199]

When all was said and done, many teenagers felt better equipped for modern life than their parents. An increasing number went on to secondary school, most found work as the Depression loosened its grip and many enjoyed the era's speedy modernity. These multi-layered characters engaged with the cultural life around them as they cut and pasted the bits they liked and discarded the rest. Traditionally minded adults failed to halt teenagers' forward march. Even so, the assertiveness of adolescence had its limits. Teens embraced a greater independence but they did not yet proclaim their collective interests on the national stage.[200] That would have to wait for the next two decades.

Chapter Five **Milk-Bar Cowboys and Rock 'n' Roll**

Queues formed in the bookshops in the winter of 1958 and the boys in stovepipe trousers and girls in slacks chattered excitedly. They were eager to get their hands on a copy of *The Bodgie*, a bright orange book about teenagers in New Zealand and Australia, and six shillings and sixpence bought them a look into other teens' lives.[1] The work of psychologist Arthur Manning, *The Bodgie* was full of jargon – 'adjustment', 'projection', 'sublimation' and 'displacement' – but persistent readers learned of others like themselves. Fay had a rough early life but discovered her people – a mix of Pākehā, Māori and Pacific Island teenagers – in a city restaurant and never looked back; Brian mucked about with other members of a loose 'gang'; Gail chewed gum, whiled away hours at her friends' houses and spent 'hilarious weekends on motorcycles'.[2] The book's line drawings showed teenagers hanging out in recognisable settings: milk bars, streets and backyards.

The Bodgie told of a restless generation in a changing world. Manning interviewed teens who lived in the shadow of two wars. Worried about the atomic threat and feeling they had little to look forward to, many seized any opportunity

OPPOSITE Four happy attendees at a tea party for teenagers, Central Park Cabaret, Wellington, 1958.

for a good time.³ Manning informed his readers that adolescents struggled against post-war conformity and adult intrusions upon their 'personal liberty', and he criticised corporal punishment in high school classrooms. A 'neurotic' modern society, he added, stifled self-development, crushed individuality and deprived teenagers of thrills.⁴ A manifesto for social change slowly took shape among the language of psychology. Teenagers made their way to the counter, carried home a book about themselves and pondered the language of protest.

Manning was not the only one who thought youth culture challenged social conventions. Teenagers leapt from newspaper headlines during the mid-1950s after hiding in the fine print during the forties. For many Māori and more than a few Pākehā, post-war migrations from the countryside to the cities picked up pace and heralded a new beginning. Rapid urban expansion pushed youth culture forward and the in-betweeners stood out like never before. Not everyone, though, was quite as understanding as Arthur Manning. Many serious-minded adults looked with horror upon the teens revving their motorbikes in the streets – and the hordes of young fans screaming at Johnny Devlin, a home-grown rock star. Small-scale rebellions grew into larger ones, and teenagers challenged earlier ideas about respectability. At the same time, an older set of tensions persisted: the constant interchange of youth-focussed recreation and mixed-age socialising, the contrast between church-based groups and free-wheeling leisure, and the tussle between moral tightening and social emancipation.

Mazengarb Investigates

In 1959 a Takapuna schoolboy showed his mates a stapled pamphlet he had found and they rifled through it looking for the 'dirty bits'.⁵ The boys were disappointed: the *Report of the Special Committee on Moral Delinquency in Children and Adolescents* contained plenty of bluster over 'immorality' and 'juvenile delinquency', a few brief mentions of teenage 'sex parties', homosexuality, condoms and the 'mechanical aspects of sex', but no real detail.⁶ In spite of its coyness, this report gained almost-legendary status.⁷ Its genesis is well known. In 1954 the government set up a committee to investigate adolescent sexuality after a fifteen-year-old girl walked into the Petone police station and told Frank Le Fort,

Dennis Turner's rendering of the erotic perils of the city, from Manning's book *The Bodgie*. Three years later, in 1961, English urban historian Lewis Mumford reminded readers that cities bring 'a constant titillation of the senses by sex'.

the duty sergeant, about a 'Milk Bar Gang' that 'met mostly for sex purposes'.[8] 'I have had it', she said. 'Sex, sex, sex. I want to get away from it.'[9] Lawyer Oswald Mazengarb QC chaired the subsequent government committee, and six others joined him: a headmaster, two church people, an officer from the children's court, a Department of Health bureaucrat and the president of the Junior Chamber of Commerce.

Mazengarb's committee mulled submissions from doctors, youth workers, educationalists and hundreds of right-thinking citizens. The submitters told of rebellious teenagers participating in under-age 'orgies' in private homes and local picture theatres, and Le Fort lodged a submission exposing the fondness of

Petone girls for the boys of the local Sea Cadets.[10] Other submission-writers fretted about nude mannikins in shops, underwear advertisements in magazines, racy comic books, and erotic novels with such titles as *The Sins of Stella* and *Forbidden Fruit*. The chairwoman of the Hastings Housewives' Union expressed her horror at boys and girls buying condoms from pie carts.[11] Another earnest submitter claimed that Coca Cola and milkshakes – especially vanilla ones – contained 'hypnotic sex stimulants' that sent teenagers into a frenzy.[12] American culture bore some responsibility for oversexed adolescents, in her mind at least.

Mazengarb's committee considered the 'evidence' before thrusting its conclusions into the letterboxes of the nation. The postal service delivered a copy of the report to every household in receipt of the family benefit, and New Zealand's parents were reminded that 'all people should, by right living and the regularity of their own conduct, afford the best example for the conduct of the rising generation'.[13] Fired up by all the fuss, the sensationalist news media focussed on young people like never before. *Truth*, that purse-lipped, scandal-loving protector of public morals, spun excited tales of excess. Far too many erotic dalliances took place in private homes, the paper claimed, and outdoors as well. Down at the beach, lipsticked lasses lured boys into the sand dunes for the most dissolute of 'orgies'.[14]

The Mazengarb Report, as the committee's deliberations quickly became known, set the scene for other investigations of juvenile immorality. The *Auckland Star* commissioned an American market research firm to find out more. Investigators from Gallup conducted interviews with school pupils and discovered boys' interest in casual sex. One lad, sixteen, mentioned his experience with 'three girls and a lady'; another said, 'like a lot of other jokers, I'm looking for my first opportunity to have sex with a girl'.[15] A third boy, fifteen, described a common order of events: 'Boys and girls meet at pictures. Boy takes girl home. They meet again in a local park and really have sex. I do. Most of my boy-friends do this too.'[16] A few of Gallup's male respondents took a different approach, planning to wait until they met a 'nice, clean-minded girl' to marry. Gallup's girls held a range of opinions. Some distanced themselves from sexually active boys, but others saw sex as exciting and recounted their experiences with great enthusiasm. A fifteen-year-old told an interviewer about her friends 'who do everything' and then gossiped about 'the boys and what they are like doing certain things'.[17] The *Star*'s editors lost their nerve and withheld such gritty details from their readers. Instead, they published sanitised morsels from the same Gallup survey, claiming that most New Zealand teenagers idolised their parents, readily agreed to the censorship of books and comics, and regretted the shortage of 'wholesome' places to spend their leisure time.[18]

What was really going on? Why did the sexual lives of young people cause such a fuss? Some cultural critics have regarded the Mazengarb investigation as a kind of 'moral panic', a collective outburst in which establishment figures denounce social groups (teenagers, in this case) or particular social patterns (loosening sexual norms) as a threat to the social order.[19] The events of 1954 do suggest a level of anxiety and a degree of political opportunism. Sid Holland's National government went looking for a populist issue on the eve of the general election, soon found it, and duly appointed a conservative committee chair – 'a notorious right wing killjoy and puritanical prude', as one wit later called Oswald Mazengarb – to lead the investigation.[20] Lurid newspaper headlines swept along the panic: 'Horrible juveniles', 'Police investigate youth cult', 'Moral delinquency said to be widespread'.[21] The panic was not confined to New Zealand. Commentators in

Young Kaitaia shoppers in front of a comics stand, 1950s. *Archie* and Disney titles are among those on display. There is no sign of the racy comics that vexed Mazengarb submitters or the men's magazines that adolescent boys sneakily perused at the barbers'.

Australia, Canada, Britain and the United States shared the disquiet about teenage behaviour and revealed widespread adult concern about sexuality, the advance of post-war consumer culture and teenagers' growing public visibility.[22]

At the same time, the Mazengarb fuss was more than a momentary panic whipped up by conservative forces for their own cathartic purposes. It also reflected deeper shifts in the structure of New Zealand society. Demographically speaking, the teenage hordes arrived in two waves that had profound effects on the age profiles of the population, the urban-rural distribution of people throughout the country, and school sizes. Parents with children born during the late 1930s moved into the rapidly growing suburbs of Auckland and the Hutt Valley, the two locations that featured in Mazengarb's deliberations, during the late 1940s.[23] The second wave, born across the country from 1943 onwards, were the true 'baby boomers' who gained notoriety during the late 1950s and early 1960s.[24] As they became teenagers, they forced a huge expansion of the secondary schools. Sixth-form enrolments doubled between 1951 and 1960; planners expected 66,000 high school enrolments in 1959 but 90,000 teens turned up. Twelve months later, in the summer of 1960, 111,000 pupils poured through the gates of New Zealand's secondary schools.[25]

The raw numbers were not the only concern. Most of the new suburban high schools were co-educational, and conservative submission-writers told Mazengarb's committee that boys and girls in co-ed settings were liable to lose control and rush headlong into moral depravity.[26] They had a point. Co-ed schools did shape adolescent intimacy, of that there is no doubt. They helped consolidate and extend the dating cultures of the thirties and forties, and frequent – if often chaste – nights out with a succession of dates now shared the stage with the more sexually charged idea of 'going steady'. American historian Amanda Littauer suggests 'going steady' was 'a pervasive site of sexual initiation [and] exploration' that 'both framed and veiled widespread heterosexual activity'.[27] New marriage patterns reflected these changes. By the 1950s, most young New Zealanders dated – and many married – those of a similar age to themselves. The average age difference between brides and grooms fell to just 2.6 years compared to 6.1 years during the pioneer period of the nineteenth century.[28]

Given these important social shifts and the hyperbolic responses to them, it is not surprising that New Zealanders are unsure how to interpret the 1950s.

Audrey Adams in Timaru, in her treasured Cole of California bathing suit that might have shocked the puriently minded. Audrey, who could not quite remember why she called herself 'Miss Copdodger 1955–56', spent a lot of her leisure time at Caroline Bay during the mid-1950s.

Were these settled and conservative years or the beginning of a large-scale social transformation?[29] This is a difficult riddle to solve, but sexual values take us to its heart. James Belich suggests that the 1950s gave rise to an early 'sexual revolution' among young city-dwellers. The average age of marriage dropped, and of those born between 1936 and 1949 nearly a quarter married before they turned twenty. To add to this precocious picture, 60 percent of all pregnancies were conceived outside of marriage.[30] During the 1960s, Belich adds, these demographic patterns broke through the city limits and rippled across the countryside.

The Sports Queen float at a blossom festival in Otago during the 1950s. These popular festivals saw clashes between mid-century ideals of respectable youth and those with little interest in such virtues. These girls' costumes emphasised a virginal femininity, but other kinds of teenage behaviour caused a scandal. In 1960 the newspapers reported 'wanton vandalism, gang violence and sex perversion' at the Hastings Blossom Festival, while local worthies told of 'young girls clad only in singlets pursued by ardent youths'.

Did these changes constitute a 'revolution'? Researchers unearthed many examples of casual sexual contact.[31] Gallup's young informants told of boys and girls (and boys and boys) 'playing with one another' in school buses and meeting 'after school to feel each other in a local park', while some older teenagers preferred serial casual encounters to relationships. 'There's not much goin' steady. If a fella goes steady, he don't hang around much, do he?', one Auckland teenager told a researcher when discussing his group of friends.[32] At the same time, marriage acted as a moral bulwark of sorts. Those who married took their place in the prescribed gender order, settling down into a respectable domesticity. Many pregnant girls became brides-to-be, some more willingly than others. 'I was just on 17 when I got married. It was in the fashion to get married', one woman said years later. 'All of my friends were getting married because a lot of them had to.'[33] Resistance to the gender order had its consequences. Some of those who remained unmarried left town to give birth in a state of shame, and many had their babies adopted out.[34] A lot of psychologists (and ordinary New Zealanders) derided young single mothers who decided to keep their babies as '"maladjusted" girls who put their own emotional needs above their child's best interests'.[35] Approved contraceptive practice fell into line with old-fashioned rules. Even in 1961, when the newfangled contraceptive pill promised sexual freedom, most doctors prescribed it only to married women. The small number of renegades included Wellington GP Erich Geiringer who dispensed contraception to Victoria University students; at the other extreme was the conservative Family Planning Association that did not give the pill to single women until 1970.[36]

This was not a revolution as such: it can be seen as the latest in a long line of intense double-movements. Old ideas about marital respectability persisted, men's sexual desires prevailed over women's and social stigma greeted rule-breakers – especially girls. The defenders of morality bossily shored up marital norms and the Mazengarb controversy gave them oxygen. Still, there could be no smoke without fire – and the moralisers' fears were not unfounded. The 'insistent undertow of new cultural forces', as Redmer Yska calls it, propelled social change.[37] Even teenagers uninterested in sex in parks and sand dunes knew about erotically charged movies, disreputable comics and banned songs. Feminist critiques of marriage and domesticity, with titles like 'Prison Without Bars: Home Life for the Married Woman', began to appear in magazines.[38] Queer cultures expanded in public and in private,[39] and the contraceptive pill became more readily available as the years wore on.[40] The young modernisers, whom we will soon meet, cut their teeth on the tussle between these conflicting forces.

A New Life in the City

Cities changed lives; members of the Mazengarb committee conceded as much. Urbanisation transformed youth cultures economically and socially as well as sexually.[40] Young workers poured into the main centres and moved into privately

Same-Sex Passions

Outraged by the case of Pauline Parker and Juliet Hulme, a pair of Christchurch girls who murdered Pauline's mother with a brick wrapped in a stocking, the Mazengarb committee reminded parents that 'sexual misbehaviour can occur between members of the same sex'.[41] Pauline and Juliet shared an intense emotional life. At one point the pair 'enacted how each Saint would make love in bed ... we felt exhausted and very satisfied', and doctors concluded the relationship 'was a homosexual one'.[42] The Parker-Hulme case called other girls' friendships into question; 'I felt sick and horrified because I realised that the relationship I was in was like theirs', one woman told an interviewer years later.[43]

While homosexuality gained an increasingly negative press during the 1950s, other teenage girls worried less and explored their options. They met new friends and potential partners in sports teams, including the women's hockey scene, even though they did not always give their shared sexuality a name.[44] Bubs Hetet left Te Kuiti High School and went farming near Tokaanu. She teamed up with Piri, who also 'liked girls', and the two of them met others: 'the romantic spot we had was the hot pools ... ride and swim all day and off to the hot pools at night. Then in the hot pools, well! That's where friendships were either cemented or broken.' Bubs and Piri later went fruit picking in Nelson, dressed as boys occasionally and met a lot more girls there.[45]

A corridor in Arohata Borstal.

Correctional institutions gave rise to specific kinds of intimate relationships.[46] Borstal girls gave one another names like 'Bosun', 'Sailor Boy', 'Cobra', 'Bicycle', 'Lovey', 'Dagger' and 'Sloppy Chops'. Tony Taylor, a therapist at Arohata Borstal near Wellington, researched the inmates' relationships in 1964. The girls spoke of 'darls' (short for 'darlings') who supplied one another with food, clothing and information, and many had a 'special darl' with whom they shared hugs, kisses and sexual intimacies. Taylor collected the notes passed between inmates: 'Sweetheart and I are just mutual friends. You are jealous because I was with her most of the other day. I accept the fact that she thinks a lot more of you than she probably ever will of me.'⁴⁷ Other notes documented physical desires:

A young Ian Hillier at home. Ian later became a well-known member of Christchurch's gay community.

> I often look (at other girls) and wonder if they are so deeply in love with their darls, as I am with you. Yes it took a lovely girl like you to steal my heart away from me, and [I] honestly thought that it would be a boy that did it, but I have just found out my thinking was wrong.
> I promise you I won't do anything out of place with other girls. Hell I wish I could come over and spend a night with you, but God I wouldn't like to know what state we would be in by next morning. Fill these empty arms of mine.⁴⁸

Many of the girls had sexual relationships with boys before their stay at Arohata and returned to heterosexual lives after they left borstal – but still they missed their special darls.

Boys explored their desires too. In 1952 Jon Dumble went to see a psychiatrist about his sexuality. For some years Jon had enjoyed easy sex in his boarding school dormitories where boys sneaked into one another's beds after lights out. The psychiatrist provided religious rather than psychological advice and suggested his patient pray harder. Unimpressed, Jon ventured into Auckland's library to ask for the books hidden away in a locked cabinet. Most of these described homosexuality as a sickness, but Jon did not feel ill. Down at Auckland's port he met a thirty-six-year-old steward off the *Monowai* and spent time on board. 'I could see by the look on all his mates' faces what they thought. I was sixteen and I thought he was heaven on Earth.' Jon soon found his way into Auckland's gay scene, dropping in on parties and travelling to Rotorua with carloads of men who set up camp near town: 'they were pretty wild and pretty raucous'.⁴⁹ As New Zealand's cities grew, so too did queer worlds that teenagers like Jon could explore.

Kahu and Kathy on the verandah of Roseneath Hostel, Christchurch, 1964. Many girls arrived at the end of the Motueka fruit-picking season to work in the city. Girls in this hostel-cum-flat lived in groups of three to five and cooked for themselves. Each had a door key, but staff carefully monitored their charges' comings and goings.

run boarding houses that officials judged little better than 'semi-brothels'.⁵⁰ The government responded by providing its own accommodation. The first cluster of state-run hostels catered for teenage girls and young women working in the ammunition factories during the Second World War. The second wave accommodated boys and girls learning a trade or working in the civil service. Dallas Moore went to Wellington from Auckland in 1962 to work as a Forest Service clerk and study at Victoria University. He took up lodgings at Orient Hostel in Oriental Bay, home to ninety government service boys. A move away from home, especially between cities, forced teenagers like Dallas to adapt to new circumstances. 'I do not yet know what the chaps in my room will be like. I do hope they are good Christian types', he wrote in his diary before leaving Auckland. 'But much more probably they will smoke and drink with the best.'⁵¹ After his arrival in

Wellington, Dallas quickly realised that his Orient room-mates were 'not the same as me' – but they were 'a nice set of fellows' nonetheless.[52] Hostels fostered their own cultures: the Orient's residents sorted themselves into 'the drinking brigade' and 'the card playing set'. Dallas did not belong to either of these groups but he made the hostel his own anyway. He played billiards in the evenings and watched television.[53] Television began broadcasting in New Zealand in 1961 and gave rise to new kinds of sociability. Dallas met a new pal, Dermont, while cheering on the heroes of the TV Westerns. 'He is quite clever, cleverer than me in scientific subjects at least, I think, and quite nice too.'[54]

Young Māori joined Pākehā in the move to the cities. Small numbers of Māori adolescents paved the way during the 1920s and 1930s when new organisations like Wellington's Ngati Poneke Young Maori Club provided a home away from home. A lonely trickle of Māori migrants turned into a flood after the war, and Ngati Poneke's membership boomed. Teenagers occupied the vanguard of this demographic shift.[55] Two complementary forces caused this movement of young Māori out of rural areas: a shortage of work and a lack of educational opportunities where they grew up, and a labour shortage in the rapidly expanding factories, government agencies and service sector that pulled them into the cities.[56]

Māori girls took jobs in hotels and the post office and many trained as nurses once they turned seventeen.[57] One young woman from the Hokianga took up her new career with her father's blessing: 'my Dad said I had to go nursing because it was a good job, you know; you had a uniform and all this hoo-ha'.[58] Churches opened hostels for Māori, supplementing those run by the state. In New Plymouth the Rangiatea Methodist Maori Girls' Hostel looked after school pupils and young female workers, and Geni Taylor had a good time there during the mid-1960s. 'I loved our nights in the Rec Room listening to music and I still have flashes of me dancing hard out thinking I was a go-go girl. I loved singing and sang in the church choir. I only joined because it meant driving through town on the bus on Friday nights and so we would be having a perv at all the boys congregated around the place.'[59] Adults tried to protect girls from wayward temptations but, as always, their control was never total. Geni sneaked down the back of the Rangiatea garden for a smoke and others hid cigarettes 'in the bar in the wardrobe that we hung our clothes on'.[60] Those looking for freedom soon moved out of hostels

TEENAGERS

LEFT Rehua boys undertake trades training during the 1960s.

OPPOSITE At Rehua Hostel, 1969.

like Rangiatea. Never again would they have to miss an episode of *Peyton Place*, a popular American prime-time soap opera, when their television privileges were suspended for bad behaviour.

Māori boys' experiences mirrored aspects of the girls'. The earliest trades training schemes began in 1952 and the first specialist trades schools opened a decade later in Auckland, the Hutt Valley and Canterbury.[61] Christchurch's Rehua Hostel housed seventy boys from the East Coast of the North Island who trained as carpenters, plumbers, painters, electricians and motor mechanics.[62] Most set out from home with mixed emotions, and one later remembered the scene at Wairoa railway station. 'I was anxious to go and see new things, my mother was bawling her head off. I must have cried all the way to Raupunga', a small settlement half an hour down the line.[63] Pākehā saw the Rehua boys as curiosities at

TEENAGERS

The New Zealand Railways had long provided apprenticeships and cadetships for boys, some of whom spent the rest of their working lives in the government department, but urban expansion provided new kinds of jobs. These photos show a cadet in the signals division, 1960s, and an apprentice trimmer making a railway carriage seat in the Otahuhu railway workshops, 1953. The railways' refreshment facilities were predominantly staffed by women, many of them young. Here Huia and Alena pose in their NZR uniforms at the Wellington railway station cafeteria in 1959.

first, and they drove past the hostel to gawp and point. When groups of Rehua lads ventured into the Square in the evenings, Pākehā 'used to look at us and say "who are they?"', but soon they became friendlier. 'Once they knew we were from the hostel we became like movie stars. People were choice, man!'[64] Still, the excitement of city living called for a careful balancing act. Migrants reassessed their new lives in light of the old, reconsidering the importance of te reo, familial connections and traditional food. Many were reluctant to appear 'too Māori-fied' in the Pākehā cities that 'whispered for them to be more Pākehā' – they would not eat eel and paraoa takakau (Māori bread) in public, for instance – but they also worried about appearing 'too Pākehā-fied' when back home among their families.[65]

Ready work and a slowly expanding range of job opportunities allowed teenagers to stretch their wings. The post-war economic boom intensified the sense of adolescent autonomy; as one woman remembered, 'you could leave a job in the morning and get a new one in the afternoon'. Wages rose rapidly. In 1951, 5 percent of young men earned over £300 each year, but within five years 44 percent did. Bank jobs were highly sought after by those who did well at school. A teller at the Bank of New Zealand in Auckland (*left*); new BNZ employees attend a training course during the 1950s (*right*).

Some hostels brought together teenagers from both Māori and Pākehā backgrounds. The Gear Meat Works hostel in Petone was one such example, the Mosgiel Woollen Mill hostel another. Sixteen-year-old Trevor Rupe, who later became the celebrity Carmen, worked at Mosgiel in 1952 and enjoyed living at the mill's hostel. He shared a room with a friendly young Pākehā chap named Arthur, and they made the most of the entertainment. There were monthly parties, a few at the hostel and others at the nearby Taieri Air Force base. 'My party piece was the "hula"', Carmen recalled. 'I would put a flower in my hair . . . and wore an artificial grass skirt to enhance my dance.'[66] He took on extra jobs – stewarding or bar work – whenever he managed to convince people he was older than he looked. A teenager from Taumarunui, Trevor took to hostel life and the city like a duck to water. He embraced the opportunity to find himself and have some fun. As they sought independence, work, money and pleasure in the ever-expanding cities, teenagers like Trevor readily adapted to city living and made the urbanisation process work for them.[67]

Bodgies, Widgies and Milk-Bar Cowboys

A growing number of social scientists investigated the effects of city life on adolescents. Gallup's researchers joined the many psychologists, sociologists and criminologists who turned their attention to young people after the Second World War. As the Mazengarb furore reveals, teenagers – especially those dubbed 'juvenile delinquents' – attracted sustained attention at times of heightened social strain.[68] New Zealand researchers tapped into international trends, producing reports with titles such as 'Catholics and Delinquency', 'The Young Incorrigible' and 'Five Case Histories of Girls Discharged from Burwood'.[69] The Girls' Training Centre at Burwood was the successor to Te Oranga, the Christchurch reformatory mentioned in Chapter 3. The authors of these dissertations searched for the causes of bad behaviour ('lying, thieving, sadism and other antisocial habits') by tabulating household incomes, educational achievement and parental circumstances.[70] They laid much of the blame at parents' feet and also suggested the government crack down on truancy, censor radio broadcasts and ban the sale of contraceptives.[71]

Psychologist Arthur Edward Manning was heavily influenced by the work of Sigmund Freud, and aspects of his analysis seem cranky to modern readers. Manning thought gum-chewing and smoking reflected sublimated desires for the nipple, and he suggested that a 'neurotic' society gave rise to a malaise among post-war youth. Still, he was sympathetic to young people's lives and his analysis of social repression and adult authoritarianism were progressive for their time. His book's cover and illustrations – by Dennis Turner who also designed cover art for Barry Crump's novels – neatly capture the zeitgeist and the image: DA ('duck's arse') hairstyle, tight trousers and brightly coloured shirts.

Dorothy Crowther's 'Street Society in Christchurch', a university report from 1956, is the most culturally rich piece of mid-century social scientific work on young New Zealanders. It closely resembles international ethnographic studies of its time, including the famous (and similarly titled) book *Street Corner Society*, sociologist William Foote Whyte's ethnography of Boston street gangs. A psychologist at the University of Canterbury, Crowther took six students into town at night to discover 'what the boys and girls on the streets were actually like'.[72] The researchers loitered on Christchurch's footpaths and inside the milk bars, eavesdropping on conversations and asking questions of any teenager willing to talk.

Some of Auckland's milk-bar cowboys in 1956, and a disapproving onlooker.

Four types of teenagers form the centrepiece of 'Street Society': the 'bodgie', the 'milk-bar cowboy', the 'widgie' and the 'Teddy boy'. These categories had a close and tense relationship to the concept of juvenile delinquency. Unlike other studies of the 1950s, though, 'Street Society' shied away from a diagnosis of moral failure. Instead, Crowther tried to understand youth culture on its own terms. She wanted to find out about social life on the streets: what did teenagers do there, where did they congregate, how did they distinguish themselves from one another? This does not mean Crowther flattered her subjects. She defined the bodgie, for instance, by his scruffy appearance and 'boisterous and attention provoking' behaviour.[73] 'Street Society' contained other idiosyncracies too. Given her apparent awareness of Whyte's research on Boston, Crowther's hazy knowledge of the overseas context is surprising. She told her readers about the bodgie's Australian counterparts – she claimed many belonged to 'a closely knit sex cult' – but forgot to mention that the broader style hailed from America where the 'greaser' wore the same slicked hair, white t-shirt and stovepipe trousers.[74] In keeping with the American theme, the bodgies' early New Zealand counterparts were Wellington boys known as 'Cuba Street Yanks'.[75] The bodgie, like the larrikin, the masher and the flapper, was an antipodean iteration of an international phenomenon.

'Milk-bar cowboys' (known as 'ton-up boys' or 'coffee-bar cowboys' in Britain, 'les blousons noirs' in France and 'die Halbstarken' in Germany) were close relatives of the bodgies: they owned the motorbikes the bodgies lacked.[76] Christchurch's milk-bar cowboys wore 'leather jackets and trousers tucked into the tops of wool-lined boots' and loitered with their bikes outside the Crystal Palace picture theatre.[77] How might we conceive of these developments? Sociologist Jarrod Gilbert thinks of bodgies and milk-bar cowboys as members of 'urban play groups' rather than 'gangs' as we now understand them.[78] There were a great many such loosely organised groups. In 1959, youth worker Allan Levett collated the titles, ages, membership details, clothing styles and activities of forty-one in Auckland alone. The black-jeans-wearing Bats, for example, hung about the milk bars and loitered in the streets, while the Epsom Boys wore tidy casual dress and met each night at a hamburger bar. The aptly named Arcade Boys dressed 'Ivy League style' and lurked in Queens Arcade. Levett's research suggests these groups shared a common set of interests: 'street meeting, trips, pictures, dances, drink, sex, fighting'.[79]

Levett and his colleagues knew of at least seventeen bodgie- and milk-bar cowboy-style groups in Wellington, but only a few (Pinocchio, the Naenae Boys and the Petone Gang) gave themselves names. The Waikato had its fair share of likely lads as well, including the Demo Gang.[80] Former lad-about-town Rob Comer remembers Hamilton's milk-bar cowboys who 'lined their bikes up along Little London Street, and the crowds of kids that would come and watch these guys. They'd have a smoke and talk among themselves. They were scary, they had a leader called Tiny who lived in Ngaruawahia and had a fearsome reputation.

When the movies finished they'd peel off and drive down the main street, but they'd throttle out in first or second gear and put their boots on the tar seal and sparks would fly off. That was amazing for us, amazing stuff.'[81]

It is unsurprising that bodgies and milk-bar cowboys garnered a bad press, for the public fuss about juvenile delinquency had set the scene. Solid citizens claimed that bodgies turned Wellington into a 'little Chicago' by fighting with knives and pushing adults off the footpaths, and they grumpily demanded the culprits be quarantined on Somes Island in the middle of the harbour.[82] There is no doubt some youths caused mayhem, fighting in the dance halls and milk bars. Paddy Black knifed a rival to death in Auckland's Ye Olde Barn café. Still, the newspapers overstated the situation, and statistics suggest that 1950s teenagers appeared in court no more often than their parents at the same age.[83] This did not stop the increasingly salacious reporting, though, and public concerns often appeared in a caricatured form. Dunedin's *South End News*, a short-lived tabloid in the *Truth* mould, claimed milk-bar cowboys and their female companions – often called 'pillion pussies' – made perversity into an art form. According to the *South End News*, the behaviour of Dunedin's miscreants 'reached the evil level of the Hutt Valley episode', and they conducted themselves in a manner reminiscent of a 'black mass'. 'The motor-cycles were in a semi-circle, around a fire. Young women in brief underwear, and some without any clothing, were dancing in front of the fire.' The article suggested that the female partygoers were far from innocent. 'Most of the girls have only recently left school, but they are already well-versed in the ways of the "cowboys". In fact, the unhappy suggestion left in one's mind is that they are keen to indulge in these ritualistic orgies.'[84]

What did teenagers make of all this ruckus? Given the heightened distinctions between troublesome and respectable youths, few readily embraced such value-laden identities as 'bodgie' or 'milk-bar cowboy'.[85] In 1958 one lad told a radio interviewer: 'we're just ordinary sensible jokers, or we try to be', it's just that 'we wear different clothes . . . so we get called a bodgie. We're not really.'[86] Others resented the idea that boys like them, who simply hung about and listened to music, should be dismissed as bodgies.[87] One lad beat up his father over it. 'My father called me a bodgie once. I was in the bathroom, all dressed up, just putting a comb through my hair, and he barged in drunk and that was the time I flattened him, laid him out. I was no bodgie.'[88] Still, a few pinned the 'bodgie' label to their t-shirts and wore it as a badge of defiance. To them 'going bodgie' meant adopting a 'loose independent way of living' associated with a particular 'appearance and behaviour'.[89] Erstwhile bodgie Rob Comer described his own look:

> I had the haircut; I had the clothes; we had the music, we had everything, I was content. I came to do the James Dean thing, I couldn't find a pair of Levis and I couldn't find the right jacket. But I had a white t-shirt, so I went and bought a beautiful black jacket, and it had a beautiful golden leopard-skin lining. Black stovepipe pants and I had white socks and black slip-on shoes. This was it, I was hot and ready to go! It was neat.[90]

Rebel Without a Cause had made James Dean a teenage hero, and the 1955 film about troubled suburban youth reinforced the connections between adolescence, new clothing styles and social resistance. As Rob said, 'It was a "look at me!" era and you dressed to impress, had the image to upset, and that was part of the thing. We were rebelling against our parents, or society in fact.'[91]

For girls, the widgie style included hair worn in a ponytail or 'bushy windswept style', a white high-collared shirt or round-necked sleeveless blouse, and a high-necked sweater or a jacket. Loose-fitting slacks served for everyday wear and a tight black skirt with a slit up the back made it easy to dance the jitterbug and the jive.[92] The avant-garde widgie look appealed to some: 'I got a bottle of peroxide and secretly bleached my fringe a little at a time . . . And I saved up and bought a bottle of white nail varnish because I really wanted to be a widgie.'[93] Some felt their widgie image, like bodgie style, meant they belonged to an edgy modern age, but others resented having the 'widgie' label foisted upon them – especially when it implied outsider status. A Wellington schoolgirl boarded a bus and beat up a group of girls when one of them called her a widgie through the window.[94] There was a difference between embracing a dangerous new look and being pilloried for it.

Teddy boys, another distinctive teen style, had slightly more complex origins than the bodgies and widgies. The true Teddy boy was an English lad who arrived here as a permanent migrant or a ship's sailor. As dandyish lads with eccentric suits and duck's arse ('DA') hairstyles, the 'Teds' grew out of London's working-class culture. The English Teds paraded around the streets

Widgies and bodgies, as depicted by Dennis Turner in Manning's book.

in search of admiration, hung about the cinemas, parks and late-night cafés, and sometimes formed gangs to defend territories.[95] They made their way to New Zealand in ones and twos and their image met with varying degrees of adulation and hostility, especially at first.[96] The Teddy boy 'twice removed', as Crowther called him, was not a British resident but a New Zealander who copied elements of the English style: the long, fancy jackets with extra pockets and flaps and the DA hairstyle.

Why was there such an explosion of youth types during the 1950s? Economic factors certainly played a role. In New Zealand, like Australia, America and Britain, young people's wages continued to climb rapidly and post-war affluence caused a degree of class convergence.[97] Increasingly well-remunerated working-class youths had the means to participate in a consumer culture previously reserved for middle-class adolescents. The flash clothes worn by bodgies, milk-bar cowboys and Teddy boys told of this growing affluence and autonomy.

Further along the spectrum, parents granted their middle-class offspring a greater degree of independence and they became freer to occupy the ambiguous spaces of the cities.[98] Teenagers from a wider range of backgrounds also mingled in the rapidly expanding secondary schools, veritable hothouses where subcultural styles emerged and circulated.

As distinctive youth styles, Teddy boys, widgies and bodgies signalled an increasing social distance between teenagers and adults. They differed from the flapper, their most recent ancestor, in one important respect. The flapper image began life among the in-betweeners but quickly spread to adult women so the sartorial line between adolescents and adults quickly blurred. During the war years most teenagers distinguished themselves from younger children but not from adults: by and large they dressed like their parents. By the 1950s, though, bodgies, widgies and Teddy boys had forged a style no parent dared appropriate, and clothing accentuated the generational divide like never before.

Modes of Address

A curious thing happened as the media clamour reached its crescendo. The jeans, leather jackets and slitted skirts that denoted the membership of a sub-group soon percolated through the wider adolescent population. Teenagers cut and pasted a mixture of overlapping styles to craft a look. Although Crowther's 'Street Society' offered definitions of the bodgie and the widgie to its curious readers, the report also revealed that other teenagers dressed in 'no set fashion' and mixed and matched different clothing items.[99] Girls around the country wore wide, brightly coloured plastic belts and the 'little skimpy tops' associated with the widgie.[100] The sketches in Manning's book *The Bodgie* showed widgies dancing in roomy mid-length skirts, which many non-widgie girls wore over layered petticoats. The ensemble was 'wonderful to dance in'.[101] Many girls slipped on the same flat ballerina shoes as Manning's widgies.[102] Boys, meanwhile, danced in sports jackets, fluorescent lime or pink ties, and beetle-crusher shoes.[103] Many forgot which hairstyle was whose. When a researcher asked one Christchurch youth 'if that was a Bodgie haircut, he shrugged his shoulders and replied "I dunno. I just went in to a place and had it out". Later I asked why he'd had it out like that

Sailor Boys

Young New Zealanders living in the port towns flocked to the wharves when the ships came in. Seamen from the USS *Colorado* showed eager Aucklanders around their ship one afternoon in 1926. 'Down in the engine room where it was so warm I nearly roasted & then when I went on deck I caught cold, now I can hardly croak', a girl named Daisy wrote in a letter to her relatives. Romances sprang up between the sailors ('our little Yankee boys') and the girls, but they ended a few days later in sorrowful partings. 'You should have been here in town last Monday night & Tuesday morning, it was all too funny for words, the sailors & their girls were saying the final goodbyes. Every one of the sailors busted out howling & most of the girls followed suit. You can't imagine how quiet and lonely it is in town now, it makes you feel sad.'[104]

The ports were libidinal gateways through which sailors passed into the lives of boys as well as girls. In 1941, sixteen-year-old Bruce Millar rang up men in the navy, met them in the vicinity of Auckland's Ferry Building and took them to a quiet spot for sex. 'There was a petty officer, a marine and one I think an ordinary seaman', he told the court after his circle of friends came to the attention of police.[105]

In 1956, under the title 'Every Girl Loves the Navy', the *South End News* published grainy photographs of grinning Dunedin girls welcoming the USS *Brough* and posing with its crew. Seamen 'changed hats with the teenagers, did a few steps of jive when the officers weren't looking, and made a list of dates a mile long. Most

Audrey Adams' friends Alex, Roy and Sammy on the *Fremantle Star*.

were ready to take their girl-friends off to a local grill-room for T-bone and porterhouse steaks which were selling in ton lots to steak-crazy seamen.'[106]

Timaru girls met the new arrivals in the main street or the town's milk bars. They slurped cold drinks together, swapped hats, went to the pictures, and made the most of the three or four days the lads spent in port.[107] 'They were lovely', Timaruvian Audrey Adams said of the young Teddy boy seamen – cabin boys and pantry boys, mostly – with their sideburns, coiffed hair and polite ways.[108] 'The blokes off the boats definitely had a more sophisticated look than the local lads', Sophie Tindall added.[109]

There is no doubt the visitors were cyphers of style. They imported new fashions.[110] Jeans began life as seamens' 'go-ashore gear' and soon found a place on landlubbers. Disreputable at first, these soon became near universal.[111] A few local lads soaked up the stylish ambience down at the docks. 'I love the American navy hat!', musician and self-described 'fashionista' Ray Columbus wrote. 'I buy cartons of Camel cigarettes cheaper than I can buy them at any store. I buy Old Spice because I'm into aftershave. I bring back stuff and sell it at school. It makes me feel international, and not someone limited to one small town.'[112]

Up until the 1960s the ports had a significant influence on teenage cultural life, but in the last half century their role in shaping fashion, friendship and pleasure has completely disappeared.

Yvonne (*left*) and Audrey try on the hats of two sailor friends in Timaru, 1954.

Michael, Audrey's English Teddy boy beau from the *Port Pirie*, 1954.

– an upswept duckstail? He said, "I dunno".'[113] A bodgie style could ultimately be worn by anybody.

The teenage clothing industry continued its expansion during the 1960s. Mohair and fawn duffle coats found ready buyers among New Zealand's girls, and long white 'go-go boots' garnered fans in the middle of the decade.[114] The first mini-skirts appeared at the same time, popularised by English fashion designer Mary Quant who reworked the 1920s flapper look for a new era. Their clean lines made them easy to sew and teenage girls whipped up their own versions.[115] They carried on the DIY clothing ethos of their Victorian predecessors, although their electric sewing machines sped up the job considerably. Pantyhose, invented in 1959 and introduced to New Zealand straight away, were the mini-skirt's perfect accompaniment.[116] To top it all off, girls of the 1960s teased and lacquered their hair, put in a stack of rollers and covered the ensemble with a layer of plastic spray. The 'beehive' hairdo was the result.[117]

The consumer revolution intensified, and teen-focussed magazines ramped up their advice about how girls should dress. American periodical *Seventeen* – the 'bible for all cool teenagers' – continued to promote glamour and charm, and local publishers added their voices too.[118] The *Mirror* provided instructions for teenage 'makeovers', while *Vogue New Zealand* told of the 'Youthquake' and 'the importation of European cool'.[119] *Playdate* offered Hollywood gossip and movie reviews; *Count Down* told of popular music and fashion – and advertised cosmetics. Make-up remained a thorny issue. Some parents approved of lipstick but others did not, and the toilets of Lower Hutt's milk bars were full of girls applying Tangee Orange well away from their mothers' prying eyes.[120] The lipstick wearer soon learned how much to put on. In 1961, when Rosalind Warburton wore her first lipstick at the age of thirteen, she 'felt like a painted Jezebel, not knowing that soon I would wear a dash of lipstick with nonchalance'.[121] Post-war consumer culture instilled freedom and discipline in equal measure, and the socially imposed line between prettiness and brazenness could be a fine one indeed.

The mini-skirt belonged to a new style: 'mod', which was an expression of the upwardly mobile British working class that enticed both girls and boys.[122] 'Mod' (short for 'modern') made its antipodean debut in 1964 as the Beatles' Australasian tour loomed.[123] The pop group brought a new aesthetic when they introduced New Zealanders to a new sound. *Count Down* told readers about this

OPPOSITE Auckland photographer John Rykenberg captured this scene. He usually zoomed in on Aucklanders who epitomised style, like the young woman on the left. This image includes half a schoolboy as well. Pupils in school uniform were ubiquitous in city streets but often ignored by photographers intent on capturing urban modernity.

classical, suited, slightly dandyish way of dressing, and its advertisers urged lads to embrace the 'Mersey look': tapered slacks, collarless jackets, thin ties and gold-plated beetle jewellery.[124] Finally, some forty years after they had first noticed adolescent girls, local advertisers turned their attention to teenage boys. This marked an important turning point, even though many New Zealand men remained reluctant shoppers for another generation or two.[125] The tailored suit – if not the Beatles' floppy hair – provided the ideal look in an urban male workforce where the number of office jobs continued to grow steadily.[126] The Beatles' visit also showed that men's handsomeness – or the lack of it – no longer escaped public scrutiny. *Count Down* reminded readers that Ringo Starr had a 'big nose' and Paul McCartney 'pulls in the screams with his babyfaced good looks'.[127]

The male body became a focus like never before, and sometimes the tensions between old and new styles erupted in violence. Jealous boyfriends pelted the Beatles with eggs during the pop group's tour, Hamilton's 'rugby club guys' picked

A Stokes Valley boy and his Beatles haircut.

fights with the local bodgies, and a group of servicemen hacked off Auckland bodgies' hair.[128] Hamilton MP Hilda Ross, no fan of the bodgie, said the young soldiers should have carried on and 'cleaned up the whole of New Zealand'.[129] Male mods clashed with the 'bikers' (also known as 'rockers' after their British counterparts), a group with little patience for dandyism.[130] Tensions escalated when a rocker arrived at a Christchurch mod party with chains and knives and began 'stirring shit'.[131] This particular episode had a tragic end: a mod fired a hunting rifle and killed the rocker.

Bodybuilding grew in popularity as growing white-collar employment undermined old associations between manliness and physical labour. Boys with sedentary jobs found other ways to put on muscle. The fitness craze of the early 1900s re-emerged in a new guise, spurred along by a deluge of ads showing skinny boys bulking up with the help of barbells, chest expanders and weights.[132] Down at the beach the newly strengthened lad stood his ground against any sand-kicking

Well-dressed lads, with their 1950s collars, in Kaitaia.

Bryan McGovern, seventeen, in his boxing get-up in 1956; Bryan's membership card for Koolman's gym, one of many established in New Zealand cities over the course of the twentieth century.

bully. Some liked the idea of bodybuilding but made their own gadgets. David Wildey used macrocarpa logs: 'When cut they were an ideal size, shape and weight for weight-lifting so I tried some exercise with them. The going was tough but not bad for a beginning.'[133] This was the start of David's lifelong interest in body-building, and it revealed a complex entanglement of body-shaping and desire. As David continued his exercise regime into young adulthood, he eagerly collected the American physique magazines – *Physique Pictorial* was the most well known – published for gay readers like him.[134]

The renewed focus on the body gave rise to its own kind of social scientific research project. Peter Smith, a physical education student at Otago University, asked teenagers what they thought of bodybuilding. His male respondents, pupils at a local boys' high school, hedged their bets. The younger lads liked the muscular look but their older peers were not so sure. 'It's all show', they said, worried that bulked-up bodies suggested self-obsession and shallowness. Several claimed bodybuilding encouraged 'the adoration of the male physique, which is unnatural'. An older boy began his answer with a high-minded principle: 'the men I admire and wish to emulate are not men who have developed their bodies but their minds', he said, before adding a confession: 'However, a naturally developed body would be desirable.'[135] Smith's female respondents, mostly students, typists and factory machinists, were more forthright in their views. Few wanted to promenade along the waterfront with an 'overdeveloped' boyfriend – 'I like men to look like men instead of a string of sausages' – and many assumed overly muscly boys to be egotistical, domineering and not very bright.[136] The girls' male ideal was slim by today's standards, with a narrow waist and relatively thin arms. Peter Smith's study reveals that 'big muscle boys', as the author called them, embodied social change. In a society where consumption increasingly defined teenage lives, externally imposed forms of bodily discipline, a legacy of early-twentieth-century militarism, gradually gave way to a newer, freely-chosen mix of self-shaping and self-expression.

Rebels and Jalopies

In 1963 Pauline Crowley, a New Plymouth fourth former, described modern teenagehood: 'We, today, live in a world of colour, and is it not natural to absorb the feeling of the age? The times, too, are a hurly-burly of rushing here and rushing there; we, too, modern teenagers, are caught up in this rush and show it in our dancing, singing and dress, driving fast motorbikes.'[137] The association between speed and teenagehood had been thirty years in the making, and it drew upon a lengthy process of change. Cultural histories of the sailing ship, the railway, the bicycle and the tram reveal something of mobility's long evolution, and the same is true of individual motorised transport. Boys competed to show who had the fastest motorbike as early as the 1920s, and Manning's book tells of 1950s teenagers embracing bikes in ever-increasing numbers. Nineteen-year-old Frank 'loved speeding on a motor-cycle and the thrill of appearing to float through space', Manning wrote, while Irene, eighteen, rode to picnics on the back of boys' motorbikes 'and was stimulated by the speed'.[138]

A Rehua boy and his motorbike, early 1960s.

The car-driving dream turned into a reality for a growing number of teenagers during the 1950s. Antipodeans lagged ten years or more behind their American counterparts and their flash sedans, and most New Zealand teenagers made do with an 'old bomb' discarded by a parent or acquaintance. Dares and fast driving feature prominently in the film *Rebel Without a Cause* and the majority of New Zealand teens, including those in Hamilton and the Hutt, imitated James Dean's races with twenty- or thirty-year-old cars.[139] The lucky few drove Fords or V8 coupés, the latest in streamlined sophistication that idled with a luxurious 'hubble bubble sound'.[140]

The distinction between 'old bombs' and something flasher was not lost on Crowther's social scientific researchers. After all, they were barely out of the teenage years themselves. Three Christchurch boys tried to tempt one young investigator to ride in a 'one-seater car of ancient vintage': 'What ya doin', love? What about comin' for a ride?' With barely disguised disdain she groaned inwardly and turned them down – 'No thanks' – and they hurried away.[141] In contrast, she could not help but admire the American sedans parked up in Gloucester Street in which youths 'dressed in open shirts, slacks or jeans' and girls 'in "Widgie" style' posed for an audience.[142]

More and more girls obtained drivers' licences by the late 1950s, and a life behind the wheel transcended divisions of gender.[143] Rosalind Warburton, a Whanganui fifth former, described 'a tingling sensation that fills me when I drive the car – pride that I am alone the master of a forty horsepower engine'.[144] A young Aucklander learned to drive in a truck: 'I roared up and down the road, crunching the gears and giving all the neighbours a thrill. You should have seen all the curtains twitching', she wrote in a letter to her brother. Once she mastered the vehicle she looked forward to a holiday: 'Think about sunny Northland

A group of Auckland lads gathers around a late-1940s Mercury.

because that's where I'm going even if I have to drive myself.'[145] Girls who drove took part in an important social transition. The independent cross-country trip had been the preserve of boys on bicycles during the thirties and forties but cars also allowed girls greater access to the countryside. The gendered mobility gap slowly began to close.

Cars also fuelled new expectations in the field of romance. Now fewer teenagers walked or took public transport to dances in groups. The twin influences of dating and car culture slowly changed patterns of social behaviour, and the new arrangements came with an informal contract: a girl who abandoned the boy who drove her to a dance broke a new set of rules.[146] On the other hand, those who drove themselves gained a profound new independence. When things progressed well, the car became a private mobile living room or bedroom.[147] Some teenagers parked up for a kiss and a cuddle – or something more – at Hamilton's lake, Wellington's Oriental Bay and countless other spots dotted around the country, and they escaped parental oversight for a while.[148] Cars signified privacy as well as speed, and they snuffed out the last vestiges of the chaperone.

Vehicles helped young New Zealanders defend territory as well as expand it. Crowther saw groups of Christchurch teenagers congregate in large groups in the Square and Colombo Street. Like previous generations of adolescents they talked among themselves, rough-housed 'in a playful sort of way' and flicked cigarette ash at passing adults.[149] Now, though, motorbikes and cars joined bodies as props in a nightly drama, a way to block roads and hold up traffic. Christchurch pedestrians had to plan their walking routes around clusters of teenagers' vehicles. Still, not every young Cantabrian took up quite as much space. Ray Columbus and his slick-haired mates leaned on parking meters and read the satirical American comic paper *Mad*. Ray had no car as such, but he fed the meter to reserve his little piece of turf.[150]

From Milk Bars to Coffee Haunts

Teenagers' territorialism expanded during the 1950s when the milk bar became a young person's space more or less exclusively. The shift from all-purpose diner to adolescent hangout, which had begun ten or fifteen years earlier, was now

complete. In none of the milk bars Crowther visited in 1956 was any patron older than twenty-five or so.[151] At the Crystal Palace boys and girls sat around and 'fooled aimlessly'; they scuffled over the top of the partitions and threw cigarette packets at each other.[152] Crowther's researchers made themselves at home, recorded conversations and captured the idiom. After bagging her seat, one nineteen-year-old went up to the counter to place her order. A lad of seventeen 'asked her if she was coming out with him tonight. She paused, posed in the manner of a Hollywood star and said, "Reg, the night I go out with you, I need my head read".'[153] Another exchange, like so many, turned to cars:

> First youth: 'What ar-ya-doin' tonight?' Second youth: 'Oh, a-dunno.' The first: 'Yi goin' to the Māori Club?' The second: 'Oh, a-dunno.' The first: 'Ave-yi-gotta car? Couldja getta car? Yiv gotta car, haven't ya?' The second: 'Me, no. I smashed mine up.' The first: 'What about yer mother's?' The second: 'Don' be silly. Takes me all ma time to get hers any night, let alone a Sunday night.' The first: 'Couldn't ya get one then?' The second: 'No, I couldn't get one'. The first: 'Oh, ____ ya'.[154]

A Kaitaia milk bar during the 1950s.

TEENAGERS

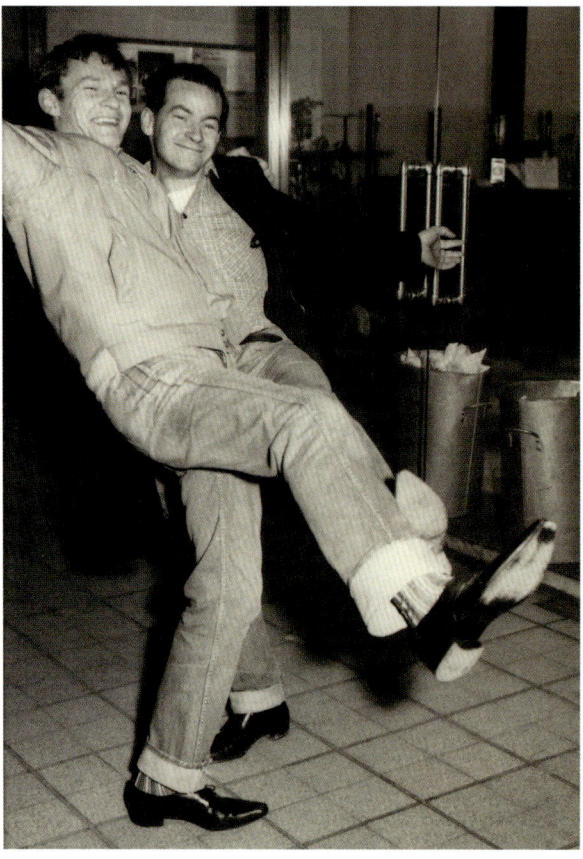

Bryan McGovern (*left*) and a mate have found a milk bar.

As a teenage-centred place to spend time, make friends and occasionally bear the brunt of humiliation, in Reg's case at least, the milk bar appealed to teenagers seeking to evade adult control. This youthful domain was not only a place to smoke and wear make-up; it offered musical freedoms too. In 1952, when the Hit Parade debuted on the radio, the New Zealand Broadcasting Corporation banned all suggestive tunes from the airwaves. Any song that violated the perceived need for 'consistent wholesomeness' faced the chop.[155] Marilyn Monroe stepped over the line when she sang 'I learned about love in the pale moonlight / And now I'm an educated gal', and Noël Coward's song about sailors' sexual partners – 'They're all alike in the dark' – outraged the censors. Milk-bar jukeboxes, though, allowed their listeners to evade state intrusion. Young patrons chose the tracks that suited them, sailors, moonlight and all, secure in the knowledge the government's busy-bodies could not interfere.

On a personal level, music afforded new freedoms and a way of finding an identity that was separate from that imbibed within families:

> Music was a leveller, it got me through a few things – people lived their lives through music then. Music allowed me to define myself and it put me in touch with emotions that I wasn't going to come across in my own life. In the words of songs I found feelings and love stories that I could hope for in my life, that were given expression in the wider world beyond my own. They told about the perfect relationship, about touch and feeling. I cherished those words.[156]

Milk-bar owners welcomed teenagers – or at least contented themselves with making money off them – but young New Zealanders did not have easy access to every post-war leisure space. The pubs were not their natural territory. Youths sauntered into Auckland's Royal and Exchange hotels in the middle of the nineteenth century but the drinking age had risen to twenty-one in 1910 and stayed there for decades afterwards. This did not stop teenagers trying, even though police raided the bars periodically. They overlooked some older teens and ejected the fresh-faced ones. Seventeen-year-old Anna Hoffmann sneaked into Wellington's Alhambra, 'a dingy den of thieves and hardened drinkers that smelt of smoke, sweat, stale beer and saturated carpets', but the police visited and threw her out.[157] Still, some publicans helped where they could. The proprietor of the Duke of Edinburgh ushered youngsters upstairs if the police looked likely to visit.[158] The New City, the Masonic and the Dominion were also popular with teenage Wellingtonians during the 1960s. They claimed the right to occupy these adult spaces only tentatively, although boys who held their nerve during a police raid considered they had passed a key test of manhood.[159]

An illicit takeaway liquor trade allowed teenagers to forge their own drinking culture. The proprietor of some Wellington pubs, including the Te Aro Hotel, sold half bottles of spirits – secreted in a brown paper bag – for teens to take to parties after the pub had closed. All that remained was to grab some food en

DIG ME

SORRENTO
COMPILED FROM RECO
PLAYED ON JUKE BOX
PRIVATE BAR
PAUL McCARTNEY

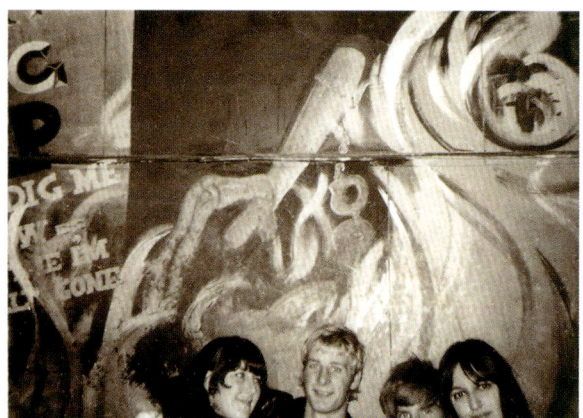

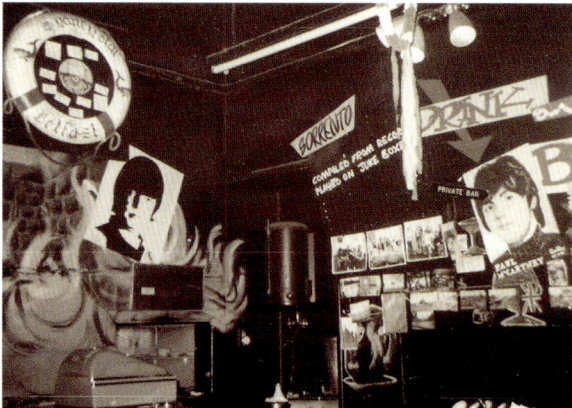

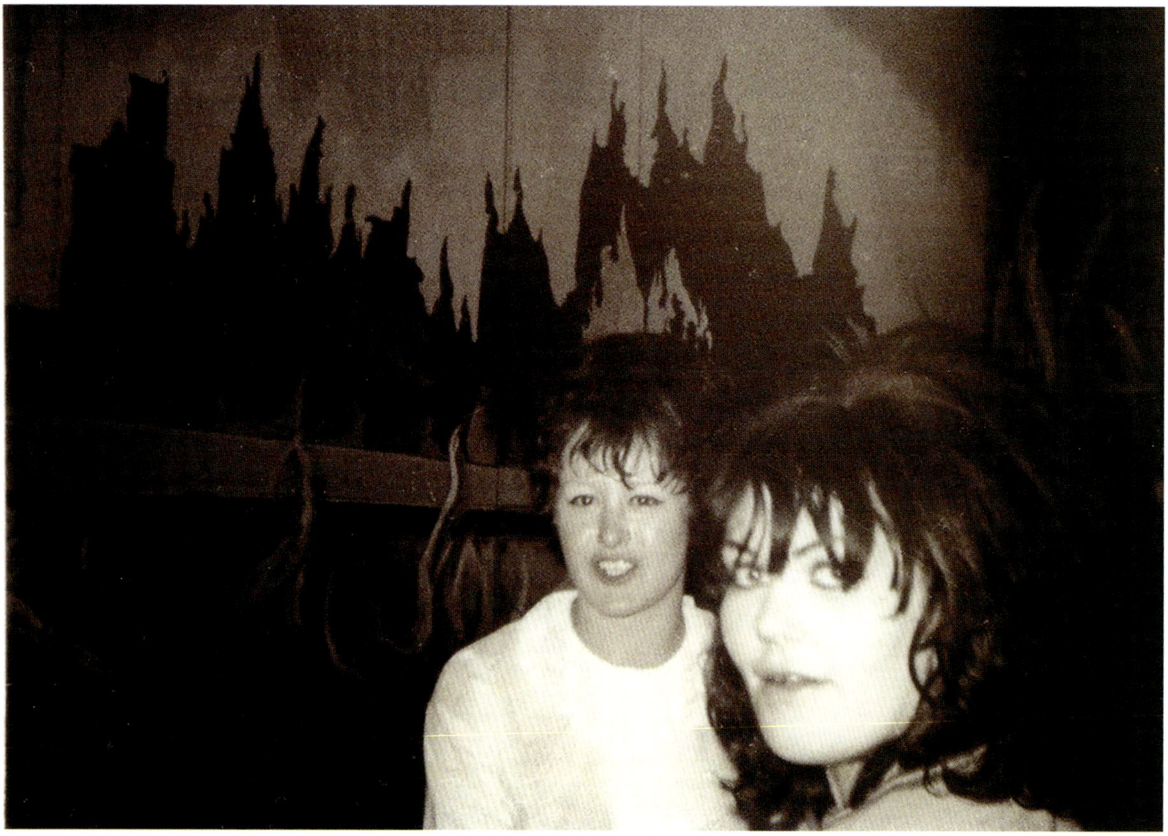

route, usually from a local burger bar or fish-and-chip shop.[160] There were private 'booze parties' in houses, cemeteries, parks and any other available spot; flat parties with drinking and jiving; and university parties where lecturers drank beer from tea pots, got every bit as drunk as their students and fell down the stairs.[161] In the suburbs of the Hutt Valley, the Petone and Naenae boys partied hard on 'Petone Hash'. Mixed together in bulk, this potent cocktail contained an idiosyncratic list of ingredients: three bottles of whisky, two of gin, two of port wine, four of sherry and twelve of beer along with six flasks of crème de menthe, one bottle of vanilla essence, one of lemonade, one of fizzy raspberry – and two eggs.[162]

Some of Crowther's research participants imbibed as well:

After general quips and fooling around Helen asked Keith, 'Did you see that love bite you gave Hilary on Saturday night?'

Keith: 'Who's she? I was so drunk I don't remember anything.'

Helen: 'I'll say you were drunk all right. Making us walk home.'

Observer: 'The boys were stinkers to leave you in the lurch.'

Helen: 'Yes, they get so drunk they don't remember what they've done.'[163]

If the milk bar represented youth-centred modernity and the pub was mostly an adult domain, coffee bars occupied the space in between. These were European in origin and some owed their existence to a wave of post-war Dutch immigration into New Zealand's larger cities. By the 1960s the coffee shop began to replace milk bars in urban teenagers' affections. Many offered live music – jazz and R'n'B, mostly – and catered to a mixed-age bohemian crowd. Some Christchurch teens mingled with military personnel and sundry beatniks at the Plainsman, 'a very cool scene'.[164] Others went to the Attic Coffee House upstairs in Cashel Street, home of Christchurch's best cappuccino and toasted sandwiches. The Silver Grill, another popular place, had little jukebox stations on every table. Most coffee bars were unlicensed so there was no age limit on entry, although teenagers and adults smuggled in small bottles of spirits to supplement the coffee, toasted sandwiches and soft drinks on offer. Some patrons at the Mexicali in Wellington

OPPOSITE The Sorrento Coffee Bar in Wellington, around 1964, as the milk bar's appeal began to wane. Note the Beatles material on the walls. The Sorrento was 'a nice place where you could have fun', one regular recalled. It had a jukebox, a band and a bouncer. Teens, like the adult patrons, smuggled in spirits.

smoked marijuana as well. 'I quickly began to "dig" the "scene" and thought I was "hip" when the "weed" was offered to me', Anna Hoffman wrote of her teenage years. 'My first "blast" was on a "reefer" shared with a couple of "muso" "cats".'[165] This distinctive atmosphere gestured towards the scenes of the 1970s.

Dance Halls and Rock 'n' Roll

Just as mid-century teenage leisure evolved out of older geographies and institutions – the street corner, the frontier hotel and the tearooms – abrupt changes in the urban scene shared the stage with older forms of socialising. As some boys headed into the coffee bars, others pressed their suits in readiness for public balls whose waltzes and formalities bore a striking resemblance to nineteenth-century dances. The debutante ball also retained its place in many young New Zealanders' transitions to adulthood. In a less solemn mode, adolescents asked one another to dance in the creaking community halls just as their ancestors had done. 'Tricia could dance beautifully', one West Coaster remembered. 'I was always hopeless.' Still, this fellow's mis-steps had an upside: 'we married three years after we met'.[166]

Other teenagers flocked to the commercial dance halls that opened for business during the jazz era and flourished after the war. Auckland's Jive Centre attracted 'tremendous bands' and a 'fast crowd' of 600 dancers on Friday and Saturday nights, all enjoying rock 'n' roll and (later) the twist.[167] The Oriental Dance Hall on Symonds Street played a wider range of music while the Surfside in Milford offered 'safe pop', as one musician described it.[168] Teenagers also poured through the doors of the Orange Hall ('the Orange') in Newton and the Maori Community Centre in Freemans Bay:

> There might be a group of us and the dances would start up at the Orange and when it finished there we all used to walk rather than pay for a taxi, we would all walk to the Maori Centre . . . and stay there until 2 or 3 in the morning . . . And just dance your life away. Maybe pick up a boyfriend, I dunno, all depends. But, that was far from my mind, we used to dance. Always had a live band [and] you could pick up a feed for 2/6 or 5 shillings. A boil up and a big cup of tea.[169]

OPPOSITE Upper Hutt had an active Youth Club during the 1960s. Local photographer Revelle Jackson snapped these self-conscious teens during one of the club's many dances.

A game of kilikiti (Samoan cricket) in Wellington in 1959. A youthful wave of Pacific migration occurred during the Second World War when boys and girls arrived from the Cook Islands to work as housemaids and in factories. Samoan migration picked up pace during the 1950s, and many young Tokelauans and Fijians arrived during the 1960s.

But the new dance trends – especially rock 'n' roll – were not confined to the commercial venues. They also found their way into leisure spaces supervised by adults. Auckland's Pacific Island Congregational Church, home to many young Samoans who arrived in the city during the 1950s, 'was always swinging with Polynesian music', while some Wellington churches embraced modern dance too.[170] 'St Francis, St Georges in Seatoun, Miramar, Newtown, everywhere there would be dances on a Sunday evening, and they'd have rock 'n' roll and everything', one regular remembered.[171] Young Cantabrians made their way to dances at the Hibernian and Caledonian halls and the Spencer Street Hall in Addington – the latter run by nuns – while Timaru teenagers enjoyed the creep ('a slow, slouchy dance'), jive and limbo at the Caroline Bay Hall on Saturday nights.[172] Those with staying power flocked to the rock 'n' roll marathons where participants kept their feet flying as long as they could: the winner of a Dunedin competition finally stopped dancing after forty-nine hours.[173]

Dancing provided a way for teens from different cultural backgrounds to meet. 'Rock 'n' roll was a very big part of my growing up', Wellingtonian Sophie Tindall recalled. She often went along to the Ngati Poneke Club where young Māori and Pākehā mingled under the watchful eye of a surly doorman. 'They had all the wonderful bands. Many of the Māori men wore blue suede shoes, and they were handsome. The atmosphere was electric, people felt very free.'[174] 'The Pākehā girls got sick of their ballroom dancing up the road', another Ngati Poneke regular remembered, and so 'they came to dance rock 'n' roll with the Māori boys'. Pākehā girls and Māori boys began to pair off.[175] Much the same happened in Christchurch where Crowther's researchers wrote of Māori and Pākehā socialising in the milk bars, pubs and private parties.[176] Post-war urban life fostered a degree of cultural contact not seen since the mid-nineteenth century when Pākehā in the village-sized towns regularly mixed with young Māori. Mixed marriages also became much more common in the two decades after the war, especially between Pākehā women under the age of twenty-one and Māori men in their early twenties.[177] These raised the eyebrows of many a parent, Māori and Pākehā alike, but the world had begun to change.[178]

New and Old Strands

Post-war teenagers attracted attention when their dress, dancing and dissolute behaviour made modernity visible. But not all aspects of teenage experience proved quite so controversial. Many young people went out of an evening but others stayed in; visiting took up more time than rock 'n' roll, especially on the weekends. Dallas Moore and his mates played soccer, tennis and marbles, went biking, and spent their evenings finishing homework.[179] Somewhat peeved by adults' views of young people as 'wicked vandals', Dallas complained that few ever mentioned 'the teenagers at the Promenade Concerts' or those who enjoyed opera.[180]

Back home, the bedroom remained a place of quiet contemplation and voracious novel-reading; British scholar Angela McRobbie suggests the 'culture of the bedroom' was particularly important in the lives of girls.[181] Privacy had its uses: one Dunedin lass lay on the bed in her family's caravan and learned a bit about sex

Making Music

Nineteen-year-old Elvis Presley debuted in January 1956 on 2YD's *Western Song Parade*. His many films – including *Jailhouse Rock* – featured the hip gyrations and pelvic thrusts that shocked many adults, but teenagers loved this American's sound and image. Eight years later, when the 'Fab Four' arrived from England, New Zealand fans greeted the Liverpool lads with yells of 'We love you Beatles!'[182] Music fandom had become a cornerstone of teenage experience.

Adolescents had been producers as well as consumers of music since the early years of the colony when boys like fourteen-year-old Richard Hay and his friend Arthur George played a violin and cornet at dances on the Otago goldfields.[183] A hundred years later, in 1962, an eighteen-year-old told a friend about his impending birthday party on the tobacco fields at Riwaka, near Nelson.

Selected Few, a band from the Hutt Valley.

I shan't get pickled (all the others will) because I don't drink but I shall sit on the table & strum a (borrowed) guitar & sing folk songs. I shall get 2–3 or perhaps 4 hours sleep before getting up at 6.15 to cook breakfast before going on the picking machine at 7.15am.[184]

Others made music professionally. Dinah Lee, born Diane Jacobs, debuted on the TV show *Time Out for Talent* at the age of sixteen. She produced a string of hits in both Auckland and Sydney. Ray Columbus also launched his music career in his mid-teens and a few years later fronted the band Ray Columbus and the Invaders.¹⁸⁵ Teenage sisters Judy and Sue Donaldson became The Chicks.¹⁸⁶

Johnny Devlin, an eighteen-year-old bank clerk, caused a stir in 1958. He borrowed James Dean's hairstyle and Elvis's moves, and made fans scream. Girls regularly ripped off his leopard-skin shirts.¹⁸⁷ Adult detractors called Devlin the 'Satin Satan' but some youths tried on the style for size. Teenage pandemonium took hold at an Invercargill restaurant when seventeen-year-old Bill Roper Smith, lead singer of local band The Skiffling Five, did his own display of 'pelvis gyrations and hip wiggling'. Several days later the city council called on Bill to explain himself. He said the music 'sort of made him want to' imitate Elvis's moves, and the mayor ordered he never do it again.¹⁸⁸

Teenagers became involved in television right from its inception. In 1962 they joined the first music show, *In the Groove*, to offer their views on the latest releases.¹⁸⁹ The same year the *Have a Shot* talent show gave aspiring stars a chance to strut their stuff, although

ABOVE Johnny Devlin dances with Mabel Howard, a Labour MP sympathetic to youth culture.

LEFT Dinah Lee.

Members of The Fourmyula, another Hutt Valley band, pose for the camera. They visited England while still in their teens, and recorded at the Abbey Road Studios – just as the Beatles had done.

the sound of the shotgun that signalled them to get off the stage brought many hopeful careers to a shuddering halt. *C'mon*, another music show, gave young singers valuable publicity. A *C'mon* road show launched the Underdogs, a blues quartet of sixteen- to eighteen-year-olds who turned up drunk and stoned, threw fish and chips at the audience, unleashed squeals of ear-splitting feedback and thrashed around 'with little regard for the actual song'.[190] Their teenage audience went wild.

Sales of guitars soared in 1964 when Beatlemania gripped the country and a great many teenagers set up high school bands. Russell Young and his Te Kuiti friends wagged school on Friday afternoons to play the Beatles' albums:

> On many occasions we would retreat to my mate's parents' bach at Mokau on the west coast of the North Island. The bach became our Abbey Road. At times we felt like John and Paul, as we wrote songs eyeball to eyeball. My mate, who did a lot of the vocals, actually sounded a bit like McCartney, particularly after a couple of bottles of DB lager.[191]

Music was a creative pursuit, an escape from school and sometimes the basis of a career.

by reading *Romeo and Juliet*.[192] Others pored over Mickey Spillane's racy detective novels, well away from their parents' prying eyes. Bedrooms also provided venues for social chit-chat, much as they had done in 1906 when Dora de Beer and her friends gossiped in front of the gas fire. New technologies – records and the radio – added to the ambience, whether friends came over or not. Soon these became more or less portable and were taken anywhere, with music fans eager to carry their audio culture into the outdoors: one day in the bedroom, the next at the beach.

Some initiatives occupied the middle ground between old and new types of leisure. 'Teenage clubs' popped up during the mid-to-late 1950s in the wake of the Mazengarb Report.[193] An antipodean version of the 'Teen Canteens' of post-war America, these clubs hybridised private and public space, adult control and adolescent self-governance.[194] While grown-ups exercised loose oversight, teenaged committee members decided who to let in and how to arrange their time. Following a vigorous debate, the Timaru Teenage Club agreed to admit young seamen into their cosy den of dance, darts, music, movies and table tennis.[195] These activities mirrored the American model, although the local versions had none of the evocative names (Jive Hive and Strut Hut) of their northern hemisphere counterparts.[196] Still, some teenage clubs broke new ground and quickly became popular with the hip crowd. In Christchurch, for instance, the Carlyle Street club became the city's first rock 'n' roll venue.[197] The teenage clubs went off like rockets – there were a dozen or more in Auckland alone – but many soon fizzled out. Gangs of disaffected youths stormed a few clubs and scared off their regulars; the Hamilton club closed down after a group of Frankton hostel boys repeatedly raided it.[198] Tensions between antagonistic factions threatened to rip apart this ambitious teenage experiment, but other clubs lived on. The Timaru Teenage Club, for instance, became the Timaru Young Citizens' Club and joined with other organisations to form the South Canterbury Recreational Association.[199]

Church youth groups built on the fifty-year-old foundations of Bible Class and Christian Endeavour, and their religious basis meant they held little appeal for marauding malcontents. Boys at Pastor Whiting's club in Christchurch talked about their day jobs, motorbikes and the beer they hid from the Pastor under a nearby bridge, and the club harboured the same friendships and enmities as any

TEENAGERS

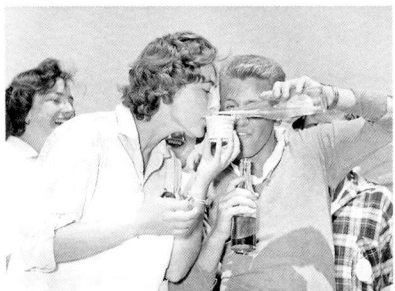

A bus trip, a Bible Class camp and a dance during the 1950s. The churches continued to play an important role in teenagers' social lives. Church hall dances introduced many to rock 'n' roll, and guitars became increasingly popular as the fifties slid into the sixties. There were tensions, of course: not all parents approved of the new moves or music. Some church leaders tried to ban disreputable kinds of clothing from functions – especially jeans – but they gave up in the face of inevitability.

other social scene. Crowther's study told of attachments, jealousies and changing allegiances. When somebody at the pastor's club noticed Dorothy's ex-boyfriend was nowhere to be seen, they asked Dorothy who replied: 'Thank God. If he walked in the door, I'd walk out.'[200]

The YMCA and YWCA set up clubs too. Each had its own small dramas. Dallas Moore went to the Auckland Y on weekday evenings to play darts, quoits, table tennis, billiards and chess: 'It was a bit rowdy. The girls got a bad time. Sandra Read got a dart stuck in her leg.'[201] YMCA personnel also carried on the outdoor activities of their turn-of-the-century counterparts. They ran camps where boys eeled, built dams, paddled kayaks, swam, played soccer and read bible stories around camp fires.[202] Meanwhile, the Bible Class movement updated itself for a new era, and teenagers made lifelong friends at the car rallies and film evenings that sprang up alongside the traditional camps and sports tournaments.[203] Religion's influence remained strong through the post-war years: when the American evangelist Billy Graham visited in 1959 he drew crowds well in excess of 100,000 people of all ages.[204]

The past constantly intersected with the present. School sports tournaments carried on their long tradition, and ski trips offered a new take on 'away games'. North Island schools sent pupils to National Park by train. They enjoyed thrills and spills during the day and impromptu rock 'n' roll in the lodge at night.[205] Air travel opened new frontiers too, allowing a lucky few to embark on school trips as far afield as Australia and the Pacific Islands. Groups of Guides and Scouts also sent delegations overseas. The eager young members of the Awakeri Scout troop, for instance, embarked on goodwill visits to Norfolk Island and Fiji.[206]

In 1962 a New Zealand contingent of twenty-six boys and seven adult Scouters set out for the Eleventh World Jamboree in Greece, travelling to Europe by ship with stops and side-trips in the ports along the way. After the Jamboree they toured Europe's capital cities and returned by air via New York. The lads thrilled to see the cradle of American culture that influenced teenage lives at home. 'The number of planes and the modern buildings, motorways, fast traffic – in fact everything just took our breath away', a Scouter wrote in his scrapbook. 'The scenery throughout the trip was magnificent and the contrast ranging from the filthy conditions of Singapore, our first stopping place, to the glamour of Honolulu in Hawaii, our final stopover, was incredible.'[207] This truly was a trip of

OVERLEAF Bike trips continued their appeal, and by the middle of the century new innovations – gears and balloon tyres – made long-distance cycling more comfortable. In these photos, members of the Wanganui Overlanders travel around the countryside during the 1950s and early 1960s. *Clockwise from top:* 'Arthur, David, Graeme', 'Mt Egmont from Te Kiri', 'In the drink.'

TEENAGERS

MILK-BAR COWBOYS AND ROCK 'N' ROLL

two halves. The long sea journey followed the same pathway as the immigrants of the 1870s, while the youths' return jet flights at 30,000 feet took a fraction of the time. Robert Baden-Powell's Scouting movement, established in the early 1900s to train boys in the ways of rustic manliness, eagerly embraced aspects of modern life. Sometimes new kinds of leisure replaced the old, but often the novel and the traditional intertwined in evocative ways.

Speaking Up, Speaking Out

The Bodgie, psychologist Arthur Manning's exposé of post-war adolescence, described a new generation straining against its parents' expectations. Manning's teenagers fired up their motorbikes, hunted for sexual opportunities and rebelled against authority. On the other hand, self-expression and youthful struggle were not new in themselves. In-betweeners of the nineteenth and early twentieth centuries expressed their 'resistance through rituals', as Dick Hebdige puts it.[208]

By the middle of the century the promise of airborne speed came true for more and more young people. At Auckland in 1955 a group of Cubs and Scouts poses next to their Pan American World Airways DC7 after a goodwill tour to Fiji.

TEENAGERS

Gesture, pose and attitude – the larrikin's slouch, the masher's smirk, the flapper's swearing and the bodgie's sneer – all reflected a desire to dissemble and transgress. Steerage passengers, physical culture fans and jazz fiends all asserted their presence in the face of wary adults.

In a political sense, though, the 1950s and 1960s represented a departure from previous decades. Some teenagers forged a sense of collective endeavour alongside their individual rebellions. A new ethos of independence, self-direction and individuality took hold during these decades.[209] The boys at Henderson High School expressed their annoyance when the school's principal told them what to wear to a school dance and forbade anything even remotely fashionable. 'We could wear any coat except windcheaters & zip jackets etc', Dallas Moore wrote in his diary. 'That left blazers, sportscoats and suits. Any socks except bright ones; any shirts except bright ones; any ties except shoestring ones. Michael Chester said, "Do we dress ourselves, or does [the headmaster] do it?"'[210] The principal

Boys and their boards. Some young women surfed during the 1920s but the sport became male-dominated during the 1950s; Taranaki, where the gender balance was more even, was an exception. Early 'longboards' were made of ply over a wooden skeleton; fibreglass boards replaced them at the end of the decade. A great many boys took up the sport in their teens, surfing before and after school. Lads at the YMCA's Camp Opoutama, on the Mahia Peninsula, found the surfing a highlight of their stay. Many regular surfers saw their culture as an escape from mainstream social expectations, with copious drinking and partying, and the tabloid media represented surfers accordingly. Surfing boomed from the mid-1960s: the magazine *New Zealand Surfer* was first published in 1965, and locally made and imported surfware became popular.

threatened to ban longer hair and crew cuts as well. Incensed, Dallas scribbled in his diary: 'If he does it he is a louse of the lowest order.'[211] While Henderson boys complained among themselves, Jon Dumble, a pupil at Auckland Grammar, performed his resistance out in the open. He peroxided his hair with supplies raided from the chemistry lab, and the headmaster said 'if you don't stop peroxiding your hair I will make you wear a gym dress to school'. Jon took up the challenge. He kept his hair as it was, turned up the next day in one of his sister's dresses and was thrashed by the headmaster for his trouble.[212]

These examples suggest that school discipline intensified after the war – visitors from America often noted its harshness – before loosening again during the 1960s.[213] Small wonder the film *Blackboard Jungle*, released in America in 1955, 'caused an enormous sensation' in New Zealand.[214] The movie appealed to teenagers who lapped up its classroom disobedience, alleyway rumbles and knife attacks. 'There was "Rock Around the Clock" on at the start, and then school kids in dirty white t-shirts defying everybody', one young viewer remembered.[215] New Zealand fans poured out of the movie theatres and stomped, clapped and jived down the streets.[216] *Blackboard Jungle* offered the mystique of America and a rebellious attitude.

Some teenagers went further and published their criticisms of adult authority. In 1968, a year of anti-authoritarian protests and riots in Europe and America, boys at Wellington College edited a magazine titled *Free Press* and circulated copies outside the school gates. They criticised New Zealand's 'anachronistic' school system built on petty regulations, drab uniforms, corporal punishment, power-crazed prefects and Hitler-like headmasters. Such conditions, they felt, churned out 'conforming, spiritless automatons' with nary a spark of individuality.[217]

While the *Free Press* encouraged teenagers to throw off their shackles, secondary school pupils engaged in other debates as well. In 1968 a sixth former wrote a piece entitled 'The Status of Women' for the *Auckland Girls' Grammar Magazine*. She denounced discrimination in the workplace, 'male dominated society' in general, and the seeming inevitability of marriage and domesticity. 'The role of today's women hinges on the institution of marriage', she wrote. 'From childhood upwards we are taught to regard marriage as an inevitable stage in our lives just like going to school or getting our second teeth. Marriage is variously, insidiously and constantly reproduced by magazines, novels, television and films as being the acme of romance, and the passport to social acceptance.'[218] Few teenagers had questioned the hegemony of matrimony during the mid-1950s, but soon the ground began to shift. Three years after the piece in the high school yearbook, the visit of Australian feminist Germaine Greer, author of the 1970 best-seller *The Female Eunuch*, created a public sensation. Greer denounced the nuclear family as suffocating and oppressive of women, and was arrested for using the words 'bullshit' and 'fuck' in public.[219]

A few young New Zealanders also criticised the booming mass culture industry. Although consumer capitalism had propelled teenage culture during the post-war years, and movies like *Blackboard Jungle* and *Rebel Without a Cause* hinted at rebellious freedoms, some suspected that Hollywood and the media enforced a dull conformity of their own. 'A concrete example of the way this "one dimensional society" works is found in the influencing or manipulation of lives and opinions through the news media', Maureen Kolff wrote in the Student Christian Movement's magazine *Charisma*. The result, she added, was a 'self-seeking materialistic' society.[220] Herbert Marcuse's *One Dimensional Man*, the basis of this critique, is a sociological analysis of the ways consumer society stealthily controls the populace.[221] Marcuse's views circulated around the English-speaking world during the late 1950s and early 1960s. They became popular among leftist critics as consumer society rapidly expanded.[222] In *New Zealand Through Young Eyes*, a 1963 compilation of teenagers' writings, Ngaruawahia teenager Suzanne Foreman added her voice to the debate. 'The world of commerce has thought up myriads of money-making ideas for our pleasure, but, as part of our growing-up process, what becomes of our individuality? Why is so much notice given to us? The word "teenager" seems to have taken the meaning of some "thing" that has been manufactured along with other mass-produced objects.'[223]

Dunedin fifth former Alistair Sloan, another contributor to the *Young Eyes* book, felt much the same way, and he expressed his views in poetry:

> Out of suburbia they come,
> Mindless creatures of a mindless world,
> Seeking elusive satisfaction

New Zealand through YOUNG EYES

edited by TERRY POWER

> In the gaudy blare of the juke-box
> – 'Sixpence in the slot
> For a three-tune lot' –
> The clatter of heels on pavements
> – 'Watch where ya goin', son' –
> The whistle at pretty girls.
> (Eyes right, eyes up and down.)
>
> Light-lost moths that are dull and grey
> Summoned by the main-street glare;
> Empty faces and empty eyes
> Deserted in their vacancy –
> Stirred only by the primeval throb
> Of guitars, the shriek of saxophones
> In tawdry smoke-filled dance-halls;
> Finding shallow excitement
> In artificial emotion.[224]

Marcuse's critique resonates between these verses, while the poem's moody quality evokes Jack Kerouac's 1957 novel *On the Road*: 'Tracy is a railroad town; brakemen eat surly meals in diners by the tracks. Trains howl away across the valley.'[225] The well-known poet James K. Baxter owned a copy of Kerouac's counterculture classic, and his teenage friends fell over one another to borrow it.[226] Kerouac inspired young New Zealanders, like their American counterparts, to experiment with the beat generation's oppositional style. 'I decided I was a beatnik', one man recalled of his younger years. 'I read Kerouac and wore black – black shirt, black fisherman's knit jersey, black cords.'[227] Teens' political awareness drew on other sources too. Brian, a nineteen-year-old whose life story appears in Crowther's 'Street Society', worked as an apprentice and professed an interest in travel, psychology and politics. 'His views are leftish, and he is very interested in racial problems', Crowther wrote. 'He has a wide Maori and Pakeha circle.' Raised a Presbyterian, Brian's religious views 'are now a mixture of Deism and Yoga'.[228] Brian embraced the new values of post-war selfhood – a belief in equality, self-expression and self-fulfilment – and his potted biography shows

OPPOSITE Those on the cover of *New Zealand Through Young Eyes* spent their weekend afternoon in Auckland Domain. Terry Power's schoolteacher friend Peter Ohms snapped the group when he wandered past.

how philosophy and personal experience helped teenagers forge a critique of their own society.[229]

Avant-gardism came slowly to the universities. Students were hardly the most radical of youth, at least at first, and few expanded their horizons like Brian did. They had the time to take part in political activity but the universities were elite institutions and many students held conservative views.[230] A handful of left-wing debating clubs had sprung up during the 1930s and small groups advocated pacifism, but their members' resolve weakened when war broke out.[231] Only the barest glimmers of political organisation shone in the universities during the early 1950s, including a yearly national congress that met in the Marlborough Sounds to discuss politics. Most students of the 1950s seemed content, as Sam Elworthy observes, to 'use sex and alcohol as an act of defiance against their parents', and they felt little need to challenge the status quo in any broader sense.[232]

Change eventually came to the ivy halls. University enrolments slowly increased from 11,600 in 1949 to 13,300 in 1959 and then swelled to 31,000 in

Two sides of university life. Many out-of-towners lived in gender-segregated halls of residence with their own quirky traditions: in Wellington, for instance, new boys from Weir House were stripped to their underwear and tied to a fence while girls from nearby Victoria House threw rubbish at them.

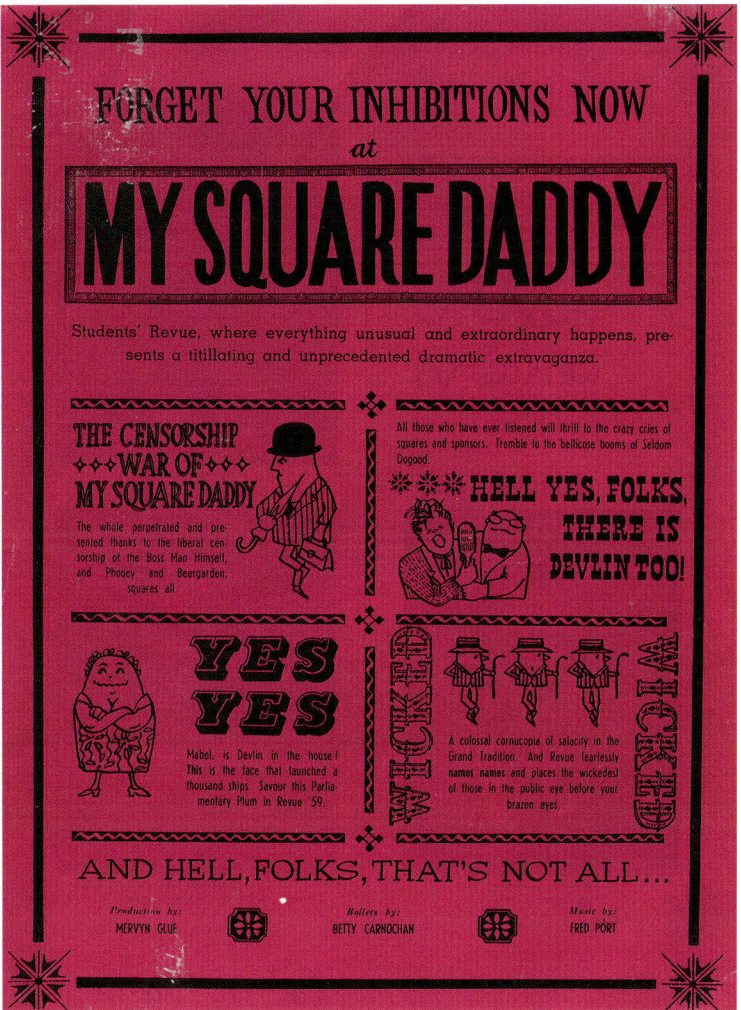

The University of Canterbury's capping magazine from 1959 hints at students pushing the boundaries. Editors rarely complied with university administrators' requests to keep sex out of the magazines.

1969.[233] This surge coincided with a growing political consciousness. Broadsides against the 'puritanism' of New Zealand society filled the front pages of alternative papers like *Falus*, produced at the University of Otago and dedicated to a new counterculture movement of hippies, weirdies, anarchists and pot smokers. 'Queen Victoria's remains are stinking rather a lot now', *Falus* declared. 'We hope

An anti-Vietnam war protest, Wellington, 1967. Young people played a central role in the politics of the movement, and television disseminated ideas and images. The new generation was keenly aware of New Zealand's place in the world. Politically inclined young people – not just students – began to focus on international issues during the mid-1960s: civil rights, racism and nuclear weapons. A few joined the Campaign for Nuclear Disarmament, the World Affairs Council and Amnesty International.

that no-one will try to dig her up.'[234] *Falus* advocated equality between men and women and supported homosexual law reform several years before second-wave feminism and gay liberation burst into life.[235] Like Manning's book *The Bodgie* and Wellington College pupils' *Free Press*, *Falus* set the scene for the anti-authoritarian and sexual liberationist literature of the 1970s.[236] Many teenagers and twenty-somethings lived conventional lives, but others drew upon the simmering discontents of the 1950s to mould the egalitarian campaign of the 1960s and the new social movements of the 1970s.

Conclusion: Modern Youth?

'It's hard to explain to someone who wasn't there just how exciting it was to be young in the 1950s and early 1960s.'[237] Ray Columbus – Elvis fan, mod and band leader – remembered his formative years fondly. In Ray's experience, and that of many other New Zealand teenagers, personal and social change came together in a heady mix. The atomic bomb was not the only explosion in the post-war world. Internal migrations and new mobilities laid bare the shifting tensions between dependence and independence, and the streets, schoolrooms, picture theatres, milk bars, dance halls and television shows provided the settings for culture-building and intergenerational conflict.

Not everything changed, though, certainly not at once. Social transitions took time, and Ray Columbus tempered his own excitement with a certain wariness. Cities enticed young New Zealanders but urban society did not treat everyone equally. Ray felt that the 'churches and women's guilds' ruled Christchurch, and he sensed a prejudice towards anyone different.[238] At first, traditional patterns of authority, including the rigorously enforced institution of marriage, resisted the new challenges that bubbled away under the surface. Soon things began to shift and the pace of change quickened. Youthful resistance, though, did not spring up out of nowhere. International influences played an important role and New Zealanders' independent-mindedness had a long local history of its own. Young people's cultures celebrated resistance, pleasure-seeking and a certain permissiveness during every decade covered in this book, and the tensions finally came to a head during the fifties and sixties.

Not everyone pushed at the barricades, at least not in the same way. Rugby lads picked fights with bodgies and sailors hacked their contemporaries' hair when new fashions transformed teenage style. Even as similarities jostled with differences, though, a new look spread throughout the teenage population. Those who attended Bible Class gatherings rarely saw themselves as widgies or bodgies but both groups shared a love of bright colours, guitars and rock 'n' roll. Few boys identified as mods during the 1960s, but the skinny tie, Beatles haircut and black jacket found a broad constituency. Young people forged a 'generational self-consciousness' in spite of their differences.[239]

TEENAGERS

The mid-twentieth-century teenager was a contradictory hybrid: a personality type ripe for analysis, a delinquent in need of firm discipline and a consumer with money to spend. Even conservative newspaper editors wove together these paradoxical elements. In 1958 *Truth* shocked its readers with stories about 'teenage bottle parties' where leopard-skin-trouser-wearing, leather-jacketed adolescents yelled, shouted and strewed broken glass in public places, but these exposés sat alongside ads for films like *Rebel Without a Cause*.[240] Newspapers reacted against the new youth culture, but they were happy to collect advertising revenues from the industries that propelled it along. Young people noticed the inconsistencies. 'Surely the teenager of today is being taken too seriously?', Suzanne Foreman

A New Year's Eve bonfire on the beach at Caroline Bay, Timaru, in 1962.

wrote peevishly in 1963. 'Weekly magazines make a feature of us, articles in the press appear almost daily, either extolling our accomplishments or bewailing our shortcomings.'[241] It did not seem to matter how much adults worried about the volatility of youth culture, they could not resist poking it with a sharp stick.

Economic forces shaped the leisure life of a generation while adolescents pondered their own feelings: in the words of one girl, it is 'no wonder the grownup cannot altogether understand the temperamental teenager, for at this in-between stage of neither child nor grownup I am sure I hardly know myself'.[242] When the media attempted to define teenagehood, it created an image for young people to embrace or to push against. At the same time, some teenagers questioned adults' smug self-satisfaction. Why did they start wars? Why were they obsessed with money? Why did they gamble and always get drunk? Weren't flapper fashions and the Charleston, the high point of their parents' youth, 'every bit as ridiculous' as the clothes and dances of the post-war decades?[243] Adult society placed teenagers firmly under the spotlight, but young people talked back louder than ever before.

Naomi Highfield, Glenys Taylor and Beverley Nicholson near the skating rink in Paraparaumu, early 1965. The girls pose with a friend's Holden FJ.

Conclusion **Back to the Future**

Until recently my own teenage diaries – a green leatherette volume from 1986, when I was a fourth former, and another from 1987, the year I sat School Certificate – lay in boxes in my parents' cupboard. I felt a tingle of trepidation as I opened them for the first time in thirty years, feeling sure they must be embarrassing or – even worse – deeply tedious. I quickly flicked through them and read about exams, prize-givings, piano lessons, reading lists, music and clothes (lime-green trousers!) before stowing them away again.

I was a bookish Hutt Valley teenager, happy but not overly sociable, interested in French and geography and Cyndi Lauper's music, with a vague idea of becoming an architect or a town planner and only half aware of being gay. At university I 'came out', discovered sociology and involved myself in environmental activism. I didn't really think I had a flair for architecture, and abandoned the idea of town planning when my summer job at the (then) Historic Places Trust revealed the ugliness of the 1980s building boom. Like the contributors to the 1963 book *New Zealand Through Young Eyes*, I had definite views about things – and these shaped my young adult life.

OPPOSITE Lance Best, a fifth former at Mana College in Porirua, in 1981.

I knew little about local teenage history during the 1980s, even though my school, Hutt Valley High, was only 700 metres from the site of the long-closed Elbe's, a well-known milk bar during the Mazengarb fuss of 1954. Some three kilometres from school were the long-closed Petone picture theatres at the centre of Frank Le Fort's investigation. I had no idea that Hutt Valley teenagers had caused a national scandal thirty years earlier. No-one ever talked about bodgies and widgies. Our only awareness of the fifties was the 1985 film *Back to the Future* whose protagonist Marty, played by Michael J. Fox, zips back to 1955 in a time machine and meets his then-teenaged parents. Our own social history meant little: the immediacy of our own lives was very much the focus, and we had half an eye on the future.

At the same time, our views, interests and self-perceptions were profoundly shaped by the years in which we came of age, years whose cultural tentacles stretched back even further. Hutt Valley High School, an amalgamation of the earlier Petone District High School and Hutt District High School, opened its doors in 1926 when there were separate entrances for boys and girls, the product of a decade unable to decide whether they should mix or not. Our own uniform reflected much older designs: the cut of the shorts, the style of the shirt and the length of the socks bore a striking resemblance to those worn at Waitaki Boys' High School in 1918 (see p. 157). Typing class was another remnant of the 1910s, a carry-over from the old commercial course. By 1985 all third formers, boys as well as girls, took typing for a term. This seemed fun to me – my mother had trained as a typist, and we compared notes on the keyboard 'drills' – but I failed to make the link between what we did in typing class and the room with a dozen boxy computers where we played around with programming. Did we learn to type in preparation for the white-collar world of word processing or the unlikely sounding 'paperless office'? Whatever the intention, we were readying ourselves for the yet-unforeseen online revolution. Other technologies made an appearance too. On the weekends we made 'mix tapes': my 1985 diary has a sketch of the plug-and-wire gadget I invented to link two electronic devices. I embraced low-tech customisable content, perfected by the iPod fifteen years later and the smartphone a few years after that. These elements of teenage experience formed links in a longer chain, from the gramophone to the jukebox, the Walkman and beyond.

BACK TO THE FUTURE

Teenagers of the 1980s.

TEENAGERS

New Zealand's education system has moulded and managed adolescence in critically important ways. While the first mission schools changed the lives of a few, late-twentieth-century mass education moulded the existence of nearly everyone. All the while, a single central tension persisted: the often-uneasy relationship between the truism that knowledge is powerful, and the forceful shaping – some might say control – of adolescent minds and bodies. For decades boys and girls grappled with arithmetic and geometry and expanded their literary horizons as they read the classics, and some teachers thrashed those – especially boys – who stepped over the line. Corporal punishment had disappeared by the early 1980s, replaced by detention, suspensions and, ten years after that, warnings about the perils of the neo-liberal marketplace that would deliver lifelong failure to those who dropped out. In order to survive and prosper in the new dog-eat-dog world, the entrepreneurial graduates of the early twenty-first century must learn how to make 'good choices'. They need to hone their marketable skills and develop a sense of personal responsibility.[1] Even so, the self-governing teenager was, and is, subject to older modes of discipline. Some teachers and principals continue to regulate personal appearance and send home those who refuse to toe the line. Remarkably, boys' hair length and the use of slickening oils and creams – popular during the 1940s, if not before – are still contentious, and some schools would rather defend their rules in court than relax their grip.[2] Regulations, freedoms and 'rights' still jostle uncomfortably.

Girls' bodies are even more tightly tangled in the knots of power. Female adolescents quietly confessed their desires to their diaries – and occasionally to one another – during the late nineteenth century, and they navigated the sexual double standard as best they could. The researchers of the 1950s revealed girls' sexual repressions and enthusiasms in equal measure. Through the 1970s, young adults' own publications – illicit underground papers like *Itch* and *Down Under the Plum Trees*, a book with sketches of sexual positions and explicit photographs taken in Wellington's student flats – urged revolution, but they paid more attention to male prerogatives than female passions.[3] Even now, forty years on, teachers keep an eye on girls' clothing and tell them how much skin they should bare, while popular media outlets vacillate between encouraging sexual empowerment, sexualising girls and maintaining taboos around their sexuality. As Auckland educationalist Louisa Allen recently observed, 'female desire

OPPOSITE At the AFS Dance in Oamaru during the 1970s.

is everywhere unofficially and yet still nowhere officially'.[4] The sexual double standard, an artefact of the nineteenth century, has not yet disappeared.

Old meets new in the age of the internet. To Google 'teenage sexuality' is to learn of the psychological perils and moral dangers lurking in sexting, selfies and social media.[5] 'Sexting Like Drug Addiction For Kiwi Teens' shrieked a not atypical headline of 2016.[6] These jeremiads mirror the old contention that 'the ever increasing complexity and high tempo of modern living seems to have resulted in a never-ending search for pleasure and excitement'.[7] This claim appears in the 1953 Hutt Valley Youth Survey which, in turn, echoed *The Evangelist*'s dire warnings from 1866. These anxieties have resonated over 150 years, and it is hard to separate the age-old themes of adult piety and techno-fear from the real challenges posed by social and technological change. After all, the social media age has ushered in a new intensity and novel kinds of accountability. Saying and doing the 'wrong thing' has become a highly public act and nobody can retract an image or idea once it has an online life. At the same time, the small size and portability of the smartphone confers a certain privacy upon the teenager and makes parental surveillance more complicated than ever before.[8]

What about labels? 'Teenager' is in many respects an elusive term. I cannot remember identifying with it, and it makes no appearance in my own high school yearbooks from the 1980s. Adults usually slapped on the classification, often dismissively. I recall my irritation when I saw a poster with this slogan: 'TEENAGERS. Tired of being harassed by your stupid parents? ACT NOW! Move out, get a job and pay your own bills while you still know everything.' Feckless, clueless know-alls, teenagers would only realise the error of their ways once they learned life's hard lessons. Recent cartoons archived on the National Library's website convey much the same message: the millennial teenager is a witless, untidy, heavy-drinking, sex-obsessed, antisocial slacker.[9] Here 'teenager' is a spoiled identity, as American sociologist Erving Goffman would have said, 'a discredited person' possessing a value system unacceptable to the adult world.[10] The same was true of the nineteenth century, when 'larrikin' was a label applied to troublesome lads and the 'dude' more a figure of fun than an identity, and seventy years later when few proclaimed themselves 'widgies' or 'milk-bar cowboys'.

Young people choose some labels and others are applied from outside; some identities are fleeting, others last longer. A recent ethnography identified twelve 'tribes' at a Christchurch high school, including 'Christians', 'Goths', 'Sporty Girls', 'Pasifika Girls' and 'Geeks', although most of the classifications were externally imposed.[11] There are other examples. The category of 'hipster' includes adolescents but has a broader meaning. 'Nobody will admit to being a hipster', observes Christchurch sociologist Ben Elley, 'but everybody is willing to say who is – it is always somebody strange, and more often than not there is an implicit criticism.'[12] Still, there are a great many self-imposed identities: 'swimmer', 'sports chick', 'prefect', 'Mormon', 'Islander' and 'Southsider' all appear in recent writing.[13] The 'can-do girl' is a twenty-first-century incarnation of the colonial girl: physically confident, outdoorsy, sometimes interested in cars and shooting. She hybridises gendered ideals just like her turn-of-the-century predecessor.[14]

At high school I wondered when I would cease to be a 'pupil' – a status we all shared with five-year-olds – and become a 'student', something far more grown up. 'Adult' was perhaps the most coveted title. The transition to adulthood has changed since the nineteenth century. Then, children acquired elements of adulthood at any time between thirteen and twenty-one: individuals' size, work capacity, and marital and educational status shaped their place in this transition. These bookends slid closer together as the twentieth century progressed: the school leaving age rose to sixteen in 1989; the voting age fell from twenty-one to twenty in 1969 and then to eighteen in 1974; and eighteen-year-olds could buy alcohol in 1999. The twenty-first birthday lost its significance as anything other than an excuse for a party, and the New Zealand Law Commission now considers eighteen to be the age of majority. The legal period of transition from childhood to adulthood shrank as the twentieth century wore on, from a wide eight-year window to the narrow two-year gap between sixteen and eighteen. There is one notable exception to this compression of boundaries: twenty-five is the age at which a tertiary student allowance is no longer means-tested against parents' income – a testament to government parsimony more than anything else.

Teenagers continue to stand up for themselves, and the recent past has seen new kinds of activism. Some young New Zealanders of earlier generations – Dunedinite Dora de Beer and her friends, for instance – would have embraced the high school feminist societies of the twenty-first century, but what would they have made of sexual diversity? Few lesbian and gay students 'came out' during the 1980s – as a fourth former I found myself on the fringes of tense

Hikoi: in 2016 this group of high school students from Te Kura Kaupapa Māori o Whakarewa i te Reo ki Tuwharetoa walked from Taupo to Wellington to present a petition that demanded all New Zealand's lakes and rivers be clean enough to swim in.

discussions over the Homosexual Law Reform Bill, not sure what to make of it all – but the prospect was wholly unthinkable before the 1970s when young gay liberationists visited schools and urged teenagers to cast aside conservative sexual values.[15] Many among the earlier generations were horrified, including the redoubtable Patricia Bartlett from the Society for the Promotion of Community Standards. *Truth*, meanwhile, complained about 'social engineering of the young by trendies and the sexually sick'.[16] The revolutionary zeal soon faded away. The legislative reforms of the 1980s required reassurances that nobody was trying to 'recruit' anybody else, and school sex education reverted to its previous (heterosexual) form.

Environmentalism made an impact too. I started learning to drive at fifteen but lost interest – for seventeen years – when I learned about pollution and fossil fuel depletion. New Zealand's environmental movement has radiated outwards, from the localised Save Manapouri campaign of the 1960s and 1970s to a wider range of concerns. Now young people play important roles in recycling initiatives, pest-trapping programmes and climate-change lobbying.[17] Work, another key theme in adolescent lives, gives rise to other kinds of activism. The continuing growth in retail and service jobs has installed a great many teenagers on the 'other side of the counter', and some agitate for better wages and conditions. Youth rates were a particular target during the mid-2000s when school students led strike action. Three out of five strike leaders at one Auckland fast-food outlet were aged under eighteen. 'I'm looking forward to going on strike to let the community know we're getting paid crap. I'm doing it for everyone', one fifteen-year-old said in 2005.[18] Technology provided a new arsenal: cellphones summoned the sudden crowd of the 'flashmob', and blogs bypassed established forms of media.[19]

Teenagers weigh up and sometimes reject the idea that they are imperfectly formed, impulsive and in need of careful management. Alongside every debate about teenagers' psychological immaturity sits another, often unspoken concern: as the foot soldiers of modernity, young adults forge new ideological paths. They are 'sucked into the vortex of social change', as sociologist Karl Mannheim wrote during the 1920s, threatening to live differently from their parents.[20] The larrikin was presumed less disciplined than his father, the flapper 'faster' than her mother, the activist of the 1970s less tolerant of authority than her parents. As the years pass by, successive generations incorporate new values into their adult lives and superimpose their own styles over what has gone before – and later in life they perceive the next generation of teenagers to be more outrageous than they possibly could have been themselves.[21]

Continuities persist in spite of it all, and teenage cultures draw upon the past as much as they supercede it. History teaches us that young people pull out and re-stitch the threads of the past. Youths made music and went drinking ('nobblerising') during the 1840s, ten-pin bowling began in the 1860s and movies date from the first decade of the twentieth century. Likewise, school camps, ski trips, milk bars and pop concerts were all built on older youth cultures. When the Hutt Valley High School First XV travelled to America in 1988, they echoed long-running traditions: the migrations of the 1840s, the 'away game' of the 1880s, and the international student exchanges of the 1950s and 1960s. In 1987, when members of the school's drama club dressed as clowns in the Queensgate shopping mall, they staged a 1920s-style burlesque in Lower Hutt's brand-new citadel of consumption. 'The most mischievous clowns jumped in a Foodtown trolley, drove down the aisles and unloaded each other at the check-out.'[22]

There is no more typical teenager now than there was in 1883 when Nelsonian Fred Gibbs criticised his masher counterparts, when youths of the 1920s clashed in Auckland's picture theatres and during the 1960s when young trades trainees hung out at Christchurch's hostels. Class, ethnicity, gender, age, sexuality and religion, diverse temperaments, various attitudes towards authority and differing degrees of general enthusiasm create different experiences of adolescence. Not everyone was (and is) socially adventurous, alienated or politically aware; many get on with making their way through life with a minimum of fuss.[23] Life has always been tougher for some than for others. Of those whose lives appear here, many recorded the gentle pleasures and mild ups-and-downs of a comfortable existence, while more than a few, including those eking out a living during the Depression or incarcerated in state care, had a rockier road and adapted as best they could.

Adolescent histories are intimate tales of thinking, feeling, being, becoming and belonging; large-scale shifts and intimate lives are closely intertwined. Everyday stories tell of more than just the individual: teenagers learn how to fit in socially, but they take their place in history too.

OPPOSITE DIY punk rockers The Suburban Reptiles who, with The Scavengers, set alight Auckland's energetic punk scene in the late seventies. Playing all their own songs to a predominantly teenage crowd wherever they could, the former Auckland University art school students showed that you didn't have to be a musician to perform on stage or release records. In a short time, they helped spawn a generation of new artists as many in their audience were quick to start their own bands.

Abbreviations

AC	Author's collection	NZFL	*New Zealand Free Lance*
AL	Auckland Libraries	NZG	*New Zealand Genealogist*
ADM	Albertland and Districts Museum, Wellsford	NZGWS	*New Zealand Gazette and Wellington Spectator*
AGGM	*Auckland Girls' Grammar Magazine*	NZH	*New Zealand Herald*
AJHR	*Appendices to the Journals of the House of Representatives*	NZL	*New Zealand Listener*
		NZPD	*New Zealand Parliamentary Debates*
AM	Auckland Museum	NZPM	New Zealand Police Museum, Porirua
ANZ	Archives New Zealand	*NZT*	*New Zealand Truth*
AS	*Auckland Star*	*NZTI*	*New Zealand Times*
ATL	Alexander Turnbull Library, Wellington	*NZWW*	*New Zealand Woman's Weekly*
BNZ	Bank of New Zealand Archive, Wellington	OBHS	Otago Boys' High School Archive, Dunedin
BPT	*Bay of Plenty Times*	*ODT*	*Otago Daily Times*
CCA	Christ's College Archives, Christchurch	OHI	Oral History Interviews (in this volume)
CCL	Christchurch City Libraries	*OM*	*Oamaru Mail*
CD	*Count Down*	*OW*	*Otago Witness*
CM	Canterbury Museum	OWM	Owaka Museum
CR	*Catholic Review*	PA	Puke Ariki, New Plymouth
CSM	Central Stories Museum, Alexandra	*PBH*	*Poverty Bay Herald*
DGG	*Dominion Girl Guide*	PC	Private collection
DHS	Dalmatian Historical Society, Auckland	PRA	Presbyterian Archives, Dunedin
DSC	*Daily Southern Cross*	RM	Riverton Museum
EP	*Evening Post*	RMTB	Rehua Marae Trust Board, Christchurch
ES	*Evening Star*	SCM	South Canterbury Museum, Timaru
FP	*Free Press*	*SDR*	*New Zealand Sporting and Dramatic Review*
FS	*Feilding Star*	*SEN*	*South End News*
GRA	*Grey River Argus*	*SEP*	*Social End Product*
HC	Hocken Collections, Dunedin	SMC	St Margaret's College Archive, Christchurch
HCL	Hamilton City Libraries	SOM	South Otago Museum, Balclutha
HHC	Hokonui Heritage Centre, Gore	*SSTM*	*Sunday Star-Times Magazine*
HN	*Here and Now*	*ST*	*Southland Times*
HNS	*Hawera and Normanby Star*	*SVCR*	*The Spike or Victoria College Review*
HT	*Human Touch*	TA	Te Ahu, Kaitaia
HTNS	*Hutt News*	*TAH*	*Te Ao Hou*
HUCL	Hutt City Libraries	*TAN*	*Te Aroha News*
HVHS	*Hutt Valley High School Magazine*	*TE*	*The Evangelist*
IL	Invercargill City Library	*TGSM*	*Takapuna Grammar School Magazine*
KCM	Kapiti Coast Museum, Waikanae	TOSM	Toitū Otago Settlers Museum, Dunedin
LDM	Lakes District Museum, Arrowtown	*TT*	*Tuapeka Times*
LT	*Lyttelton Times*	UHL	Upper Hutt Library
LWM	*Lake Wakatip Mail*	*WD*	*Wairarapa Daily*
MA	Methodist Archives, Christchurch	*WDT*	*Wairarapa Daily Times*
MB	Macmillan Brown Library, Christchurch	*WI*	*Wellington Independent*
ME	*Marlborough Express*	WMRC	Whakatane Museum and Research Centre
MS	*Manawatu Standard*	*WR*	*White Ribbon*
NENZC	*Nelson Examiner and New Zealand Chronicle*	WRM	Whanganui Regional Museum
NLA	National Library of Australia	*WT*	*Waikato Times*
NOM	North Otago Museum, Oamaru	*YMM*	*Young Man's Magazine*
NPM	Nelson Provincial Museum		

Notes

Introduction: Finding the Teenage

1. Gertie Brookes to Ella Marsh, 18 June 1890, ADM.
2. Gertie Brookes to Ella Marsh, 11 September 1889, ADM.
3. Gertie Brookes to Ella Marsh, 29 November 1888, ADM.
4. Daisy Brookes to Ella Marsh, 7 August 1893, ADM.
5. Yska, *All Shook Up*; Dalley, 'The Golden Weather'.
6. A number of international authors make similar arguments about the slow emergence of the teenager, although their timeframes vary: see Gillis, *Youth and History*; Savage, *Teenage*; Schrum, *Bobby Sox*.
7. Gertie Brookes to Ella Marsh, 29 November 1888, 18 June 1890, ADM.
8. Savage, *Teenage*, xiii.
9. Gillis, *Youth and History*, 55.
10. Belich, *Paradise Reforged*; Coney, *Every Girl*; Cumming and Cumming, *History of State Education*; Dalley, *Family Matters*; Daley, *Leisure and Pleasure*, ch. 6; Gregory, 'Saving the Children'; Smyth, *Rocking the Cradle*; Somers, 'The Politics of Social Discourses'.
11. On cultural history, see Burke, *What is Cultural History?*; Salmi, 'Cultural History'.
12. Tindall, Interview, AC.
13. On the limitations and possibilities of oral histories, see Boyd, 'Who is the Subject?'.
14. Helm, undated letter, ATL.
15. Helm, undated letter, ATL.
16. Daisy Brookes to Ella Marsh, 5 October 1893, ADM.
17. On assumptions about the gendering of diaries, see McNeill, 'Teaching an Old Genre New Tricks', 25.
18. Clogstoun, Diary, HC, passim.
19. Clogstoun, Diary, 6 January 1881, HC.
20. Porter and Macdonald, *My Hand Will Write*, 13; Fairburn, *Nearly Out of Heart and Hope*, 2–5.
21. MacGregor, Diary, Undated entry c. 1881–1883, HC.
22. MacGregor, Diary, 6 June 1886, HC.
23. Hargreaves, Diary, 18 March 1872, CM.
24. Burdon, Diary, 24 December 1910, ATL.
25. MacGibbon, Diary, 1 September, 5 September 1918, CM.
26. Byrnes, 'Introduction'; Gibbons, 'The Far Side of the Search for Identity'.
27. Rowland, *Dining Out*, 4; Fairburn, 'Is There a Good Case'.
28. Shiel, Diary, 16 March, 11 April 1921, HC.
29. Fairburn offers a comprehensive discussion of travelling culture in 'Is There a Good Case', passim.
30. On the importance of considering local differences as well as international connections, see Pickles, 'Transnational History and Cultural Cringe', 658.
31. McLeod, Diary, ATL, passim.
32. Singer, *Melodrama and Modernity*, ch. 1. For further discussion, see Felski, *The Gender of Modernity*; Matthews, *Dance Hall and Picture Palace*.
33. Macdonald, *Strong, Beautiful and Modern*, 17.
34. Barker et al., 'The Road Less Travelled'.
35. Jensen, 'Flows of Meaning, Cultures of Movements'.
36. Certeau, *The Practice of Everyday Life*, xii.
37. De Beer, Diary, 17 January 1910, HC; Gibbs, Transcript, 27 April 1884, NPM; Clogstoun, Diary, 8 December 1880, HC.
38. For a similar argument in the British context, see Weight, *Mod*, 11 and passim.
39. On this recursive approach to culture and history, see Fraser, *To Tara via Holyhead*, 8–9.
40. Graff, 'Introduction', xiv.
41. McLeod, Diary, 22 December 1936, ATL.

One: Setting the Scene

1. Port Albert settlers were granted forty acres with an additional allotment for extra family members: Borrows, *Albertland*, 20.
2. Halfpenny, *Bachelor Block*, 66.
3. Halfpenny, *Bachelor Block*, 67.
4. Ell and Ell, *Explorers, Whalers and Tattooed Sailors*.
5. Wright, *Convicts*, 42–45.
6. Bentley, *Cannibal Jack*, 40.
7. Hine, *Rise and Fall*, 16.
8. Bentley, *Cannibal Jack*, 40.
9. Halfpenny, *Bachelor Block*, 52.
10. Halfpenny, *Bachelor Block*, 66.
11. Wanhalla, *Matters of the Heart*, 4. See further discussion in Salmond, *Between Worlds*, 121. The exact ages of these young women are rarely specified in the historic record but, as Wanhalla shows, the accounts often feature the term 'young' or 'girl'.
12. Wanhalla, *Matters of the Heart*, 10–11. See also the discussion in Porter and Macdonald, *My Hand Will Write*, 188.
13. Bentley, *Pākehā Māori*, 62, 65.
14. http://whalerswahine.com/pdfs/Tokitoki.pdf

15 There are a few slivers of information in Best, *Maori Agriculture*, and Firth, *Economics of the New Zealand Maori*.
16 Ballantyne, *Entanglements of Empire*, 40.
17 http://whalerswahine.com/pdfs/Tokitoki.pdf
18 Belich, *Making Peoples*, 144; O'Malley, *Haerenga*, 19.
19 Craik, *New Zealanders*, ch. 14.
20 Craik, *New Zealanders*, ch. 14.
21 Wilson, *Flying Kiwis*, 20–21; see also Belich, *Making Peoples*, 144.
22 McLean, 'Nga Tamariki o Te Roho o Waikato', 109.
23 Hughes, Transcript, 1 December, 8 November 1860, PA.
24 Grace, 'A Fencible's Grand-daughter', *NZG*, 17, 169, 1986, 545–47.
25 Gillis, *Youth and History*, ch. 1.
26 Gillis, *Youth and History*, 2.
27 Phillips, *A Man's Country*, 4–5.
28 Cited in Forth, *Masculinity in the Modern West*, 158.
29 Bourdieu, 'The Forms of Capital'.
30 Wakefield, *Adventure in New Zealand*, 13.
31 Wakefield, *Adventure in New Zealand*, 171.
32 Temple, *A Sort of Conscience*, 358; see also 279.
33 Brookes, *History of New Zealand Women*, 29.
34 http://www.nzhistory.net.nz/culture/immigration/home-away-from-home/summary
35 Sinclair, *A History of New Zealand*, 96.
36 McKirdy, Diary, 14 January 1862, HC.
37 McKirdy, Diary, 'Wednesday 29th', 1862, HC.
38 Prouten, 'Copy of Diary', ATL, 1, 15. For a discussion of gender segregation on these ships, see Hastings, 'Women at Sea', 29–44; Fraser, *To Tara via Holyhead*, 2.
39 Prouten, 'Copy of Diary', ATL, 1.
40 Prouten, 'Copy of Diary', ATL, 2.
41 Prouten, 'Copy of Diary', ATL, 5–6.
42 Prouten, 'Copy of Diary', ATL, 4.
43 Prouten, 'Copy of Diary', ATL, 7.
44 Prouten, 'Copy of Diary', ATL, 8.
45 Prouten, 'Copy of Diary', ATL, 12.
46 Prouten, 'Copy of Diary', ATL, 12.
47 Prouten, 'Copy of Diary', ATL, 14.
48 Prouten, 'Copy of Diary', ATL, 17.
49 Steele, 'Uncharted Waters?', 141. On trans-Tasman circuits, migration and the 'perennial interchange' between New Zealand and Australia, see Arnold, 'The Dynamics and Quality of Trans-Tasman Migration', 1–20.
50 New Zealand Statistics, 1848, no volume number or pagination.
51 Stone, *Logan Campbell's Auckland*, ch. 9.
52 Cited in Buddee, *Fate of the Artful Dodger*, 93; see also *DSC*, 14 September 1844, 2; 3 February 1844, 2.
53 *DSC*, 3 February 1844, 2.
54 Swainson, Newspaper clippings, AL.
55 Cited in Buddee, *Fate of the Artful Dodger*, 84.
56 Cited in Wright, *Convicts*, 165; see also Philips, *Memories of the Past*, 6.
57 *DSC*, 28 September 1844, 3.
58 Felton Mathew, cited in Buddee, *The Fate of the Artful Dodger*, 85.
59 Jones, *Ngā Tohuwhenua Mai Te Rangi*, 29. On pre-contact gardening practices, see Leach, *1,000 Years of Gardening in New Zealand*, 61–65.
60 Gorst, *Māori King*, 22, 132.
61 Gorst, *Māori King*, 23.
62 May, *The West Coast Gold Rushes*, 282; Olssen, 'Families and the Gendering', 44; Dickinson, 'Picks, Pans and Petticoats', 15; Eldred-Grigg, *Diggers, Hatters & Whores*, 225, 251.
63 Strachan, 'James Strachan's Experiences', HC, 40–41.
64 Fraser, *To Tara via Holyhead*, 54.
65 Wilson, *Reminiscences of the Early Settlement of Dunedin and South Otago*, 48.
66 Belich, *Making Peoples*, 379.
67 Strachan, 'James Strachan's Experiences', HC, 11, 26 and passim. For a similar kind of account, see Bryant, 'Memoirs and Reminiscences', HC.
68 Connell, *Gender and Power*, 112.
69 Elwell, *The Boy Colonists*, 46–47.
70 Tiffen, Transcript, AM, 6.
71 Strachan, 'James Strachan's Experiences', HC, 11, 26 and passim.
72 *OW*, 11 June 1864, 7.
73 Trial File, AR, ANZ. On sex between men and boys in New Zealand and Australian history, see Brickell, '"Waiting for Uncle Ben"'; Smaal, 'Boys and Homosex'.
74 Halfpenny, *Bachelor Block*, 45.
75 Fisher, Transcript, AM, 1.
76 Fisher, Transcript, AM, 11.
77 Fisher, Transcript, AM, 11.
78 Fisher, Transcript, AM, 19.
79 Fairburn, *The Ideal Society and its Enemies*; Olssen, 'Families and the Gendering of European New Zealand', 42.
80 Fisher, Transcript, 19, AM.
81 Gillis, *Youth and History*, 5–6. Other historians have also forgotten to question whether the category of 'youth' may have been gendered: Davis, *Youth and the Condition of Britain*, ch. 2; Springhall, *Coming of Age*, 7–8.
82 Pickens, 'Marriage Patterns', 182.
83 Malone, 'What's Wrong with Emma?', 73.
84 Bathgate, *Colonial Experiences*, 58–66.

85   Macdonald, *A Woman of Good Character*, 52–53; *LT*, 8 May 1861, 4.
86   Belich, *Making Peoples*, 377–78; Millen, *Colonial Tears and Sweat*, 69. On domestic servants during the early twentieth century, see Pickles, 'Pink Cheeked and Surplus'.
87   Sangster, Transcript, HC, 4.
88   Macdonald, *A Woman of Good Character*, 105, 125.
89   Macdonald, *A Woman of Good Character*, 175; *LT*, 20 June 1863, 4.
90   Quoted in Millen, *Colonial Tears and Sweat*, 74.
91   Gertie Brookes to Ella Marsh, 18 June 1890, ADM.
92   Gertie Brookes to Ella Marsh, 6 December 1893, ADM.
93   *OW*, 26 May 1877, 9.
94   Millen, *Colonial Tears and Sweat*, 86.
95   Cited in Porter and Macdonald, *My Hand Will Write*, 391.
96   Haselden, Transcript, AM, 13.
97   Haselden, Transcript, AM, 15.
98   Macdonald, *A Woman of Good Character*, 119.
99   Godley, *Letters from Early New Zealand*, 31, 53.
100 Macdonald, *A Woman of Good Character*, 121; Porter and Macdonald, *My Hand Will Write*, 401; Bathgate, *Colonial Experiences*, 58–66.
101 Sinclair, *A New Zealand History*, 96.
102 Godley, *Letters from Early New Zealand*, 53.
103 Dickinson, 'Picks, Pans and Petticoats'; Eldred-Grigg, *Diggers, Hatters & Whores*, ch. 11, 380; Upton, *Wanted*, ch. 2.
104 Arbury, *Prostitution*, np.
105 May, *West Coast Gold Rushes*, 324.
106 Lévesque, 'Prescribers and Rebels', 8. See also Upton, *Wanted*, 42–43.
107 Arbury, *Prostitution*, np.
108 Carr, 'Regulating Sexuality in Early Otago', 35–37; *Observer*, 21 March 1896, 2.
109 *LT*, 11 March 1863, 5; 12 July 1865, 2; 29 July 1865, 2.
110 McLaren, 'The Politics of Secondary Education', 64.
111 Cumming and Cumming, *History of State Education*, ch. 2.
112 Moon, *Māori Transition to a Literate Society*, 19.
113 Rountree, 'Remaking the Māori Female Body', 49–66.
114 Cited in McKenzie, 'The Sociology of a Text', 341.
115 Simon, *Ngā Kura Māori*, 5.
116 Simon, *Ngā Kura Māori*, 2–3.
117 'A portion of the diary of Charles Henry Brookes', ADM, 3.
118 Cumming and Cumming, *History of State Education*, 6.
119 *DSC*, 1 July 1848, 4.
120 Ward, *Early Wellington*, 327; *OW*, 29 September 1855, 2; Trotter, *Dunedin's Spiteful Socrates*, 14.
121 *NZGWS*, 19 December 1940, 2.
122 Dyhouse, *Girls Growing Up*, 46.
123 Cumming and Cumming, *History of State Education*, 9.
124 Davidson, *Selwyn's Legacy*, 64.
125 Cumming and Cumming, *History of State Education*, 9–10. Governor George Grey also supported the idea of teaching European and Māori side by side, and 'civilising' Māori in the process: Alexander, *The Story of Te Aute College*, 27.
126 Greenwood, Diary, Entries for December 1850, ATL.
127 Greenwood, Diary, 12 February 1851, ATL.
128 Greenwood, Diary, 14 January 1851, ATL.
129 Greenwood, Diary, 30 July 1851, ATL.
130 Davidson, *Selwyn's Legacy*, 78.
131 Davidson, *Selwyn's Legacy*, 78; Cumming and Cumming, *History of State Education*, 9.
132 *New Zealander*, 21 December 1850, Supplement, 1.
133 Phillips, *Social History of Auckland*, 43.
134 Arthur and Buttle, *Tale of Two Colleges*, 10.
135 Davidson, *Selwyn's Legacy*, 66.
136 On age grading in American schools during this period, see Kett, *Rites of Passage*, 124.
137 Philips, *Memories of the Past*, 5.
138 Licensing was legislated on a provincial government basis but minimum ages do not seem to have been specified. For a background discussion, see Scott, 'Public Control of the Liquor Trade'.
139 *NENZC*, 16 July 1856, 1.
140 *DSC*, 15 May 1860, 1; Belich, *Making Peoples*, 371.
141 Tiffen, Transcript, AM, 6.
142 Swainson, Letters, ATL, 17.
143 White, *Light Fantastic*, 23.
144 Mary Haselden, Transcript, AM, 18–20.
145 Strachan, 'James Strachan's Experiences', HC, 22.
146 Greenwood, Diary, 11 September 1851, ATL.
147 Petre, Diary, 25 February 1843, ATL.
148 Petre, Diary, 11 April 1843, ATL.
149 Petre, Diary, 8 March 1843, ATL.
150 Petre, Diary, 9 March 1843, ATL.
151 Petre, Diary, 16 May 1843, ATL.
152 Petre, Diary, 15 May 1843, ATL.
153 Downes, *Shadows on the Stage*, 10.
154 Phillips, *Social History of Auckland*, 255.
155 Rosenman, *Unauthorized Pleasures*, 80–81.
156 Dougherty, *Vauxhall Gardens*, 45.
157 Nead, *Victorian Babylon*, 109.
158 Dougherty, *Vauxhall Gardens*, 14.
159 Nead, *Victorian Babylon*, 121.
160 Dougherty, *Vauxhall Gardens*, 20.
161 Dougherty, *Vauxhall Gardens*, 22.
162 Demos and Demos, 'Adolescence', 633–34.

163 Jones, 'Jones Family Letterbook', ATL.
164 Grant, *Colonial Characteristics*, 12.
165 Dunedin Mayor's Court Record Book, ANZ.
166 *TE*, 1 June 1869, 9.
167 *TE*, 1 June 1869, 9.
168 *TE*, 1 June 1869, 9.
169 I offer a more sustained analysis in Brickell, 'Sensation and the Making of New Zealand Adolescence'.
170 Gustav-Wrathall, *Take the Young Stranger by the Hand*, 2.
171 Taylor, *Body, Mind and Spirit*, 37. On the history of the YMCA, see also McLennan, *YMCA New Zealand*.
172 On mid-nineteenth-century letter reading as a social occasion, see Schrader, *Big Smoke*, 129.
173 Taylor, *Body, Mind and Spirit*, 63.
174 Scott, 'The Popular Lecture and the Creation of a Public', 801.
175 Christchurch Young Men's Literary Association Minute Book, 23 March 1865, 5 January 1865, CCL.
176 *Colonist*, 9 May 1862, 3.
177 *Colonist*, 9 May 1862, 3.
178 Greg Rawlings encouraged me to think about regional variation; see also Graham, 'Settler Society', 120.
179 Hughes, Transcript, 24 February 1861, PA.
180 *WI*, 26 August 1857, 6.
181 *WI*, 26 August 1857, 6.
182 *New Zealand Statutes*, 1865, Master and Apprentice Act, 142; Murray, 'A History of Apprenticeship in New Zealand', 38–39.
183 Campbell, *Educating New Zealand*, 110.

Two: Adolescent Stirrings

1 Clogstoun, Diary, 16 November 1880, HC.
2 Clogstoun, Diary, 22 November 1880, HC.
3 Clogstoun, Diary, 30 November 1880, HC.
4 Wood, Unpublished memoir, PA, 22.
5 Wood, Unpublished memoir, PA, 32.
6 Demos and Demos, 'Adolescence', 632.
7 *New Zealand Statistics*, 1881. These figures include the cities' surrounding boroughs. On the growth of New Zealand's cities during these decades, see Schrader, *Big Smoke*, ch. 2.
8 On the rise of factory work in Dunedin, see Olssen, *Building the New World*; and for Christchurch, see Pickles, 'Workers and Workplaces'.
9 Martin, *Holding the Balance*, 378–80.
10 Nolan, 'Constantly on the Move', 364; Olssen, *Working Lives*, 100.
11 Olssen, 'Working Gender', 71.
12 Olssen, *Building the New World*, 4; Brown, *Scottish Mother*, 77.
13 Graham, 'Child Employment', 63.
14 Olssen, *Building the New World*, 131.
15 Coney, *Every Girl*, 19. Eldred-Grigg, *New Zealand Working People*, ch. 3, offers an especially evocative account.
16 Sweating Commission, 53.
17 Sweating Commission, 42.
18 Sweating Commission, 26.
19 On a domestic servant's daily tasks, see Coney, *Standing in the Sunshine*, 226.
20 Sweating Commission, 22, 43.
21 Quoted in Millen, *Colonial Tears and Sweat*, 144.
22 *NZH*, 25 May 1897, 6.
23 Olssen, *Building the New World*, 53.
24 Olssen, *Working Lives*, 21.
25 Sweating Commission, 9.
26 Sweating Commission, 9.
27 Sweating Commission, 47.
28 Gillis, *Youth and History*, 102.
29 Dakin, *Education in New Zealand*, 21, 32, 59; Arrowtown School General Registers, LDM.
30 See the Annual Reports of the Minister of Education, *AJHR*, 1879, 1882.
31 'Report of the Royal Commission into the University of New Zealand', 10.
32 Annual Reports of the Minister of Education, *AJHR*, various years.
33 Gillis, *Youth and History*, 102–3.
34 Graham, 'Settler Society', 114, 138.
35 Gibbs, Transcript, 16 March 1883, NPM.
36 Gibbs, Transcript, 16 March 1883, NPM.
37 Gibbs, Transcript, 23 May 1883, NPM.
38 Gibbs, Transcript, 25 September 1883, 24 October 1883, NPM.
39 Belich, *Paradise Reforged*, 141. On the age overlap between primary and secondary schools, see Lee, 'The Junior Civil Service Examination Reconsidered'.
40 Beattie, 'Notebook Concerning Herries Beatties' Schooldays', HC.
41 Beattie, 'Notebook Concerning Herries Beatties' Schooldays', HC.
42 Beattie, 'Notebook Concerning Herries Beatties' Schooldays', HC.
43 King, *The Evils of Cram*, 27.
44 King, 'A Plea for Stringent Legislation', 1891, 149; King, 'A Plea for Stringent Legislation', 1890, 19. On the emergence of this belief more broadly, see Kett, *Rites of Passage*, 113, 135.
45 Gibbs, Transcript, 29 August 1885, NPM.
46 Gibbs, Transcript, 5 December 1885, NPM.

47 Gibbs, Transcript, 5 December 1885, NPM.
48 Gibbs, Transcript, 29 August 1885, 1 October 1883, NPM.
49 Forth, *Masculinity in the Modern West*, 115, 137.
50 King, *Evils of Cram*, p. 27.
51 Annual Reports of the Minister of Education, *AJHR*, various years. For the enrolments in particular schools, see 'Report of the Royal Commission into the University of New Zealand', 10.
52 Tennant, 'Natural Directions', 143.
53 Fry, 'The Curriculum and Girls' Secondary Schooling', 41.
54 Morris Matthews, *In Their Own Right*, 60.
55 Morris Matthews, *In Their Own Right*, 40–41.
56 Simon, *Ngā Kura Māori*, 2.
57 Hetherington, 'Numbering My Days', ATL, 11.
58 Hooper, Diary, 13 December 1874, HC. On Watson's Dining Room, see Rowland, *Dining Out*, 1–2.
59 Kett, *Rites of Passage*, 111.
60 Cumming and Cumming, *History of State Education*, 114–15.
61 Kennedy, 'Educating Our Nurses'; Roberts, Diary, 14 September 1897, HC.
62 Dougherty, *Bricklayers*, 15; 'Education: Manual and Technical Instruction', *AJHR*, E-5, 1901, 6–7.
63 Dougherty, *Bricklayers*, 28.
64 On female students at Otago's medical school, see Page, 'Dissecting a Community'.
65 Hargreaves, Diary, CM, 84.
66 Roberts, Diary, 11 August, 16 October 1896, HC.
67 Morpeth, Diary, 16 March 1927, PA.
68 Hetherington, 'Numbering My Days', 17, ATL.
69 Hetherington, 'Numbering My Days', 17, ATL.
70 Hetherington, 'Numbering My Days', 17, ATL.
71 Morris Matthews, *In Their Own Right*, 12.
72 Gardner, *Colonial Cap and Gown*, 105–7.
73 Bannerman, Unpublished memoir, ATL, np.
74 Olssen, 'Families and the Gendering of European New Zealand', 43.
75 Graham, 'My Brother and I', 7.
76 Hetherington, 'Numbering My Days', ATL, np.
77 Clogstoun, Diary, 22 December 1880, 29 November 1880, HC.
78 See, for instance, *OW*, 2 April 1902, 69.
79 Anderson, Diary, no date, HC.
80 Cited in Porter and Macdonald, *My Hand Will Write*, 383.
81 Malthus, '"Bifurcated and Not Ashamed"', 41. Scott makes this point for nineteenth-century America too: Scott, *Fresh Lipstick*, 37.
82 Clogstoun, Diary, 9 December 1880, HC.
83 Gibbs, Transcript, 27 April 1884, NPM.
84 Gibbs, Transcript, 27 April 1884, NPM.
85 Hargreaves, Diary, 21 July 1872, CM.
86 Hargreaves, Diary, 19 June, 25 June, 11 August 1872, CM.
87 Gertie Brookes to Ella Marsh, 11 September 1889, ADM.
88 Clogstoun, Diary, 28 March 1881, HC.
89 Clogstoun, Diary, 29 March 1881, HC.
90 Clogstoun, Diary, 29 March 1881, HC.
91 Gibbs, Transcript, 29 March 1883, NPM.
92 Hargreaves, Diary, 6 September, 7 September 1872, CM.
93 Hargreaves, Diary, 18 September 1872, CM.
94 Swainson, Letters, ATL, passim.
95 Hargreaves, Diary, 3 October 1872, CM.
96 Dyer, Diary, HC, 125. On Braithwaites, see *ODT*, 21 January 1890, 3.
97 Stock, *Glorious Technicolor*, 8; Pascoe, 'Spectacular Flâneuse'.
98 Singer, *Melodrama*, 103; Fox and Lears, 'Introduction', x. On the crowd in New Zealand's cities, see Schrader, *Big Smoke*, ch. 5.
99 *ST*, 10 March 1885, 4; *ODT*, 22 November 1887, 4; Sweating Commission, passim; Olssen, *Working Lives*, 116.
100 *ODT*, 10 April 1889, 4. On similar hardships endured by British shop assistants, see Springhall, *Coming of Age*, 93.
101 *Monthly Review by the City Youths Association*, 1 October 1872, HC.
102 Schlör, *Nights in the Big City*, 10.
103 *Tablet*, 30 August 1873, 8.
104 Cohen, 'Policing the Working-Class City'; Savage, *Teenage*, 34–35.
105 *EP*, 28 February 1880, 1.
106 Cited in Gregory, 'Saving the Children', 6; *EP*, 12 August 1889, 3; *ES*, 8 August 1890, 4; *AS*, 15 August 1894, 8.
107 *GRA*, 13 October 1892, 4. For other examples, see Shuker, 'Moral Panics and Social Control', 123. On sensation and the larrikin, see *NZFL*, 23 February 1901, 8; 21 May 1904, 6; *EP*, 22 February 1887, 2; *WD*, 13 April 1888, 2.
108 Gregory, 'Saving the Children', 19.
109 *ES*, 23 May 1878, 4.
110 See, for instance, *PBH*, 11 October 1894, 3.
111 *AS*, 8 October 1894, 3.
112 *NZH*, 6 November 1897, 1; Phillips, *Man's Country*, 49. On the evangelical zeal of the emerging middle-classes, see also Bongiorno, *Sex Lives of Australians*, 23; Shuker, 'Moral Panics', 129; Harrison, 'Victorian Gospel', 160.

113 William Porter to William Porter, 20 May 1843, AL.
114 Tebbutt, *Making Youth*, 9.
115 Schrader, *Big Smoke*, 292–93; Tulloch, 'State Regulation of Sexuality', 277.
116 Platt, *Child Savers*, 36.
117 Lears, *Fables of Abundance*, 137; Tulloch, 'State Regulation of Sexuality', 277.
118 Taylor, *Body, Mind and Spirit*, 71, 83.
119 Dalley, *Family Matters*, 15; Hebdige, 'Posing', 73. On the history of the concept of juvenile delinquency, see Magarey, 'Invention of Juvenile Delinquency'.
120 Hebdige, 'Posing', 86.
121 *WDT*, 12 January 1895, 2. On Australian larrikins' style, see Bellanta, *Larrikins*, 110; Bellanta and Sleight, 'Leary Larrikin', 263–83.
122 'Larrikinism at Manutahi North', ANZ.
123 Savage, *Teenage*, 36.
124 *AS*, 8 October 1894, 3.
125 Hoare, *Faces of Boyhood*, 15.
126 Bellanta, *Larrikins*, 32; see also DuBois and Gordon, 'Seeking Ecstacy on the Battlefield'; Bellanta, 'Larrikin Girl'.
127 *Observer*, 15 August 1891, 17.
128 *AS*, 5 April 1892, 5.
129 *OW*, 24 November 1892, 43.
130 *ODT*, 18 November 1889, 4; *EP*, 1 June 1891, 2.
131 *Monthly Review by the City Youths Association*, 1 January–31 March 1873, HC; Hargreaves, Diary, CM, 67.
132 Beattie, 'Notebook Concerning Herries Beattie's Schooldays', Volume 2, HC.
133 Gore Young Men's Literary Society, First Journal Session 1898, HHC, 2.
134 *TT*, 12 September 1896, 2. Ninety-seven percent of all New Zealanders over the age of fifteen could read by 1881: *Census of New Zealand*, 1881, 141.
135 Gore Young Men's Literary Society, Journal No. 1, 30 April 1895, HHC, 10–11; Gore Young Men's Literary Society, First Journal Session 1898, HHC, 2. On the genre, see Herr, 'Introduction', 10; Springhall, *Youth, Popular Culture and Moral Panics*.
136 *Observer*, 11 August 1883, 10.
137 *Observer*, 7 February 1885, 4; 6 October 1883, 2; Sleight, *Young People*, 125.
138 Forth, *Masculinity in the Modern West*, 156.
139 *OW*, 13 June 1889, 32.
140 *Observer*, 25 July 1885, 6; *TAN*, 26 November 1887, 2.
141 *Observer*, 25 July 1885, 6.
142 *Observer*, 18 August 1883, 16.
143 *OW*, 13 June 1889, 32.
144 Lizzie Sorenson to Ella Marsh, 2 September 1891, ADM.
145 *Observer*, 15 November 1890, 18; 25 August 1890, 26; Knight, Diary, 4 August 1893, ATL.
146 *WD*, 9 January 1889, 2.
147 On the sensuality of the West End, see Cook, *London and the Culture of Homosexuality*, 23–25.
148 Brickell, *Manly Affections*, 34.
149 *ODT*, 29 December 1888, 2; *ODT*, 24 December 1888, 2; *OM*, 2 November 1888, 3.
150 *ODT*, 8 November 1888, 4; *ODT*, 24 December 1888, 2.
151 *ST*, 24 December 1888, 2.
152 Phillips, *A Man's Country*, 4–6, 17; Lee, 'The Junior Civil Service Exam Reconsidered', passim. Yorick Smaal suggested the phrase 'masks of modernity'.
153 Gibbs, Transcript, 24 June 1885, NPM.
154 Gibbs, Transcript, 10 May 1883, NPM.
155 *OW*, 13 June 1889, 32.
156 *Observer*, 27 October 1883, 11.
157 *NZH*, 21 July 1883, 3; *Observer*, 27 October 1883, 11; 9 January 1892, 12.
158 *Press*, 12 May 1894, 10.
159 Coney, *Standing in the Sunshine*, 15.
160 Foucault, *History of Sexuality*, 1–15.
161 Patient Case File, Percy Ottywell, ANZ, 3. On the broader context of this example, see Brickell, 'Same-sex Desire'.
162 Christoffel, *Censored*, 4.
163 King, 'A Plea for Stringent Legislation', 1890; King, 'Plea for Stringent Legislation', 1891.
164 Muchembled, *Orgasm and the West*, 160; Kett, *Rites of Passage*, 137.
165 King, 'Plea for Stringent Legislation', 1890, 25.
166 *NZTI*, 25 November 1902, 3.
167 Barraclough, 'Causation of Insanity', 336.
168 Barraclough, 'Causation of Insanity', 336.
169 Girls' Friendly Society, 'A History', ATL.
170 Harrison, 'For Church, Queen and Family'; Woods, 'Re/producing the Nation', 70–73.
171 *BPT*, 25 December 1891, 2.
172 *MS*, 17 April 1885, 2; *EP*, 24 September 1889, 3; *Observer*, 17 September 1892, 20; *WR*, 15 June 1896, 7. See also the discussion in Gregory, 'Saving the Children', 14–15.
173 Gertie Brookes to Ella Marsh, 11 September 1889, ADM.
174 On these kinds of assumptions in European cities, see Schlör, *Nights in the Big City*, 190–92.
175 Gertie Brookes to Ella Marsh, 29 November 1888, ADM.
176 Hettie Stott to Ella Marsh, 16 March 1897, ADM.
177 Tulloch, 'State Regulation of Sexuality', 291; Brookes, 'Weakness for Strong Subjects', 145.
178 See also Bongiorno, *Sex Lives of Australians*, 49.

179 Clogstoun, Diary, 22 January 1881, HC.
180 Anderson, Diary, 26 December 1899, HC.
181 Anderson, Diary, 26 December 1899, HC.
182 See also Brookes, 'Weakness for Strong Subjects'.
183 Cited in Gillingham, 'Sexual Pleasures and Dangers?', 8; Tulloch, 'State Regulation of Sexuality', 251.
184 Brookes, 'Weakness for Strong Subjects', 146; see also Beckson, *London in the 1890s*, 129.
185 Bunkle, 'Origins of the Women's Movement in New Zealand', 60.
186 Gibbs, Transcript, 29 June 1883, NPM.
187 D'Emilo and Freedman, *Intimate Matters*, 121–30; Brickell, *Mates and Lovers*, ch. 1.
188 Gibbs, Transcript, 29 June 1883, NPM.
189 Gibbs, Transcript, 27 April 1884, NPM.
190 Gibbs, Transcript, 27 April 1884, NPM. For a more substantial discussion of feeling in Fred Gibbs' diaries, see Brickell, 'Affect and the History of Masculinities'.
191 Gibbs, Transcript, 27 April 1884, NPM.
192 Gibbs, Transcript, 24 October 1883, 18 October 1883, NPM.
193 Gibbs, Transcript, 9 July 1887, NPM.
194 Brickell, *Mates and Lovers*, ch. 1.
195 Trial File, WK, ANZ.
196 Brickell, *Mates and Lovers*, ch. 1.
197 Brickell, *Mates and Lovers*, ch. 1.
198 Pool, Dharmalingam and Sceats, *The New Zealand Family*, 71–72. See also Pickens, 'Marriage Patterns'.
199 Pool, Dharmalingam and Sceats, *New Zealand Family*, 85.
200 *ME*, 27 May 1882, 2.
201 Olssen, 'Families and the Gendering of European New Zealand', 48.
202 Harding, Journal, ATL, 58.
203 D'Emilo and Freedman, *Intimate Matters*, 42.
204 Knight, Diary, 18 August 1893, ATL.
205 Knight, Diary, 1 April 1892, 2 April 1892, ATL.
206 Daisy Brookes to Ella Marsh, 7 August 1893, ADM.
207 Dewson, 'Off to the Dance', 05-5. In 1881 the *Observer*'s gossip column berated young Thames men who neglected to provide chaperones for young women after a dance, accusing them of 'a flagrant breach of etiquette': *Observer*, 24 December 1881, 237.
208 Harding, Journal, ATL, 65.
209 *Monthly Review by the City Youths Association*, 1 January–31 March 1873, HC.
210 Singer, *Melodrama*, 61.
211 Clogstoun, Diary, 23 December 1880, HC.
212 Clogstoun, Diary, 30 November 1880, HC.
213 Graham, 'Child Employment', 63.
214 *ODT*, 9 April 1880, 3; *WT*, 17 June 1886, 3; 5 November 1885, 2. On the emergence of adolescent 'girlhood' in Britain, see Tebbutt, *Making Youth*, 134.
215 Various correspondence in Jessie Mackersey, Letters, ATL.
216 *Monthly Review by the City Youths Association*, 1 January–31 March 1873, HC.
217 *OW*, 13 June 1889, 32. The term 'flash' originates with the costermongers, London street traders of the mid-nineteeth century: Hebdige, 'Posing', 73.
218 Bellanta, *Larrikins*, xviii, 10. See also Sleight, *Young People*, ch. 4.
219 Srebnick, *Mysterious Death of Mary Rogers*, 34.
220 *Star*, 13 September 1880, 3.
221 Hooper, Diary, 16 November, 29 December 1875, HC.
222 MacGregor, Diary, Undated entries, HC.
223 Clogstoun, Diary, 31 January 1881, HC.

Three: Jazz Age Youth

1 Brown, 'Female Office Workers in Auckland', 24; see also Olssen, 'Working Gender, Gendering Work', 72–75; Coney, *Standing in the Sunshine*, 228.
2 *AS*, 8 November 1924, 22. For an early account of the impending significance of the typewriter, see the reprint of an overseas story in *ST*, 11 November 1884, 4.
3 *Star*, 22 April 1905, 3.
4 *EP*, 13 February 1914, 9.
5 *EP*, 10 January 1913, 6; 13 February 1914, 9.
6 *HNS*, 8 January 1921, 4.
7 *GRA*, 8 May 1914, 8. For similar sentiments, see *EP*, 28 April 1914, 2.
8 On these continuities in the Australian context, see Sleight, *Young People*, 161.
9 Bland, *Modern Women on Trial*, 3–4.
10 Sprecher, 'Good Clothes are Good Business', 152–53.
11 Brookes, *History of New Zealand Women*, 5, 223.
12 Belich, *Paradise Reforged*, 157.
13 For an apposite critique of Belich, see Daley, 'Puritans and Pleasure Seekers'; see also Burgess 'Looking to the Heart', 2–8, 138.
14 De Beer, Diary, 30 December 1906, HC.
15 Erle Crawford to Tommy, Letters, 7 October 1910, ATL; see also Ennor, Diary, 14 June 1907, ATL.
16 *OW*, 22 July 1908, 73. On the figure of the 'New Woman' in Britain, see Dyhouse, *Girl Trouble*, 49–51.
17 Savage, *Teenage*, 103.
18 *Clansman*, April 1907, CM.
19 De Beer, Diary, 15 February 1903, HC.
20 De Beer, Diary, 15 June 1908, HC.
21 *Star*, 10 April 1909, 3.

22 *OW*, 3 April 1901, 65.
23 Daley suggests the Sandow system was popular among both girls and boys, many of whom did the same types of exercises at school: Daley, *Leisure and Pleasure*, 200–3.
24 *Clansman*, 5 August 1907, 6 October 1907, CM.
25 Trial File, DJ, ANZ. For more on this case, see Brickell, 'On the Case of Youth', 61–62.
26 Belich, *Paradise Reforged*, 166.
27 On eugenics, see Tennant, *Children's Health*, 20; Wanhalla, 'To "Better the Breed of Men"'; Taylor, 'Thomas Hunter and the Campaign Against Eugenics'.
28 Dharmalingham et al., *A Demographic History. Tables*, 1.
29 On the light application of make-up, see Daley, *Girls & Women*, 125. On cosmetics, the gender order and boundaries of acceptability in the British context, see Houlbrook, '"The Man With the Powder Puff"', 145–71.
30 Fyfe, 'Topsy-Turvy Twenties', 61.
31 Schrum, *Some Wore Bobby Sox*, 19.
32 On these coy and sometimes sexualised poses, see Fyfe, *Topsy-Turvy Twenties*, 74.
33 *Mirror*, 1 September 1926, 2.
34 *DGG*, 2 August 1926, 17.
35 Daley, *Girls & Women*, 125.
36 Seddon Memorial Technical College, School reports, 1914–16, AL.
37 Fyfe, 'Topsy-Turvy Twenties', 65; McIndoe, 'Cockabully Story', HC, 107.
38 McIndoe, 'Cockabully Story', HC, 107.
39 *Dominion*, 29 January 1913, 9.
40 *NZT*, 3 November 1927, 4; 29 August 1925, 19.
41 *NZT*, 20 June 1925, 3.
42 *NZT*, 20 June 1925, 3.
43 *NZT*, 6 May 1922, 5.
44 Belich, *Paradise Reforged*, 179.
45 Courage, Diary, 28 July 1920, HC.
46 Courage, Diary, 12 March 1921, HC.
47 Courage, Diary, 28 February 1921, HC.
48 Bongiorno, *Sex Lives of Australians*, 154; Savage, *Teenage*, 84; Taylor, 'Thomas Hunter', 204.
49 Fisher, 'The Physical Needs of the Empire', ATL. See also the discussion in Morris Matthews, *In Their Own Right*, 20.
50 Taylor, 'Tales of Early Kilbirnie', ATL, 6.
51 Shiel, Diary, 24 February 1921, HC.
52 Cooke and Crawford, *The Territorials*, ch. 5.
53 Taylor, 'Tales of Early Kilbirnie', ATL, 39.
54 Taylor, 'Tales of Early Kilbirnie', ATL, 40.
55 Taylor, 'Tales of Early Kilbirnie', ATL, 40.
56 Baker, *King and Country Call*, 144–45.
57 Cooke and Crawford, *The Territorials*, ch. 5.
58 Ross, Memoir, PC, 54.
59 Paulin, Diary, 28 June, 30 June, 8 July 1917, HC.
60 Aitken, 'Book I New Zealand Infantryman, 1915–16', HC. Aitken later published a full memoir: Aitken, *Gallipoli to the Somme*, London, 1963.
61 Bennett, '"Now the War is Over"'.
62 Cited in Bennett, '"Now the War is Over"', 27.
63 Rosen, *Armies of the Young*, 8.
64 http://muse.aucklandmuseum.com/databases/cenotaph/RecordDetail.aspx?OriginalID=8029
65 Gillies, 'Playing Private Spencer'.
66 Spencer, NZDF Personnel File, ANZ.
67 Pugsley, *On the Fringe of Hell*, 263.
68 Dalley, *Family Matters*, ch. 1.
69 Dalley, *Family Matters*, 23–25.
70 Wanhalla, 'To "Better the Breed of Men"', 178; Taylor, 'Thomas Hunter', 198; Coney, *Standing in the Sunshine*, 172.
71 'Te Oranga Home: Report of Commission', 16, 19 and passim. For further discussion, see Dalley, 'Demi-Mondes to Slaveys'; Hughes, 'Inquiry into the Te Oranga Girls' Home, 1908'.
72 Coney, *Standing in the Sunshine*, 172.
73 Goodland, 'Five Case Histories of Girls Discharged from Burwood', 22–24.
74 See, for example, *Press*, 18 October 1923, 2; 13 November 1928, 7; 13 August 1927, 8.
75 Trial File, MM, ANZ.
76 *Press*, 2 January 1930, 5.
77 *NZH*, 14 March 1927, 14.
78 Bellanta, *Larrikins*, 149–50.
79 Beagle, 'Children of the State', 93–96.
80 Lee, *Delinquent Days*, 5.
81 Bardsley, 'Otekaieke Special School', 123–36; Roydhouse, 'Otekaieke Special School'.
82 Otekaieke Special School, Principal's Case Book, ANZ, 61.
83 Cited in Bardsley, 'Otekaieke Special School', 128.
84 Otekaieke Special School, Principal's Case Book, ANZ, 14.
85 'Burnham Industrial School: Report of Commissioner'.
86 Otekaieke Special School, Principal's Case Book, ANZ, 7.
87 Otekaieke Special School, Principal's Case Book, ANZ, 37, 65. For further analysis of these cases, see Brickell, 'On the Case', 55–57.
88 Otekaieke Special School, Principal's Case Book, ANZ, 1.
89 Martin, *Holding the Balance*, 378–80.
90 Orchard and Porterfield, 'Industrial Survey of the Chocolate Factory', 33.

91 Bamford, 'Wax Vesta Match Factory', HC.
92 Belich, *Paradise Reforged*, 187; Eldred-Grigg, *New Zealand Working People*, 46.
93 Olssen, 'Working Gender, Gendering Work', 78; Law, 'On the Streets of Southern Dunedin', 280; Olssen, *Working Lives*, 109.
94 Fyfe, 'Topsy-Turvy Twenties', 82; Goodyear, 'Overworked Children?', 80; Daley, *Girls & Women*, 34; Brown, 'Female Office Workers', 157.
95 See, for instance, Thwaites, *The Wyndham Story*, ch. 4.
96 Downey, *Telegraph Messenger Boys*, 11.
97 Trial File, JL, ANZ.
98 Stringer, Notes of Evidence, ANZ.
99 Lee, *Delinquent Days*, 15.
100 Bell, Interview, CSM.
101 Toynbee, *Her Work and His*, 51, 58.
102 Gillis, *Youth and History*, 15–19; Toynbee, *Her Work and His*, 36, 40.
103 Hugh McMaster, Transcript, HC; Simpkin, Transcript, AM.
104 Hugh McMaster, Transcript, 28 January 1907, HC.
105 Bradford, Diary, OWM.
106 Daley, *Girls & Women*, 47.
107 Toynbee, *Her Work and His*, 1.
108 Pearson, *Johnsonville*, 24.
109 'Sargood Social Experiment', Notebook, HC, np.
110 Elizabeth McMaster, Transcript, 18 January 1907, HC.
111 Elizabeth McMaster, Transcript, 25 January 1907, HC.
112 McKenzie, Diary, HC; Alston, Diary, CM.
113 McLeod, Diary, 7 September 1918, CM.
114 Currie, *Report of the Commission on Education*, 170; Morris Matthews, *In Their Own Right*, 19.
115 Currie, *Report of the Commission on Education*, 170.
116 Schrum, *Some Wore Bobby Sox*, 12.
117 McIndoe, 'Cockabully Story', HC, passim.
118 Christ's College Register, August 1920, CCA, 357.
119 Ramson, *Hutt Valley High School*, 14.
120 Courage, Diary, 29 July 1920, HC; Christ's College Registers, August 1920, 355; April 1921, 493; December 1921, 558, CCA.
121 Courage, Diary, 29 July 1920, HC.
122 Burdon, Diary, Thursday [otherwise undated], ATL.
123 Lunbeck, *The Psychiatric Persuasion*, 187.
124 Barraclough, 'Human Instincts', 208–9; Field, 'Consideration of The Problem of Sex Education', 72.
125 McGeorge, 'Sex Education in 1912'; *HNS*, 25 August 1906, 7; on the English antecents, see Morgan, 'Knights of God'.
126 *NZT*, 6 April 1912, 5; Watson, 'The Perils of Impurity'.
127 Committee of the Board of Health, *AJHR*, 12–13.
128 See, for instance, *TT*, 30 October 1907, 3; *NZT*, 21 April 1923, 3.
129 Keith, *New Zealand Yesterdays*, 220.
130 King, 'A Plea for Stringent Legislation', 1890, 24; King, 'A Plea for Stringent Legislation', 1891, 155.
131 Trial File, DJ, ANZ.
132 Trial File, DJ, ANZ; see also Brickell, 'On the Case of Youth', 61–62; Gillingham, 'Sexual Pleasures and Dangers?'.
133 *NZT*, 11 July 1914, 6.
134 Brookes, 'Weakness for Strong Subjects', 146.
135 Brickell, *Mates and Lovers*, 109.
136 Tennant, 'Natural Directions', 144.
137 Cited in Tennant, 'Natural Directions', 144.
138 *Dominion*, 14 February 1914, 11.
139 For details of curricula in girls' secondary schools at the turn of the century, see Fry, 'Curriculum', 41–43; Duncan, 'What Katy Did at School'; Day, 'Women in Technical Education', 73.
140 Daley, *Girls & Women*, 63.
141 Dharmalingham et al., *A Demographic History. Tables*, 1.
142 Duncan suggests schools developed their curricula in response to the needs and demands of their own communities: *What Katy Did at School*, 9.
143 Taylor, 'Tales of Early Kilbirnie', ATL, 53.
144 Morris Matthews, *In Their Own Right*, 140; Brookes, *History of New Zealand Women*, 223.
145 Morris Matthews, *In Their Own Right*, 143; Gardner, *Colonial Cap and Gown*, 106.
146 Mason, 'Cockabully Story', HC, 107.
147 Coney, *Standing in the Sunshine*, 205–6; Page, 'Dissecting a Community', 122; Fyfe, 'Topsy-Turvy Twenties', 76–77.
148 Gillis, 'Evolution of Juvenile Delinquency', 97.
149 Kett, *Rites of Passage*, 190–98.
150 Blamires, *Youth Movement*, ch. 1.
151 Donnelly, *Heritage of Methodist Youth*, Wellington, 1954, 9. There was no organised youth movement in the Catholic Church until the 1940s. Most young Catholics went to Catholic schools which taught the religious doctrine that young Protestants would go on to learn in Bible Class. On women's Bible Class, see also Cook, *History of the Young Women's* . . . ; Brabyn, *Life Upon Life*.
152 Young People's Society of Christian Endeavour, Syllabus, MA; Woodville Methodist Young People's Society Journal, 2 August 1916, MA.
153 Blamires, *Youth Movement*, ch. 1, 28.
154 Olssen, 'Working Gender, Gendering Work', 72.
155 Troughton, 'Jesus and the Ideal of the Manly Man', 53. On the international context, see Putney, *Muscular Christianity*.
156 *YMM*, 4, 5, 1905, 120–22.

157 Blamires, *Youth Movement*, 12.
158 Warren, 'Popular Manliness'.
159 Culliford, *New Zealand Scouting*; Tennant, *Children's Health*, 35.
160 Belich, *Paradise Reforged*, 365–66. See also Gillis, *Youth and History*, 146; Savage, *Teenage*, 86.
161 Ashby, 'Scouting and the Mohicans', HC.
162 *Kelburne Scout*, ATL, 10.
163 Dyhouse, *Girl Trouble*, 74.
164 Iles, *65 Years of Guiding*, 2; Woods, 'Re/producing the Nation', 62–67.
165 Girl Guiding New Zealand, *Te Rama*, ATL, 8–9.
166 Girl Guiding New Zealand, 'The Campers' Leaflet', ATL.
167 Moruzi and Smith, 'Colonial Girlhood', 10; Alexander, 'Picturing Girlhood and Empire'.
168 YMCA, Camp Journal, Bright Brighton Camp, 1919, HC.
169 *Paerata Pie*, MA.
170 Culliford, *New Zealand Scouting*, 33.
171 Ross, Memoir, PC, 59.
172 Anonymous, 'Diary of a Wellington Schoolboy', 20 August 1921, ATL.
173 Taylor, 'Tales of Early Kilbirnie', ATL, 6, 36.
174 Toynbee, 'Dancing Between the Showers', 7.
175 McLeod, Diary, 18 December 1918, CM.
176 McLean, Memoir, HC, 20 (1).
177 De Beer, Diary, 23 June 1906, HC.
178 Brookes, Olssen and Beer, 'Spare Time', 177–78; Brickell, 'Badness Personified'.
179 Churchman, *Celluloid Dreams*, 7.
180 Stock, *Glorious Technicolor*, 13.
181 *WDT*, 1 June 1907, 6.
182 Churchman, *Celluloid Dreams*, 10. Most New Zealanders talked of going to 'the pictures' but the American term 'movie' was in circulation by the end of World War I: *Sun*, 20 July 1918, 12.
183 McQueen, 'A Preliminary Inquiry', 50.
184 Ennor, Diary, 1 January 1907, ATL.
185 Ennor, Diary, 22 January 1907, ATL.
186 Ennor, Diary, 28 February 1907, ATL.
187 Ennor, Diary, 5 January 1907, ATL.
188 Ennor, Diary, 11 February 1907, ATL.
189 Ennor, Diary, 27 January 1907, ATL.
190 Price, *New Zealand's First Talkies*, 12. On adolescent movie fandom in the US, see Schrum, *Some Wore Bobby Sox*, 154–64; Daley, *Girls & Women*, 110.
191 Anonymous, 'Diary of a Wellington Schoolboy', 12 July, 22 July 1921, ATL.
192 McLeod, Diary, 27 March 1918, CM.
193 McQueen, 'Preliminary Inquiry', 47, 49.
194 McQueen, 'Preliminary Inquiry', 39.
195 McQueen, 'Preliminary Inquiry', 44.
196 'The Young Delinquent', ANZ, 3; Daley, *Girls & Women*, 126. On 'hyperstimulus', see Singer, *Melodrama*, 65.
197 'The Young Delinquent', ANZ, 3.
198 Christoffel, *Censored*, 11; Eldred-Grigg, *Pleasures of the Flesh*, 5.
199 Piess, *Cheap Amusements*, 155–56.
200 On the industry, see Jacobs, *The Rise of the American Film*.
201 Kelly, 'Beauty and the Market', 101.
202 Kelly, 'Beauty and the Market', 112.
203 Brookes, Olssen and Beer, 'Spare Time', 169–70.
204 *EP*, 31 December 1926, 4; Phillips, *A Man's Country*, 230.
205 Ross, Memoir, PC, 59.
206 Iversen, Interview, CSM.
207 Ross, Memoir, PC, 61.
208 White, *Light Fantastic*, 55.
209 *ST*, 17 July 1915, 11.
210 Mason, 'Cockabully Story', HC, 42–43.
211 Heap, *Slumming*, 130.
212 *NZT*, 7 June 1919, 6.
213 On increasingly permissive practices of sexuality and intimacy in American culture during the 'roaring twenties', see Fass, *Damned and the Beautiful*, ch. 6.
214 Piess, *Cheap Amusements*, 106; Griffiths, 'Popular Culture', 611.
215 Sinfield, *Literature*, 159.
216 Griffiths, 'Popular Culture', 615, 617.
217 Mason, 'Cockabully Story', HC, 44.
218 *NZT*, 26 July 1928, 9.
219 Olssen, 'Working Gender, Gendering Work', 69.
220 Gillis, *Youth and History*, 106.
221 Marsh, Diary, 2 March, 22 October 1928, PC.
222 Burgess, 'Looking to the Heart', ch. 2.
223 *FS*, 11 April 1917, 1; see also *Sun*, 20 June 1916, 4.
224 *ODT*, 26 October 1915, 10; see also *PBH*, 19 October 1920, 6.
225 *Press*, 10 April 1926, 2. On the 'teen-age girl' and 'teen-age boy', see also *EP*, 6 October 1927, 22.
226 *Press*, 15 March 1926, 2.
227 Olssen, 'Working Gender, Gendering Work', 53.

Four: The Teenager is Here!

1 Wildey, Transcript, 24 January 1940, HC.
2 Wildey, Transcript, 24 June, 6 December 1940, HC.
3 Wildey, Transcript, 30 September 1939, HC.
4 Wildey, Transcript, 2 January 1940, HC.
5 Schrum, *Some Wore Bobby Sox*, 183, note 25.

6 Fox, 'Epitaph for Middletown', 103.
7 Simpson, *Sugarbag Years*, 6; Coney, *Standing in the Sunshine*, 230.
8 Rankin, *Unemployment in New Zealand*, 4; McKinnon, *Broken Decade*, 179 and passim.
9 Rankin, *Unemployment in New Zealand*, 2.
10 *NZH*, 20 January 1938, 4; see also *AS*, 22 November 1930, 4; Broughton et al., *Silent Migration*, 11.
11 Mackay, Unpublished memoir, PA, 10.
12 Frank, 'Bread Queues and Breadwinners', 113, 123.
13 Morrison, Interview, SCM. For an account of a lad working in the milling industry during the Depression, see Griffin, *Book of Mills and Men*.
14 Morris Matthews, *Who Cared?*
15 Stapleton, Interview, SCM.
16 Findlay, *Tooth and Nail*, 9, 13, 14, 66. For more examples of attempted sexual assault on domestic servants, see Dawson, 'Don't Just Go Through It', IL, 10; Mackay, Unpublished memoir, PA, 11. On similar dangers in the British context, see Dyhouse, *Girl Trouble*, 99.
17 Findlay, *Tooth and Nail*, 39. On department store jobs more generally, see Pickles, 'Workers and Workplaces', 154–58.
18 Stevenson, 'One of Seven', ATL, 42.
19 Dawson, 'Don't Just Go Through It', IL, 12, 15.
20 Stevenson, 'One of Seven', ATL, 43.
21 Simpson, *Sugarbag Years*, 12; Rankin, *Unemployment in New Zealand*, 24.
22 NZ Vocational Guidance Association, Annual Reports of Vocational Work, ATL.
23 Sutch, *The Quest for Security*, 267; NZ Vocational Guidance Association, 'Article for "Times"', ATL.
24 Nolan, *Breadwinning*, 167.
25 Aitken, 'Wives and Mothers First'. On primary school enrolments, see Currie, 'Report of the Commission', 47. Legislation enabling education boards to refuse to hire married teachers was repealed in 1938 but memories of its existence persisted into the late 1940s: *Mirror*, November 1947, 56–57.
26 Nolan, *Breadwinning*, 167.
27 Albiston, Diary, 14 October 1936, ATL. All subsequent dates refer to those pre-printed in the diaries, not Albiston's own idiosyncratic and inconsistent dating system.
28 Albiston, Diary, 3 May 1937, ATL.
29 Albiston, Diary, 12 May 1938, ATL.
30 Albiston, Diary, 30 May 1938, ATL.
31 Albiston, Diary, 30 May 1938, 1 June 1938, ATL.
32 Albiston, Diary, 20 February 1941, ATL.
33 Savage, *Teenage*, 104–5.
34 Macdonald, *Strong, Beautiful and Modern*, 75.
35 Sunlight League Papers, Miscellaneous Speech Notes, MB.
36 Collins, Diary, 13–14 January 1933, PC.
37 Collins, Diary, 14 January 1933, PC.
38 Parnell, 'South Island Road Trip', WRM. See also Wildey, Diary, 17 September 1939 and passim, HC.
39 Mackay, Unpublished memoir, PA, 12.
40 Page, Letter to parents, 25 June [ny], SMC.
41 St Paul's Rangers Camp Log Book, ATL.
42 Maclean, *Tararua*, 132–34. On the growth of tramping, see also Sunlight League Papers, Minister of Education to Cora Wilding, MB.
43 Parnell, 'South Island Road Trip', WRM. For a published account of boys' bike trips during this period, see Geering, *On Me Bike*.
44 Collins, Diary, 25 November 1930, PC.
45 Broughton et al., *The Silent Migration*, 44.
46 Mackay, Unpublished memoir, PA, 13.
47 Gale, 'The Gully Boys', AL, 25.
48 Courtis, 'Milk Bars in Wellington', np.
49 Barson and Heller, *Teenage Confidential*, 30.
50 Barson and Heller, *Teenage Confidential*, 12.
51 Cupit, 'Juvenile Delinquency', 19, 94.
52 Gale, 'The Gully Boys', AL, 23.
53 Gale, 'The Gully Boys', AL, 24.
54 Hill, Interview, HCL.
55 *EP*, 19 July 1939, 4; *AS*, 13 March 1945, 6.
56 Albiston, Diary, 18 June 1937, ATL.
57 Albiston, Diary, 19 June 1938, ATL.
58 Matthews, *Dance Hall and Picture Palace*, 7.
59 Wildey, Transcript, 12 August 1940, HC.
60 McLean, 'Hurrah for Playland!', 89.
61 *NZH*, 11 January 1939, 24. On peep shows, see Daley, 'Puritans and Pleasure Seekers', 58.
62 Collins, Diary, 5 January, 5 April 1930, PC.
63 Stonyer, Diary, 23 March 1934, ATL.
64 Stryker, *Queer Pulp*, 7.
65 *NZT*, 8 December 1937, 1.
66 *Korero*, 3, 10, 1945, 11; see also *Korero*, 3, 11, 1945, 7–10.
67 Finnane, 'Censorship and the Child'; Openshaw and Shuker, '"Worthless and Indecent Literature"', 1–12.
68 Sutch, *Quest for Security*, 455.
69 *NZWW*, 16 December 1948, 8–9; *AS*, 16 October 1945, 7; *AS*, 31 August 1944, 2; *NZH*, 27 June 1945, 4; *NZWW*, 4 November 1948, 19.
70 Albiston, Diary, 20 April 1941, ATL.
71 Stock, *Glorious Technicolor*, 83.
72 Barson and Heller, *Teenage Confidential*, 15; *LWM*, 19 November 1940, 3.
73 Mirams, *Speaking Candidly*, 6.
74 Albiston, 2 May 1938, ATL.

75 Greenhalgh, 'Bush Cinderellas', 13; see also Burgess, 'Looking to the Heart', ch. 1.
76 McLeod, Diary, 22 February 1936, ATL.
77 Bailey, *From Front Porch to Back Seat*, 7–8; Schrum, *Some Wore Bobby Sox*, 154–55.
78 Hill, Interview, HCL.
79 McLeod, Diary, 31 May 1936, ATL.
80 McLeod, Diary, 8 March 1936, ATL.
81 Lears, 'From Salvation to Self-Realization', 27.
82 McLeod, Diary, 5 July 1936, ATL.
83 McLeod, Diary, 14 February 1936, ATL.
84 McLeod, Diary, 17 February 1936, ATL.
85 Mirams, *Speaking Candidly*, 81–82.
86 On the origins and impacts of imported films on New Zealand culture, see Fairburn, 'Is There a Good Case', 155.
87 Collins, Diary, 2 November 1930, PC.
88 Page, Letter to parents, undated, SMC.
89 McLeod, Diary, 11 July 1936, ATL.
90 Carne, Interview, AC.
91 McCahon, Diary, 20 February 1938, HC.
92 Gale, 'The Gully Boys', AL, 24.
93 Bourke, *Blue Smoke*, 100.
94 Collins, Diary, 15 May, 17 May 1933, PC.
95 Collins, Diary, 25 January 1936, PC.
96 Collins, Diary, 30 December 1936, PC.
97 Schrum, *Some Wore Bobby Sox*, 17; Bailey, 'Rebels Without a Cause?', 28.
98 Collins, Diary, 16 November 1936, PC.
99 Collins, Diary, 19 February, 17 September 1936, PC.
100 Collins, Diary, 3 April, 5 May 1936, PC.
101 Currie, *Report of the Commission on Education*, 54.
102 Collins, Diary, 18 November 1930, PC.
103 Page, Letter to parents, 2 July [ny], SMC.
104 Page, Letter to parents, 30 June [ny], SMC.
105 Schrum, *Some Wore Bobby Sox*, 4.
106 Kett, *Rites of Passage*, 111. On the suggestion that the New Zealand teaching profession had become increasingly authoritarian by the 1940s, see 'In Memoriam', *SVCR*, 1946, 7.
107 Bryan Helm to Dad and Herbert, 6 February 1941, ATL.
108 Bryan Helm to Dad and Herbert, 6 February 1941, 1 August 1942, ATL.
109 Bryan Helm to Dad and Herbert, 18 April 1942, ATL.
110 Whakatane District High School Magazine, 1941, MS 71 Box 2, WMRC, np.
111 Whakatane District High School Magazine, 1944, MS 71 Box 2, WMRC, np.
112 Whakatane District High School Magazine, 1945, MS 71 Box 2, WMRC, 23.
113 Whakatane District High School Magazine, 1945, MS 71 Box 2, WMRC, 11.
114 Page, Letter to parents, Sunday 2 July [ny], SMC.
115 Page, Letter to parents, undated, SCM.
116 Albiston, Diary, 7–8 March 1936, 19 July 1936, ATL.
117 Albiston, Diary, 13 June 1936, ATL.
118 O'Donnell, *When Nelson Had a Railway*, 74–75.
119 Albiston, Diary, 29 March 1936, ATL. On courting on Melbourne trams, see Sleight, *Young People*, 125.
120 Albiston, Diary, 25 September 1936, ATL.
121 Albiston, Diary, 4 July 1936, ATL.
122 Gale, 'The Gully Boys', AL, 27.
123 Gale, 'The Gully Boys', AL, 27.
124 Mackay, Unpublished memoir, PA, 11.
125 Cited in Broughton et al., *Silent Migration*, 27.
126 Stevenson, 'One of Seven', ATL, 45.
127 Carne, Interview, AC.
128 Carne, Interview, AC.
129 Coyle and Van Dyke, 'Sex, Smashing and Storyville', 60.
130 Albiston, Diary, 17–18 March 1938, ATL.
131 Albiston, Diary, 16 November 1936, ATL.
132 Albiston, Diary, 6 May 1936, ATL.
133 Albiston, Diary, 25 February 1937, ATL.
134 Albiston, Diary, 25 September 1936, ATL.
135 Albiston, Diary, 27 June 1938, ATL.
136 Vickers, *Queen and Country*, 130.
137 Ellis, *Psychology of Sex*, 368. See the discussion in Chauncey, 'From Sexual Inversion to Homosexuality'.
138 *EP*, 22 July 1929, 13.
139 YWCA, 'Notes for Camp Leaders', ATL.
140 Albiston, Diary, 3 April 1937, ATL.
141 Albiston, Diary, 16 February 1936, ATL.
142 Wildey, Transcript, 12 December 1939, HC.
143 Wildey, Transcript, 7 July 1940, HC.
144 Wildey, Transcript, 24 March 1940, HC.
145 Sentencing File, PB, ANZ. For a further discussion, see Brickell, *Southern Men*, 23.
146 Sentencing File, TN, ANZ.
147 On similar assumptions in the British context, see Vickers, *Queen and Country*, 143–44.
148 Brickell, 'Queens Gardens', 1949'; Brickell, *Mates and Lovers*, 152–53.
149 Gertie Brookes to Ella Marsh, 11 September 1889, ADM.
150 Mason, 'Cockabully Story', HC, 105.
151 Porter and Macdonald, *My Hand Will Write*, 339.
152 Coney, *Standing in the Sunshine*, 97.
153 Dawson, 'Don't Just Go Through It', IL, 9b.
154 Cochran and Cochran, *Sex, Love and Marriage*; Horn, *Digest of Hygiene for Father and Son*; Dalby, *Young Manhood*.
155 Gornall, *Biosex M*, 9.
156 'Purity', *Needful Knowledge*, 10.

157 *HT*, June 1936, 20–22. On psychology as 'a science still in the making', see *HT*, August 1936, 7–8.
158 Trial File, JS, ANZ.
159 On Wildey's career and his time in the military, see Brickell, *Southern Men*, ch. 2 and Brickell, 'Networks of Affect'.
160 Martin, *NZPD*, 1943, vol. 262, 1002.
161 Parr, *Home*, 54, 72, 79.
162 Hutchinson, Memoir, AL, 1.
163 Hutchinson, Memoir, AL, 2.
164 Cooke and Crawford, *The Territorials*, 254, 260, 276.
165 Lovell, Unpublished memoir, PA.
166 Parnell, Unpublished memoir, WRM.
167 Foote, *Going Uphill Backwards*, 45.
168 Hall, 'Women at War', 7, 28 and passim.
169 Tyson, 'Adolescent Years', PA, 4.
170 Tyson, 'Adolescent Years', PA, 4.
171 Day, 'Women in Technical Education', 74.
172 Connelly, Interview, HCL.
173 Montgomerie, *The Women's War*, 87; Parr, *Home*, ch. 5.
174 Ebbett, *When the Boys*, 52.
175 Ebbett, *When the Boys*, 54; Nolan, *Breadwinning*, 217.
176 Grace Johnson, cited in Bardsley, *The Land Girls*, 66.
177 Ruth Atchison, cited in Bardsley, *The Land Girls*, 49–50.
178 Jenny Gibson, cited in Bardsley, *The Land Girls*, 71.
179 *NZWW*, 15 January 1948, 26. See also *Mirror*, June 1946, 12–14; *NZWW*, 7 October 1948, 1; 12 December 1948, 1.
180 *NZWW*, 8 January 1948, 10, 37–38; Bardsley, *Land Girls*, ch. 2; Coney, *Standing in the Sunshine*, 293–94.
181 Montgomerie, *Women's War*, 96.
182 Bioletti, *The Yanks are Coming*, 21.
183 Spedding, cited in Coney, *Standing in the Sunshine*, 316.
184 Taylor, *Home Front*, 642–43.
185 Jones, 'Paekakariki Marines', HC; Taylor, *Home Front*, 642–43.
186 Rowland, *Dining Out*, 106; Griffiths, 'Popular Culture', 622; Bourke, *Blue Smoke*, 93.
187 Griffiths, 'Popular Culture', 622; Bourke, *Blue Smoke*, 93; *HTNS*, 30 July 1941, 5.
188 Wanhalla and Stevens, '"I Don't Like Māori Girls Going Out with Yanks"'.
189 Gale, 'The Gully Boys', AL, 19; Griffiths, 'Popular Culture', 616.
190 Edwards, *Mihipeka*, 126–27.
191 *EP*, 19 April 1944, 4; Bourke, *Blue Smoke*, 122.
192 Montgomerie, *Women's War*, 166; see also Ebbett, *When the Boys*, 156.
193 McLeod, Diary, 2 March 1936, ATL.
194 McLeod, Diary, 11 June 1936, ATL.
195 McLeod, Diary, 31 March 1936, ATL.
196 *EP*, 2 July 1932, 10; NZ Vocational Guidance Association, 'Vocational Guidance in New Zealand', ATL; see also Lunbeck, *Psychiatric Persuasion*, 37; Schrum, *Some Wore Bobby Sox*, 4.
197 'The Catholic Youth Movement', *CR*, 4, 1, 1948, 82; Brickell, 'Politics of Consumer Culture', 146.
198 *AS*, 30 August 1941, 8; *EP*, 10 July 1941, 10; *EP*, 19 April 1944, 4; see also Barson and Heller, *Teenage Confidential*, 44.
199 Savage, *Teenage*, 445.
200 Palladino makes the same point for America: *Teenagers*, 55.

Five: Milk-Bar Cowboys and Rock'n'Roll

1 On queues for copies of the book, see Yska, *All Shook Up*, 207.
2 Manning, *The Bodgie*, 51, 55.
3 Manning, *The Bodgie*, 13.
4 Manning, *The Bodgie*, 8, 11, 86.
5 John Webster, email to Chris Brickell, 10 August 2015.
6 'Report of the Special Committee on Moral Delinquency in Children and Adolescents', 19, 20, 30, 41, 47.
7 See, for instance, Molloy, 'Science, Myth and the Adolescent Female'; Soler, 'Incredible Document'; Yska, *All Shook Up*.
8 'Committee on Moral Delinquency', 12. Concerns had been expressed about the youth of the Hutt Valley and nearby Porirua since the start of the decade: *NZT*, 1 March 1950, 18; 31 January 1951, 7; Dalley, *Family Matters*, 189.
9 Cited in Yska, *All Shook Up*, 65.
10 F.W. Le Fort, Submission, Special Committee Evidence, ANZ, 6.
11 May Corter, Submission, Special Committee Evidence, ANZ; Hastings Housewives' Union, Submission, Special Committee Evidence, ANZ.
12 Elsie Wells, Submission, Special Committee Evidence, ANZ.
13 'Committee on Moral Delinquency', 12, 68.
14 *NZT*, 4 March 1958, 9.
15 Report by Public Opinion and Gallup Polls, Special Committee Evidence, ANZ, 3.
16 Report by Public Opinion and Gallup Polls, Special Committee Evidence, ANZ, 3.
17 Report by Public Opinion and Gallup Polls, Special Committee Evidence, ANZ, 1–2.
18 *AS*, 10 August 1954, 1; 11 August, 1; 14 August, 1. *Woman's Weekly* also published a similar set of

findings from the Gallup survey: *NZWW*, 9 September 1954, 20, 21.
19 Cohen, *Folk Devils and Moral Panics*, 9; Soler, 'Incredible Document', 22; Openshaw and Shuker, '"Worthless and Indecent"', passim.
20 https://longwhitekid.wordpress.com/category/mazengarb-report/
21 *NZT*, 10 March 1954, 24; 26 May 1954, 1; 14 July 1954, 9.
22 Finnane, 'Censorship and the Child'.
23 Pool et al., *New Zealand Family*, 207.
24 Pool et al., *New Zealand Family*, 168; see also Neville, 'Trends and Differentials'.
25 Currie, *Report of the Commission on Education*, 204; Middleton, 'A Short Adventure', 82; Nolan, 'Constantly on the Move, But Going Nowhere?', 379.
26 'Committee on Moral Delinquency', 29.
27 Littauer, *Bad Girls*, 112.
28 Pool et al., *New Zealand Family*, 180. This mirrors the European experience as well: Gillis, *Youth and History*, 189.
29 For a range of perspectives on this question, see Glamuzina and Laurie, *Parker and Hulme*; Labrum, *Real Modern*, 11–12; McKergow, 'Opening the Wardrobe of History'; *NZL*, 28 November 2015, 48. I offer a comparison of differing approaches to the decade in Brickell, 'Moral Panic or Critical Mass?'.
30 Belich, *Paradise Reforged*, 506; Dharmalingham et al., *A Demographic History. Tables*, 13.
31 Molloy, 'Science, Myth and the Adolescent Female', 2.
32 Report by Public Opinion and Gallup Polls, Special Committee Evidence, ANZ, 3; Levett, *Gangs in Auckland*, AC.
33 Barrington and Gray, *Smith Women*, 69.
34 Brookes, 'Shame and its Histories', 48.
35 Molloy, 'Science, Myth and the Adolescent Female', 16.
36 May, *Minding Children*, 196; Brookes, Gooder and de Castro, 'Uptake of the Contraceptive Pill', 225; Smyth, *Rocking the Cradle*, 106–9.
37 Yska, *All Shook Up*, 16.
38 Coney, *Standing in the Sunshine*, 80–81; see also *NZT*, 12 June 1950, 37.
39 Brickell, 'Moral Panic or Critical Mass?'.
40 For statistics on urban growth, see Carlyon and Morrow, *Changing Times*, 25.
41 'Committee on Moral Delinquency', 20.
42 Cited in Laurie and Glamuzina, *Parker and Hulme*, 63; *NZT*, 1 September 1954, 21.
43 Cited in Laurie and Glamuzina, *Parker and Hulme*, 170.
44 Laurie, 'Lady-Husbands', 347.
45 Laurie, 'Lady-Husbands', 339, 340.
46 Kunzel, *Criminal Intimacy*, ch. 4.
47 Taylor, 'The Significance of "Darls"', 413.
48 Taylor, 'The Significance of "Darls"', 414.
49 Dumble, Interview, AC.
50 'Report of Wellington Citizens' Committee on Questions of Morality and Social Conduct', 1943, ATL, 1–3.
51 Moore, Transcript, 8 January 1963, PC. These privately held transcripts relate to the diaries held in the ATL under the reference number MS-Group-0980.
52 Moore, Transcript, 23 January 1963, PC.
53 Moore, Transcript, 7 June 1963, PC.
54 Moore, Transcript, 13 June 1963, PC.
55 Woods, 'Integrating the Nation', 35, 73.
56 Woods, 'Integrating the Nation', 65–68; Pearson, *A Dream Deferred*, 113.
57 Woods, 'Integrating the Nation', 201; Williams, *Panguru*, 80, 81.
58 Cited in Williams, *Panguru*, 58.
59 Cited in Taylor and Goldsmith, *Nga Kakano o Rangiatea*, MA, 67.
60 Taylor and Goldsmith, *Nga Kakano o Rangiatea*, MA, 68; Woods, 'Integrating the Nation', 186; Williams, *Panguru*, 130.
61 *TAH*, June 1966, 7; Williams, *Panguru*, 95.
62 Woods, 'Integrating the Nation', 78.
63 Alan Barnes, *White Sheep*, Television documentary, 2000.
64 Alan Barnes, *White Sheep*, Television documentary, 2000.
65 Williams, *Panguru*, 126
66 Rupe and Martin, *Carmen*, 43.
67 Williams, *Panguru*, 36–37, 55.
68 Finnane, 'Censorship and the Child', 234, 236–37; see also Hebdige, 'Posing', 77; 'Report of the Hutt Valley Youth Survey', 1953, ATL.
69 Bardwell, 'Young Incorrigible'; Goodland, 'Five Case Histories'; O'Neill, 'Catholics and Delinquency'.
70 Cupit, 'Juvenile Delinquency', 9.
71 Cupit, 'Juvenile Delinquency', 57.
72 Crowther, 'Street Society', 1. On the wider context of mid-century social science and Crowther's study, see Brickell, 'The Teenager and the Social Scientist'.
73 Crowther, 'Street Society', 3.
74 Crowther, 'Street Society', 2; Stratton, 'Bodgies and Widgies'.
75 Yska, *Wellington*, 173.
76 On the international dissemination of this style, see Phillips, 'Blue Jeans, Black Leather Jackets, and a Sneer'.
77 Crowther, 'Street Society', 5.
78 Gilbert, *Patched*, 7.

79 Appendix to Levett, *Gangs in Auckland*, AC.
80 'Gang Misbehaviour in Wellington', AC.
81 Comer, Interview, HCL.
82 Keith, *New Zealand Yesterdays*, 200–1.
83 'Summary of Analyses of Children's Court Appearances', ANZ. A 1960s report is Blizard, *Juvenile Delinquency*. For detailed discussions of juvenile delinquency during this period, see Dalley, *Family Matters*; Lavelle, 'Youth Without Purpose'; Peters and George, *Showband!*, 23.
84 *SEN*, 2 February 1956, 1.
85 Hebdige, 'Posing', 78; Stratton, 'Bodgies and Widgies', 10; Ritchie, 'Shaken', 15.
86 'Teddy Boys', 81.
87 Stratton, 'Bodgies and Widgies', 19; Genn, 'Christianity and the Teenager', 29.
88 Ginny Sullivan in conversation with Howard Dunn, 28 November 2016.
89 Levett, *Gangs in Auckland*, AC, 2.
90 Comer, Interview, HCL.
91 Comer, Interview, HCL.
92 Crowther, 'Street Society', 5; Manning, *The Bodgie*, 9; see also Yska, *All Shook Up*, 176; Stratton, 'Bodgies', 17.
93 Cited in McGill, *Kiwi Baby Boomers*, 156.
94 Yska, *All Shook Up*, 171.
95 Mort, *Capital Affairs*, 86–89; see also Davis, *Youth and the Condition of Britain*, ch. 7.
96 *HN*, March 1956, 14–15. The *South End News* agreed about the relative rarity of the Teddy boy: *SEN*, 27 October 1955, 6.
97 Hebdige, 'Posing', 78; Gillis, *Youth and History*, 187.
98 Gillis, *Youth and History*, 187.
99 Crowther, 'Street Society', 5.
100 On overlapping styles see Crowther, 'Street Society', 6; Smith, *Twist and Shout*, 12.
101 Wilkie, Interview, AC.
102 Tindall, Interview, AC.
103 Hopkins, 'My Life', HC, np.
104 Daisy Marsh to Aunt G & Uncle H, 26 August 1926, ADM.
105 Trial File, BS, ANZ. Millar is a pseudonym. For further details on this friendship group, see Brickell, *Mates and Lovers*, 151–53.
106 *SEN*, 11 October 1956, 8–9.
107 Adams, Interview, AC.
108 Adams, Interview, AC.
109 Tindall, Interview, AC.
110 Tindall, Interview, AC.
111 Phillips, 'Blue Jeans'; Thomson, *An Innocent Aboard*, 109; Wolfe, *The Way We Wore*, 21.
112 Columbus, *Ray Columbus*, 70.
113 Crowther, 'Street Society', 11.
114 Cited in Barrington and Gray, *Smith Women*, 31.
115 Smith, *Twist and Shout*, 74.
116 Weight, *Mod*, 13; Wolfe, *The Way We Wore*, 27.
117 Coney, *Every Girl*, 253.
118 Columbus, *Ray Columbus*, 106.
119 *Mirror*, March 1962, 46; cited in Lloyd Jenkins, *Frank Carpay*, 58.
120 Wilkie, Interview, AC.
121 Warburton, 'The Teenager', 25.
122 McRobbie and Garber, 'Girls and Subcultures', 182.
123 Weight, *Mod*, 42.
124 *CD*, 29 May 1964, 10.
125 On the 1960s fashion moment for American boys, see Brooks, *Last Season of Innocence*, 110, 114.
126 Weight, *Mod*, 49–51; Andrewes, 'Man in the Grey Flannel Suit'.
127 *CD*, 12 June 1964, 4, 6.
128 *HN*, March 1956, 14–15; Comer, Interview, HCL.
129 *HN*, March 1956, 14–15.
130 Perone, *Mods, Rockers*, ch. 1; Weight, *Mod*, 214–17.
131 Shadbolt, *Bullshit & Jellybeans*, 45; 'Mods Killed Lightning', *SEP*, 1, 1, 1996, 34–35.
132 Moore, Transcript, 31 December 1962, PC; Amon, 'The Time of My Life', HC, 10.
133 Wildey, Transcript, 21 January 1941, HC.
134 Brickell, *Southern Men*, ch. 5.
135 Smith, 'Big Muscle Boys', 62.
136 Smith, 'Big Muscle Boys', 45.
137 Crowley, 'The 1961 Teenager', 34.
138 Manning, *Bodgie*, 50; 63.
139 McGill, *Kiwi Baby Boomers*, 131; Honnibal, Interview, HCL.
140 Tindall, Interview, AC; Crowther, 'Street Society', 6.
141 Crowther, 'Street Society', 13.
142 Crowther, 'Street Society', 6.
143 On cars and gender, see Law, 'On the Streets of Southern Dunedin'.
144 Warburton, 'The Teenager', 25.
145 Aldene Moore to Dallas Moore, Transcript of letter, 15 July 1963, PC.
146 Law, 'On the Streets of Southern Dunedin', 282.
147 Howard, 'The Library, the Park and the Pervert'; see also Bailey, *From Front Porch to Front Seat*.
148 Honnibal, Interview, HCL.
149 Crowther, 'Street Society', 7.
150 Columbus, *Ray Columbus*, 69.
151 Crowther, 'Street Society', 10.
152 Crowther, 'Street Society', 8.
153 Crowther, 'Street Society', 10.
154 Crowther, 'Street Society', 14.
155 Bourke, *Blue Smoke*, 263–65.
156 Ginny Sullivan in conversation with Howard Dunn, 28 November 2016.

157 Hoffmann, *Tales of Anna Hoffman*, 20.
158 Hart, Interview, AC.
159 Phillips, *Man's Country*, 80.
160 Hart, Interview, AC.
161 Crowther, 'Street Society', 20, 25; *NZT*, 5 April 1950, 11; Jeremy Lowe to Dallas Moore, Transcript of letter, late August 1963, PC.
162 'Gang Misbehaviour in Wellington', AC, 9.
163 Crowther, 'Street Society', 26.
164 Columbus, *Ray Columbus*, 117.
165 Hoffman, *Tales*, 60.
166 Cited in White, *Light Fantastic*, 149.
167 Williams, *Panguru*, 138.
168 Dix, *Stranded in Paradise*, 59; Bourke, *Blue Smoke*, 291.
169 Williams, *Panguru*, 138.
170 Cited in White, *Light Fantastic*, 174.
171 Tindall, Interview, AC.
172 Bourke, *Blue Smoke*, 295; Columbus, *Ray Columbus*, 102; Adams, Interview, AC.
173 White, *Light Fantastic*, 169.
174 Tindall, Interview, AC.
175 Cited in White, *Light Fantastic*, 161.
176 Crowther, 'Street Society', 9, 35.
177 Harré, 'Māori-Pākehā Intermarriage'.
178 Wanhalla, *Matters of the Heart*, 146–47, 153.
179 Moore, Transcript, PC, passim.
180 Moore, Transcript, 1 March 1963, PC.
181 McRobbie and Garber, 'Girls and Subcultures', 181.
182 Hutchins, *Eight Days a Week*, 38; *CD*, 28 August 1964, 4.
183 White, *Light Fantastic*, 29.
184 Jeremy Lowe to Dallas Moore, Transcript of letter, 30 January 1962, PC.
185 Columbus, *Ray Columbus*, 104.
186 Dix, *Stranded in Paradise*, 81; for other examples, see Bourke, *Blue Smoke*, ch. 6.
187 Yska, *All Shook Up*, 198; White, *Light Fantastic*, 170–71.
188 McKelvie and Chilton, *45 South in Concert*, 159.
189 Dix, *Stranded in Paradise*, 76.
190 Dix, *Stranded in Paradise*, 60.
191 Hutchins, *Eight Days a Week*, 88.
192 Holden, Interview, AC.
193 Dalley, *Family Matters*, 186; Ritchie, 'Shaken', 25.
194 Savage, *Teenage*, 447.
195 Timaru Teenage Club minute book, SCM.
196 Savage, *Teenage*, 448.
197 Dix, *Stranded in Paradise*, 28.
198 Comer, Interview, HCL; see also *ODT*, 24 September 1960, 2.
199 Timaru Teenage Club minute book, SCM.
200 Crowther, 'Street Society', 28.
201 Moore, Transcript, 25 March 1957, 6 April 1957, 6 June 1959, PC.
202 Moore, Transcript, 19 January 1957, PC.
203 Wilkie, Interview, AC.
204 'Evangelist Billy Graham Arrives for 11-day Crusade', http://www.nzhistory.net.nz/page/evangelist-billy-graham-arrives-11-day-crusade
205 Whakatane District High School Magazine, 1957, WMRC, 35–36.
206 'A History of Scouting at Awakeri', WMRC.
207 Watson, '11th World Scout Jamboree', AC.
208 Hebdige, 'Posing', 86.
209 Gillis, *Youth and History*, 207.
210 Moore, Transcript, 19 August 1959, PC.
211 Moore, Transcript, 13 August 1959, PC.
212 Dumble, Interview, AC.
213 Winks, *These New Zealanders*; Ausubel, *Fern and the Tiki*.
214 Columbus, *Ray Columbus*, 67.
215 McGill, *Kiwi Baby Boomers*, 144.
216 Bourke, *Blue Smoke*, 278.
217 *FP*, 8 November 1968.
218 *AGGM*, November 1968, 12.
219 Brookes, *History of New Zealand Women*, 342.
220 *Charisma*, 10, November 1968, 2. New Zealand movie critic Gordon Mirams also criticised the role of the film industry, calling it 'the biggest dope racket on earth': Mirams, *Speaking Candidly*, 39, 54, 122.
221 Marcuse, *One Dimensional Man*.
222 Tebbutt, *Making Youth*, 148–49.
223 Foreman, 'Profile of a Teenager', 26.
224 Sloan, 'Saturday Night', 34–35.
225 Kerouac, *On the Road*, 77.
226 Hoffmann, *Tales*, 23.
227 Cited in McGill, *Kiwi Baby Boomers*, 153. On the figure of the beatnik in British youth culture, see Tebbutt, *Making Youth*, 161.
228 Crowther, 'Street Society', 37.
229 Hughes, 'The Struggle of the Male Self', 901.
230 Elworthy, *Ritual Song of Defiance*, 85.
231 Elworthy, *Ritual Song of Defiance*, 62–63.
232 Elworthy, *Ritual Song of Defiance*, 84, 91.
233 *AJHR*, E-7, 1950, 3; *AJHR*, E-1, 1960, 114; Gilbert, *Patched*, 28.
234 *Falus*, 3, 1967, 1; also *Falus*, 4, 1967, 2.
235 *Falus*, 9, 1967, 1; Dann, *Up From Under*, ch. 1.
236 Brickell, 'Sex Education, Homosexuality and Social Contestation'.
237 Columbus, *Ray Columbus*, 65.
238 Columbus, *Ray Columbus*, 71.
239 Tebbutt, *Making Youth*, 144.
240 *NZT*, 17 June 1958, 5; 22 May 1956, 6.

241 Foreman, 'Profile of a Teenager', 27.
242 Warburton, 'The Teenager', 26.
243 Crowley, 'The 1961 Teenager', 34; *TGSM*, 1960, 23.

Conclusion: Back to the Future

1 Somers, 'The Politics of Social Discourses about Youth', ch. 7.
2 'Lucan Battison Wins Long-hair Court Battle', 27 June 2014, http://www.stuff.co.nz/national/education/10207087/Lucan-Battison-wins-long-hair-court-battle
3 Brickell, 'Sex Education', 392–94.
4 Allen, 'Girls' Portraits of Desire', 299.
5 Moran-Ellis, 'Sexting, Intimacy and Criminal Acts'.
6 'Sexting Like Drug Addiction for Kiwi Teens with Kids as Young as 11 Taking Part', 9 February 2016, http://www.stuff.co.nz/national/health/76672892/sexting-like-drug-addiction-for-kiwi-teens-with-kids-as-young-as-11-taking-part
7 'Report of the Hutt Valley Youth Survey', 1953, ATL, 8.
8 *SSTM*, 1 May 2016, 10–15.
9 http://natlib.govt.nz/photos
10 Goffman, *Stigma*, 19.
11 Katie Drager, 'Language, Stance, and Identity at Selwyn Girls' High', unpublished, undated paper available at http://katiedrager.com/papers/Drager_IGALA.pdf
12 Elley, 'The New Gnostics', 6.
13 Ward, Freeman and McGee, 'The Influence of Transport on Well-being Among Teenagers', 417; Belinda Borrell, 'Living in the City Ain't So Bad: Cultural Identity for Young Māori in South Auckland', unpublished paper, online; Nairn, Higgins and Sligo, *Children of Rogernomics*.
14 Nairn, Higgins and Sligo, *Children of Rogernomics*, 129.
15 Brickell, 'Sex Education', 391.
16 *NZT*, 10 July 1979, 4.
17 http://www.radionz.co.nz/news/regional/290788/climate-activists-in-nationwide-protests; Wood, 'Youth Participation in Society'.
18 https://libcom.org/library/super-size-my-pay-fast-food-workers-new-zealand-organise-better-pay-and-conditions
19 Beals and Wood, 'Negotiating Agency'.
20 Mannheim, 'The Problem of Generations', 303.
21 Mannheim, 'The Problem of Generations', 315.
22 'Drama Camp, 1987', *HVHS 1987*, 38.
23 Graff, *Conflicting Paths*, 340.

Bibliography

PRIMARY SOURCES

Government Reports
'Burnham Industrial School: Report of Commissioner', *Appendices to the Journals of the House of Representatives* (*AJHR*), E-3B, 1906.
Committee of the Board of Health. 'Venereal Diseases in New Zealand', *AJHR*, H-31A, 1922.
Currie, George. *Report of the Commission on Education in New Zealand*, Wellington, 1962.
'Report of the Royal Commission into the University of New Zealand and its Relations to the Secondary Schools of the Colony', *AJHR*, H1, 1880.
'Report of the Special Committee on Moral Delinquency in Children and Adolescents', *AJHR*, H-47, 1954.
Sweating Commission. 'Report of the Royal Commission Appointed to Inquire into Certain Relations Between the Employers of Certain Kinds of Labour and the Persons Employed Therein', *AJHR*, H5, 1890.
'Te Oranga Home: Report of Commission', *AJHR*, H-21, 1908.

Manuscripts
Albertland and Districts Museum (ADM)
'A portion of the diary of Charles Henry Brookes'.
Brookes and Marsh family letters.

Alexander Turnbull Library (ATL)
Albiston, Isobel Shirley, Diary, 1936, MSX-6387.
——. 1937, MSX-6388.
——. 1938, MSX-6389.
——. 1941, MSX-6392.
Anonymous. 'Diary of a Wellington Schoolboy', 1921, MS-0683.
Bannerman, Jane. Unpublished memoir, qMS-0131.
Burdon, Randal. Diary, 1910, 85-109-4/20.
Crawford, Erle. Letters, 1910–1912, MS-Papers-4140-4.
Ennor, Harrold. Diary, 1907, qMS-0674.
Fisher, Francis. 'The Physical Needs of the Empire From a Military Standpoint', 1905, MS-0772.
Girl Guiding New Zealand. Records, 88-130-01/01.
Girls' Friendly Society. 'A History of the Society', 85-075-3/05.
Goldsworthy, Russell. Papers re Wanganui Collegians' activities, MS-Papers-5434.
Greenwood, John. Diary, 1850–1851, MS-Copy-Micro-0194-5.
Harding, Ruth. Journal, 1861–1881, qMS-0581.
Helm, Bryan. Letters, 1941–1942, MS-Papers-7843.
Hetherington, Jessie. 'Numbering My Days', Unpublished memoir, MS-Papers-0644-2.
Jenner, Maurice, 'Saturday Sixpence', Unpublished memoir, MS-Papers-7104.
Jones, John. 'Jones Family Letterbook', 1860–1861, MSY 3936.
Kelburne Scout. Handwritten magazine, MS-Papers-1013.
Knight, Charles. Diary, 1892–1893, 90-362.
Mackersey, Jessie. Letters from her children at boarding school, 1899–1903, MS-Papers-10251-09.
McLeod, Jean. Diary, 1936, MS-Papers-11255-1.
New Zealand Vocational Guidance Association. Records, 82-086-31.

OPPOSITE Typing class at King Edward Technical College, Dunedin, c. 1963.

BIBLIOGRAPHY

Petre, Mary. Diary, 1843, MS-1772.
Prouten, Bessie. 'Copy of Diary Written by Bessie Prouten', 1876–1877, MS-Papers-5337.
'Report of Wellington Citizens' Committee on Questions of Morality and Social Conduct', 1943, 77-206-06/21.
Swainson, Mary. 'Letters of Mary Swainson to her Grandparents in England', 1840–1854, qMS-1339.
St Paul's Rangers. Camp Log Book, 1931–1935, MSX-5937.
Stevenson, Margaret. 'One of Seven', Unpublished memoir, MS-Papers-5415.
Stonyer, Cyril. Diary, 1934, MSX-6219.
Taylor, Charles. 'Tales of Early Kilbirnie', Unpublished memoir, MS-Papers-3794.
YWCA. 'Notes for Camp Leaders', 1942, 85-013-09/15.

Archives New Zealand (ANZ)
Dunedin Mayor's Court Record Book, 1866–1870, DAAC 20881 D438/1.
'Larrikinism at Manutahi North', 1883, AANN W4250 1 38.
New Zealand Defence Force Personnel File, Victor Manson Spencer, AABK 18805 W5553 0108055.
Otekaieke Special School. Principal's Case Book, 1908–1916, CAJG D16 129.
Patient Case File, Percy Ottywell, 1891, DAHI D264 86 2714.
Sentencing File, PB, 2 February 1945, CAHX 173 S5.
Sentencing File, TN, 2 February 1945, CAHX 173 S3.
Special Committee on Moral Delinquency in Children and Adolescence Evidence, AAFD 7523 W4198 Box 172 part 1.
Stringer, J. Notes of Evidence, TH, Civil Criminal and Circuit, 1922, Vol. 3, BBAE A304 888.
'Summary of Analyses of Children's Court Appearances', SS W2363 5 8/10/7 1.
'The Young Delinquent', CW W 1982 12 4/19/21.
Trial File, AR, 1864, DAAC D256 250 18.
Trial File, DJ, 1909, AAOM W3265 2297, C414 425.
Trial File, WK, 1896, DAAC D256 395 13.
Trial File, JL, 14 May 1917, AAOM W3265.
Trial File, MM, May 1908, DAAC D256 318.
Trial File, BS, May 1941, BBAE 5609 29.
Trial File, JS, 1948, DAAC D256 426 25.

Auckland Libraries (AL)
Gale, Len. 'The Gully Boys', Unpublished memoir, NZMS 1520.
Hutchinson, Jack. Memoir, NZMS 1443.
Porter, William. Letters to William Porter Jnr, 1843, NZMS 1256.
Seddon Memorial Technical College. School reports, 1914–1916, NZMS 823.
Swainson, William. Newspaper clippings, GNZMS 225.

Auckland Museum (AM)
Fisher, Alder. Transcript of diary, 1862–1863, MS-372.
Haselden, Mary. Transcript of diary, 1860–1864, MS-1385.
Simpkin, Joseph Alvan. Transcript of diary, Volume 1, 1915–1920, 2003/103.
Tiffen, Frederick. Transcript of diary, 1842–1850, MS-469.

Author's Collection (AC)
Adams, Audrey. Interview with Chris Brickell, 2014.
Carne, Doris. Interview with Chris Brickell, 2010.
Dumble, Jon. Interview with Chris Brickell, 2011.
Hart, Angela. Interview with Chris Brickell, 2015.
'Gang Misbehaviour in Wellington: Report Prepared for the Inter-departmental Committee on Adolescent Offenders', April 1959.

Holden, Jennifer [pseudonym]. Interview with Chris Brickell, 2009.
Levett, Allan. *Gangs in Auckland*, Unpublished report, 1959.
Tindall, Sophie [pseudonym]. Interview with Chris Brickell, 2010.
Watson, Lloyd. '11th World Scout Jamboree 1963 Held at Marathon, Greece: A Personal Reflection', Unpublished memoir.
Wilkie, Yvonne. Interview with Chris Brickell, 2016.

Canterbury Museum (CM)
Alston, Isabella. Diary, 1876, ARC 190.55.
Clansman. Handwritten magazines, Box 7, Folder 37, ARC 1988.88.
Hargreaves, Mary Annie. Diary, 1872, 68/52.
McLeod, Alison. Diary, 1918–1919, ARC 1994.34, Box 1, Folder 2, Item 2.

Central Stories Museum, Alexandra (CS)
Bell, Isobel ('Ivy'). Interview, no date.
Iversen, Mrs. Interview, 1961.

Christchurch City Libraries (CCL)
Christchurch Young Men's Literary Association. Minute Book, 1865, ARCH 30.

Christ's College Archive (CCA)
Christ's College Registers, August 1920, April 1921, December 1921.

Hamilton City Libraries (HCL)
Comer, Rod. Interview with Megan Peinell, 1995, OH 0276.
Connelly, Dorrie. Interview with Christene Mauchline, 1995, OH 235.
Hill, June. Interview with Jan Lindsay, 1995, OH 0227.
Honnibal, Heather. Interview with Sarah Smith, 1995, OH 0256.

Hocken Collections (HC)
Aitken, Alexander Craig. 'Book I New Zealand Infantryman, 1915–16. Gallipoli to the Somme', MS-0717/001.
Anderson, Helen. Diary, 1899, Misc-MS-1331.
Amon, Lew. 'The Time of My Life', Unpublished memoir, 97-231.
Ashby, Ernie. 'Scouting and the Mohicans', Audio-taped memoir, no date, AG-107/020.
Bamford, Anthony. 'Wax Vesta Match Factory', Unpublished report, MS-2690/032.
Beattie, Herries. 'Notebook Concerning Herries' Schooldays', Volume 2, 1897–1898, MS-582/L/20.
Bryant, James. 'Memoirs and Reminiscences of JT Bryant', Misc-MS-0917.
Clogstoun, Elsie. Diary, 1880–1881, MS-0978.
Courage, James. Diary, 1920–1921, MS-999/78.
De Beer, Dora. Diary, 1903, MS-1392/005.
——. Diary, 1905–1906, MS-1392/007.
——. Diary, 1906–1909, MS-1392/007.
——. Diary, 1910, MS-1392/008.
Dyer, Gertrude. Diary, 1895–1899, MS-0117.
Hooper, Harold Kendal. Diary, 1874–1875, MS-1400/002.
Hopkins, Doug. 'My Life', Unpublished memoir, Misc-MS-2014.
Jones, Sinclair. 'Paekakariki Marines, Boyhood Memories', Unpublished memoir, Misc-MS-1808.
MacGregor, Agnes. Diary, 1881–1886, Misc-MS-1291.
Mason, Elizabeth. 'Cockabully Story: The Memoirs of Elizabeth Mason (née Mabel McIndoe), Part 1: New Zealand', MS-1400/001.
McCahon, Beatrice. Diary, 1938–1940, MS-3891.

McKenzie, Alice. Diary, 1890–1891, MS-0137.
McKirdy, Charles. Diary, 1862, MS-0985-036/002.
McLean, Gavine. Unpublished memoir, 96-007/1.
McMaster, Elizabeth. Transcript of diary, 1907, MS-4212/002.
McMaster, Hugh. Transcript of diary, 1907, MS-4212/004.
Monthly Review by the City Youths Association. Handwritten magazines, Misc-MS-1985.
Paulin, Thomas Gerald. Diary, 1917, AG-777/01.
Roberts, Edward Fletcher. Diary, 1896–1897, MS-0485/001.
Sangster, Elizabeth. Transcript of diary, 1877–1878, Misc-MS-1668.
'Sargood Social Experiment', Notebook, 1914, MS-0577.
Shiel, Gerald. Diary, 1921, AG-870/018.
Strachan, James. 'James Strachan's Experiences: The First Twelve Years on My Own', Unpublished memoir, ARC-0415.
Wildey, David. Transcript of diary, 1939, MS-3549/006.
——. Transcript of diary, 1940, MS-3549/008.
——. Transcript of diary, 1941, MS-3549/009.
YMCA. Camp Journal, Bright Brighton Camp, 1919, AG-039/034.
——. Camp Journal, Buttercup Farm, 1919–1920, MS-2503/054.

Hokonui Heritage Centre (HHC)
Gore Young Men's Literary Society. Journals, 1895–1898, GO 78/159.

Invercargill City Libraries (IL)
Dawson, Ailsa. 'Don't Just Go Through It, Grow Through It: An Autobiography', Unpublished memoir.

Lakes District Museum (LDM)
Arrowtown School. General Registers, 1881–1892.

Macmillan Brown Library (MB)
Sunlight League Papers, MB 1186-18.

Methodist Archives (MA)
Paerata Pie. Handwritten magazine, 1928.
Taylor, Glenis and Joyce Goldsmith. *Nga Kakano o Rangiatea: Memoirs From Our Time at Rangiatea Methodist Maori Girls' Hostel, New Plymouth, 1940–1977*, Unpublished manuscript, 2004.
Woodville Methodist Young People's Society. Journal, 1916, 5081 Box 2.
Young People's Society of Christian Endeavour. Syllabus, 5081/914.

Nelson Provincial Museum (NPM)
Gibbs, Fred. Transcript of diary, 1883–1885, A657.

Owaka Museum (OWM)
Bradford, Willie. Diary, 1908, CT3094i.

Private Collections (PC)
Collins, Burton. Diary, 1930.
——. Diary, 1933.
——. Diary, 1936.
Marsh, Belle. Diary, 1928.
Moore, Dallas. Transcript of diary, 1957.
——. Transcript of diary, 1959.
——. Transcript of diary, 1962.

——. Transcript of diary, 1963.
Moore, Dallas. Transcripts of letters from friends and family, 1962–1963.
Ross, Arthur Leslie. Memoir, Book 2.

Puke Ariki (PA)
Hughes, Robert. Transcript of diary, 1860–1861, ARC 2001-140.
Lovell, Ken. Unpublished memoir, ARC 2004-1509.
Mackay, Dorothy. Unpublished memoir, ARC 2002-977.
Morpeth, John. Diary, 1927, ARC 2003-541.
Tyson, Valda. 'Adolescent Years During WW2', Unpublished memoir, ARC 2004-1509.
Wood, Henry. Unpublished memoir, ARC 2002-412.

St Margaret's College Archives (SMC)
Page, Elizabeth. Letters to parents, 1942–1944, SMC 145-170w.

South Canterbury Museum (SCM)
Morrison, Sam [pseudonym]. Interview, 1999, OH 1999RV.
Stapleton, Robert [pseudonym]. Interview, 1989, OH 1989RS.
Timaru Teenage Club minute book, 992/53 Box 2/2.

Whakatane Museum and Research Centre (WMRC)
'A History of Scouting at Awakeri', MS 68.
Whakatane District High School Magazine, 1941–1945, MS 71 Box 2.
——. 1957, MS 71, Box 3.

Whanganui Regional Museum (WRM)
Parnell, Jim. Unpublished memoir, 2004.139.2.
——. 'South Island Road Trip', 1949–1950, 2004.139.2.

Oral History Interviews
Adams, Audrey. Interview with Chris Brickell, 2014, Author's Collection (AC).
Ashby, Ernie. 'Scouting and the Mohicans', Audio-taped memoir, no date, AG-107/020, Hocken Collections (HC).
Bell, Isobel ('Ivy'). Interview, no date, Central Stories Museum, Alexandra (CSM).
Carne, Doris. Interview with Chris Brickell, 2010, AC.
Comer, Rod. Interview with Megan Peinell, 1995, OH 0276, Hamilton City Libraries (HCL).
Connelly, Dorrie. Interview with Christene Mauchline, 1995, OH 235, HCL.
Dumble, Jon. Interview with Chris Brickell, 2011, AC.
Hart, Angela. Interview with Chris Brickell, 2015, AC.
Hill, June. Interview with Jan Lindsay, 1995, OH 0227, HCL.
Holden, Jennifer [pseudonym]. Interview with Chris Brickell, 2009, AC.
Honnibal, Heather. Interview with Sarah Smith, 1995, OH 0256, HCL.
Iversen, Mrs. Interview, 1961, CSM.
Morrison, Sam [pseudonym]. Interview, 1999, OH 1999RV, South Canterbury Museum (SCM).
Stapleton, Robert [pseudonym]. Interview, 1989, OH 1989RS, SCM.
Tindall, Sophie [pseudonym]. Interview with Chris Brickell, 2010, AC.
Wilkie, Yvonne. Interview with Chris Brickell, 2016, AC.

BIBLIOGRAPHY

SECONDARY SOURCES

Books, Book Chapters, Journal Articles, Pamphlets and Theses
Aitken, Alexander. *Gallipoli to the Somme*, London, 1963.
Aitken, Jo. 'Wives and Mothers First: The New Zealand Teachers' Marriage Bar and the Ideology of Domesticity, 1920–1940', *Women's Studies Journal*, 12, 1, 1996, 83–98.
Alexander, Kristine. 'Picturing Girlhood and Empire: The Girl Guide Movement and Photography', in Kristine Moruzi and Michelle Smith (eds), *Colonial Girlhood in Literature, Culture and History, 1840–1950*, Houndmills, 2014, 197–213.
Alexander, R.R. *The Story of Te Aute College*, Wellington, 1951.
Allen, Louisa. 'Girls' Portraits of Desire: Picturing a Missing Discourse', *Gender and Education*, 25, 3, 2012, 295–310.
Andrewes, Frazer. 'The Man in the Grey Flannel Suit: White-Collar Masculinity in Post-War New Zealand', in Caroline Daley and Deborah Montgomerie (eds), *The Gendered Kiwi*, Auckland, 1999, 191–212.
Arbury, David. *Prostitution on the Goldfield*, Thames, 2001.
Arnold, Rollo. 'The Dynamics and Quality of Trans-Tasman Migration, 1885–1910', *Australian Economic History Review*, 26, 1, 1985, 1–20.
Arthur, Aylesbeare and Nora Buttle. *Tale of Two Colleges (Wesley College and Seminary and Prince Albert College): A Centenary Survey*, Auckland, 1950.
Ausubel, David. *The Fern and the Tiki: An American View of New Zealand National Character, Social Attitudes and Race Relations*, New York, 1965.
Bailey, Beth. *From Front Porch to Back Seat: Courtship in Twentieth-Century America*, Baltimore, 1988.
——. 'Rebels Without a Cause? Teenagers in the 1950s', *History Today*, 40, February, 1990, 25–31.
Baker, Paul. *King and Country Call: New Zealanders, Conscription and the Great War*, Auckland, 1988.
Ballantyne, Tony. *Entanglements of Empire: Missionaries, Māori and the Question of the Body*, Auckland, 2015.
Bardsley, Dianne. *The Land Girls: In a Man's World, 1939–1946*, Dunedin, 2000.
Bardsley, Sandy. 'The Otekaieke Special School for Boys, 1908–1950', in Barbara Brookes and Jane Thompson (eds), *"Unfortunate Folk": Essays on Mental Health Treatment*, Dunedin, 2001, 123–36.
Bardwell, N.E. 'The Young Incorrigible', Diploma of Social Science dissertation, Victoria University College, 1953.
Barker, John, Peter Kraftl, John Horton and Faith Tucker. 'The Road Less Travelled: New Directions in Children's and Young People's Mobility', *Mobilities*, 4, 1, 2009, 1–10.
Barraclough, Herbert. 'The Causation of Insanity', *New Zealand Medical Journal*, 3, 2, 1904, 335–51.
——. 'Human Instincts, Normal and Pathological', *New Zealand Medical Journal*, 4, 16, 1905, 199–213.
Barrington, Rosemary and Alison Gray. *The Smith Women: 100 New Zealand Women Talk About Their Lives*, Auckland, 1981.
Barson, Michael and Steven Heller. *Teenage Confidential: An Illustrated History of the American Teen*, San Francisco, 1998.
Bathgate, Alexander. *Colonial Experiences or, Sketches of People and Places in the Province of Otago*, Glasgow, 1874.
Beagle, J.M. 'Children of the State: A Study of the New Zealand Industrial School System, 1880–1925', MA thesis, Auckland University, 1974, 93–96.
Beals, Fiona and Bronwyn Wood. 'Negotiating Agency: Local Youth Activism in Aotearoa New Zealand', in Susan Dewey (ed.), *Super Girls, Gangstas, Freeters, and Xenomaniacs: Gender and Modernity in Global Youth Cultures*, New York, 2010, 193–210.
Beckson, Karl. *London in the 1890s: A Cultural History*, New York, 1992.
Belich, James. *Making Peoples: A History of the New Zealanders from Polynesian Settlement to the End of the Nineteenth Century*, Auckland, 1996.
——. *Paradise Reforged: A History of the New Zealanders from the 1880s to the Year 2000*, Auckland, 2001.

OPPOSITE These girls were photographed in the Taranaki area during the 1910s.

BIBLIOGRAPHY

Bellanta, Melissa. 'The Larrikin Girl', *Journal of Australian Studies* 34, 4, 2010, 499–512.
——. *Larrikins: A History*, St Lucia, 2012.
Bellanta, Melissa and Simon Sleight. 'The Leary Larrikin', *Cultural and Social History*, 11, 2, 2014, 263–83.
Bennett, Charlotte. '"Now the War is Over, We Have Something Else to Worry Us": New Zealand Children's Responses to Crises, 1914–1918', *Journal of the History of Childhood and Youth* 7, 1, 2014, 19–41.
Bentley, Trevor. *Pākehā Māori: The Extraordinary Story of the Europeans Who Lived as Māori in Early New Zealand*, Auckland, 1999.
——. *Cannibal Jack: The Life and Times of Jacky Marmon, Pākehā Māori*, Auckland, 2010.
Best, Elsdon. *Maori Agriculture*. Wellington, 1925.
Bioletti, Harry. *The Yanks are Coming: The American Invasion of New Zealand 1942–1944*, Auckland, 1995.
Blamires, E.P. *Youth Movement*, Auckland, 1952.
Bland, Lucy. *Modern Women on Trial: Sexual Transgression in the Age of the Flapper*, Manchester, 2013.
Blizard, Peter. *Juvenile Delinquency in New Zealand*, Wellington, 1967.
Bongiorno, Frank. *The Sex Lives of Australians: A History*, Collingwood, 2012.
Borrows, J.L. *Albertland: The Last Organised British Settlement in New Zealand*, Wellington, 1969.
Bourdieu, Pierre. 'The Forms of Capital', in John Richardson (ed.), *Handbook of Theory and Research for the Sociology of Education*, New York, 1986, 241–58.
Bourke, Chris. *Blue Smoke: The Lost Dawn of New Zealand Popular Music, 1918–1964*, Auckland, 2010.
Boyd, Nan Alamilla. 'Who is the Subject? Queer Theory Meets Oral History', *Journal of the History of Sexuality*, 17, 2, 2008, 177–89.
Brabyn, Isabella. *Life Upon Life: A History of the Presbyterian Young Women's Bible Class Union*, Christchurch, 1954.
Brickell, Chris. 'Same-sex Desire and the Asylum: A Colonial Experience', *New Zealand Journal of History*, 39, 2, 2005, 158–78.
——. 'The Politics of Consumer Culture', *New Zealand Journal of History*, 40, 3, 2006, 133–55.
——. 'Sex Education, Homosexuality and Social Contestation in 1970s New Zealand', *Sex Education*, 7, 4, 2007, 387–406.
——. *Mates and Lovers: A History of Gay New Zealand*, Auckland, 2008.
——. 'Moral Panic or Critical Mass? The Queer Contradictions of 1950s New Zealand', in Heike Bauer and Matt Cook (eds), *Queer 1950s: Rethinking Sexuality in the Postwar Years*, Houndmills, 2012, 94–114.
——. 'Queens Gardens, 1949: The Anxious Spaces of Post-war New Zealand Masculinity', *New Zealand Geographer*, 68, 2012, 81–91.
——. '"Waiting for Uncle Ben": Age-structured Homosexuality in New Zealand, 1920–1950', *Journal of the History of Sexuality* 21, 3, 2012, 467–95.
——. *Manly Affections: The Photographs of Robert Gant, 1885–1915*, Dunedin, 2012.
——. 'On the Case of Youth: Case Files, Case Studies and the Social Construction of Adolescence', *Journal of the History of Childhood and Youth*, 6, 1, 2013, 50–80.
——. 'The Teenager and the Social Scientist', *New Zealand Sociology*, 28, 1, 2013, 36–61.
——. 'Affect and the History of Masculinities', *Qualitative Research Journal*, 14, 1, 2014, 28–40.
——. 'Sensation and the Making of New Zealand Adolescence', *Journal of Social History*, 47, 4, 2014, 994–1020.
——. *Southern Men: Gay Lives in Pictures*, Dunedin, 2014.
——. 'Badness Personified: Nola Pratt's Photograph Album', in Annabel Cooper, Lachy Paterson and Angela Wanhalla (eds), *The Lives of Colonial Objects*, Dunedin, 2015, 262–67.
——. 'Networks of Affect: Male Homoeroticism and the Second World War: A Soldier's Archive', *Social & Cultural Geography*, 16, 2, 2015, 183–202.
Brookes, Barbara. 'A Weakness for Strong Subjects: The Women's Movement and Sexuality', *New Zealand Journal of History*, 27, 2, 1993, 140–56.

——. 'Shame and its Histories in the Twentieth Century', *Journal of New Zealand Studies*, 9, 2010, 37–54.
——. *A History of New Zealand Women*, Wellington, 2016.
Brookes, Barbara, Annabel Cooper and Robin Law (eds). *Sites of Gender: Women, Men & Modernity in Southern Dunedin, 1890–1939*, Auckland, 2003.
Brookes, Barbara, Erik Olssen and Emma Beer. 'Spare Time? Leisure, Gender and Modernity', in Barbara Brookes, Annabel Cooper and Robin Law (eds), *Sites of Gender: Women, Men and Modernity in South Dunedin, 1890–1939*, Auckland, 2013, 151–89.
Brookes, Barbara, Claire Gooder and Nancy de Castro. 'Uptake of the Contraceptive Pill in New Zealand', *New Zealand Journal of History* 47, 2, 2013, 208–31.
Brooks, Victor. *Last Season of Innocence: The Teen Experience in the 1960s*, Lanham, 2012.
Broughton, Agnes et al. *The Silent Migration: Ngāti Pōneke Young Māori Club, 1937–1948*, Wellington, 2001.
Brown, Esther. *Scottish Mother*, New York, 1957.
Brown, Shannon. 'Female Office Workers in Auckland, 1891–1936', MA thesis, Auckland University, 1993.
Buddee, Paul. *The Fate of the Artful Dodger: Parkhurst Boys Transported to Australia and New Zealand*, Perth, 1984.
Bunkle, Phillida. 'The Origins of the Women's Movement in New Zealand: The Women's Christian Temperance Union, 1885–1895', in Phillida Bunkle and Beryl Hughes (eds), *Women in New Zealand Society*, 1980, 52–76.
Burgess, Charlotte. 'Looking to the Heart: Young People, Romance and Courtship in Interwar New Zealand', MA thesis, Auckland University, 2007.
Burke, Peter. *What is Cultural History?*, Cambridge, 2004.
Byrnes, Giselle. 'Introduction: Reframing New Zealand History', in Giselle Byrnes (ed.), *The New Oxford History of New Zealand*, Melbourne, 2009, 1–18.
Campbell, A.E. *Educating New Zealand*, Wellington, 1941.
Carlyon, Jenny and Diana Morrow. *Changing Times: New Zealand Since 1945*, Auckland, 2013.
Carr, Sarah. 'Regulating Sexuality in Early Otago, 1848–1867', *New Zealand Journal of History*, 50, 1, 2016, 30–46.
Certeau, Michel de. *The Practice of Everyday Life*, Berkeley, 1988.
Chauncey, George. 'From Sexual Inversion to Homosexuality: Medicine and the Changing Conceptualization of Female Deviance', *Salmagundi*, 58/59, 1982/1983, 114–46.
Christoffel, Paul. *Censored: A Short History of Censorship in New Zealand*, Wellington, 1989.
Churchman, Geoffrey. *Celluloid Dreams: A Century of Film in New Zealand*, Wellington, 1997.
Cochran, Joan and Bruce Cochran. *Sex, Love and Marriage*, Wellington, 1943.
Cohen, Phil. 'Policing the Working-Class City', in Mike Fitzgerald, Gregor McLennan and Jennie Pawson (eds), *Crime and Society: Readings in History and Theory*, London, 1981, 95–108.
Cohen, Stanley. *Folk Devils and Moral Panics: The Creation of the Mods and Rockers*, Oxford, 1980.
Columbus, Ray. *Ray Columbus, The Modfather: The Life and Times of a Rock 'n' Roll Pioneer*, Auckland, 2011.
Coney, Sandra. *Every Girl: A Social History of Women and the YWCA in Auckland*, Auckland, 1986.
——. *Standing in the Sunshine: A History of New Zealand Women Since They Won the Vote*, Auckland, 1993.
Connell, R.W. *Gender and Power*, Stanford, 1987.
Cook, Matt. *London and the Culture of Homosexuality, 1885–1914*, Cambridge, 2003.
Cook, Olive. *History of the Young Women's Methodist Bible Class Movement, 1906–1927*, Christchurch, 1927.
Cooke, Peter and John Crawford. *The Territorials: The History of the Territorial and Volunteer Forces of New Zealand*, Auckland, 2001.
Courtis, G.B. 'Milk Bars in Wellington', Preventive Medicine dissertation, University of Otago, 1928.
Coyle, Katy and Nadiene Van Dyke. 'Sex, Smashing and Storyville in Turn-of-the-Century New Orleans', in John Howard (ed.), *Carryin' On in the Lesbian and Gay South*, New York, 1997, 54–72.

BIBLIOGRAPHY

Craik, George. *The New Zealanders*, London, 1830.
Crowley, Pauline. 'The 1961 Teenager', in Terry Power (ed.), *New Zealand Through Young Eyes*, Auckland, 1963, 33–34.
Crowther, Dorothy. 'Street Society in Christchurch', Christchurch, 1956.
Culliford, Stanley. *New Zealand Scouting: The First Fifty Years, 1908–1958*, Wellington, 1958.
Cumming, Ian and Alan Cumming. *History of State Education in New Zealand, 1840–1975*, Wellington, 1978.
Cupit, Barbara. 'Juvenile Delinquency: An Illustration of the Position Obtaining in New Zealand at Present', Preventive Medicine dissertation, University of Otago, 1949.
Dakin, J.C. *Education in New Zealand*, Auckland, 1973.
Dalby, Ross. *Young Manhood*, Wellington, 1943.
Daley, Caroline. *Girls & Women, Men & Boys: Gender in Taradale, 1886–1930*, Auckland, 1999.
——. *Leisure and Pleasure: Reshaping and Revealing the New Zealand Body 1900–1960*, Auckland, 2003.
——. 'Puritans and Pleasure Seekers', in Allison Kirkman and Pat Moloney (eds), *Sexuality Down Under: Social and Historical Perspectives*, Dunedin, 2005, 47–62.
Dalley, Bronwyn. 'From Demi-Mondes to Slaveys: Aspects of the Management of the Te Oranga Reformatory for Delinquent Young Women, 1900–1918', in Barbara Brookes, Charlotte Macdonald and Margaret Tennant (eds), *Women in History 2*, Wellington, 1992, 148–67.
——. *Family Matters: Child Welfare in Twentieth-century New Zealand*, Auckland, 1998.
——. 'The Golden Weather, 1949–1965', in Bronwyn Dalley and Gavin McLean (eds), *Frontier of Dreams: The Story of New Zealand*, Auckland, 2005, 307–36.
Dann, Christine. *Up From Under: Women and Liberation in New Zealand, 1970–1985*, Wellington, 1985.
Davidson, Allan. *Selwyn's Legacy: The College of St John the Evangelist, Te Waimate and Auckland, 1843–1992: A History*, Auckland, 1993.
Davis, John. *Youth and the Condition of Britain: Images of Adolescent Conflict*, London, 1990.
Day, Barbara. 'Women in Technical Education: An Historical Account', in Sue Middleton and Alison Jones (eds), *Women and Education in Aotearoa 2*, Wellington, 1992.
D'Emilo, John and Estelle Freedman. *Intimate Matters: A History of Sexuality in America*, New York, 1988.
Demos, John and Virginia Demos. 'Adolescence in Historical Perspective,' *Journal of Marriage and the Family*, 31, 4, 1969, 632–38.
Dewson, Emma. 'Off to the Dance: Romance in Rural New Zealand Communities, 1880s–1920s', *History Australia*, 2, 1, 2004, 05/1–05/9.
Dharmalingam, Arunachalam, Ian Pool and Janet Sceats. *A Demographic History of the New Zealand Family From 1840: Tables*, 2007, www.auckland.ac.nz/uoa/aup/nzfamily/nzfamily_home.cfm
Dickinson, Jennifer. 'Picks, Pans and Petticoats: Women on the Central Otago Goldfields', BA (Hons) dissertation, University of Otago, 1993.
Dix, John. *Stranded in Paradise: New Zealand Rock 'n' Roll, 1955–1988*, Wellington, 1988.
Donnelly, W.E. *Heritage of Methodist Youth*, Wellington, 1954.
Dougherty, Ian. *Bricklayers and Mortarboards: A History of New Zealand Polytechnics and Institutes of Technology*, Palmerston North, 1999.
——. *Vauxhall Gardens: Dunedin's Notorious Victorian Pleasure Gardens*, Dunedin, 2007.
Downes, Peter. *Shadows on the Stage: Theatre in New Zealand – The First 70 Years*, Dunedin, 1975.
Downey, Gregory. *Telegraph Messenger Boys: Labor, Technology, and Geography, 1850–1950*, New York, 2002.
DuBois, Ellen and Linda Gordon. 'Seeking Ecstacy on the Battlefield: Danger and Pleasure in Nineteenth-Century Feminist Thought', *Feminist Review*, 13, 1983, 42–54.
Duncan, A.L. 'What Katy Did at School: A Study of Curriculum Development in Dunedin Girls' Secondary Schools 1900–1920', BA (Hons) dissertation, University of Otago, 1982.
Dyhouse, Carol. *Girls Growing Up in Late Victorian and Edwardian England*, London, 1981.
——. *Girl Trouble: Panic and Progress in the History of Young Women*, London, 2013.
Ebbett, Eve. *When the Boys Were Away*, Auckland, 1984.

Edwards, Mihi. *Mihipeka: Time of Turmoil*, Auckland, 1992.
Eldred-Grigg, Stevan. *Pleasures of the Flesh: Sex and Drugs in Colonial New Zealand, 1840–1915*, Wellington, 1984.
——. *New Zealand Working People 1890–1990*, Palmerston North, 1990.
——. *Diggers, Hatters & Whores: The Story of the New Zealand Gold Rushes*, Auckland, 2008.
Ell, Gordon and Sarah Ell. *Explorers, Whalers and Tattooed Sailors*, Auckland, 2008.
Elley, Benjamin. 'The New Gnostics: The Semiotics of the Hipster', MA thesis, Canterbury University, 2014.
Ellis, Havelock. *Studies in the Psychology of Sex*, 3rd edition, Philadelphia, 1923.
Elwell, E. Simon. *The Boy Colonists: Eight Years of Colonial Life in Otago, New Zealand*, London, 1878.
Elworthy, Sam. *Ritual Song of Defiance: A Social History of Students at the University of Otago*, Dunedin, 1990.
Fairburn, Miles. *The Ideal Society and its Enemies: The Foundations of Modern New Zealand Society, 1850–1900*, Auckland, 1989.
——. *Nearly Out of Heart and Hope: The Puzzle of a Colonial Labourer's Diary*, Auckland, 1995.
——. 'Is There a Good Case for New Zealand Exceptionalism?', in Tony Ballantyne and Brian Moloughney (eds), *Disputed Histories: Imagining New Zealand's Pasts*, Dunedin, 2006, 143–67.
Fass, Paula. *The Damned and the Beautiful: American Youth in the 1920s*, Oxford, 1979.
Felski, Rita. *The Gender of Modernity*, Cambridge, Massachusetts, 1995.
Field, Henry ('Aglow'). 'A Consideration of The Problem of Sex Education With Special Reference to New Zealand Conditions', Honours in Education thesis, University of New Zealand, 1927.
Findlay, Mary. *Tooth and Nail: The Story of a Daughter of the Depression*, Auckland, 1974.
Finnane, Mark. 'Censorship and the Child: Explaining the Comics Campaign', *Australian Historical Studies*, 23, 92, 1989, 220–40.
Firth, Raymond. *Economics of the New Zealand Maori*, Wellington, 1959.
Foote, W.J. *Going Uphill Backwards: Foote-notes from a Storied Life*, Wellington, 2002.
Foreman, Suzanne. 'Profile of a Teenager', in Terry Power (ed.), *New Zealand Through Young Eyes*, Auckland, 1963, 26–27.
Forth, Christopher. *Masculinity in the Modern West: Gender, Civilization and the Body*, Houndmills, 2008.
Foucault, Michel. *The History of Sexuality, Volume 1: An Introduction*, London, 1990.
Fox, Richard. 'Epitaph for Middletown: Robert S. Lynd and the Analysis of Consumer Culture', in Richard Fox and T.J. Jackson Lears (eds), *The Culture of Consumption: Critical Essays in American History, 1880–1980*, New York, 1983, 101–42.
Fox, Richard and T.J. Jackson Lears. 'Introduction', in Richard Fox and T.J. Jackson Lears (eds), *Culture of Consumption: Critical Essays in American History, 1880–1980*, New York, 1983, vii–xvii.
Frank, Tim. 'Bread Queues and Breadwinners: Gender in the 1930s', in Caroline Daley and Deborah Montgomerie (eds), *The Gendered Kiwi*, Auckland, 1999, 113–40.
Fraser, Lyndon. *To Tara Via Holyhead: Irish Catholic Immigrants in Nineteenth-Century Christchurch*, Auckland, 1997.
Fry, Ruth. 'The Curriculum and Girls' Secondary Schooling, 1880–1925', in Sue Middleton (ed.), *Women and Education in Aotearoa*, Sydney and Wellington, 1988, 41–43.
Fyfe, Sarah. 'The Topsy-Turvy Twenties: Urban Society 1921–1928', BA (Hons) dissertation, University of Otago, Dunedin, 1984.
Gardner, W.J. *Colonial Cap and Gown: Studies in the Mid-Victorian Universities of Australasia*, Christchurch, 1979.
Geering, Lloyd. *On Me Bike: Cycling Round New Zealand 80 Years Ago*, Wellington, 2015.
Genn, Philipa. 'Christianity and the Teenager', in Terry Power (ed.), *New Zealand Through Young Eyes*, Auckland, 1963, 29–30.
Gibbons, Peter. 'The Far Side of the Search for Identity: Reconsidering New Zealand's History', *New Zealand Journal of History*, 37, 1, 2003, 38–49.
Gilbert, Jarrod. *Patched: The History of Gangs in New Zealand*, Auckland, 2013.

Gillies, Jade. 'Playing Private Spencer', *The Life: Southland Culture and Lifestyle*, edition 2, 32–33.
Gillingham, Mary. 'Sexual Pleasures and Dangers?: A History of Sexual Cultures in Wellington 1900–1920', MA thesis, Massey University, 1998.
Gillis, John. *Youth and History: Tradition and Change in European Age Relations 1770–Present*, New York, 1974.
——. 'The Evolution of Juvenile Delinquency in England 1890–1914', *Past and Present*, 67, 1975, 96–126.
Glamuzina, Julie and Alison Laurie. *Parker and Hulme: A Lesbian View*, Auckland, 1981.
Godley, Charlotte. *Letters from Early New Zealand*, Christchurch, 1951.
Goffman, Erving. *Stigma: Notes on the Management of Spoiled Identity*, Englewood Cliffs, 1963.
Goodland, R. 'Five Case Histories of Girls Discharged from Burwood', School of Social Science dissertation, Victoria University College, 1953.
Goodyear, Rosemary. 'Overworked Children?: Child Labour in New Zealand, 1919–1939', *New Zealand Journal of History*, 40, 1, 2006, 75–90.
Gornall, A.E. *Biosex M: Sex Instruction for the Adolescent Boy and Young Man*, Auckland, 1944.
Gorst, John. *The Maori King: Or, the Story of Our Quarrel with the Natives of New Zealand*, Hamilton, 1959.
Graff, Harvey. 'Introduction', in Harvey Graff (ed.), *Growing Up in America: Historical Experiences*, Detroit, 1987, xi–xix.
——. *Conflicting Paths: Growing Up in America*, Cambridge Massachusetts, 1995.
Graham, Jeanine. 'Settler Society', in W.H. Oliver (ed.), *The Oxford History of New Zealand*, Wellington, 1981, 112–39.
——. 'Child Employment in New Zealand', *New Zealand Journal of History*, 21, 1, 1987, 62–78.
——. 'My Brother and I: Glimpses of Childhood in Our Colonial Past', Hocken Lecture, Dunedin, 1991.
Grant, J.G.S. *Colonial Characteristics*, Dunedin, 1874.
Greenhalgh, Charlotte. 'Bush Cinderellas: Young New Zealanders and Romance at the Movies, 1919–1939', *New Zealand Journal of History*, 44, 1, 2010, 1–21.
Gregory, Penelope. 'Saving the Children of New Zealand: A Study of Social Attitudes Towards Larrikinism in the Later Nineteenth Century', BA (Hons) dissertation, Massey University, 1975.
Griffin, R.W. *The Book of Mills and Men*, Totara Flat, 2002.
Griffiths, John. 'Popular Culture and Modernity: Dancing in New Zealand Society 1920–1945', *Journal of Social History*, 41, 3, 2008, 611–32.
Gustav-Wrathall, John. *Take the Young Stranger by the Hand: Same-sex Relations and the YMCA*, Chicago, 1998.
Halfpenny, Edward. *Bachelor Block: A Story of Albertland as Related in the Letters & Manuscripts of the Brookes Family*, Wellsford, 1995.
Hall, D.O.W. 'Women at War', in Department of Internal Affairs War History Branch (ed.), *New Zealand in the Second World War, 1939–1945, Episodes and Studies Volume 1*, Wellington, 1954.
Harré, John. 'Maori-Pakeha Intermarriage', in Eric Schwimmer (ed.), *The Maori People in the Nineteen-Sixties*, Auckland, 1968, 118–31.
Harrison, Brian. 'The Victorian Gospel of Success', *Victorian Studies*, 1, 2, 1957, 155–64.
——. 'For Church, Queen and Family: The Girls' Friendly Society, 1874–1920', *Past and Present*, 61, November 1973, 107–38.
Hastings, David. 'Women at Sea, 1870–1885', in Lyndon Fraser and Katie Pickles (eds), *Shifting Centres: Women and Migration in New Zealand History*, Dunedin, 2002, 29–44.
Heap, Chad. *Slumming: Sexual and Racial Encounters in American Nightlife, 1885–1940*, Chicago, 2009.
Hebdige, Dick. 'Posing. . . . Threats, Striking Poses: Youth, Surveillance, and Display', *SubStance*, 11/12, 1982/3, 68–88.
Herr, Curt. 'Introduction', in James Malcolm Rymer, *Varney the Vampire; Or, the Feast of Blood*, Crestline, California, 2008.
Hine, Thomas. *The Rise and Fall of the American Teenager*, New York, 1999.
Hoare, Michael. *Faces of Boyhood: An Informal Pictorial Record of the Boys' Brigade in New Zealand, 1886–1982*, Wellington, 1982.
Hoffmann, Anna. *Tales of Anna Hoffman, Volume Two, Part Three*, Nelson, 2010.

Horn, M.A. *The Digest of Hygiene for Father and Son*, Wellington, 1947.
Houlbrook, Matt. '"The Man With the Powder Puff" in Interwar London', *The Historical Journal*, 50, 1, 2007, 145–71.
Howard, John. 'The Library, the Park and the Pervert: Public Space and Homosexual Encounter in Post-World War II Atlanta', *Radical History Review*, 62, 1995, 166–87.
Hughes, Beryl. 'The Inquiry into the Te Oranga Girls' Home, 1908', *New Zealand Women's Studies Journal*, 4, 1, 1988, 27–38.
Hughes, Celia. 'The Struggle of the Male Self: A New Left Activist and His 1961 Diary', *Journal of British Studies*, 54, 4, 2015, 898–925.
Hutchins, Graham. *Eight Days a Week: The Beatles' Tour of New Zealand, 1964*, Auckland, 2004.
Iles, Marie. *65 Years of Guiding, 1908–1973: The Official History of the Girl Guides Association NZ*, Christchurch, 1976.
Jacobs, Lewis. *The Rise of the American Film*, New York, 1930.
Jensen, Ole. 'Flows of Meaning, Cultures of Movements: Urban Mobility as Meaningful Everyday Life Practice', *Mobilities*, 4, 1, 2009, 139–58.
Jones, Kevin. *Ngā Tohuwhenua Mai Te Rangi: A New Zealand Archaeology in Aerial Photographs*, Wellington, 1994.
Keith, Hamish. *New Zealand Yesterdays: A Look at Our Recent Past*, Sydney, 1984.
Kelly, Veronica. 'Beauty and the Market: Actress Postcards and their Senders in Early Twentieth-Century Australia', *New Theatre Quarterly*, 20, 2, 2004, 99–116.
Kennedy, Angela. 'Educating Our Nurses: Nelson College for Girls, 1892–1910', in Norma Chick and Jan Rogers (eds), *Looking Back, Moving Forward: Essays in the History of New Zealand Nursing and Midwifery*, Palmerston North, 1997, 17–22.
Kerouac, Jack. *On the Road*, Melbourne, 2008 [1957].
Kett, Joseph. *Rites of Passage: Adolescence in America, 1790 to the Present*, New York, 1977.
King, F. Truby. 'A Plea for Stringent Legislation in the Matter of Corrupt and Immoral Publications', *New Zealand Medical Journal*, October 1890, 16–25.
——. 'A Plea for Stringent Legislation in the Matter of Corrupt and Immoral Publications', *New Zealand Medical Journal*, January 1891, 145–58.
——. *The Evils of Cram*, Dunedin, 1906.
Kunzel, Regina. *Criminal Intimacy: Prison and the Uneven History of Modern American Sexuality*, Chicago, 2010.
Labrum, Bronwyn. *Real Modern: Everyday New Zealand in the 1950s and 1960s*, Wellington, 2015.
Laurie, Alison. 'Lady-Husbands and Kamp Ladies: Pre-1970 Lesbian Life in Aotearoa-New Zealand', PhD thesis, Victoria University of Wellington, 2003.
Lavelle, Bernadette. 'Youth Without Purpose: Juvenile Delinquency in New Zealand in the 1950s', MA thesis, University of Otago, 1990.
Law, Robin. 'On the Streets of Southern Dunedin: Gender in Transport', in Barbara Brookes, Annabel Cooper and Robin Law (eds), *Sites of Gender: Women, Men and Modernity in South Dunedin, 1890–1939*, Auckland, 2013, 258–84.
Leach, Helen. *1,000 Years of Gardening in New Zealand*, Wellington, 1984.
Lears, T.J. Jackson. 'From Salvation to Self-Realization: Advertising and the Therapeutic Roots of the Consumer Culture, 1880–1930', in Richard Fox and T.J. Jackson Lears (eds), *The Culture of Consumption: Critical Essays in American History, 1880–1980*, New York, 1983, 1–38.
——. *Fables of Abundance: A Cultural History of Advertising in America*, New York, 1994.
Lee, Howard. 'The Junior Civil Service Examination Reconsidered: A Study of the Changing Function of a Competitive Examination, 1900–1912', in Roger Openshaw and David McKenzie (eds), *Reinterpreting the Educational Past*, Wellington, 1987, 107–21.
Lee, John A. *Delinquent Days*, Auckland, 1967.
Lévesque, Andrée. 'Prescribers and Rebels: Attitudes to European Women's Sexuality in New Zealand, 1860–1916', in Barbara Brookes, Charlotte Macdonald and Margaret Tennant (eds), *Women in History: Essays on European Women in New Zealand*, Wellington, 1986, 1–12.

Littauer, Amanda. *Bad Girls: Young Women, Sex, and Rebellion Before the Sixties*, Chapel Hill, 2015.
Lloyd Jenkins, Douglas. *Frank Carpay*, Napier, 2003.
Lunbeck, Elizabeth. *The Psychiatric Persuasion: Knowledge, Gender, and Power in Modern America*, Princeton, 1994.
Macdonald, Charlotte. *A Woman of Good Character: Single Women as Immigrant Settlers in Nineteenth-Century New Zealand*, Wellington, 1990.
——. *Strong, Beautiful and Modern: National Fitness in Britain, New Zealand, Australia and Canada, 1935-1960*, Wellington, 2011.
Magarey, Susan. 'The Invention of Juvenile Delinquency in Early Nineteenth-Century England', *Labour History*, 34, May, 1978, 11–27.
Malone, Judith Elphick. 'What's Wrong with Emma?: The Feminist Debate in Colonial Auckland', in Barbara Brookes, Charlotte Macdonald and Margaret Tennant (eds), *Women in History: Essays on European Women in New Zealand*, Wellington, 1986, 69–86.
Malthus, Jane. '"Bifurcated and Not Ashamed": Late Nineteenth-Century Dress Reformers in New Zealand', *NZJH*, 23, 1, 1989, 32–46.
Mannheim, Karl. 'The Problem of Generations', in Paul Kecskemeti (ed.), *Essays on the Sociology of Knowledge*, New York, 1952, 276–322.
Manning, A.E. *The Bodgie: A Study in Psychological Abnormality*, Wellington, 1958.
Marcuse, Herbert. *One Dimensional Man: Studies in the Ideology of Advanced Industrial Society*, Boston, 1964.
Martin, John. *Holding the Balance: A History of New Zealand's Department of Labour 1891–1995*, Christchurch, 1996.
Matthews, Jill Julius. *Dance Hall and Picture Palace: Sydney's Romance with Modernity*, Strawberry Hills, NSW, 2005.
Maxwell, Aileen and Ada Gilling. 'The Working Girl of New Zealand', Preventive Medicine dissertation, University of Otago, 1942.
May, Helen. *Minding Children, Managing Men: Conflict and Compromise in the Lives of Postwar Pakeha Women*, Wellington, 1992.
May, Philip. *The West Coast Gold Rushes*, Christchurch, 1962.
McGeorge, C. 'Sex Education in 1912', *New Zealand Journal of Educational Studies*, 12, 2, 1977, 133–41.
McGill, David. *Kiwi Baby Boomers: Growing Up in New Zealand in the 40s, 50s and 60s*, Lower Hutt, 1989.
McKelvie, Neil and Chris Chilton. *45 South in Concert*, Invercargill, 2006.
McKenzie, D.F. 'The Sociology of a Text: Orality, Literacy and Print in Early New Zealand', *The Library*, 6, 4, 1984, 333–65.
McKergow, Fiona. 'Opening the Wardrobe of History: Dress, Artefacts and Material Life of the 1940s and 1950s', in Bronwyn Dalley and Bronwyn Labrum (eds), *Fragments: New Zealand Social and Cultural History*, Auckland, 2000, 163–87.
McKinnon, Malcolm. *The Broken Decade: Prosperity, Depression and Recovery in New Zealand, 1928-39*, Dunedin, 2016.
McLaren, Ian. 'The Politics of Secondary Education in Victorian New Zealand', in Roger Openshaw and David McKenzie (eds), *Reinterpreting the Educational Past: Essays in the History of New Zealand Education*, Wellington, 1987, 64–81.
McLean, Chris and Chris Barnett. *Tramping: A New Zealand History*, Nelson, 2014.
McLean, Gavin. 'Hurrah for Playland!', in William Renwick (ed.), *Creating a National Spirit: Celebrating New Zealand's Centennial*, Wellington, 2004, 87–98.
McLean, Sally. 'Nga Tamariki o te Rohe o Waikato: Māori Children in the Waikato Region, 1850–1900: A Case Study', MA thesis, Waikato University, 1990.
McLennan, Barbara. *YMCA New Zealand: The First 25 Years*, Wellington, 1981.
McNeill, Laurie. 'Teaching an Old Genre New Tricks: The Diary on the Internet', *Biography*, 26, 1, 2003, 24–47.
McQueen, H.C. 'A Preliminary Inquiry into the General Affects of Attendance at Moving Pictures by Children of Dunedin', MA thesis, University of Otago, Dunedin, 1927.

McRobbie, Angela and Jenny Garber. 'Girls and Subcultures', in Stuart Hall and Tony Jefferson (eds), *Resistance Through Rituals: Youth Subcultures in Post-war Britain*, Abingdon, 2006 [1975], 177–88.

Middleton, Sue. 'A Short Adventure Between School and Marriage?: Contradictions in the Education of the New Zealand "Post-war Woman"', in Sue Middleton (ed.), *Women and Education in Aotearoa*, Sydney and Wellington, 1988, 72–88.

Millen, Julia. *Colonial Tears and Sweat: The Working Class in Nineteenth Century New Zealand*, Wellington, 1984.

Mirams, Gordon. *Speaking Candidly: Films and People in New Zealand*, Hamilton, 1945.

Molloy, Maureen. 'Science, Myth and the Adolescent Female: The Mazengarb Report, the Parker-Hulme Trial and the Adoption Act of 1955', *Women's Studies Journal*, 9, 1, 1993, 1–25.

Montgomerie, Deborah. *The Women's War: New Zealand Women 1939–45*, Auckland, 2001.

Moon, Paul. *Maori Transition to a Literate Society in the Nineteenth Century*, Wellington, 1997.

Moran-Ellis, Jo. 'Sexting, Intimacy and Criminal Acts: Translating Teenage Sexualities', in Paul Johnson and Derek Dalton (eds), *Policing Sex*, Abingdon, 2012, 115–32.

Morgan, Sue. 'Knights of God: Ellice Hopkins and the White Cross Army, 1883–1895', *Studies in Church History*, 34, 1998, 431–45.

Morris Matthews, Kay. *In Their Own Right: Women and Higher Education in New Zealand Before 1945*, Wellington, 2008.

——. *Who Cared? Childhoods Within Hawke's Bay Children's Homes and Orphanages, 1892–1988*, Napier, 2012.

Mort, Frank. *Capital Affairs: London and the Making of the Permissive Society*, London, 2010.

Moruzi, Kristine and Michelle Smith. 'Colonial Girlhood/Colonial Girls', in Michelle Smith and Kristine Moruzi (eds), *Colonial Girlhood in Literature, Culture and History, 1840–1950*, Houndmills, 2014, 1–11.

Muchembled, Robert. *Orgasm and the West: A History of Pleasure from the Sixteenth Century to the Present*, Cambridge, 2008.

Murray, Nicky. 'A History of Apprenticeship in New Zealand', MSocSci thesis, Lincoln University, 2001, 38–39.

Nairn, Karen, Jane Higgins and Judith Sligo. *Children of Rogernomics: A Neoliberal Generation Leaves School*, Dunedin, 2012.

Nead, Lynda. *Victorian Babylon: People, Streets and Images in Nineteenth-Century London*, New Haven, 2000.

Neville, W. 'Trends and Differentials in the Age-Sex Structure', in United Nations/ESCAP Population Division (eds), *Population of New Zealand: Country Monograph Series No. 12*, New York, vol. 1, 29–53.

Nolan, Melanie. *Breadwinning: New Zealand Women and the State*, Christchurch, 2000.

——. 'Constantly on the Move, But Going Nowhere? Work, Community and Social Mobility', in Giselle Byrnes (ed.), *The New Oxford History of New Zealand*, Melbourne, 2009, 357–88.

O'Donnell, Barry. *When Nelson Had a Railway: The Life and Death of New Zealand's Last Isolated Railway, 1876–1955*, Wellington, 2005.

Olssen, Erik. *Building the New World: Work, Politics and Society in Caversham, 1880s–1920s*, Auckland, 1995.

——. 'Families and the Gendering of European New Zealand in the Colonial Period, 1840–80', in Caroline Daley and Deborah Montgomerie (eds), *The Gendered Kiwi*, Auckland, 1999, 32–62.

——. 'Working Gender, Gendering Work: Occupational Change and Continuity in Southern Dunedin', in Barbara Brookes, Annabel Cooper and Robin Law (eds), *Sites of Gender: Women, Men and Modernity in South Dunedin, 1890–1939*, Auckland, 2013, 50–90.

——. *Working Lives c. 1900: A Photographic Essay*, Dunedin, 2014.

O'Malley, Vincent. *Haerenga: Early Māori Journeys Across the Globe*, Wellington, 2015.

O'Neill, D.P. 'Catholics and Delinquency', Diploma of Social Science dissertation, Victoria University College, 1950.

Openshaw, Roger, and Roy Shuker. '"Worthless and Indecent Literature": Comics and Moral Panic in Early Post-war New Zealand', *History of Education Review*, 16, 1, 1987, 1–12.
Orchard, D.E. and N.N. Porterfield. 'An Industrial Survey of the Chocolate Factory of R. Hudson & Co. Ltd, Dunedin', Preventive Medicine dissertation, University of Otago, 1928.
Page, Dot. 'Dissecting a Community: Women Medical Students at the University of Otago, 1891–1924', in Barbara Brookes and Dot Page (eds), *Communities of Women: Historical Perspectives*, Dunedin, 2002, 111–27.
Palladino, Grace. *Teenagers: An American History*, New York, 1996.
Parr, Alison. *Home: Civilian New Zealanders Remember the Second World War*, Auckland, 2010.
Pascoe, Judith. 'The Spectacular Flâneuse: Mary Robinson and the City of London', *The Wordsworth Circle*, 23, 3, 1992, 165–71.
Pearson, David. *Johnsonville: Continuity and Change in a New Zealand Township*, Auckland, 1980.
——. *A Dream Deferred: The Origins of Ethnic Conflict in New Zealand*, Wellington, 1990.
Perone, James. *Mods, Rockers and the Music of the British Invasion*, Westport, 2009.
Peters, Mahora and James George. *Showband! Mahora and the Maori Volcanics*, Wellington, 2005.
Philips, P.A. *Memories of the Past: Auckland from 1847*, Auckland, 1897.
Phillips, Jock. *A Man's Country? The Image of the Pakeha Male: A History*, Auckland, 1997.
Phillips, J.R. 'A Social History of Auckland, 1840–53', MA thesis, Auckland University, Auckland, 1966.
Phillips, Lily. 'Blue Jeans, Black Leather Jackets, and a Sneer: The Iconography of the 1950s Biker and its Translation Abroad', *International Journal of Motorcycle Studies*, March 2005, online, no pagination.
Pickens, K.A. 'Marriage Patterns in a Nineteenth-Century British Colonial Population', *Journal of Family History*, 5, 2, 1980, 180–96.
Pickles, Katie. 'Workers and Workplaces', in John Cookson and Graeme Dunstall (eds), *Southern Capital: Christchurch: Towards a City Biography, 1850–2000*, Christchurch, 2000, 138–61.
——. 'Pink Cheeked and Surplus: Single British Women's Inter-war Migration to New Zealand', in Lyndon Fraser and Katie Pickles (eds), *Shifting Centres: Women and Migration in New Zealand History*, Dunedin, 2002, 63–80.
——. 'Transnational History and Cultural Cringe: Some Issues for Consideration in New Zealand, Australia and Canada', *History Compass*, 9, 9, 2001, 657–73.
Piess, Kathy. *Cheap Amusements: Working Women and Leisure in Turn-of-the-Century New York*, Philadelphia, 1986.
Platt, Antony. *The Child Savers: The Invention of Delinquency*, Chicago, 1969.
Plummer, Ken. *Cosmopolitan Sexualities: Hope and the Humanist Imagination*, Cambridge, 2015.
Pool, Ian, Arunachalam Dharmalingam and Janet Sceats. *The New Zealand Family From 1840: A Demographic History*, Auckland, 2007.
Porter, Frances. *Away From Home: The Story of Victoria House*, Wellington, 2002.
Porter, Frances and Charlotte Macdonald. *My Hand Will Write What My Heart Dictates: The Unsettled Lives of Women in Nineteenth-Century New Zealand as Revealed to Sisters, Family and Friends*, Auckland, 1996.
Price, Simon. *New Zealand's First Talkies: Early Film-making in Otago and Southland*, Dunedin, 1996.
Pugsley, Christopher. *On the Fringe of Hell: New Zealanders and Military Discipline in the First World War*, Auckland, 1991.
'Purity', *Needful Knowledge on Social and Sexual Hygiene*, Wellington, 1941.
Putney, Clifford. *Muscular Christianity: Manhood and Sports in Protestant America, 1880–1920*, Cambridge, 2001.
Ramson, Frederick. *Hutt Valley High School: The First 42 Years: A Personal Memoir*, Lower Hutt, 1976.
Rankin, Keith. *Unemployment in New Zealand at the Peak of the Great Depression*, Auckland, 1995.
Ritchie, Megan. 'Shaken But Not Stirred?: Youth Cultures in 1950s Auckland', MA thesis, Auckland University, 1997.
Rosen, David. *Armies of the Young: Child Soldiers in War and Terrorism*, New Brunswick, 2005.
Rosenman, Ellen. *Unauthorized Pleasures: Accounts of Victorian Erotic Experience*, Ithaca, 2003.

Rountree, Kathryn. 'Remaking the Maori Female Body: Marianne Williams' Mission in the Bay of Islands', *Journal of Pacific History* 35, 1, 2000, 49–66.
Rowland, Perrin. *Dining Out: A History of the Restaurant in New Zealand*, Auckland, 2013.
Roydhouse, N. 'Otekaieke Special School', Preventive Medicine dissertation, University of Otago, 1949.
Rupe, Carmen and Paul Martin. *Carmen: My Life*, Auckland, 1988.
Salmi, Hannu. 'Cultural History, the Possible, and the Principle of Plenitude', *History and Theory* 50, 2, 2011, 171–87.
Salmond, Anne. *Between Worlds: Early Exchanges Between Māori and Europeans 1773–1815*, Auckland, 1997.
Savage, Jon. *Teenage: The Creation of Youth 1875–1945*, London, 2008.
Schlör, Joachim. *Nights in the Big City: Paris, Berlin, London, 1840–1930*, London, 1998.
Schrader, Ben. *The Big Smoke: New Zealand Cities, 1840–1920*, Wellington, 2016.
Schrum, Kelly. *Some Wore Bobby Sox: The Emergence of Teenage Girls' Culture, 1920–1945*, New York, 2004.
Scott, Donald. 'The Popular Lecture and the Creation of a Public in Mid-Nineteenth-Century America', *The Journal of American History*, 66, 4, 1980, 791–809.
Scott, Linda. *Fresh Lipstick: Redressing Fashion and Feminism*, Houndmills, 2005.
Scott, Robert. 'Public Control of the Liquor Trade in New Zealand, 1840–1899', MA thesis, Victoria University of Wellington, 1952.
Shadbolt, Tim. *Bullshit & Jellybeans*, Wellington, 1971.
Shuker, Roy. 'Moral Panics and Social Control: Juvenile Delinquency in Late Nineteenth Century New Zealand', in Roger Openshaw and David McKenzie (eds), *Reinterpreting the Educational Past: Essays in the History of New Zealand Education*, Wellington, 1987, 122–31.
Simon, Judith. *Ngā Kura Māori: The Native Schools System 1867–1969*, Auckland, 1998.
Simpson, Tony. *The Sugarbag Years*, Martinborough, 1974.
Sinclair, Keith. *A History of New Zealand*, Auckland, 1988.
Sinfield, Alan. *Literature, Politics, and Culture in Postwar Britain*, Oxford, 1993.
Singer, Ben. *Melodrama and Modernity*, New York, 2001.
Sleight, Simon. *Young People and the Shaping of Public Space*, Farnham, 2013.
Sloan, Alistair. 'Saturday Night', in Terry Power (ed.), *New Zealand Through Young Eyes*, Auckland, 1963, 34–35.
Smaal, Yorick. 'Boys and Homosex: Danger and Possibility in Queensland, 1890–1914', in Shirleene Robinson and Simon Sleight (eds), *Children, Childhood and Youth in the British World*, Houndmills, 2016, 221–36.
Smith, Paul. *Twist and Shout: New Zealand in the 1960s*, Auckland, 1991.
Smith, Peter. 'The Big Muscle Boys: A Study of Physical Culture', Special Study in Physical Education, University of Otago, 1958.
Smyth, Helen. *Rocking the Cradle: Contraception, Sex and Politics in New Zealand*, Wellington, 2000.
Soler, Janet. 'That Incredible Document Commonly Known as the Mazengarb Report', *Sites*, 19, 1989, 22–32.
Somers, Jean-Christopher. 'The Politics of Social Discourses About Youth in New Zealand, 1950–1965 and 1990–2005', PhD thesis, Victoria University of Wellington, 2015.
Sprecher, Danielle. 'Good Clothes are Good Business: Gender, Consumption and Appearance in the Office, 1918–39', in Caroline Daley and Deborah Montgomerie, *The Gendered Kiwi*, Auckland, 1999, 141–62.
Springhall, John. *Coming of Age: Adolescence in Britain, 1860–1960*, Dublin, 1986.
——. *Youth, Popular Culture and Moral Panics: Penny Gaffs to Gangsta Rap, 1830–1996*, Houndmills, 1998.
Srebnick, Amy Gilman. *The Mysterious Death of Mary Rogers: Sex and Culture in Nineteenth Century New York*, New York, 1995.
Steele, Frances. 'Uncharted Waters? Cultures of Sea Transport and Mobility in New Zealand Colonial History', *Journal of New Zealand Studies*, 12, 2011, 137–54.

Stock, Francine. *In Glorious Technicolor: A Century of Film and How it Has Shaped Us*, London, 2011.
Stone, R.C.J. *Logan Campbell's Auckland: Tales From the Early Years*, Auckland, 2007.
Stratton, Jon. 'Bodgies and Widgies: Youth Cultures in the 1950s', *Journal of Australian Studies*, 8, 15, 1984, 10–24.
Stryker, Susan. *Queer Pulp: Perverted Passions from the Golden Age of the Paperback*, San Francisco, 2001.
Sutch, W.B. *The Quest for Security in New Zealand*, Wellington, 1966.
Taylor, A.J.W. 'The Significance of "Darls" or "Special Relationships" for Borstal Girls', *British Journal of Criminology*, 5, 4, 1965, 406–18.
Taylor, Colin. *Body, Mind and Spirit: YMCA Auckland Celebrating 150 Years 1855–2005*, Auckland, 2005.
Taylor, Nancy. *The Home Front*, volume 1, Wellington, 1986.
Taylor, Tony. 'Thomas Hunter and the Campaign Against Eugenics', *New Zealand Journal of History*, 39, 2, 2005, 195–214.
Tebbutt, Melanie. *Making Youth: A History of Youth in Modern Britain*, Basingstoke, 2016.
'Teddy Boys', in Stephen Barnett and Jim Sullivan (eds), *In Their Own Words: From the Sound Archives of Radio New Zealand*, Wellington, 1988, 78–83.
Temple, Philip. *A Sort of Conscience: The Wakefields*, Auckland, 2002.
Tennant, Margaret. 'Natural Directions: The New Zealand Movement for Sexual Differentiation in Education During the Early Twentieth Century', *New Zealand Journal of Educational Studies*, 12, 2, 1977, 142–53.
——. *Children's Health, the Nation's Wealth: A History of Children's Health Camps*, Wellington, 1994.
Thomson, Warwick. *An Innocent Aboard*, Auckland, 2003.
Thwaites, Agnes. *The Wyndham Story 1854–2000: Life Between the Three Rivers*, Wyndham, 2003.
Toynbee, Claire. *Her Work and His: Family, Kin and Community in New Zealand, 1900–1930*, Wellington, 1995.
——. 'Dancing Between the Showers: Growing Up in New Zealand in the Inter-war Years', *ANZALS Leisure Research Series*, 3, 1996, 36–55.
Trotter, Olive. *Dunedin's Spiteful Socrates: James Gordon Stuart Grant*, Dunedin, 2005.
Troughton, Geoffrey. 'Jesus and the Ideal of the Manly Man in New Zealand after World War One', *Journal of Religious History*, 30, 1, 2006, 45–60.
Tulloch, Tracy. 'State Regulation of Sexuality in New Zealand, 1880–1925', PhD thesis, University of Canterbury, 1997.
Upton, Susan. *Wanted: A Beautiful Barmaid: Women Behind the Bar in New Zealand, 1830–1976*, Wellington, 2013.
Vickers, Emma. *Queen and Country: Same-Sex Desire in the British Armed Forces, 1939–45*, Manchester, 2013.
Wakefield, Edward Jerningham. *Adventure in New Zealand from 1839 to 1844*, Christchurch, 1908 [1845].
Walker, Ranginui. *He Tipua: The Life and Times of Sir Āpirana Ngata*, Auckland, 2001.
Wanhalla, Angela. 'To "Better the Breed of Men": Women and Eugenics in New Zealand, 1900–1935', *Women's History Review*, 16, 2, 2007, 163–82.
——. *Matters of the Heart: A History of Interracial Marriage in New Zealand*, Auckland, 2013.
Wanhalla, Angela and Kate Stevens. '"I Don't Like Maori Girls Going Out with Yanks": Māori-American Encounters in New Zealand', in Judith Bennett and Angela Wanhalla (eds), *Mothers' Darlings of the South Pacific: The Children of Indigenous Women and US Servicemen, World War II*, Hawaii, 2016, 202–37.
Warburton, Rosalind. 'The Teenager', in Terry Power (ed.), *New Zealand Through Young Eyes*, Auckland, 1963, 25–26.
Ward, Aimee, Claire Freeman and Rob McGee. 'The Influence of Transport on Well-being Among Teenagers: A Photovoice Project in New Zealand', *Journal of Transport and Health*, 2, 2015, 414–22
Ward, Louis. *Early Wellington*, Auckland, 1928.

Warren, Allen. 'Popular Manliness: Baden Powell, Scouting and the Development of Manly Character', in J.A. Mangan and James Walvin (eds), *Manliness and Morality: Middle-Class Masculinity in Britain and America, 1800–1940*, Manchester, 1987, 199–219.
Watson, Lindsay. 'The Perils of Impurity: The New Zealand Purity Crusades of Henry Bligh, 1902–1930', *New Zealand Journal of History*, 49, 2, 2015, 110–35.
Weight, Richard. *Mod: A Very British Style*, London, 2013.
White, Georgina. *Light Fantastic: Dance Floor Courtship in New Zealand*, Auckland, 2007.
Williams, Melissa Matutina. *Panguru and the City, Kāinga Tahi, Kāinga Rua: An Urban Migration History*, Wellington, 2015.
Wilson, John. *Reminiscences of the Early Settlement of Dunedin and South Otago*, Dunedin, 1912.
Wilson, Jude. *Flying Kiwis: A History of the OE*, Dunedin, 2014.
Winks, Robin. *These New Zealanders*, Christchurch, 1956.
Wolfe, Richard. *The Way We Wore: The Clothes New Zealanders Have Loved*, Auckland, 2001.
Wood, Bronwyn. 'Youth Participation in Society: Everyday Citizenship Perspectives from Young People in New Zealand', *New Zealand Sociology*, 25, 2, 2010, 103–25.
Woods, Megan. 'Re/producing the Nation: Women Making Identity in New Zealand, 1906–1925', MA thesis, University of Canterbury, 1997.
——. 'Integrating the Nation: Gendering Māori Urbanisation and Integration, 1942–1969', PhD thesis, University of Canterbury, 2002.
Wright, Matthew. *Convicts: New Zealand's Hidden Criminal Past*, Auckland, 2012.
Yska, Redmer. *All Shook Up: The Flash Bodgie and the Rise of the New Zealand Teenager in the Fifties*, Auckland, 1993.
——. *Wellington: Biography of a City*, Auckland, 2006.

Illustration Credits

Introduction Chapter opener: 48/1, OBHS; page 2: ADM; page 5: BC43, SOM; page 6: PC; page 7: 1952.68.92, CM; page 8: 48/1, OBHS; page 10: PC; page 13: G3-31, TA.

Chapter 1 Page 16: A-050-032, ATL; page 18: NZG-18910530-10-1, AL; page 21, left: E-216-f-011, ATL; page 21, right: A-286-009, ATL; page 22, left: PUBL-0022-258, ATL; page 22, right: E-452-f-009-2, ATL; page 23: A-042-006, ATL; page 26: S15-647b, HC; page 27: S15-647a, HC; page 28: B-064-022, ATL; page 31: E-455-f-014, ATL; page 37: ESBrookesLetter004, ADM; page 41: PA1-f-019-19-3, ATL; pages 44-45: PA1-o-530-25, ATL; page 48: PUBL-0153-1865-189, ATL; A-220-008-a-1, ATL; page 49: A-220-008-a-2, ATL; page 51: A-252-027, ATL; page 52, top: PAColl-8850, ATL; page 52, bottom: CCA; page 54: B-176-003, ATL; Philips, *Memories of the Past*, 12; page 55: 1944.78.291, CM; page 57: 1/2-047261-F, ATL; page 58: S-L-1425-92, ATL; page 62: 1/4-006418-G, ATL.

Chapter 2 Page 66: PA1-q-962-13-1, ATL; page 68, top left: PA1-q-962-17, ATL; page 68, top centre: A0209_S0381_Vol1e, IL; page 68, top right: A0209_S0381_Vol1e, IL; page 68, middle left: PA1-q-962-17-6, ATL; page 68, middle centre: PA1-q-962-20-4, ATL; page 68, A0209_S0381_Vol1e, IL; page 68: bottom left: KCM; page 68, bottom centre: PA2-0439, ATL; page 68, bottom right: PA1-q-630-07-4, ATL; page 70: RM; page 72: 00.122, CS; page 75: 0703_01_001A, HC; page 76, left: E-783-051, ATL; right: E-783-059, ATL; page 79: PA3-0053, ATL; Gibbs, Diary, 11 December 1883, NPM; page 81: 181099, NPM; page 82: PA1-q-962-13-3, ATL; page 84: E-061-006, ATL; Goldsworthy, Papers, 9; page 85: 1448-4696, MB; page 88: 2014/45, NOM; page 89: 03.128, CS; page 91: PA1-q-963-10-9, ATL; page 92: E-423-q-017, ATL; Clogstoun, Diary, HC; Hetherington, 'Numbering My Days', ATL; Knight, Diary, ATL; page 93: S16-634b, HC; Clogstoun, Diary, 20 May 1881; page 94: 47_5-1, TOSM; page 96: 28_23-1, TOSM; page 100: ACGB 8306 CW 15 5/8, ANZ; page 101, left: NZPM; page 101, right: NZPM; ODT, 18 Nov 1889, 4; Hebdige, 'Posing', 74; page 105: NZPM; page 106: PA1-q-962-18-3; ATL; page 107: 1/4-008097-G, ATL; page 108: E-311-q-018-2, ATL; page 110: *Dead Bird*, 10 November 1889; page 113: S16-634a, HC; page 116: PC; page 118: 1/4-030179-G, ATL; page 119: Crawford, Diary, ATL, 82; page 120: PA1-q-963-10-2, ATL; page 122: PA1-q-962-21-1/2, ATL; King, 'A Plea for Stringent Legislation', 1890, 18; page 124, left: PA1-q-962-18-5; ATL; page 124, right: 2014/45, NOM.

Chapter 3 Page 126: PA1-1372-02-3, ATL; page 129: PA1-0-833-027-2, ATL; page 131: 1/1-002943-G, ATL; page 132: 2004-2-97-396, ADM; page 133: 1375, SCM; page 134, left: 88-130-1-05/3, ATL; page 134, right: 88-130-1-05/1, ATL; page 136, left:1/2-163671-G, ATL; page 136, right: 1/2-118389-G, ATL; page 137: S12-664b, HC; page 138: PHO2012-0267, PRA; page 141: P0025.301, NOM; page 144: P27/4/4254, ANZ; page 148: D016a, HUCL; page 149: 2014-43, NOM; page 151: Milne1, SOM; page 152: 48/1, OBHS; page 153: S11-523a, HC; page 155: PAColl-4262-02, ATL; Erle Crawford to Edith Crawford, 7 October 1910, ATL; page 156: 1/2-092651, ATL; page 157: 2012-730, NOM; page 159: 48/1, OBHS; page 160: 2012-730, NOM; page 161: 1/1-017707-G, ATL; pages 162-3: 1448-4330, MB; page 166, left: 18page29, MA; page 166, top right: 18page29, MA; page 166: bottom right: 18page23, MA; page 167, top left: 18page33, MA; page 167, bottom left: Albums5, MA; page 167, right: Albums5, MA; page 169: S16-634d, HC; YWCA, Buttercup Farm Journal, HC; page 170: AG-039/037, HC; page 172: PA1-1372-21-4, ATL; page 174: 7074-1/1, ATL; page 175: 48/1, OBHS; page 176: EP-1721-1_2-G, ATL; Jenner, 'Saturday Sixpence', ATL, 5-6; page 179, left: 12-1031-1, NOM; page 179, right: 12-1031-2, NOM; page 181: 2004-2-98-265, ADM; page 183: 8979, NOM; page 184: BC41, SOM; page 185: 48/1, OBHS; page 186: 1/2-045580-G, ATL.

OPPOSITE 'Miss Heather Wilson, Photo Snapping' at a Methodist camp, c. 1939.

ILLUSTRATION CREDITS

Chapter 4 Page 188: PA1-0-742, ATL; page 190: S12-625c, HC; page 192: PAColl-5800-55, ATL; page 193: PA1-q-566-027-01, ATL; page 195: IB1, SOM; Honnibal, Interview, HCL; page 197: S14-551d, HC; page 199, top: MSY-6127/2, ATL; page 199, bottom: MSY-6127/1, ATL; page 200: EP53, ATL; page 201: 161071, NPM; Helm, Letter to Father, 8 Apr 1942, ATL; page 203: 1/2-212744-F, ATL; page 205, top left: EP-0629-1_2-G, ATL; page 205, bottom left: PAColl-0224-18, ATL; page 205, top right: 1/1-031912-F, ATL; page 205, bottom right: 1/1-031828-F, ATL; page 206: P0021.626, NOM; page 207: AC; page 210: AC; page 212: PA1-0-1029, ATL; John Marsh to parents, 1933, ADM; page 214: 2004-2-99-483, ADM; Carne, Interview, AC; page 216: P0001.11-1, NOM; Carne, Interview, AC; page 217: PC; page 218: 2008-3-75-18, ADM; Page, Letter to parents, Sunday 15th [no month], 1945, SMC; page 219: 1/4-000846-F, ATL; page 220: 118313, NPM; page 221: CT3085, OM; page 222: DHS; email from Marian Tolich to author, 10 October 2016; page 226: 320869, NPM; page 228: S12-652b, HC; page 229: AC; page 230: PA1-0-1290-34-4, ATL; page 231: PA1-0-724-11-5, ATL; page 233: PAColl-4161-01-144-3, ATL; pages 234-5: 154218, NPM; page 237: F966-1/1, ATL; page 238, all: Maxwell and Gilling, 'Working Girl'; the written information can be found in Maxwell and Gilling, 'Working Girl', 19-30; Carne, Interview, AC; page 241, KM; page 243: AC; page 244: P0025.506, NOM.

Chapter 5 Page 246: EP/1958/1469-F, ATL; page 249: *Manning, The Bodgie*, reproduced courtesy of family of Dennis Turner; Mumford cited in Plummer, *Cosmopolitan Sexualities*, 62; page 251: C117-15, TA; page 253: PC; page 254: 2015-450-3, NOM; Keith, *New Zealand Yesterdays*, 201; page 256: EP/1959/0490-1-F, ATL; page 257: AC; page 258: PC; page 260: Box 51, RMTB; page 261: Box 51, RMTB; page 262, top left: AAVK/6390/B19098, ANZ; page 262, top right: AAVK/6390/B3642, ANZ; page 262, bottom: PC; page 263, left: BNZ; page 263, right: BNZ; Adams, Interview, AC; page 265: *Manning, The Bodgie*, reproduced courtesy of family of Dennis Turner; page 266: NZH; page 269: *Manning, The Bodgie*, reproduced courtesy of family of Dennis Turner; page 272: PC; page 273, top: PC; page 273, bottom: PC; page 274: 1269-Z331-5, AL; page 276: AC; page 277: C117-6, TA; page 278, left: PC; page 279, right: PC; page 280, Box 51, RMTB; page 281: PC; page 283: C117-2, TA; page 284: PC; page 286, top left: PC; page 286, top right, PC; page 286, bottom, PC; page 287: Hart, Interview, AC; page 289: P1-1698-4088, UHL; page 290: EP/1959/0050-F, ATL; page 292: F-37406-35mm; page 293, top: PAColl-5679-01, ATL; page 293, bottom: PA1-f-167-17/10-11-12, ATL; page 294: F- 47518-35mm, ATL; page 296, top left: P-A285.1-2, PA; page 296, middle left: P-A23-20-26001, PRA; page 296, top right: P-AH-60.45-47001, PRA; page 296, middle right, P-AH1.17-17, PRA; page 296, bottom: P-AH23.28-28, PRA; page 298, top: 2007.87.2, WRM; page 298, bottom left: 2007.87.2, WRM; page 298, bottom right: 2007.87.2; page 299: MS526-5, WMRC; page 300: NAA/9710622/0001, NLA; page 301: EP/1957/0011-F, ATL; page 304: HC; page 306, left: EP/1956/2453c-F, ATL; page, 306, right: EP/1959/4001-F, ATL; page 307: MB; page 308: EP/1967/3661/1A-F, ATL; page 310, 3690, SCM; page 311, PC.

Conclusion Page 312: EP/1981/2700/8A-F, ATL; page 315, all: PC; page 317: 8.1, NOM; page 320: PC, reproduced by permission of Dylan Owen; page 323: PC, reproduced by permission of Jeremy Templer.

Bibliography Page 342: S14-551c, HC; Page 349: PHO2012/0269, PA

Illustrations Reference List Page 362: Album5, MA

Acknowledgements Page 366: EP/1960/1762-F, ATL

Acknowledgments

I started thinking about this book in 2008 when an earlier project – *Mates & Lovers: A History of Gay New Zealand* – was about to be published. My first forays into the possibility of creating a volume on young New Zealanders were pictorial. As I sat in the photographic reading room at the Alexander Turnbull Library in Wellington, archivist Walter Cook brought out photo albums by the trolley-load: I pored through them and was hooked. Over tea and cake in the since-disappeared downstairs café, Walter, who has since retired, listened to my musings and worked out what else to show me. Some of his images ended up in the book.

A great many other people have guided me along the way. Three research assistants have worked on this project at various points. Louise Pearman-Beres, Joey Macdonald and Raelene Inglis all spent countless hours in the Hocken Collections, unearthing diary treasures and trawling through newspapers, magazines and archives. Ian Watt and Robert Aldrich encouraged me during the early stages of writing, and John Webster sent me snippets of useful information through the post. Laurence Senelick provided information on theatre history, Judith Collard inspired me to look closely at the flapper and Graham Willett engaged me in conversation on the importance of the port cities. David Herkt suggested I pay attention to young people's slang – 'teenagers are such coded creatures', he said. What was to have been a glossary found its way into the main part of the book. Chris Bourke introduced me to the photographer Revelle Jackson. Colin Hayes read and responded to an endless stream of eccentric emails, sent almost daily over the period of a year, in which I declared the manuscript was nearly ready – it wasn't – and just needed a bit more 'polishing'.

I had a lot more help with photographs too. Katy Yiakmis looked through many of my photos with her keen artist's eye, and shared her thoughts about their visual significance. Bronwyn McGovern generously loaned me photos from her family collection, several of which appear in Chapter 5, and put me in touch with her mother, Audrey Adams, who told me about her life as we worked our way through a pile of images. Angela Hart, Jeremy Templer, Dylan Owen, and Claire White also provided wonderful pictures from their collections. At various stages Les O'Neill, Paul Renata and Richard Schofield prepared photos for publication.

My own research has taken me to 50-odd museums, libraries and archives around New Zealand, from the north to the south. Curators and archivists greeted me warmly; some offered tea and biscuits as well as access to their collections. Many put up with numerous emails and some welcomed repeated visits. I am especially grateful to Lynda and Don Hammond, Te Ahu in Kaitaia; Keith Giles, Auckland Libraries; George Mihaljevich, Dalmatian Genealogical and Historical Society in Auckland; Wayne Marriott, Whakatane Museum and Research Centre; Gareth Winter, Wairarapa Archive; Rowan Carroll, New Zealand Police Museum; Reid Perkins, Upper Hutt City Library; Jessica Ward, BNZ Archive; Tony Rippin, South Canterbury Museum; Jo Smith, Methodist Archives; Geraldine Pickles, St Margaret's College Archive; Terry Ryan and Jill Durney, Te Rūnanga o Ngāi Tahu; Marguerite Hill, Canterbury Museum; Jane Teal, Christ's College Archive; Kathleen Stringer, Ashburton Museum; Chris Meech, North Otago Museum; Yvonne Wilkie and Myke Tymons, Presbyterian Archives; Richard Germon, University of Otago Medical Library; Emma Knowles, Toitū Otago Settlers Museum; Susan Madden-Grey, Otago Boys' High School Archive; Kaaren Mitcalfe, Owaka Museum; and Gary Ross at the South Otago Museum. Lyn Johnston at the Albertland and Districts Museum in Wellsford really went the extra mile. She looked among her family records for letters and diaries that might be of interest, transcribed sections of them for me, and provided photographs from her own collection. Heather Mathie and Joce Chalmers at the Alexander Turnbull Library cheerfully fielded my messages and pointed me in the right direction, and the friendly team at the Hocken Collections in Dunedin greeted me with a smile – and a kindly

ACKNOWLEDGEMENTS

ribbing when I asked annoying questions. Ali Clarke always enquired how the book was going, and she shared tales of her own writing projects. My sister Diane Richards is a stalwart of the Kapiti Coast Museum, and she fished out two photographic treasures for me.

Some wonderful sources for this book come from private collections. As well as Lyn Johnston's family letters, Ross Scott shared the unpublished memoir of his grandfather, Les Ross; Dallas Moore loaned me the transcripts of his own diaries and letters to and from friends and family; and Jill Goodwin sent me her transcripts of Burton Collins' diaries.

The University of Otago is a supportive and collegial setting to embark on a wide-ranging and long-running project like this. My colleagues in the Department of Sociology, Gender and Social Work have provided support and encouragement, and they knew when (and when not) to ask. As it turned out, the final push on the manuscript coincided with a six-month-long stint as Head of Department in the second half of 2016. Gwenda Crawford, our able and unflappable Department Manager, did not mind when I vanished into a writing haze – or if she did, she did not let on. My wonderful office mates in 'the little house' in Leith Street provided guidance, amusement – and food – right on cue. Marcelle Dawson took me out for cake and wine; Rebecca Stringer offered reassurance about my conceptual framework; Annabel Cooper pointed me in the direction of the 'colonial girl'; Fairleigh Gilmour brought baking and searched through several years of *Woman's Weekly* for me; Patrick Vakaoti let me raid his stash of mandarins; Anita Gibbs exuded sympathy whenever I appeared, agitated, at her office door waving pages of recalcitrant drafts; and Martin Tolich enthusiastically asked me to write about this book for an edited collection he was working on: the third edition of *Social Science Research in New Zealand*. Several University of Otago Research Grants, two study leave allowances and a Head of Department's allowance have funded research assistance, travel, accommodation, archival costs, digital images and a subvention to support publication.

Sam Elworthy at Auckland University Press exuded enthusiasm for this project from the moment he heard me present a paper on teenagers and social science. His insightful suggestions on a very early draft helped shape the final version, even though he warned me to don some 'body armour' before sitting down to read them. Robust comments often make for a much better final product, and this book is no exception. Ginny Sullivan expertly copy-edited the manuscript and provided some useful tidbits of information that I eagerly incorporated, and Katrina Duncan's smart, spacious design gives the text and images room to breathe.

Mashing this manuscript into shape would have been extremely difficult without the help of two friends in particular: Greg Rawlings and Yorick Smaal. Greg worked his way through one draft, and his anthropological insights helped strengthen my account of New Zealand history. He also offered advice on an especially troublesome chapter, peering at it with me as we spread it across our meeting-room table. Over the past several years Yorick has proffered thoughts and suggestions from across the Tasman, and he read two drafts. The first of these was very rudimentary, the second not-quite-ready, and Yorick's wide-ranging comments proved invaluable. When I was tentative he urged me to be bolder.

My partner Jeffrey Vaughan always provides cheerful support for my writing. We road-tripped across the country together during this book's research phase, guided by the battered map book we take everywhere. Rain storms, hot springs, bush walks, cheap-and-cheerful restaurants, hospitable archivists and irascible motel owners, we discovered, are the basis of a good New Zealand research trip.

My parents Kerry and Brian have supported my scholarly endeavours as long as I can remember, in a multitude of ways. They nurtured me as a child and a teenager and have cheered me along ever since. They have been eagerly waiting for this book, and I dedicate it to them.

Chris Brickell, January 2017

OPPOSITE **At the Glide Rink, Kilbirnie, Wellington, in 1960.**

Index

Italics are used to indicate illustrations as well as information contained in the captions.

Abbey Road Studios, 294, *294*
Abdallah, Ruby, 135
acrobatic troupes, 9
activism and activists: environmental, 313, 321; feminist, 132, 319; work, 321; *see also* Campaign for Nuclear Disarmament; nuclear weapons, protests against; racism, protests against; Save Manapouri Campaign; Vietnam war, protest against; youth pay rates, strike action against
Adams, Audrey, *253*, *272*, 273, *273*
Addington railway workshops, Christchurch, 74
adolescence, as concept, 3, 14, 19, 32, 47, 54, 63, 64–65, 69–70, 72, 73, 75–76, 80, 82, 83, 87, 111, 117, 121–23, *122*, 125, 128, 158, 171, 190, 243, 245, 269–70, 299–300, 322
adult surveillance, 12, 40, 74, 93, 101, 146, 149, 216, 244, 318; *see also* shipboard matrons
adulthood, as concept, 1, 3, 14, 20, 24, 33, 39, 46, 60, 63, 73, 117, 121, 125, 147, 190, 288, 319
adventurousness, 22, 23, *23*, 25, 38, 59, 89–90, 141, 143, 154, 165, 168–69, 177, 182, 187, 198, 201, 224, 239–40, 322a
advertising, 15, 208, 211, 249, 310; targeting boys, 135, 158, 276, *277*; targeting girls, 128, *128*, *134*, 134–35, 178, 183, 187, 208, 230, 275
aeroplanes, 204, *299*
AFS Dance, Oamaru, *317*
Air Training Corps, *233*, 236
Aitken, Alexander, 142
Albert Park, Auckland, 98
Albiston, Shirley, 196–98, 204, 208, 209, 222–23, 225–27
alcohol, 3, 38, 43, 54, 116, *195*, 285, *286*, 287, 306, 319, 321; and national drinking age, 54, 319; and takeaway liquor trade, 285, 287
Alexandra, Central Otago, 179–80
Alhambra Hotel, Wellington, 285
Allen, Louisa, 316, 318
Amberley, Canterbury, 139
American influences, on New Zealand and New Zealanders, 15, *92*, 102–3, 115, 176, 180, 181, 190–91, 198, 202–3, 204, 207, 208–9, 212, 225, 237, 240–41, 243, *243*, 250, 267, 280–81, 295, 297, 302; *see also* dating; films and movies; Hollywood; slang, American; USA
American servicemen in New Zealand, 240–42
Amnesty International, *308*
ANA (Army, Navy and Fir Force) club, New Plymouth, 236–37
Anderson, Helen, 113–14
anti-authoritarianism, 302, 308; *see also* authoritarianism, adult
Apiti Bible Class Rally, Manawatu, *167*
apprentices and apprenticeships, 32–33, 39, 65, 73–74, *75*, 143, 172, 202, *262*, 305; *see also* cadetships
Archerfield School, Dunedin, 135, 155
Archie (comic), 202–3, 207, *251*
Arohata Borstal, Wellington, *256*, 256–57
Ashby, Ernie, 168
Ashwell, Benjamin, *48*
Atchison, Ruth, 239
Attic Coffee House, Christchurch, 287
Auckland, 50, *54*, 74, 203, 240, 241–42, 252, 257, 258–59, 260, *263*, *266*, 272, *272*, *274*, *304*, 316, 322; as destination for teenagers, 1, 3, *10*, 14, 17, 24, 32–33, 38, 42, 56, 60, 98, 99, 105, 111–12, *116*, 123, *144*, 182, *218*, *222*, 224, 254, *266*, 267, *274*, 276, *276*, 281, *281*, 295; eating establishments in, *10*, 202, 321; entertainment in, *54*, 173, 288, 292, *320*, 322; gay scene in, 257; population of, 32, 71; transport in and from, 94, 204, 223–24; *see also* Albert Park; College of St John the Evangelist; Dixieland Dance Hall; Exchange Hotel; Ferry Building; Henderson High School; Jive Centre; Karangahape Road; Leys Institute, Ponsonby; Maori Community Centre, Freemans Bay; Newmarket railway workshops; *Observer*; Orange Hall, Newton; Oriental Dance Hall, Symonds Street; Otahuhu railway workshops; Pacific Island Congregational Church; Paerata Dominion Camp; Prince Albert College; Queen Victoria School for girls; Royal Hotel; Rutland Street Drill Hall; Seddon Memorial Technical College; St Stephen's Native Girls' School, Kohimarama; *Star*; Surfside dance hall, Milford; Takapuna; The Scavengers; The Suburban Reptiles; University of Auckland; Waiheke Island; Watson's Exchange Coffee Rooms; Wesley Young Men's Institute; Wesleyan College and Seminary; West End Picture Theatre; Western Springs speedway; Ye Olde Barn café; Young Men's Christian Association
Auckland Academy, 49
Auckland Airport, *299*
Auckland Domain, 191, *304*
Auckland Girls' Grammar Magazine, 302
Auckland Girls' High School, 84
Auckland Grammar School, 302
Auckland Star (newspaper), 250
Auckland University College, 87, 164; *see also* University of Auckland

Auckland Weekly News (newspaper), 207, 211
Australasian White Cross League, 158
Australia, 9, 19, 22, 97, 98, 109, 145, 158, 173, *229*, 270, 297; and disquiet about teenage behaviour, 252; bodgies in, 247, 267; concept of masculinity in, 98; criticism of comics in, 208, 247; teenagers in, 100, 247, 270; urbanisation in, 3; *see also* Greer, Germaine; Sydney; *The Bodgie*; *The Dead Bird*
authoritarianism, adult, *265*
authority, adult, 74, 299, 302, 309, 322
avant-gardism, 12, 270, 306; *see also* rebellion
Awakeri Scout troup, 297

'baby boomers', 252
Baden-Powell, Agnes, 168–69
Baden-Powell, Lieutenant-General Robert, 167–68, 299
Balclutha, Otago, *151*
Baldwin, Jessie, 78
Ballantyne's Department Store, Christchurch, 74–75
balls and ballrooms, 56, 57, 59, 92, *93*, 164, 185, 216, 222, 288
bands, popularity and setting up of, 28–29, 288, 291, 292–94, *294*, *320*; *see also* guitars, popularity of; Selected Few; The Fourmyula; The Scavengers; The Skiffling Five; The Suburban Reptiles; Underdogs
Bank of New Zealand, *263*
banks, jobs in, 124, *263*, 293
Banks Peninsula, Canterbury, 198, 209
Bannerman, Jane, 87
barmaids, 43, 59
Barraclough, Herbert, 111, 158
Barrett's Hotel, Wellington, 56
Bartlett, Patricia, 320
basketball, 156, 169, *199*, *243*
Baxter, James K., 305
Bay of Islands, 20, 22, *23*
beaches and beach-going, 9, 11, 169, *172*, 173, 185, 186, 189, 224, *228*, 250, 277, 277–78, 295, *310*; *see also* Caroline Bay; Fitzroy Beach; Sumner; swimming and bathing; sunbathing
Beatles, 275–76, *276*, 286, 292, 294, 309
beatniks, 287, 305

Beattie, Herries, 78–79, 102
beauty pageants, *133*
beauty, concept of, 100, 103–4, 130, 139, 169, 183
bedrooms: as private space, 172, 282, 291, 295; decoration of, 211, 214–15
Belich, James, 128, 132, 139, 147, 168, 253
Bell, Ivy, 150
Benstead, George, 146–47, 187
Best, Lance, *312*
Bible Class, 128, 165, *166*, 166–68, *167*, 171, 173, 174, 182, 185, 186, 295, 297, 309; *see also* Apiti Bible Class Rally; camps: Bible Class
Bicknell sisters, *88*
bicycles, 11, 12, 130, *136*, 148–49, *149*, 174, 189, 193, 198, 199–200, 202, 244, 279, 282, 291, *298*; racing, *207*; *see also* Wanganui Overlanders cycle club
bikers, 277; *see also* rockers
billiards and billiard rooms, 54, *54*, 259, 297
Bing Harris and Co., 109
Black, Paddy, 268
Blackboard Jungle (film), 302, 303
Blackburn, Charlie, *91*, *120*
Blackmore, Edward, 61, 63
Blenheim, 117
Bligh, Richard, 158
boarding and boarding houses, 34, 35, 38, 39, 40, 111, 150, 255, 258; *see also* Christchurch Female Home; Cook's Boarding House; hostels; Magdalen Asylum
boats, for leisure, 90, 113–14, 171–73, *174*, 174–75, 223–24
bodgies, 247–48, *265*, 266–69, *270*, 270–71, 275, 276, 299–300, 309, 314; *see also* Australia, bodgies in; *The Bodgie*
bodybuilding, 130–31, *131*, 277–79
Boer War, 140, 168
bohemianism, 128, 135, 139, 202, 287
boisterousness, 3, *54*, 97, 148, 266–67
book clubs, 55
books and reading, 9, 55, *55*, 92, 96, 102, 146, 233, 247, 257; risqué, 109, *110*, 111, 207–8, 247, 250–51, 295, 303–5; *see also* Braithwaites bookshop; censorship: of books and comics; comics; magazines; *New Zealand*

Through Young Eyes; penny dreadfuls; *The Bodgie*
bookshops, 191, 211, 247
bootmakers, 72, *238*
borstals and special schools, *see* reformatories
boxing, *278*
boy flappers, 135, 139, 157, 179
Boy Scouts, 15, 128, 167–68, 171, 173, 182, 185, 198–99, *199*, *200*, 207, 297, 299, *299*; *see also* Awakeri Scout troup; camps: Boy Scouts; Takatuma Scout Crew
Boys' Brigade, 99
Boy's Own (magazine), 86, 92
Braithwaites bookshop, Dunedin, 96, 97, 109
Brickell, John, 24
Brickell, Robert, 24
bricklaying, 33
British influences, on New Zealand and New Zealanders, 56, 58, 61, 102–3, 158, 270, 275, 277; *see also* Beatles; Great Britain; slang, British
Brookes, Barbara, 26, 114
Brookes, Charlie, 17–18, *18*, 19, 20, *36*, 36–37, 47
Brookes, Daisy, 2–3, 4–5, 119
Brookes, Edwin, 17–18, *18*, 19, 20, 36–37
Brookes, Gertie, 1–2, *2*, 3, 4–5, 40, *93*, 111–12, 230
Brookes, Hovey, 17–18, *18*, 19, 20, 37
Brooks, Emily, *101*, 101–2
brothels, 43, 46, 258; *see also* prostitution
Brough, USS (destroyer escort), 272–73
Brown Ewing drapery, Dunedin, 95
Buck, Peter, *155*
Buller, Reverend J., 64–65
Burdon, Randal, 8–9, 158
burglary and theft, 101–2, 105, *144*, 145–46
Burnham Industrial School, Christchurch, 99, *100*, *144*, 145–46, 150, 165
Burnham military camp, 232
Burwood school, *see* Girls' Training Centre, Burwood
buses: school, 254, 270; trips on, *231*, 296
bush felling, 70, 71
Buttercup Farm YWCA camp, Otago, 169

INDEX

cabarets, 182, 241; *see also* Central Park Cabaret
Caddell, James, 21, 22
cadets, 15, 140–41, 168, *183*, 184, *233*
cadetships, 153, 183, *262*; *see also* apprentices and apprenticeships
Caledonian Hall, Christchurch, 290
camera clubs, 156, 219
cameras, availability and popularity of, 8–9, 173, *210*; *see also* Kodak Brownie camera; photograph albums; photographs; photography
Camp Opoutama, Mahia Peninsula (YMCA), *300*
Campaign for Nuclear Disarmament, *308*
camping, 8–9, 11, *175*, 198–99, 202, 223, 244
camps: Bible Class, 4, 15, 166–67, *166*, *167*, 170, 185–86, *296*, 297; Boy Scouts, 199, *199*, 200; Christian, 165–66, 178, 297, *364*; gender differences in, 199–201; Girl Guides, 169, 200; military, 140–41, 142, 232, 236, 240; Rangers, 200; school, 321; YMCA, 190, 191, 297, *300*; YWCA, 169–70, *169*, *170*, 200, 227; *see also* Burnham military camp; Buttercup Farm YWCA camp; Camp Opoutama; Kia Ora camp; Ohakea Air Force Station; Otago Young Women's Bible Class camp; Paerata Dominion Camp; Trentham army camp
Canada: and disquiet about teenage behaviour, 252; criticism of comics in, 208
Canterbury, *52*, 67, 69, 73, 89, *133*, 154, 260; *see also* Amberley; Banks Peninsula; Christchurch; Geraldine; Orari; South Canterbury Recreational Association; Timaru
Canterbury Agricultural College, 87; *see also* Lincoln University
Canterbury College, *85*, *92*, 162–63, 164
car culture, 182, 204, 280–82, 283; *see also* motorcars
car rallies, *296*, 297
Carlyle Street teenage club, Christchurch, 295
Carmen (Trevor Rupe), 264
Carmen, Pollie, 30, 31–32
Carne, Doris, *216*, 225

Caroline Bay, Timaru, *253*, *310*, *311*
Caroline Bay Hall, Timaru, 290
carpentry, 33, *48*
Carr, Sarah, 46
Catlins, Southland, *175*
censorship: of books and comics, 251; of film, 178; of radio and songs, 255, 264, 284–85; of words, 212, 303
Centennial Exhibition, Wellington, 206
Central Otago, *72*, *89*, 209; *see also* Alexandra; Ophir
Central Park Cabaret, Wellington, *246*
Challenger, HMS (survey ship), 159
chaperones and chaperonage, 56, 92–93, 119–21, 165, 173, 182, 216, 224, 282
Charisma (student Christian magazine), 303
chess clubs, 55, 297
Chester, Michael, 300
childhood, 1, 3, 20, 46, 63, *72*, 75, 121, 123, 147, 319
child-savers and organisations, 98–99, 111, 121, 144, 146–47, 164–65
Christchurch, 9, 46, 69, 99, 124, *136*, 139, 141, 189, 256, 280–81, 309, 319; as destination for teenagers, 46, 64, 105, 130–31, *144*, 145, 172, 198–99, *217*, *218*, 218, 222, 267, 277, 282, 291, 295, 322; eating establishments in, 172, 202, 287; entertainment in, *55*, *58*, 176, 177, 287, 295, 297; gay scene in, 227–29, *228*, *229*, *257*; transport in and from, 69, 94; *see also* Addington railway workshops; Attic Coffee House; Ballantyne's Department Store; Banks Peninsula; Burnham Industrial School; Burnham military camp; Caledonian Hall; Canterbury College; Carlyle Street teenage club; Christ's College; Cooke's Tudor Tearoom; Cook's Boarding House; Crystal Palace picture theatre and milk bar; Girls' Training Centre, Burwood; Hagley Park; Hibernian Hall; Industries Fair; Kohler's pleasure gardens; Magdalen Asylum; Milky Way milk bar, High Street; Pastor Whiting's youth group; Plainsman coffee bar; Roseneath Hostel; Regent Theatre; Rehua Hostel; Roseneath Hostel; Silver Grill; Spencer Street Hall, Addington; St Margaret's College; 'Street Society in Christchurch'; Sumner; Te Oranga reformatory; *The Press*; Young Men's Christian Association; Young Men's Literary Association
Christchurch Boys' High School, 219
Christchurch Female Home, 39–40
Christchurch Girls' High School, *85*
Christchurch Physical Culture Society, 140
Christchurch School of Domestic Instruction, *161*
Christchurch Technical College, *161*
Christian Endeavour, *see* Young People's Society of Christian Endeavour
Christ's College, Christchurch, *52*, *53*, 76, 157
Christ's College Register, 156
Church Missionary Society, *23*
church organisations and youth groups, 165–66, 187, 245, 248, 295–96; *see also* Bible Class; Pastor Whiting's youth group
cigarettes and smoking, 12, 56, 64, 97, 103, 124, 135, 137, 145, 146, 153, 171, 178, *210*, 240, 241, 258, 259, *265*, 267, 273, 282–83, 284, 285, 305
cinemas and picture theatres, 128, 173, *176*, 176–79, 186, 208–9, 212–13, 216, 223, 244, 268, 270, 302, 309, 322; *see also* Crystal Palace picture theatre and milk bar; fan cultures: film; film stars; films and movies; Hollywood; Regent Theatre, Christchurch; Regent Theatre, Masterton; Regent Theatre, Wellington; West End Picture Theatre
'cissy boys', 136–37, 139, 179, 184, 187, 221
citizenship: female, 169; legal, 63
civil rights, *308*
civil service jobs, 77, 102, 195, 196, 197–98, 258; *see also* Junior Civil Service exam
class, concepts and effects of, 14, 27–28, 43, 67, 69, 77, 82, 83, 98–99, 102, *110*, 117, 119–21, 123–24, 139, 144–45, 149, 322; convergence of, 270–71, 275
clerical jobs, *see* office work and workers

cliques, friendships and groups, 75, 155–56, 164, 165, 172, 174–75, 184, 186–87, 189, 191, 196, 198–99, 202, 219, 225–29, 242, 247, 254–55, 256–57, 272, 273, 284, 295, 319
Clogstoun, Elsie, 5–6, 8, 67, 69, 89, 90, 92, *92*, *93*, 94, 113, *113*, 121, 125
Clogstoun, Ina, 5–6, 90, *93*, 113
clothing: and class, *41*, 43, *72*; and disrobing, 90, 171, 224, 268; for dancing, *93*, 135, 181, *181*, 268, 271, *289*, 300, 302; for sports, 8, *81*, *131*, 136, *160*, 201, 207, 243, *278*, *290*; for work, *72*, *148*, *149*, *151*, *193*, 239; formal and informal, *172*, *173*, *197*, *216*; home-made, 90, 275; identified with groups, 99, 104, *107*, 108–9, 127, 128, *129*, 129–30, 133, 135–37, *137*, 139, 140, 184, 213, 224–25, *254*, 265, 267, 268–71, *269*, 275–76, *275*, *296*, 305, 311, 313; imported, 95; restrictive, 12, 90, 130–31, *132*; smart, *13*, *133*, *137*, *138*, *184*, *197*, *274*, *277*; *see also* duffle coats; fashion; jeans; mini-skirts; pantyhose; school uniforms
clothing industry, 71–72, 73–74, 95, *238*, 275
clothing retailers, 109, 208, 211
Clouston, Thomas, *122*
clubs: military, 242; religious, 295, 297; school, 87, 219; sports, 232, 276; teenage and youth, *289*, 295; university, 306; YMCA and YWCA, 297; *see also* ANA (Army, Navy and Air Force) club; book clubs; camera clubs; Carlyle Street teenage club; drama clubs and dramatic societies; glee clubs; Meccano club; Ngati Poneke Young Maori Club; Pastor Whiting's youth group; surf lifesaving clubs; Timaru Teenage Club; tramping clubs; Upper Hutt Youth Club
C'Mon (television music show), 294
coffee bars and cafés, 94, 202, *262*, 270, 286, 287–88; *see also* Attic Coffee House; Mexicali coffee house; Plainsman coffee bar; Sanitarium café; Sorrento Coffee Bar; Watson's Exchange Coffee Rooms; Ye Olde Barn café

College of St John the Evangelist, *48–49*, 50–51, 53, 56
Collins, Burton, 198–99, 206, 207, 213, 215, 216–18, *217*, 219
Collins, Noel, 206
'colonial girl', as concept, 64, 87–90, *89*, 131, 154, 168–69, 201, 244–45, 319
Colonist (newspaper), 63
Colorado, USS (battleship), 272
Columbus, Ray, 273, 282, 292, 309
Comer, Rob, 267–68, 269–70
comics, *110*, 207–8, 243, 249–50, 251, *251*, 255; *see also Archie*; Australia, criticism of comics in; Canada, criticism of comics in; censorship: of books and comics; Great Britain, criticism of comics in; *Mad*; USA, criticism of comics in
commercial education, 135, 161, 314
commercialisation, 128, 173, 178, 211, 215, 244; *see also* advertising; consumer culture, growth of; leisure, commercial
communication, mass, 11
concerts, 56, 84–85, 102, 104, 113, 116, 170, 185, 291, 321
conflict, intergenerational, 309
conformity, 135, 248, 302, 303
Connon, Helen, *85*
Connell, Raewyn, 34–35
conscription: industrial, 238–39; military, 25, 232
consent, age of, 114
consumer culture, growth of, 3, 95–96, 134–35, 139, 178, 190–91, 208, 211, 244, 252, 270, 275, 279, 303, 310
contraceptives, 208, 242, 248, 250, 255, 264
control, adult, 31, 43, 46, 64, 114, 117, 121, 145, 236, 245, 259–60, 284, 295, 316, 318
convicts, 14, 19, 32–33
Cook, Charles ('Cooky'), 102
Cook, Charlie, 153, *153*
Cook Islands, migration and students from, *155*, *290*
Cooke's Tudor Tearoom, Christchurch, 172, 202
Cook's Boarding House, Christchurch, 56
cosmopolitanism, 14, 140
Cossgrove, Colonel David, 168, 169,

170–71, 182
Cossgrove, Muriel, 169, 182
Count Down (music and fashion magazine), 275–76
counterculture, 305, 307–8; *see also* rebellion
Courage, James, 139, 140, 157, 160
courtship and choices, 117, 119–21, 209; *see also* dating
Coutts, Lulu, 78
Crawford, Erle, *155*
Crawford, Jim, *118*
Crawford, Jessie, *41*
cricket, 9, 50, 99, 170, 174, 190, 245, *290*
criminologists, and attitudes to adolescence, 264
cross-cultural contact, 18, 20–21, 65; *see also* Māori–Pākehā relationships
Crowley, Pauline, 279
Crowther, Dorothy, 265–67, 270, 271, 280–83, 287, 291, 297, 305–6; *see also* 'Street Society in Christchurch'
Crystal Palace picture theatre and milk bar, Christchurch, 267, 283
cultural capital, 24–25, 83
culture-building, 172, 191, 309
culture, popular, 136–37, 176, 190, 208, 212, 214, 243
cultures, age-specific, 53, 77

Daily Mirror (newspaper), 211
Daley, Caroline, 150, 152
Dalrymple, Learmonth, 83
D'Arcy, Minnie May, *91*, *120*
dance halls and cabarets, 59, 92, 182, 187, 225, 242, 268, 288, 290, 295, 309; *see also* balls and ballrooms; Caledonian Hall; Hibernian Hall; Jive Centre; Orange Hall, Newton; Oriental Dance Hall, Symonds Street; Spencer Street Hall, Addington; Surfside dance hall, Milford; The Hydro, St Clair
dances and dancing, 2, 6, 9, 12, 14, 29, 56, 57, *58*, 58–59, 87, 93, *93*, 99, 100, 114, 115, 142, 179–82, *181*, 185, 187, 213, 217–18, *217*, *218*, 222, 224, 236, 241–42, 259, 267, 279, 282, 288, *289*, 290–91, 292, 295, *296*, 309, 311; ballroom, 225, 288, 291; Black Bottom, 180; Bunny Hug, 180, 181–82; Charleston, 180, 181, 311; creep, 290; foxtrot, 180;

INDEX

dances and dancing (cont.), jazz, 180, 181–82, 187; jitterbug, 191, 241–42, 269; jiving, 2, 242, 243, 269, 272, 287, 290, 302; limbo, 290; Peabody, 180; rock 'n' roll, 3, 182, 288, 290, 291, 295, *296*, 297; Tango, 180; twist, 288; *see also* balls and ballrooms

dances, church, 225, 290, *296*

dances, school, 142, 180, 218, *218*, 220–21, 222, 300, 302

dancing girls, 43, *45*

Daniells family, 57

Dare, Phyllis, 178, *179*

darts, 295, 297

dating, 215–25, 232, 237, 243, 252, 255, 282; *see also* courtship and choices; friendships, romantic

Dawson, Ailsa, 230–31

Days Bay, Wellington, *126*, 171

de Beer, Dora, 129, 130, 172–73, 295, 319

de Certeau, Michel, 12

Dean, James, 269, 280, 293

debutantes, *216*, 288

Defence Act 1909, 140

delivery boys, 148–50, *149*

Department of Health, 249

department stores, 95, 96, 194, 208; *see also* Ballantyne's Department Store

dependency: among boys, 18, 24, 39, 65, 123–23, 309; among girls, 19, 39–40, 46–47, 63–64, 65, 309

Devlin, Johnny, 248, 293, *293*

diaries, as information sources, 5–7, *5*, *6*, 8–9, 12, 14, 28–29, 38, 50–51, 57, 64, 67, 69, 77, 80, 86, 90–91, 94, 106, 113, *113*, 115, 125, 139, 140, 157, 158, 171–72, 174–75, *175*, 176, 186, 189, 197–99, 204, 213, 215, 216–18, *217*, 219, 221–24, 226–27, 230, 258–59, 300, 302, 313, 314, 316; *see also* farm diaries

discipline, 11, 12, 28–31, 59, 60, 65, 74, *100*, 145, 153, 171, 236, 275, 279, 310, 321; *see also* Boy Scouts; militarism; school discipline

Dixieland Dance Hall, Auckland, 182

doctors, and attitudes to adolescence, 69, 109, 111, *122*, 227, 245, 249, 256; *see also* Barraclough, Herbert; Blackmore, Edward; Ellis, Havelock; King, Truby; Scott, Dr Jessie

domestic service, 1, 3, 15, 32, 39–43, 46, 51, 64, 69, *72*, 73, 74, 97, 111, 119, 145, 161, *161*, 191, 194, 239

domesticity, as concept, 38, *48*, 49–50, 64, 69, *72*, 90, 128, 160–61, 196, 215, 237, 254–55, 302

Dominion (Wellington newspaper), 135, 160

Dominion Girl Guide, *134*, 135

Dominion Hotel, Wellington, 285

Donaldson, Judy and Sue, *see* The Chicks

Dovey's gym, Wellington, 140

Downey, Gregory, 148–49

drama clubs and dramatic societies, 156–57, 160, 322

driving, 280–82, 321

Drummond, Tommy, *see* Mowhee

dudes, 102–4, 108, 123, 139, 318

dudines, *108*, 108–9

duffle coats, 275

Duke of Edinburgh Hotel, Wellington, 285

Duke of Portland (migrant ship), *31*

Dumble, Jon, 257, 302

Dunedin, 9, 14, 34, 74, *96*, 101, 102, 105, 120, 142, 168, 169, 172, 180, *214*, 215, *216*, 268, 291, 303, 319; as destination for teenagers, 35, 39, 42, 73–74, 87, 95–96, *96*, 97, 98, 101–2, 109, 123, 129, 130, 133, 145, 147, 177, 181, 202, 214, 225, 229, *238*, 272, 290; eating establishments in, 164, 202; entertainment in, *58*, 58, 84–85, 177; population of, 71; transport in and from, 94, *110*; *see also* Archerfield School; Braithwaites bookshop; Brown Ewing drapery; *Evening Star*; Farley's Arcade; Hillside railway workshops; Hopkins' bakery; Hudson chocolate factory; King Edward Technical College; Mosgiel Woollen Mill hostel; Otago Boys' High School; *Otago Daily Times*; Otago Girls' High School; *Otago Punch*; Otago University; *Otago Witness*; Queens Gardens; Ross & Glendining clothing factory; Seacliff Lunatic Asylum; *South End News*; Taieri Air Force base; The Hydro, St Clair; Vauxhall Gardens; Watson's Dining Rooms; Wax Vesta factory; Young Men's Christian Association

Dunedin Academy, 49, 59

Dunedin Railway Station, *94*

Dunedin School of Art, *92*

Dyer, Gertrude, 95–96

Dyer, H.B., *68*

Earle, Augustus, 22

East Town railway workshops, Whanganui, 74

education, *see* schools and schooling

Edwards, Mihipeka, 242

egalitarianism, 77, 308

Elbe's milk bar, Lower Hutt, 314

Elley, Ben, 319

Ellis, Havelock, 227

Elworthy, Sam, 306–7

Empire Hotel, Oamaru, 229

Employment of Females Act 1873, 72; and amendment 1875, 72

Employment of Females and Others Act 1881, 72

Ennor, Harrold, 174–75, *174*, *175*, 186–87, 202

entertainment, 9, 11, 15, 54–55, *54*, *55*, 56, 104, *163*–64, 264; commercial, 225; mixed-age, 55, 56, 60, 124; youth-focussed, 55–56, 63, 124; *see also* Auckland, entertainment in; balls; billiards; books and reading; bowling, ten-pin; chess clubs; Christchurch, entertainment in; cinemas and films; concerts; dances and dancing; Dunedin, entertainment in; horse racing; leisure; 'penny gaffs'; picnics; shooting galleries; speedways; theatres

environmentalism, 313, 321

eugenics, 132, 144–45, 160, 166, 168, 183, 232

Evangelist (Presbyterian magazine), 55, 59–60, 318

Evening Post (Wellington newspaper), 97, 127

Evening Star (Dunedin newspaper), 75, 98

examinations, school, 77, 80, 82, 83, 154, 174, 219, 313; *see also* Junior Civil Service exam

Exchange Hotel, Auckland, 54, 285

exhibitions and fairs, 141, 204–5, *206*; *see also* Centennial Exhibition; Industries Fair

extra-curricular activities, 56, 156–57, 160, 219, 294; *see also* camera clubs; dramatic societies; glee clubs
Ewing, John, *137*

Factories Act 1891, 72, 121
factories and factory workers, 3, 12, 20, 69, 71–75, 77, 92, 96, 97, 102, 114, 122, 123, 147–50, *148*, 171, 191, 192, 196, 214, *229*, 231, *238*, 239, 245, 258, 259, 279, *290*; *see also* Lever Bros plant; Ross & Glendining clothes factory; Wax Vesta factory
Falus (Otago University Magazine), *307*, 307–8
Family Planning Association, 255
fan cultures: film, 178–79, *179*, 187, 209, 211, 244; music, 187, 292, 295; *see also* posters and pin ups, film
Farley, Henry, 59
Farley's Arcade, Dunedin, 98
farm diaries, 150, 152, 154
farms and farming, 4, 14, 15, 20, 36–37, *48*, 69–71, 150, 152, 154, 191, *192*, 193, 239–40, *244*, 245, 256; *see also* sheep stations and farms
fashion, 11, 12, 178, 183, 275, 309; *see also* clothing; Quant, Mary
Featherstone family, 57
Feaver, Sam, *138*
femininity, concepts and ideals of, 49, 90, 108, *134*, 134–35, 147, 165, 168–69, 183, 214, 245, *254*
feminism and feminists, *92*, 255, 303, 319; first-wave, 15, 114, 130, 132, 183; second-wave, 308
Ferry Building, Auckland, 229, 272
fertility rates, Pakeha, 132
festivals and floats, *254*
Field, Henry, 158
fighting and violence, 98, 145, 212, 267–68, 276, 309; *see also* murder
Fiji: migration from, *290*; travel to, 297, *299*
film stars, 11, *205*, 209, 211, 212, 214, 263; *see also* fan cultures: film; posters and pin ups, film
films and movies, 2, 9, 173, 178–79, 182, *192*, 215, 243–44, 295, *296*, 297, 321; crime thriller, 177–78; erotic, 178, 255; moral criticisms of, 177–78, 186; romantic, 177; silent, 176, *176*, 177,

209; talkies, 86, 191, 208–9; westerns, 177; *see also Blackboard Jungle*; censorship: of films; cinemas and picture theatres; *Rebel Without a Cause*
Findlay, Mary, 191, 194
First Otago Battalion, 143
First World War, *8*, 9, 12, 133, *141*, 142–43, 156, 173, 202, 223, 224, 232, 233, 242
fish and chips, *195*, 287, 294
Fisher, Alder, 38, 63
Fisher, Francis, 140
Fitzgerald family, 57
Fitzroy Beach, New Plymouth, 237–38
FitzRoy, Robert, 25
flâneuses, 96
flappers, 12, 15, 127–28, 129, *129*, 133–35, 176, 181, 182, 183, 184, 187, 267, 271, 275, 300, 311, 321; *see also* boy flappers
food, 95, 150, 202, 240, 263, 285, 287; takeaway, 267, 285, 287, 321; *see also* Auckland, eating establishments in; Christchurch, eating establishments in; Dunedin, eating establishments in; fish and chips; hamburgers; hotdogs; pie carts; Wellington, eating establishments in
Foreman, Suzanne, 303, 310
Forest Service, 258
Foucault, Michel, 109
Free Press (Wellington College magazine), 302, 308
freedom, 12, 24, 25, 38, 43, 50, 57, 87, 89, 97, 123, 128, 135, 142, 145, 149, 154, 182, 183, 194, 224, 244, 259–60, 275, 303, 316; musical, 284–85; sexual, 181–82, 255
Freedom (National Party newspaper), 242
Fremantle Star (ship), *272*
friendships, romantic, 20, 114–15, 117, 119, 209, 215; *see also* dating
Fry, Oscar, 146
Furlong, Miss, 115

Gale, Jim, 215
Gale, Len, 204, 215
Gallipoli, 142, 143
Gallup research and surveys, 250–51, 254, 264
gangs, 97–98, 145, 204, 212–13, 247, 248, *254*, 265, 267–68, 270, 287

Gant, Robert, *122*
gardening, 15, 34, 50, 147, *152*, *192*
Garland's Restaurant, Wellington, 172
gay liberation, 308, 320
gay teenagers, *see* homosexuality
Gear Meat Works hostel, Petone, 264
Geiringer, Erich, 255
gender differences and divisions, 14, 27–29, 30, 46, 47, 60, 61, 64, 109, 122, 123–24, 151–52, 160, 170, 177–78, 182–83, 225, 242
gender ideals: transformation of, 100–1, 121, 122, 154, 182–83, 201, 237–38, 245, 281–82, 319; upholding of, 121, 137, 161, 182, 201, 319
'gender order', 34–35, 39, 40, 43, 46–47, 64, 87, 102–9, 135, 154, 169, 196, 240, 242, 254–55; *see also* Connell, Raewyn
generational divides, 60, *172*, 271, 309
George, Arthur, 292
Geraldine, Canterbury, 5, 67
Germany, influences from, 130–31, 198; *see also* Wandervogel
Gibbs, Dick, 230
Gibbs, Fred, 77, *79*, 80, 82, 90–92, 94, 106, 108, 115, 230, 322
Gibbs, Resa, 115
Gibbs, Sid, 80
Gilbert, Jarrod, 267
Gilbert, Robert Grant, *144*
Gilby's Commercial College, Wellington, 196
Gillis, John, 24, 39, 75–76
Girl Guides, 15, 128, 169, 171, 182, 185, 187, 297; *see also* camps: Girl Guides; *Dominion Girl Guide*
girl mashers, 69, 108, 114, 128
Girl Scouts, 168–69, 170–71
Girls' Friendly Society, 111
Girl's Own (magazine), 86, *92*
Girls' Training Centre, Burwood, 264
Gisborne, *174*, 174–75, 186, 202
glee clubs, 156, 187
Gleeson, Thomas, 105, *105*
Glen, Margaret, 46–47, 64
Glide Rink, Kilbirnie, Wellington, *366*
Goffman, Erving, 318
goldfields, 34, 43, *44*, *45*, 46, 59, 64, 292
goldmining, 34, 63, 71
Gore, Southland, 102, 124; *see also* Young Men's Literary Society
Gore School, 78

373

INDEX

Gorrie, John, 49
Gorst, John, 34
governesses, 42, 56
government reports, as information source, 4, 177–78
government service, *see* civil service jobs
Grace, Charles, 49
Grace, John, *68*
Graff, Harvey, 14
Graham, Billie, 297
Graham, Jeanine, 77, 121
gramophones, *see* records and record players
Grant, James, 49, 59
Great Barrier Island, 33
Great Britain, 9, 33; and disquiet about teenage behaviour, 252; criticism of comics in, 208; teenagers in, 270; urbanisation in, 3; *see also* British influences, on New Zealand and New Zealanders
Great Depression, 15, 190, 191–96, *192*, 204, 232, 239, 245, 322
Greenwood, John, 24, 50–51, *51*, 53, 56
Greenwood, Sarah, 42, *51*
Greer, Germaine, 303
Grey River Argus (Greymouth newspaper), 97–98, 127–28
guitars, popularity of, 57, 292, 294, *296*, 309; *see also* bands, popularity and setting up of
gymnasiums and gym equipment, 4, 80, 140, 189, 191, *192*, 227; *see also* Dovey's gym; Koolman's Gymnasium; Leys Institute, Ponsonby

Haddon Hall (migrant ship), *26*
Hadley, Gladys, 182, 187
Hagley Park, Christchurch, 117, 141
hairstyles: boys', 220–21, *265*, 267, 269, 271, 273, 275–76, *276*, 302, 309, 316; girls', 129, *129*, 133, 178, 214, *216*, 270, *286*
hamburgers, 240, 267
Hamilton, *149*, *195*, 209, 239, 267–68, *276*, 280, 282, 295
Harding, Ruth, *118*, 120
Harding, William, *62*, *118*
Hardy, Andy, 209, 215, 243–44

Hargreaves, Mary Annie, 7, 86, 92–93, 95–96, 102
Haselden, Mary, 42, 56
Hastings, 122
Hastings Blossom Festival, *254*
Hastings Housewives' Union, 250
Have a Shot (television talent show), 293–94
Hawke's Bay, 50, *129*, 193; *see also* Hastings; Napier
Hay, Richard, 292
Hebdige, Dick, 99, *101*, 299
hedonism, 60, 182
Helm, Bryan, 4, *201*, 219–20
Henderson High School, Auckland, 300, 302
heterosexuality, 133, 227, 252, 257, 320
Hetet, Bubs, 256
Hetherington, Jessie, 83, 87, 89, *92*
Hibernian Hall, Christchurch, 290
Hikurangi College, Wairarapa, 155, *156*
Hill, June, 209
Hillier, Ian, *257*
Hillside railway workshops, Dunedin, 74
Hine, Thomas, 20
hipsters, 319
Hit Parade, 284
Hodgkins, Frances, *92*, *108*
Hoffmann, Anna, 285, 288
Hogben, George, 144, 145–46
Hokianga, 191, 259
Holland, Sid, 251
Hollywood, as image and aspiration, 178, 209, 212, 240, 275, 283, 303
Home Guard, 233, 236
homo-erotic dalliances, 51–52, 227
homosexual law reform, 308
Homosexual Law Reform Bill, 320
homosexuality, 225, 231, 248, 255; and police involvement, 117, 227–29, *229*, 232, 272; female, 114–15, 225–27, 228, 256–57, 319–20; male, 115–17, *116*, 146, 157, 160, 225, 227–29, *228*, *229*, 232, 257, *257*, 272, 319–20; 'repressed', 231; *see also* Auckland, gay scene in; Christchurch, gay scene in
Honekai, 21
Hooper, Harold Kendell, 26, 27, 83–84, 125
Hooper, Mr, *107*

Hope Gibbons Building, Wellington, 204
Hopkins' bakery, Dunedin, 73
horse racing, 55–56
hostels, 54, 55; church-run, 259–60, *261*, 263; state-run, 258–59, 260, *260*, *261*, 264, 322; work-based, 264, 322; *see also* boarding and boarding houses; Gear Meat Works hostel; Mosgiel Woollen Mill hostel; Orient Hostel, Oriental Bay; Rangiatea Methodist Maori Girls' Hostel; Rehua Hostel; Roseneath Hostel
hotdogs, 240
hotel work, 239, 259
houses, 93, 95
Howard, Mabel, *293*
Hudson chocolate factory, Dunedin, 147
Hughes, Robert, 23–24, 64
Hukarere College, Napier, 83, *155*
Hulme, Juliet, 256
hunting, 4, 15, 89
Hursthouse, Charles, 24, 25, 43
Hutchison, Jack, 232–33
Hutt District High School, 314
Hutt Valley, 252, 260, 268, 280, 287, 313–14; *see also* Lower Hutt; Mazengarb Report; Selected Few; The Fourmyula; Upper Hutt; Upper Hutt Youth Club
Hutt Valley High School, 314, 321–22
Hutt Valley Tramping Club, 201
Hutt Valley Youth Survey, 318

identity-making, 11, 12, 14, 15, 46, 86, 211, 243, 285, 308
immigration, to New Zealand: nineteenth-century, 5, 9, 14, 17–20, 24, 26–33, 35, 38, 39, 43, 46, 47, 57, 60, 64, 65, 87, 111, 299, 322; post-Second World War, 287, *290*; *see also* Cook Islands, migration and students from; Fiji: migration from; Pacific migration; Samoa, migration from
immorality, 111, 158, 248, 250; *see also* Mazengarb Report
In the Groove (television music show), 293
in-betweeners, 20, 47, 64, 73, 86, 96, 123–25, 165, *172*, 173, 202, 224, 248, 271, 299–300, 311

independence, 4, 11, 39, 63, 65, 71, 74, 97, 122–23, 173, 193, 224, 244, 245, 264, 269, 271, 300, 309; among girls, 65, 74, 90, 99, 108, 114, 121, 128, 147–48, 183, 197, 223–24, 242, 282; financial, 24, 39, 46–47, 147–48, 183, 187, 196, 197
individualism and individuality, 245, 248, 303
industrialisation, 11, 14, 65, 71, 73, 150, 198
Industries Fair, Christchurch, 204
interwar period, 12, 198, 240
Invercargill, 105, *137*, 293; transport in and from, 94
itinerant labour, 34–35, 38, 46, 51, 56, 61, 150, 191, 192

Jackson, Revelle, *289*
Jacobs, Diane, *see* Lee, Dinah
Jamieson, Syd, 116
jazz, 187, 287, 288, 300
jazz boys, 135, 140, 184
jeans, 267, 271, 273, *280*, 281, *281*, *284*, *296*
Jive Centre, Auckland, 288
John Wickliffe (migrant ship), 34
Johnstone, Sybil, 164
Jones, Kevin, 34
jukeboxes, 202, *203*, 204, 285, *286*, 287, 314
Junior Civil Service exam, 77, 154
juvenile delinquency, 3, 33, 146, 203, 245, 248, 252, 264, 266, 268, 310

Kaipara Harbour, *16*, 17
Kaitaia, *13*, *251*, *277*, *283*
Kaitangata, South Otago, *195*
Kaniere, West Coast, 43
Karangahape Road, Auckland, 100
Kawhia, Eruera, 143
Kelly, Fred, 115
Kelly, Ned, and Ned Kelly gang, 98, 99, 173
Kemsley family, *68*
Kendell, Thomas, *23*
Kerouac, Jack, 305
Korero (magazine for WWII armed forces), 208
Kia Ora camp (YWCA), Otago, *170*
King Edward Technical College, Dunedin, *197*
King, Truby, 77, 80, 82, 109, 111, 122, *122*, 158, 160–61, 182

Kissling, Reverend and Mrs, 53
Knight, Charles, *92*, 104, *110*, 117, 119
Kodak Brownie camera, 8
Kohler's pleasure gardens, Christchurch, *58*
Kolff, Maureen, 303
Koolman's Gymnasium, Wellington, *278*

labour, gendered divisions of, 69–70, 150, 152, 154, 196
Labour government, 195, 198
Lady Egidia (migrant ship), 28–29
Lakeman, Henry, 78
Lambert, Eliza, 46–47, 64
land girls, 15, 239–40
land wars, 23–24
larrikinesses and larrikinism, 69, 99–102, 108, 109, 114, 123, 128
larrikins and larrikinism, 14, 69, 97–99, 100, *101*, 102, 105, *107*, 123, 145, 146, 173, 267, 300, 318, 321
Lawrence, Otago, 59
Lawry, Reverend Walter, 53
Lawson, Kate, 164
Le Fort, Frank, 248–49, 314
Lee, Dinah, 292, *293*
Lee, John A., 146, 150
Lee, Reverend, 117
leisure, 3, 54, 57, 69, 74, 87, 89, 95, 121–23, 164–71, 174–75, 187, 198, 211, 213, 248, *253*, 299, 311; commercial, 176–82, 198, 204, 211, 225, 244, 288, 290; gender-segregated, 63–64, 173, 175, 182, 185–86, 199–200, 223, 225; independent, 173; mixed-age, 55, 56, 60, 185; mixed-gender, 223; organised, 128, 164–65, 171, 173, 181, 185–86, 187, 198, 295, *296*, 297; youth-focussed, 55, 63, 87, 123–24, 184, 185, 248, 288; *see also* entertainment
leisure culture, 199, 211, 213
leisure organisations and spaces, *10*, 19, 92–93, 92–93, 189, 251, 285, 290
leisure, types of, *see* billiards and billiard rooms; boats; dances and dancing; darts; gymnasiums; marbles; Meccano club; netball; photography, as hobby and leisure pursuit; roller skating; shooting galleries; swimming and bathing; sunbathing; table tennis; ten-pin bowling
lesbian teenagers, *see* homosexuality
letters, as information source, 1–2, 3, 4–5, 17–18, 30, 36–37, 40, 60, 111–12, 119, *155*, *201*, 213, *218*, 219–20, 272, 281–82
Lever Bros plant, Petone, *148*
Levett, Allan, 267
Lewis, Bevan, *122*
Leys Institute, Ponsonby, Auckland, *131*
Lincoln University, 87
literary societies, 61, 63, 165; *see also* Young Men's Literary Association; Young Men's Literary Society
Littauer, Amanda, 252
loneliness, 35, 38, 193
Lovell-Smith, Hilda, 130
Lower Hutt, 275, 322; *see also* Elbe's milk bar; Hutt Valley High School; Queensgate shopping mall
Lush, Reverend Vicesimus, 74
Lyttelton, 46, *55*, 200

Macdonald, Charlotte, 11
MacGregor, Agnes, 6–7, 125
Mackay, Dorothy, 200
Mackenzie Country, 192, 193
Mackersey, Jessie, 122–23
Mackersey, Lindsay, 122–23
Mackersey, Norman, 122–23
Macklin, Kathleen, *172*
MacMillan, Thelma, *133*
Mad (comic), 282
Magdalen Asylum, Christchurch, 111
magazines, 9, *92*, 207–8, 211, 230, 231, 249, *251*, 255, 275, 303, 311; *see also Boy's Own*; *Count Down*; *Dominion Girl Guide*; *Girl's Own*; *Korero*; *Meccano Magazine*; *Mirror*; movie magazines; *New Zealand Girl*; *New Zealand Surfer*; *New Zealand Woman's Weekly*; physique magazines; *Playdate*; religious magazines; school magazines and yearbooks; *Seventeen*; sports magazines; *The Clansman*; *Vogue New Zealand*; university magazines
make-up, 105, 194, 211, 214, 222, 275, 284
Mana College, Porirua, *312*
Manawatu, *see* Apiti Bible Class Rally; Palmerston North

INDEX

Mandarin (migrant ship), 32
manhood, concept of, 24, 25, 34, 35, 46, 64–65, 103, 139, 141, 146–47, 183–84, 277, 285
Mannheim, Karl, 321
Manning, Arthur, 247–48, *249*, *265*, *269*, 271, 279, 299, 308
'manpowering', *see* conscription, industrial
Manse, Mary, 231
manufacturing, 71, 74–75, 95, 195
Māori, 22, *138*; literacy of, 47; schooling, 21, 47, 48–50, *48*, *49*, 51, 53, 83, 155–56, *155*, *156*; urbanisation of, 248, *258*, 259, 260, *260*, *261*, *262*, 263, 264; work and work practices of, 34, 42, 259–60; youth, 21–23, *21*, *22*, *23*, 25, 33–34, *138*, *155*
Maori Community Centre, Freemans Bay, Auckland, 288
Māori–Pākehā relationships, 9, 14, 20–21, 25, 33, 34, 35, 50, 56, 65, 71, *84*, 260, 263–64, 288, 291
marbles, 291
marching and drill, 15, 99, 140, 141, 142, 145, 155, 168, 171, 175, 187, 232, *233*, *234*, 236; *see also* Rutland Street Drill Hall
Marcuse, Herbert, 303, 305
marijuana, 288, 307
Marmon, Jacky, 19–20, 24
marriage, 39, 128, 182, 253–55, 309; ages at, 114, 117, 252–53; customary, 21; inevitability of, 302–3, 309; mixed, 225, 291; parental involvement in, 117, 224–25; rates of for young female immigrants, 39; rates of for young male immigrants, 38; status, 64
Marsden, Samuel, 22, *23*
Marsh, Belle, *6*, 185
Marsh, Dot, *214*
Marsh, Doug, *214*
Marsh, Ella, 1–2, *3*, 4–5, 111–12, 119, 230
Marsh, John, *212*, *213*
Marshall, Katie, 119–20
masculinity, concepts of, 25, 82, 103, 106, 108, *136*, 137, 139, 140, 165, 183–84, 187; and war, 140, 183–84, 242; and sports, 80, 82; colonial, 35, 38, 78; in films, 178–79; *see also* Australia, concept of masculinity in
mashers, 12, 14, 69, 102–4, 105, 106, *106*, *107*, 108, 123, 135, 139, 184, 221, 267, 300, 322; *see also* girl mashers
Mason, Elizabeth, 230
Masonic Hotel, Wellington, 285
Masterton, 11, 66, 104, *106*, *122*, *124*, 209, 211, *243*, 244–45; *see also* Regent Theatre; Theatre Royal
masturbation, 146, 147, 158–59, 231
materialism, 245; *see also* consumer culture, growth of
Matilda Wattenbach (migrant ship), 17, *18*, 19
Maunsell, Diana, 222
Mazengarb Report, 248–55, *251*, 252, 256, 264, 295, 314
Mazengarb, Oswald, 249, 251
McCahon, Beatrice, 214–15
McCassie, Pat, 182
McGovern, Bryan, *278*, *284*
McIndoe, Mabel, 135, 155, 180, 182
McKay, Michael, 145
McKenzie, William, 78
McLay, Adam Henry Pearson, *136*
McLeod, Alison, 9, 11, 177
McLeod, Jean, 11, 14, 209, 211, 213, 214, 244–45
McLeod, Nev, 211, 214, 245
McLeod, Norn, 211, 245
McMaster, Hugh, 150, 154
McMaster, Lizzie, 154
McRobbie, Angela, 291
meat works, *151*; *see also* Gear Meat Works hostel
Meccano club, 206
Meccano Magazine, 206–7
memoirs, 4, 15, 20, 21, 25, 71, 87, 89, 120, 164
menstruation, 230–31
Mexicali coffee house, Wellington, 287–88
middle class, expansion of, 14, 77, 98, 102
militarism, 15, 85, 121, 128, 140–43, 166, 168, 183–84, 187, 219, 232–33, *234–35*, 236, 279; *see also* marching and drill
milk-bar cowboys, 266–68, *266*, 270, 318
milk bars, *10*, 202–4, *203*, 216, 223, 243, 245, 247, 249, 265, 267, 268, 273, 275, 282–85, *283*, *284*, 287, 291, 309, 321; *see also* Crystal Palace picture theatre and milk bar; Elbe's milk bar; Milky Way milk bar, High Street; Sunshine Milk Bar
Milky Way milk bar, High Street, Christchurch, 189, 191
Millar, Bruce, 272
Mills, Barton, 113
Mills, Dudley, 113
mini-skirts, 275
Mirror (magazine), 128, 134–35, 240, 242, 275
Miss New Zealand competition, *133*
missionaries, 47; *see also* Church Missionary Society; Marsden, Samuel; schools and schooling, missionary; Williams, Jane; Williams, Marianne
Mitchell, Witarina, 224
mobility, 11–12, 38, 167; boys', 33, 148–49, 174–75, 199; educational, 164; gender differences in, 199–201, 281–82; geographical, 11–12, 32, 94, 130, 148–49, 189, 201, 279; girls', 130–31, 182, 199–200; occupational, 164; social, 33, 83, 164
modernity, 11, 15, 96, 106, 128, 130, 135, 178, 179, *181*, 182–83, 202, 203–4, 245, *274*, 279, 287, 291, 299, 321
mods, 275, 277, 309
Molesworth, Francis, 57
Moore, Dallas, 258–59, 291, 297, 300, 302
Moore, George, *see* Gilbert, Robert Grant
More, James, *70*
Morpeth, John, 86
Morris Matthews, Kay, 83
Morrison, Sam, 192–93
Mosgiel Woollen Mill hostel, Dunedin, 264
motorbikes, 2, 3, 4, 11, 191, 204, *205*, *212*, 213, 215, *217*, 247, 248, 267–68, 279, *280*, 282, 295, 299
motorcars, 11, 191, 201, 204, 280–82, *281*, 282, 283; stealing of, 204, 245; *see also* car culture; car rallies; driving
motorways, 297
Motueka, 42, *201*, *258*; *see also* Swan Inn
movie magazines, 209, 211; *see also* *Playdate*
Mowhee (Tommy Drummond), 22–23, *23*, 24
Mumford, Lewis, *249*

murder, 256, 268, 277
Murihiku, 19, 20
Muscular Christianity, 165–66
music: as identity, 268, 269, 321; home-made, *214*, *321*; importance of, 139, 285, 294; live, 29, 56, 57, 58, 149, 171, *286*, 287, 288, 291, 292–94, *294*, 320; popular, 9, 123, 215, 242, 275, 295, *296*; professional, 104, 173, 292–93; recitals of, 84; *see also* bands, popularity and setting up of; censorship: of radio and songs; *C'Mon*; *Count Down*; fan cultures: of music; guitars, popularity of; *Have a Shot*; Hit Parade; *In the Groove*; jazz; jukeboxes; pop concerts; radio; records and record players; R'n'B; rock 'n' roll; singing
music halls, 116, 146
mustering, 15, 154
mutual improvement societies, 19, 60–61, 63–64, 165; *see also* Woodville Methodist Young People's Society; Young Men's Christian Association; Young Men's Literary Association; Young Men's Mutual Improvement Society

Naenae, 267, 287
Napier, 83, 174; *see also* Hukarere College
National Broadcasting Service, 206, *219*; *see also* New Zealand Broadcasting Corporation
National government, 251–52
Nelson, *21*, 59, 61, 94, 106, 115, 202, *207*, 223, 256, 292, 322; *see also* Motueka; Young Men's Mutual Improvement Society
Nelson College, 4, 53, 77, *79*, 80, *81*, 84, 115, *201*, 219, *234–35*
Nelson College for Girls, *79*, 84–85, *220*, *226*
netball, 155, *243*, *296*
New City Hotel, Wellington, 285
New Plymouth, 82, 236, 279; *see also* ANA (Army, Navy and Air Force) club; Fitzroy Beach; Rangiatea Methodist Maori Girls' Hostel
New Zealand Broadcasting Corporation, 284; *see also* National Broadcasting Service

New Zealand Company, 25
New Zealand Expeditionary Force, 143
New Zealand Girl (magazine), 134
New Zealand Herald (newspaper), 74
New Zealand Law Commission, 319
New Zealand Medical Journal, 122
New Zealand Railways, *262*
New Zealand Surfer, *300*
New Zealand Through Young Eyes (compilation of teenage writings), 303–4, *304*, 313
New Zealand Truth (tabloid newspaper), 135–37, 139, 140, 157, 158, 181, 182, 207, 208, 250, 268, 310, 320
New Zealand Woman's Weekly (magazine), 240, 242
Newmarket railway workshops, 74
newspaper industry, *75*
newspapers, as source of commentary and information, 4, 15, 40, 42, *58*, 63, 69, 77, 98, 102–4, *105*, 109, 118, 119–20, 121–22, 124, 127, 130, 145, 159, 178–79, 207–8, 227, 242, 248, 251, *254*, 268, 310–11; *see also* individual newspapers
Ngaruawahia, 267, 303
Ngata, Āpirana, *155*
Ngati Poneke Young Maori Club, Wellington, 259, 291
Nicholson, Jean, *72*
Niue, students from, *155*
Nolan, Melanie, 196
Norfolk Island, 23, 24, 297
North Otago, 34, 146, *183*, *244*; *see* Otekaieke Special School
Northampton (migrant ship), 29, 30–32
nuclear weapons, protests against, *308*
Nunweek, Trevor, *229*
nurses and nursing, *195*, 202, 259

Oamaru, 88, *110*, *124*, *141*, 148, *149*, *179*, *216*, 229, 232, *317*; *see also* AFS Dance; Empire Hotel; Opera House; Waitaki Boys' High School
Oamaru (migrant ship), 39
Observer (Auckland newspaper), 46, 99–100, 102, 103–4, 106, 108
OE, *see* overseas experience
office work and workers, 4, 12, 14, 77, 97, 102, 123, 127, 135, 147, 153, 161, 164, 165, 191, 195–96, 204, 239, 242, 276, *344*; *see also* Gilby's Commercial College

Ohakea Air Force Station, 236
Ohms, Peter, *304*
Olssen, Erik, 89, 165, 182–83
Opera House, Oamaru, 229
Ophir, Central Otago, *89*
Opunake, Taranaki, *138*, 202
oral histories, 4, 150, 152
Orange Hall, Newton, Auckland, 288
Orari, Canterbury, 8–9, 69, 94
'orgies', 181, 249, 250, 268
Orient Hostel, Oriental Bay, Wellington, 258
Oriental Dance Hall, Symonds Street, Auckland, 288
Otago, 26, 28, 150, *159*, *185*, 292; population of, 32; *see also* Balclutha; Buttercup Farm YWCA camp; Central Otago; Kia Ora camp; Lawrence; North Otago; Outram; South Otago; Sports Queen float; Taieri Air Force base; Wanaka
Otago Boys' High School, *8*, 53, 83–84
Otago Daily Times (Dunedin newspaper), 96
Otago Girls' High School, 83, 84
Otago Punch (magazine), *58*
Otago Witness (Dunedin newspaper), 100, 103–4, 108, 123, 130, 143
Otago Young Women's Bible Class camp, 166
Otahuhu railway workshops, Auckland, 262
Otautau, Southland, 143
Otekaieke Special School, Kurow, North Otago, 146–47, 165, 187
Outram, Otago, 150, 152, 154
overseas experience, 23
Owaka, South Otago, 150
Owaka District High School, *221*

Pacific Island Congregational Church, Auckland, 290
Pacific migration, *290*
Paerata Dominion Camp, *166*, 169, 170
Page, Lizzy, 213, 218, *218*, 222
pantyhose, 275
Pare, 42
parental involvement in and overseeing of children's lives, 224–25; *see also* adult surveillance; marriage, parental involvement in
Parker, Pauline, 256

INDEX

Parkhurst Prison, Isle of Wight, 32–34
Parnell, Jim, 199, 202
parties, 57, 95, 102, 120, 133, 164, 202, 241–42, *246*, 257, 264, 268, 277, 285, 287, 291, 292, *300*, 310, 319
'pashes', 225–27
Pastor Whiting's youth group, Christchurch, 295, 297
Pendry, Mark, 35
Penn, Edith, 30, 31–32
penny dreadfuls, 102, 124, 207–8
'penny gaffs', 56, 58
permissiveness, 309
Petone, 57, 172, 248, 249, 267, 287, 314; *see also* Gear Meat Works hostel; Lever Bros plant
Petone District High School, 314
Petone railway workshops, 74
Petre, Henry, 57
Petre, Mary Ann, 57, *57*
Peyton Place (television programme), 260
philanthropists and philanthropy, 153
photograph albums, *172*, 173
photographs, as information sources, 7, 7–9, *72*, *82*, *101*, 139, 186–87, 275
photography: as hobby and leisure pursuit, 8–9, 11, 156, 169, 175; professional, 7–8, *62*, *138*
physical culture craze, 130–31, *131*, 140, 165, 183, 300; *see also* Sandow, Eugene
physical size and strength, 20, 23, 34, 35, 121, 140, 277
physical training and exercise, 82, 130–31, *131*, *132*, 143, 165, 168, 183, 198, 232, 277, 300; *see also* bodybuilding; gymnasiums and gym equipment; physical culture craze; Sandow, Eugene; sport, and connection with manliness
physique magazines, 278
picnics, 9, 84, 87, *129*, *132*, 174, 185, 279
pie carts, 219, 232, 250
pioneering mentalities and values, 9, 11, 103, 139
Plainsman coffee bar, Christchurch, 287
Playdate (movie magazine), 275
Plaza tearooms, Wellington, 202
pleasure gardens, commercial, *58*, 58–59
pleasure-seeking, 59–60, 90–92, 96, 98, 104, 135, 178, 182, 203–4, 209, 211, 215, 244, 264, 273, 309, 318
Pollock, Jeanie, 78
polytechnics, 85
pop concerts, 321
Port Albert (Wellsford), *16*, 17, 20, *132*
Port Albert Hall (Wellsford), *181*
Port Pirie (ship), *273*
post office, work in, 148, 149, 239, 259
postcard craze, 178, *179*
posters and pin ups, film, 209–10
poverty, 14, 32, 194
Power, Terry, *304*
Pratt, Nola, *129*
pregnancy: marital, 255; premarital, 112, 253–55
Presley, Elvis, 2, 292, 293, 309
Prince Albert College, Auckland, 83
promiscuity, sexual, 145
prostitution, 43, 46, 59, 102; *see also* brothels
protests and marches, 302, *308*; *see also* activism and activists; nuclear weapons, protests against; racism, protests against; Save Manapouri Campaign; Vietnam war, protest against;
Prouten, Bessie, 29–30, 31–32
psychiatrists, and sexuality, *122*, 257
psychologists, and attitudes to adolescence, *122*, 255, 264; *see also* Crowther, Dorothy; Manning, Arthur
psychology, and ideas about adolescence, 227, 231, 248
puberty, 14, 111, 230–31
punk rockers, *320*
Pycroft, Mavis, *133*
Pyke, Leslie, 78
Pyke, Vincent, 78

Quant, Mary, 275
Queen Victoria School for girls, Auckland, 155
Queens Gardens, Dunedin, 229
Queensgate shopping mall, Lower Hutt, 322

racism, protests against, *308*
radio, 11, 206–7, 215, 284, 295; *see also* censorship: of radio and songs; Hit Parade; request programmes
railways, 11–12, 94, *110*, 139, 150, 189, 198, 223, 224, 262, 279, 297; *see also* New Zealand Railways
railways, employment with, 74, 202, *262*; *see also* Addington railway workshops; East Town railway workshops; Hillside railway workshops; Newmarket railway workshops; Otahuhu railway workshops; Petone railway workshops
Rangers, 200
Rangiatea Methodist Maori Girls' Hostel, New Plymouth, 259–60
Rebel Without a Cause (film), 269, 280, 303, 310
rebellion, 2, 130, 248, 249–50, 270, 299–300, 302–3, 309; *see also* avant-gardism; counterculture
records and record players, 180, 201, 210, 219, 259, 295, 314, *320*
reformatories, 143–47, *144*, 165, 256–57, 264; *see also* Arohata Borstal; Burnham Industrial School; Otekaieke Special School; Parkhurst Prison; Te Oranga reformatory
Regent Theatre, Christchurch, *176*
Regent Theatre, Masterton, 209
Regent Theatre, Wellington, *176*
Rehua Hostel, Christchurch, 260, *260*, *261*, 263, *280*
religious magazines, *see Charisma*; *Evangelist*; *The Young Man's Magazine*
Report of the Special Committee on Moral Delinquency in Children and Adolescents, *see* Mazengarb Report
request programmes, 215
research projects and studies, 74, 150, 152, 177–78, 196, *238*, 256–57, 264–67, 278–79, 316, 318; *see also* Crowther, Dorothy; Manning, Arthur; Mazengarb Report; 'Street Society in Christchurch'; Sweating Commission; *The Bodgie*
respectability, 12, 40, 46–47, 64, 74, 90, 99, 100, 102, 114, 119, 121, 144–45, 147, 148, 170, 248, *254*
restaurants and tearooms, 149, 172, 175, 202, 288; *see also* Auckland, eating establishments in; Christchurch, eating establishments in; coffee bars

and cafés; Cooke's Tudor Tearoom; Dunedin, eating establishments in; Garland's Restaurant; milk bars; Plaza tearooms; Ritz tearooms; Silver Grill; Watson's Dining Rooms; Wellington, eating establishments in
restraint and regulation, 101, *122*, 128, 135, 158, 170–71; *see also* rules and limits
Ritz tearooms, Wellington, 202
Riverton, Southland, *70*
R'n'B, 287
road-building, 33, 71
Roberts, Edward, 86
rock 'n' roll, 3, 182, 248, 309; *see also* dances and dancing, rock 'n' roll
rockers, 277
roller skating, 89, *366*
Roper Smith, Bill, 293
Roseneath Hostel, Christchurch, *258*
Ross, Arthur, 142, 180
Ross, Hilda, 276
Ross & Glendining clothing factory, Dunedin, *238*
Rotorua, 224, 257
Rout, Ettie, 132
Rowing, *81*
Royal Dane (migrant ship), *28*
Royal Hotel, Auckland, 54, 285
rugby, *8*, 80, 89, *155*, 156, *167*, 176, 201, 276, *296*, 309
Ruhe, *21*
rules and limits, 12, 14, 27–32, 40, 46, 113–14, 120, 153, 182, 187, 255; *see also* restraint and regulation
Rupe, Trevor, *see* Carmen
Rutland Street Drill Hall, Auckland, 233
Rye, Maria, 40
Rykenberg, John, *274*

Samoa, migration and students from, *155*, 290, *290*
Sandow, Eugene, 130, *131*, 165
Sangster, Elizabeth, 39
Sanitarium café, Wellington, 194
Sargood, Percy, 153
Savage, Jon, 245
Savage, Michael Joseph, 195, 198
Save Manapouri Campaign, 321
school cultures, 3, 14, 171, 218, 219

school curriculum, gender-neutral, 53, 160–61, 164
school discipline, 83–85, 219, *234–35*, 248, 302, 316
school leaving ages, 49, 76, 154, 319
school magazines and yearbooks, 156, 219, 220, 302–3, 308, 318; *see also Auckland Girls' Grammar Magazine*; *Christ's College Register*; *Free Press*
school sports and other trips, 80, *219*, 220, 297; *see also* camps, school
school uniforms, 76, 90, *155*, *156*, *157*, *219*, *274*, 302, 314
schooling statistics, 82–83, 154–55, 196, 218, 252
schools and schooling, 14, 19, 47–53, 75–77, 78, *79*, 83, 123, 171, 213; boarding, 4, 78, 122–23, 129, *156*, 218, 219–20, 222, *226*, 257; boys', 50–51, *52*, 53, 71, 76–77, 219–20; church (denominational), 50–53, *155*, *156*; co-educational, 53, 164, 219–20, 252; district high schools, 77, 220; girls', 49–50, 71, *79*, 82–83, 90, 160, 222, 225; industrial, 99, *100*; missionary, 47, *48–49*, 49, 316; primary, 75–76, 196; private, 155; secondary, 3, 12, 47, 65, 69, 75–82, 83–85, 87, 92, 140, 154–55, 183, 212, 218, 220, 245, 248, 252, 271; single-sex, 77, 218, 219–20; state, 49, 53, 76, 82; technical, 85, 220; *see also* camps: school; dances, school; examinations; extra-curricula activities; individual schools; marching and drill; militarism; reformatories; sports, school; truancy
Scott, Dr Jessie, 227
scrapbooks and scrapbooking, 191, 211, 214–15, 297
Sea Cadets, 249
Seacliff Lunatic Asylum, Dunedin, 77, 80, 109, 146
sealers, 19, 21
Second World War, 9, 15, 191, 192, 207, 232; boys' involvement in, 15, 242; gendered effects of, 242; girls' involvement in, 15, 236, 239–40, 242, 258; *see also Korero*
Seddon Memorial Technical College, Auckland, 135
Selected Few (band), *292*

self-discipline, 46, 59, 60, 99, 248, 300, 316
self-expression, 224, 279, 299, 305
self-gratification, 245
Selwyn, Bishop George, 50–51, 53
Seventeen (girls' magazine), 207, 275
sewing and sewing machines, 39, 90, 95, 130, 152, 275
sex education, 158–59, 231, 295, 320
sexual diversity, 319–20
sexual double standard, 46, 112, 316, 318
sexual liberation, 308; *see also* freedom, sexual; gay liberation
sexuality, youthful, 3, 109–14, *122*, 131, 159, 227–29, 248–55, 316, 318, 322; *see also* contraception; dating; heterosexuality; homosexuality; prostitution
Shalders, Richard Barcham, 60
sheep stations and farms, as source of work, 35, 56, 63, 239–40; *see also* mustering
Sherwill, Cecilia, *68*
Sherwill, Markham, *68*
Shiel, Gerald, 9
Ship Hotel, Wellington, 38
shipboard matrons, 29–32, 39, 43, 64
ships: coastal, 38; migrant, 5, 18–19, 26–32, 39, 47, 64, 100, 279; naval, 159, 241, 272–73; *see also Brough*, USS; *Challenger*, HMS; *Colorado*, USS; *Duke of Portland*; *Fremantle Star*; *Haddon Hall*; *John Wickliffe*; *Lady Egidia*; *Mandarin*; *Matilda Wattenbach*; *Northampton*; *Oamaru*; *Port Pirie*; *Royal Dane*; *St George*; *Sydney Cove*; *Thomas Sparks*
shooting galleries, 58, 149, 206
shops and shopping, 94, 95–97, 99, 123, 172, 194, 207, 208, 229, 249, *251*, 276, 277; *see also* bookshops; department stores
shop assistants, 73, 96–97, 124, 196, 208, 239
Silcock, Mr, *107*
Silver Grill, Christchurch, 287
singing, 279; at camps, *199*; at parties, 242, 292; at school, *219*; at work, *238*; in choirs, 259
slang, 86, 108, 123, 147, 191; American, 212–13, 215; British, 86, 212; Victorian, 102; *see also* swearing

INDEX

Sloan, Alistair, 303, 305
smartphones and cellphones, 11, 314, 318, 321
Smith, Mary, 112
Smith, Peter, 278–79
smoking, *see* cigarettes and smoking
soccer, 156, 190, 291
social controls, *see* control, adult
social distinctions, 11, 12, 14, 19, 27–28, 60, 77, 98–99, 124, 187, 215, 268
social media, 318, 321
socialising: mixed-age, 55, 248; mixed-gender, 1, 167, 202, *222*, 225, 236, 237, 248
Society for the Promotion of Community Standards, 320
sociologists, and attitudes to adolescence, 12, 264, 318, 319, 321; *see also* Connell, Raewyn; Gilbert, Jarrod; Goffman, Erving; Toynbee, Claire; Whyte, William Foote
Soper, Eileen, 133
Sorrento Coffee Bar, Wellington, *286*
South Canterbury Recreational Association, 295
South End News (tabloid newspaper), 268, 272–73
South Otago, *5*, *184*; *see also* Balclutha; Kaitangata; Owaka
Southland, 70, 171, 180; *see also* Catlins; Gore; Gore School; Otautau; Riverton; Wyndham
Southland Boys' High School, 78
special schools, *see* reformatories
speed, thrills of, 15, 191, 204, *207*, 215, 245, 279–80, 282, *299*
speedways, 191, 204, *205*, 215; *see also* Western Springs speedway
Spencer Street Hall, Addington, Christchurch, 290
Spencer, Victor Manson, 143
Spinks, Charlie, *205*
sports magazines, *300*; *see also New Zealand Surfer*
Sports Queen float, Otago, *254*
sports, as leisure activity, 15, 130, 167, 297; *see* basketball; bicycles; boxing; cricket; netball; rowing; rugby; soccer; surfing; swimming; table tennis; tennis
sports, school, *155*, 156, 213, 215, 218, 220
Srebnick, Amy, 123

St George (migrant ship), 32
St Ignatius' College, Sydney, 9
St John the Evangelist school, Tamaki, *see* College of St John the Evangelist
St Margaret's College, Christchurch, 200, 218, *218*, 219
St Stephen's Native Girls' School, Kohimarama, Auckland, 53
Stapleton, Robert, 193
Star (Auckland newspaper), 100, 127, 130
Stephen, Mary, 131, 159
Stevenson, Margaret, 194
Stewart Island, 21, 50, 90, 113
Stott, Hettie, 112
Strachan, James, 34, 35, 38, 56, 63
Stoddart, Arthur, *221*
'Street Society in Christchurch' (sociological research report, Crowther), 265–67, 271, 275, 280–81, 282, 291, 297; *see also* Crowther, Dorothy
Strong, Austin, 76
Strutt, William, 22
Stryker, Susan, 208
Student Christian Movement, 303; *see also Charisma*
subcultures, 14, *107*
suffragists, 109
Sumner, Christchurch, 189, 228
sunbathing, 15, 127, *172*, 186, 190, *210*; *see also* beaches and beach-going; swimming and bathing
Sunday School, 187
Sunshine Milk Bar, Wellington, *203*
surf lifesaving clubs, 237–38
surfing, 127, 237, *300*, *301*; *see also New Zealand Surfer*
Surfside dance hall, Milford, Auckland, 288
Swan Inn, Motueka, 54
swearing, 99, 127, 178, *300*; *see also* slang
Sweating Commission, 73–75, 96
swimming and bathing, 80, 125, *126*, 127, 171, *241*, 256, *296*; at pools, 58, *210*, *217*; at the beach, 174, 189; in streams and rivers, 94, 168, 198; naked, 90–91, 171
swimsuits, *126*, 159, *210*, 238, *241*, *253*
Sydney, 19, 22, 23, *23*, 24, 104, 292; *see also* St Ignatius' College
Sydney Cove (sealing vessel), 21

table tennis, 232, 295, 297
Taieri Air Force base, Otago, 264
Takapuna, Auckland, 248
Takarangi, Tenga-o-te-Rangi Te Hore, *155*
Takatuma Scout Crew, *199*
talent shows, television, 292, 293–94; *see also Have a Shot*
Taranaki, 22, 23, 25, 70, 99, 191, 200, 202, 235–36, 239, *300*; *see also* New Plymouth; Opunake
Taumarunui, King Country, 194, 264
Taupiri, Waikato, *48*
Taylor, Charles, 140–41, 164, 171–72, 173
Taylor, Geni, 259
Taylor, Tony, 256–57
Taylour, Fay, *205*
Te Ahiaruhi station, Wairarapa, 35
Te Aro Flat horse races, Wellington, 56
Te Aro Hotel, Wellington, 285
Te Aroha, Waikato, 99
Te Aute College, Hawke's Bay, 50, *155*
Te Kuiti High School, King Country, 256, 294
Te Oranga reformatory, Christchurch, 145, 146, 165, 264
Te Rangi Whakarurura, 25
teaching, as a profession, 42, 87, 150, 164, 196, 200, 219; *see also* governesses
Teddy boys, 266, 269–71, 273, *273*
teenager, idea of, 2–3, 15, 187, 190, 228, 303, 310–11, 318–19; emergence of, 9, 187, 238, 240, 243–45, 247–48
telegraph boys, *see* delivery boys
telephones, 11; *see also* smartphones and cellphones
television, 11, 259–60, 293–94, 303, *308*, *309*; *see also C'Mon*; *Have a Shot*; *In the Groove*; *Peyton Place*
Telfer, Katherine, 42
temperance, 78, 128
tennis, 69, 130, *155*, 291
ten-pin bowling, 54, 321
territorialism and spaces, teenage, 282–86; *see also* bedrooms: as private space
Territorials, 15, *141*, 142, 233
Thames, Coromandel, 46, 64
The Bodgie (sociological study, Manning), 247–48, *249*, 265, 269, 271, 279, 299, 308

The Chicks, 293
The Clansman (hand-written magazine), 130–31
The Dead Bird (Australian newspaper), 109, *110*
The Fourmyula (band), *294*
The Hydro, St Clair, Dunedin, 182
The Press (Christchurch newspaper), 108
The Scavengers (band), *320*
The Skiffling Five (band), 293
The Suburban Reptiles (band), *320*
The Young Man's Magazine (Christian magazine), 165
Theatre Royal, Masterton, 104
theatres, 9, *55*, 59, 123; *see also* Thomas Sparks (migrant ship), 57
Tiffen, Fred, 35, 55–56, 63
Timaru, South Canterbury, 94, *133*, 193, 273, *273*, 290; *see also* Caroline Bay; Caroline Bay Hall
Timaru Teenage Club, 295
Tindall, Sophie, 4, 273, 291
Tokaanu, Waikato, 256
Tokelau, migration from, *290*
Tokitoki, 21, 22
Tokomaru Bay School, East Coast, *219*
Toynbee, Claire, 152
traders, 19, 20, 22
trades training and schools, 85, 258, 260, *260*, *261*, *262*, 263, 322
trains, *see* railways
tramping and trampers, 34, 94, *188*, 189, 198; gender differences in, 199–201
tramping clubs, 201
trams, 12, 94, *96*, 189, 194, 198, 223, 224, 228, 240, 279
transport, 11–12, 94, *213*, 223, 279; *see also* aeroplanes; Auckland, transport in and from; bicycles; buses; Christchurch, transport in and from; Dunedin, transport in and from; Invercargill, transport in and from; motorbikes; motorcars; railways; trams; Wellington, transport in and from
travel, overseas, 9, 23, 297, 299, *299*, 321–22
Trentham army camp, 142
truancy, 264
Tucker, Frank, 142
Turner, Dennis, *249*, *265*, 269

typing and typewriters, 11, 127, 161, 314, *344*
Tyson, Valda, 236–38

Underdogs (band), 294
Undine (sailboat), 50
universal franchise, 109
universities, 85, *85*, 87, 287, 306–7, *306*, *307*; *see also* Lincoln University; University of Auckland; University of Canterbury; University of Otago; Victoria University of Wellington
university halls of residence, 306
university magazines, 307, *307*; *see also* Charisma; Falus
University of Auckland, 87, *306*, *320*
University of Canterbury, 87, 217, 265, *307*; *see also* Canterbury College; Crowther, Dorothy
University of New Zealand, 85, 87
University of Otago, 85, 164, 177, 278–79, *307*; *see also* Falus
university student culture, *162–63*, 164, 306, 306–7
Upper Hutt, 139, 157
Upper Hutt Youth Club, 289
urban growth, 95
urban/rural divide and differences, 11, 69, 71, 123, 125, *138*, 147, 154, 194–95, 253
urbanisation, 3, 15, 128, 150, 194–95, 198, 248, 255, 258–59, *262*, 263–64, 309; *see also* Australia, urbanisation in; Great Britain, urbanisation in; Māori, urbanisation of; USA, urbanisation in;
USA, 9; and disquiet about teenage behaviour, 203, 252; criticism of comics in, 208; teenagers in, 202–3, 270; urbanisation in, 3; youth culture in, 20, 84, 270

vandalism, *254*, 291
Valentino, Rudolph, 177, 178–79, 180
Vauxhall Gardens, Dunedin, *58*, 58–59
venereal disease, 158
Vernor, Miss, *179*
Victoria College Tramping Club, 201
Victoria House, Victoria University of Wellington, *306*
Victoria University of Wellington, 87, 255, 258, *306*

Victorian culture and sensibilities, 8, 69, 90, 92, 94, 109, *110*, 114, 117, 159, 185, 275; *see also* slang, Victorian
Vietnam war, protest against, *308*
visibility, public, 123, *164–65*, 252
visiting, house to house, 172, 175, 291
Vocational Guidance Association, 196
Vogue New Zealand, 275
von Sturmer, Alice, *68*
von Sturmer, Jack, *106*, *107*, *124*

wages, 73, 148, 149; adolescents', 191; climbing, *263*, 270; equal, 240; female minimum, 196; girls', 196; minimum, 208; strike action against, 321
Waiheke Island, 223–24
Waikanae River, *241*
Waikato, 24, 34, 267; *see also* Te Aroha; Taupiri; Tokaanu
Wairarapa, 56, *82*, *91*, 104, *243*; *see also* Hikurangi College; Masterton; Te Ahiaruhi station
Waitaki Boys' High School, Oamaru, 86, *157*, *160*, 314
Wakefield, Edward Gibbon, 24
Wakefield, Jerningham, 24–25, 26, 47
Wakefield, William, 25
Walkman, 314
Walter, Christiana, 119
Wanaka, Otago, 153
Wandervogel, 198, 244
Wanganui Collegiate, *84*, *155*
Wanganui Overlanders cycle club, *298*
Wanganui Technical College, 236
Wanhalla, Angela, 20–21
Warburton, Rosalind, 275, 281
Waretotara, Maketu, *21*
Watson's Dining Rooms, Dunedin, 83, 202
Watson's Exchange Coffee Rooms, Auckland, 58
Wax Vesta factory, Dunedin, 147
Webber, Ernie, *137*
Weir House, Victoria University of Wellington, *306*
Wellington, 7, 20, 25, 29, 30, 35, *41*, 43, 57, 80, 95, *101*, 102, 111, 131, 139, 142, 149, 168, *186*, 191, *193*, *199*, 219, 240, 242, 255, 270, *290*, *308*; as destination for teenagers, 4, 12, 14, 35, 38, 56, 92–93, 131, 140, 159, 170–2, 173, 176, *186*, 194,

Wellington (cont.), 202, 208–9, 229, 258–59, *262*, 267–69, 285, *286*, 287–88, 290, *291*, 316; eating establishments in, 202; population of, 71; transport in and from, 94, 139, 204, 224; *see also* Alhambra Hotel; Arohata Borstal; Barrett's Hotel; Centennial Exhibition; Central Park Cabaret; Days Bay; *Dominion*; Dominion Hotel; Dovey's gym; Duke of Edinburgh Hotel; *Evening Post*; Garland's Restaurant; Gilby's Commercial College; Glide Rink, Kilbirnie; Hope Gibbons Building; Koolman's Gymnasium; Masonic Hotel; Mexicali coffee house; New City Hotel; Ngati Poneke Young Maori Club; Orient Hostel, Oriental Bay; Petone; Plaza tearooms; Port Nicholson; Regent Theatre, Wellington; Ritz tearooms; Sanitarium café; Ship Hotel; Sorrento Coffee Bar; Sunshine Milk Bar; Takatuma Scout Crew; Te Aro Flat horse races; Te Aro Hotel; Trentham army camp; Victoria College Tramping Club; Victoria House; Victoria University of Wellington; Weir House; Young Men's Christian Association, Wellington

Wellington Academy, 49
Wellington Battalion, 142
Wellington College, 53, *76*, 80, 302, 308; *see also* Free Press
Wellington East Girls' College, 196, 222, 225
Wellington Executive Young Women's Bible Class, *167*
Wellington Girls' High School, *79*
Wellington Technical School, 164, 195
Wellsford, *6*, 17; *see also* Port Albert; Port Albert Hall
Wesley Young Men's Institute, Auckland, 165
Wesleyan College and Seminary, Auckland, 53
West End Picture Theatre, Ponsonby, Auckland, 145

Western Springs speedway, Auckland, 203, 204
Whakatane, 42
Whakatane High School, 220
whalers, 19
Whanganui, 25, *62*, *107*, 117, 120, *192*, 199, 281; *see also* East Town railway workshops; Wanganui Collegiate; Wanganui Overlanders cycle club; Wanganui Technical College
Wharehine, 1
white blouse revolution, *see* office work
Whyte, William Foote, 265, 267
widgies, 266, 269–71, *270*, 281, 309, 314, 318
Wildey, David, 189–90, *190*, 191, 204, 227, *228*, 232, 278
Wilkinson, Ruby, *89*
Williams, Eva, *72*
Williams, Jane, 47
Williams, Marianne, 47
Wilson, Heather, *364*
Wilson, Jeanie, 78
Wilson, Jude, 23
womanhood, concept of, 34, 46–47, 63, 130, 211
Women's Auxiliary Air Force (WAAF), 236
Women's Auxiliary Army Corps (WAAC), 236, *237*
Women's Christian Temperance Union (WCTU), 114
Women's Land Service, 239–40
Women's Royal New Zealand Naval Service (Wrens), 236
Wood, Henry, 70–71
Woodville Methodist Young People's Society, 165
work cultures, 15, 74, 147–50, 194–98, 238–39
workforces, 71–72; female, 39–46, 71–72, 73–74, 147–48, 150, 152, 154; male, 73, 148–50, 276
working-class street culture, 98, 270
workplaces, *10*, 14, 15, 63, 71, conditions in, 73–74, *151*; discrimination in, 302; *see also* Sweating Commission
World Affairs Council, *308*
Wraight, Doug, *137*

Wrigglesworth and Binns, Photographers, 7
Wright, William, *101*
Wyndham, Southland, 142, 230

Ye Olde Barn café, Auckland, 268
Young Men's Christian Association (YMCA), 60–61, 63, 174–75, 185, 186, 189, 191, *192*, 297; Auckland, 60, 297; Christchurch, 60, 189–90, 227; Dunedin, 60; London, 60; USA, 156, *243*; Wellington, 64; Whanganui, 192; *see also* Camp Opoutama; camps: YMCA; clubs: YMCA and YWCA
Young Men's Literary Association, Christchurch, 61
Young Men's Literary Society, Gore, 102, 124–25
Young Men's Mutual Improvement Society, Nelson, 61
Young People's Society of Christian Endeavour, 165, 174, 295
Young Women's Christian Association (YWCA), 64, 169, 185, 187, 227; *see also* camps: YWCA; clubs: YMCA and YWCA; *New Zealand Girl*
youth, as concept, 19, 24, 39, 60, 61, 63, 65, 69, 122, 243
youth-centred cultures, 3, 11, 14, 15, 19, 32, 38, 47, *52*, 53, 60, 64, 69, 73, 86, 87, 92, 95, 99, 102, 104, 107, 123, 124–25, 128, 139, 155–56, *166*, 171, 172, 184, 185–86, 187, 190, 203, 232, 248, 255, 266, 270–71, 293, 303, 309, 310–11, 321–22; *see also* bodgies; boy flappers; dudes; dudines; flappers; girl mashers; larrikinesses and larrikinism; larrikins and larrikinism; mashers; milk-boy cowboys; widgies
youth hostel movement, 198
youth workers, 227, 249, 267
Yska, Redmer, 255
Yugoslav Society Kolo group, Auckland, *222*